v

# Contents

# Contents of Volume 1

# INTRODUCTION TO
# PSYCHOLOGY

## VOLUME 2

# *Introduction to Psychology* Course Team

Steve Best   *Graphic Artist*
Gillian Cohen   *Senior Lecturer in Psychology, Faculty of Social Sciences*
Rudi Dallos   *Staff Tutor, Faculty of Social Sciences*
Ann Davey   *Print Production Co-ordinator*
Harry Dodd   *Print Production Controller*
Judith Greene   *Professor of Psychology, Faculty of Social Sciences*
Fiona Harris   *Editor*
Siân Lewis   *Graphic Designer*
Paul Light   *Professor of Psychology, School of Education*
Vic Lockwood   *Senior BBC Producer*
Dorothy Miell   *Lecturer in Psychology, Faculty of Social Sciences*
John Oates   *Lecturer in Education, School of Education*
Hugh Phillips   *BBC Producer*
Ortenz Rose   *Secretary*
Ilona Roth   *Lecturer in Psychology, Faculty of Social Sciences (Course Team Chair)*
Ingrid Slack   *Course Manager, Faculty of Social Sciences*
Jon Slack   *Lecturer in Psychology, Faculty of Social Sciences*
Richard Stevens   *Senior Lecturer in Psychology, Faculty of Social Sciences*
Kerry Thomas   *Senior Lecturer in Psychology, Faculty of Social Sciences*
Frederick Toates   *Senior Lecturer in Biology, Faculty of Science*
Pat Vasiliou   *Secretary*
Margaret Wetherell   *Lecturer in Psychology, Faculty of Social Sciences*
David Wilson   *Editor*

## Consultants

Andrew M. Colman   *Reader in Psychology, Department of Psychology, University of Leicester*
Chris Cullen   *Professor of Learning Difficulties, Department of Psychology, University of St Andrews*

## External assessor

Antony J. Chapman   *Professor of Psychology, University of Leeds*

The Open University's

# INTRODUCTION TO
# PSYCHOLOGY

# VOLUME 2

Lawrence Erlbaum Associates in association with The Open University

## Edited by Ilona Roth

Lawrence Erlbaum Associates Ltd.
27 Palmeira Mansions, Church Road
Hove, East Sussex BN3 2FA
*in association with*
The Open University
Walton Hall
Milton Keynes MK7 6AB

First published 1990

**British Library Cataloguing in Publication Data**
Introduction to psychology.
  Vol. 2.
  1. Psychology
  I. Roth, Ilona     II. Open University
  150

  ISBN 0 86377 137 8 (Hardback)
  ISBN 0 86377 139 4 (Paperback)

Designed by the Graphic Design Group of the Open University
Typeset by Phoenix Photosetting, Chatham, Kent
Printed and bound in Great Britain by Mackays of Chatham PLC, Chatham, Kent

*Introduction to Psychology* Volumes 1 and 2 form part of the Open University course DSE202 *Introduction to Psychology*. For further information about this course, please write to Open University Educational Enterprises Limited, 12 Cofferidge Close, Stony Stratford, Milton Keynes MK11 1BY, Great Britain. Further information about Open University courses may be obtained from The Admissions Office, The Open University, PO Box 48, Milton Keynes MK7 6AB, Great Britain.

# PART V
## COGNITIVE PROCESSES

# Introduction to Part V

The chapters in Part IV were mainly concerned with theories about people as whole individuals, investigating the factors that account for intelligence and personality, and exploring the full range of personal experience. In contrast, the chapters in Part V focus on certain specific aspects of human functioning: the ability to perceive the environment, to attend to what is going on around us and to remember events. Attempts to identify precisely how these processes work will be described in the following three chapters.

Chapter 10 introduces the area known as perception. This term refers to the process by which people become aware of the environment through their senses. It may seem obvious that objects and events exist 'out there', but we can only become aware of them through our ability to see, hear, touch, taste and smell. There have been many approaches to studying the way we perceive the world, ranging from investigations of the physiological functioning of sensory systems to studies of the knowledge which enables us to identify objects. Chapter 10 will be concerned mainly with vision, but it is recognized that other senses play an equally important role.

Chapter 11 outlines theories of attention. Although people are capable of perceiving a wide variety of things, on the whole they are more likely to concentrate on those aspects of the environment which initially catch their attention. Psychological studies of attention have therefore investigated people's ability to focus attention on particular activities, such as, for instance, reading a book or listening to music. Equally important is the ability to attend to two or more things at once. It is possible to drive a car and carry on a conversation at the same time, for example, until circumstances arise in which driving should necessarily become the main focus of attention.

The theme of Chapter 12 is the importance of memory in everything we do. Without memory, it would be impossible to learn anything or to profit from experience. Psychologists have mainly been interested in the way memory works in general. For example, they have investigated the role of 'short-term memory' in the learning of such things as lists of words. They have also investigated the way in which information is stored more permanently in 'long-term memory'. This concern with memory *processes* has been typical of psychological studies of memory. There has, however, recently been a revival of interest in memories for natural events in everyday life.

# chapter 10 | PERCEPTION

Judith Greene

## Contents

# 1 | Introduction: what is perception?

This may seem an odd question to ask. If **perception** is defined as seeing, hearing, touching, tasting and smelling, what more is there to explain? We experience the environment around us, seeing walls and trees, hearing birdsong and speech, touching a cup or crushing a flower, tasting a lemon or a well-cooked dish, smelling perfume or escaping gas. In all these ways we *perceive* the environment.

## 1.1 Perceptual experiences

Everyone perceives an environment full of objects. We know what things are and how they are likely to behave. Some remain much the same size; some are constantly changing, like water turning into steam; some move about of their own accord; some try to communicate with us. The desk I am writing on is a continuous surface, even where it is hidden by papers. A friend looks the same person whether she is smiling or frowning. Desks do not suddenly leap out at us, dogs often do. Because we have a reasonably accurate picture of the world, we can move confidently around in what is normally a very predictable environment.

ACTIVITY 1

Stop and think of all the ways in which you have perceived the environment in the past hour. Those of you who have a visual handicap or a hearing impairment, or suffer from some other sensory deficit, will be even more aware of the importance of using other senses to experience the environment.

In doing Activity 1, you may have thought of many different kinds of perceptions which occur throughout your daily life. In this activity, you were asked to reflect about your *conscious* awareness of perceptual experiences. Most of the time we do not think consciously about what we see and hear, simply taking the environment for granted. But we are quick enough to notice anything unexpected: a new chip on a mug, a crooked picture, fallen leaves that need to be swept up in autumn, a red mark on my nose when I look in the mirror, a lion in my garden instead of safely caged in the zoo. Examples like this imply that we must have been unconsciously monitoring the environment. Without all this information about the environment we would be unable to behave appropriately, to learn to tailor our responses to the demands of the current environment: to buy food in shops, to run away from a bull.

Usually, perception seems so immediate and instantaneous that it is difficult to understand that there is anything to be explained. But there is, and psychologists see this explanation of how we are able to perceive the world around us through our senses—through vision, hearing, touch, taste and smell—as a *problem*. The major difficulty in understanding psychological theories about perception is to grasp what questions psychologists are trying to answer. Our aim in this chapter is to enable you to see why perception is not as easy as it looks.

## 1.2 Perceptual processes

In order to receive information from the environment, animals are equipped with sense organs. The function of the **sense organs**, like the eye, nose or ear, is to receive information from the environment. In each of the sense organs there are **sensory receptors** which are stimulated by different types of physical energy (e.g. light reflected off objects, sound waves). Sensory receptors receive **sensory inputs** (often referred to as **sensory stimuli**). These provide **sensory information** about the environment. Each sense organ is part of a **sensory system** which receives sensory inputs and transmits sensory information to the brain. One special problem for psychologists is to explain the process by which the *physical* energy received by sense organs forms the basis of perceptual *experience*. Somehow sensory inputs are converted into perceptions of chairs and tables, trees and buildings, trains and aeroplanes; into sights, sounds, smells, tastes and touch experiences.

SAQ 1  (*SAQ answers are given at the end of the chapter*) Can you think of any examples of when perceptual experiences appear to occur in the absense of sensory inputs?

Let us start by considering the remarkable fact that all vision is based on the light that enters our eyes. So the first problem is to explain how light rays provide enough information for us to see a world full of separate objects, including other people. How does the human visual system operate so that it can distinguish the outline of my mug from the desk surface on which it is standing when all the eye receives are light rays coming in from all directions? What *processes* are involved in extracting information about the environment from the inputs to our senses?

In order to study complex activities, psychologists often break them down into component processes. In the case of perception, psychologists have identified different levels of perception. These include detecting the presence of a stimulus, deciding whether two sensory inputs are the same or different, and judging the sizes, shapes and distances of objects. The problem is to explain how all these component processes 'add up' to produce the experience of perceiving instantly recognizable objects.

## 1.3 Perceptual representations

Psychologists are also interested in the question of how perceptions are *represented*. When we see a mug, a desk or a dog, how are we able to distinguish exactly which objects we are seeing? When I see a mixture of black, green and yellow coloured shapes on my desk, I perceive a vase of daffodils. But if I had never seen a daffodil before, I would have no **mental representation** in my mind of what daffodils are or what they look like. How could I recognize the sensory inputs of colours and shapes without any prior knowledge of the objects they might represent?

Even if we do not know what an unfamiliar object is, someone will soon tell us what it is. But consider what happens when a newborn infant first opens its eyes. To us the environment so obviously consists of recognizable objects that it is almost impossible to visualize how it would appear to someone who has no idea what walls, tables or chairs are. For the infant, the environment is probably not even divided into separate objects. Where do what we know as a floor and what we know as a wall and what we know as a person begin and end? In order to convey the almost unimaginable prospect of a totally featureless environment, William James used the phrase 'blooming buzzing confusion' to describe a baby's perceptual world. Figure 10.1 shows a well-known example of what the 'buzzing' confusion might look like. If I tell you it is a dalmation, you are likely to 'see' it immediately. But an infant who has never seen a dog, not even a toy dog, much less a dalmation, presumably would continue to see only an unco-ordinated scatter of dots.

**Figure 10.1**
(Source: Lindsay and Norman, 1972, p. 146)

Chapter 2 described how babies very gradually become aware of other people, even of their own reflections in a mirror. Chapter 3 discussed Piaget's theory that at first babies do not realize that an object continues to exist when they do not see it. The ability to recognize objects as having a continuous existence, known as **object permanence**, develops only as a result of sensori-motor experiences during the first 6 months of life. There is no way that a newborn baby can start life with any past experiences of what particular objects look like or what they should be used for. It is only through interactions with the environment that infants can form mental representations of people, objects and events.

## 1.4 Why do psychologists study perception?

I hope that by now you feel you have a greater understanding of why perception has fascinated so many biologists and psychologists. Physiologists have studied the visual system from the reception of light by the eye to the integration of information in the brain. Psychologists have considered what perceptual cues have to be extracted from sensory inputs in order to distinguish objects and to recognize them for what they are. The aim of all these researchers is to try to 'unpack' our apparently effortless and instantaneous perceptions of the world in which we live. You should notice, too, that nearly all the theories we will be describing are concerned with **visual perception**. This is partly because vision is a dominant sense, at least for humans, enabling us to interact with the physical environment, and partly because much more research has been done into the workings of the visual system than into the workings of the other perceptual systems.

To end this introductory section, it might be helpful to recap some of the main questions raised in it:

1   How are perceptions derived from the multitude of inputs received by sensory receptors?

2   How is sensory information processed to provide mental representations of the environment?

3   What is the role of past experience in perception? What would our perceptions be like if we knew nothing about the environment?

I will come back to these questions in Section 6.6 at the end of the chapter. However, one point you should bear in mind is that psychologists do not always agree about what is meant by perception. Does it mean the sensory experience of feeling a soft piece of velvet, the sensation of wind on your cheek, the detection of a moving object, the recognition of an object as a mug or tree, the identification of my own mug? Or does it mean the processes in the eyes and the brain which convert light into meaningful perceptions? You will find all these levels studied as examples of perception in the rest of this chapter.

## Summary of Section 1

- Perceptual experience includes all the ways in which we become aware of objects and events in the environment.

- Perceptual processes extract information about the environment from the sensory inputs received by sensory receptors.

- Perceptual representations are based on past experiences of objects which are necessary for recognizing them.

- Psychologists study perception at different levels, including the physiology of the sensory system, and the ability to detect and make judgements about objects.

# 2 | The physiology of the visual system

You may wonder why a whole section of this chapter is devoted to the physiological studies of the visual system. This is because a great deal is known about the anatomy and physiological activity of the nerve cells in the eye and of the neural connections from eye to brain. Compared with this, very little is known in detail about the connections between nerve cells which underlie the development of a particular personality trait.

## 2.1 Sensory receptors

Sense organs are capable of receiving energy from the environment. Not all forms of energy can be detected by human senses, however. Those which cannot include X-rays and ultraviolet rays. These rays obviously have effects on our bodies. But they are not involved in perception because none of our sensory receptors is capable of picking them up. Some types of energy which stimulate human sensory receptors are pressures on the skin, reflected light from objects, and sound waves.

Within any sensory system there are a number of components. First there are the nerve cells (neurons) whose specialized function is to convert energy in the environment into electrical activity in the nervous system. In vision, the environmental energy is in the form of light which enters the eye through the pupil. As light rays come through the lens in the front of the eye they are focused on to the retina (see Figure 10.2). The **retina** consists of millions of nerve cells which line the back of the eye. Light-sensitive cells called *rods* and *cones* act as sensory receptors to light. The area of the retina which is currently stimulated by light rays entering the eye is called the **retinal image**.

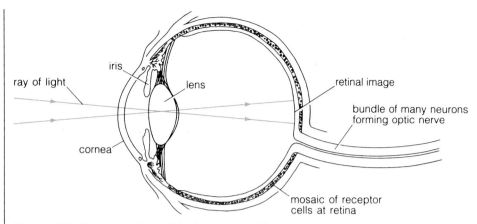

**Figure 10.2** The physiology of the human eye. The optic nerve conveys information from the eye to the visual cortex in the brain

Figure 10.3 shows an enlargement of a small section of the retina at the back of the eye. As this figure shows, the retina contains not only the specialized rod and cone receptor cells but also many other layers of cells. These include layers of bipolar and ganglion cells. Notice that these other cell layers are located in front of the light receptors so that light has to pass through them to reach the light receptors at the back of the eye. All these cells are neurons, the function of which is to process information received by the sensory receptors.

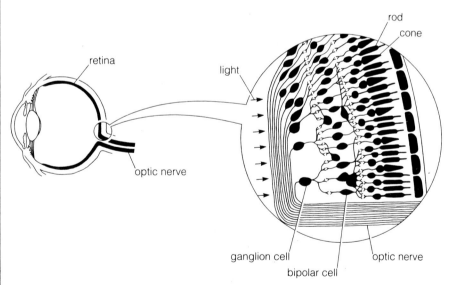

**Figure 10.3** An enlargement of a small section of the retina to show layers of nerve cells (neurons)

In Section 2 of Chapter 5 the function of a **neuron** (nerve cell) was defined as handling information and passing it on from neuron to neuron through the junctions between them (termed **synapses**). Within the retina, information is transmitted from one layer of neurons to another, from light receptors (rods and cones) at the back of the retina to the bipolar cells and on to the ganglion cells. The many ganglion cells are then gathered up as the **optic nerve**. As shown in Figure 10.4, the ganglion cells in the optic nerve from each eye transmit information further up the visual system, from where it finally converges on the area of the brain called the **visual cortex**. In this way sensory information from both eyes is passed on to the brain.

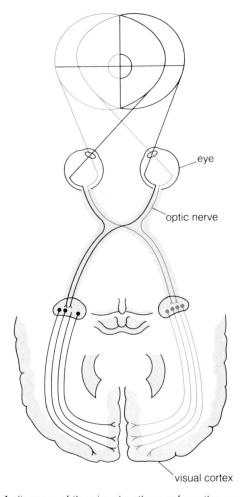

**Figure 10.4**  A diagram of the visual pathways from the eye to the cortex

The function of this complex visual system is to extract information from the numerous light receptors in the retinas of each eye, and to pass this information up to the cortex. Both eyes are constantly moving, receiving slightly different stimulation, and adapting to different intensities of light. Many objects also move about. The visual system has the colossal task of interpreting all this incoming information to provide an adequate representation of the world around us. So it is not surprising that there are many complex layers of neurons in the retina and further up towards the visual cortex, all designed to integrate and transmit information derived from sensory inputs.

## 2.2 Measuring activity in the visual system

The structure of the visual system, as shown in Figures 10.3 and 10.4, indicates the kinds of connections that are possible between various layers of neurons. But it is only in the past few decades that methods have been developed for investigating the firing activity of particular neurons in response to visual stimulation. The method of implanting micro-electrodes in single cells to record the electrical activity of those cells has made it possible to chart exactly the kinds of sensory inputs that result in activity in a particular cell. Box A describes the measurement of such activity.

### BOX A   Measuring activity in single cells

A micro-electrode is implanted in a single cell in the retina (e.g. a ganglion cell) of an anaesthetized cat (see Figure 10.5). Since there is some activity in every cell, even in its 'resting' state, the first step is to record this background level of activity in the cell. A screen is placed in front of the cat. The cat's head is fixed so that a pin-point of light projected on to a particular location on the screen stimulates a particular location on the surface of the cat's retina. The electrical activity of the cell is measured on an oscilloscope. The light is moved around the screen to see what effect this has on the firing rate of the cell.

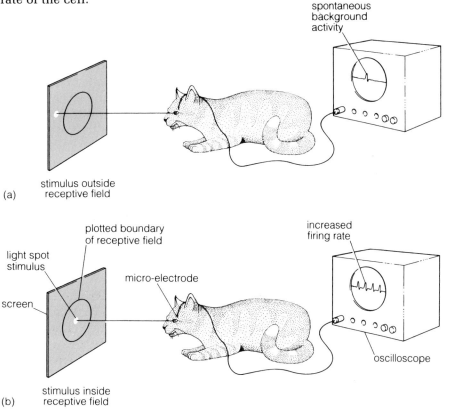

**Figure 10.5** Technique used by Hubel and Wiesel for recording the activity of single cells

Using the method of micro-electrode recordings in single cells, described in Box A, researchers were able to study whether light falling on an area of the retina would stimulate a particular ganglion cell to fire. The crucial assumption is that the area of the screen illuminated with a spot of light is exactly equivalent to a particular area of the cat's retina. As shown in Figure 10.5(a), when the spot of light is shone outside a certain area of the screen (and thus a certain area of the retina), only background electrical activity is observed. However, when the spot of light is shone anywhere within the circle on the screen, as in Figure 10.5(b), the firing rate of the cell increases considerably.

The area on the retina where light stimulation increases the firing rate of a single cell can be precisely measured. The **receptive field** of a cell is defined as the particular location of the retina which, when stimulated by light, causes a change in firing activity in that particular cell. In this way each cell picks up information about light falling on a particular area of the retina.

One important point to remember is that cells are never quite dormant. There is always a small amount of 'spontaneous' background electrical activity even in their resting state. When a ganglion cell is stimulated in response to a pattern of light falling within its receptive field on the retina, this causes a *change* in its firing rate. Sometimes a cell will *increase* its firing rate above its background spontaneous activity; at other times it will *decrease* its firing rate to an even lower rate than its background spontaneous activity. The micro-electrode picks up changes in firing rates in the single cell which it is recording.

Using micro-electrode techniques, Kuffler (1953) demonstrated some characteristic receptive fields of ganglion cells in the cat. First, he moved a spot of light around the screen until he found an area which affected the firing rate of a single cell (see Figure 10.5). In this way he identified the receptive field on the cat's retina of that particular cell. He then went on to chart the effect of moving the light around *within* the receptive field. Figure 10.6 shows typical circular receptive fields for two ganglion cells in the cat's retina.

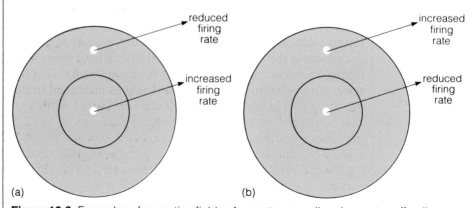

**Figure 10.6** Examples of receptive fields of a centre-on cell and a centre-off cell

First look at the cell shown in Figure 10.6(a). When a spot of light is pointed at the screen in a location that corresponds to the *centre* of the receptive field on the retina in the cat's eye, the recorded firing rate of the ganglion cell increases from its normal background rate of firing. However, if a light is pointed at the location on the screen corresponding to the outer surround of the receptive field on the cat's retina, firing is *inhibited*—that is, reduced—until the light is turned off. This is known as a **centre-on cell**.

Figure 10.6(b) shows an opposite kind of cell in which light stimulation of the outer surround of the receptive field on the retina increases firing rate, and stimulation of the centre reduces firing. This is known as a **centre-off cell** because light shone at the centre of its field *decreases* firing.

SAQ 2  In Figure 10.7, which of (a) and (b) represents the receptive field of a centre-on cell and which the receptive field of a centre-off cell? (*Note:* (+) means that, in response to light falling on the retina, the cell's firing rate increases; (−) means that firing is inhibited.)

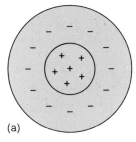 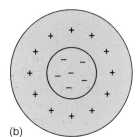

(a)  (b)

**Figure 10.7**

## 2.3 Feature detector cells in the cortex

Kuffler (1953) had studied activity in ganglion cells in the *retina*. Hubel and Wiesel (1959) carried out some famous experiments in which they implanted micro-electrodes in single cells in the cat's *visual cortex*. They were able to demonstrate the existence of cortical cells which respond to patterns of light falling on the retina. They charted the receptive fields of these cells using the same micro-electrode recording techniques described in Box A. Changes in the firing rate of each cortical cell were measured while patches of light were moved around a screen. Again the cat's head was fixed so that there was a one-to-one correspondence between the screen and the cat's retina. In this way Hubel and Wiesel could investigate those patterns of light falling on the light receptors in the retina that would activate a single cell in the visual cortex.

Like the ganglion cells in the retina, each cell in the visual cortex fired in response to light stimulation on some areas of the retina while firing was inhibited in other areas. So these cells also functioned as on–off cells. The main difference was that more complex patterns of light stimulation were necessary to increase or decrease firing activity. Figure 10.8 shows the receptive fields of four cortical cells.

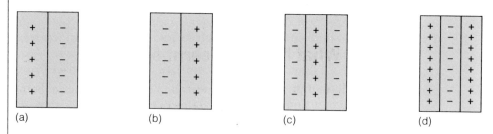

(a)                    (b)                    (c)                    (d)

**Figure 10.8** Slit-like receptive fields on the retina which stimulate four types of cortical cell

One point to notice is that the receptive fields of cortical cells are often of a slit-like shape, compared with the circular receptive fields of ganglion cells. The slit-shaped receptive fields of cortical cells means that they are optimally stimulated by long thin bars of light falling on the retina. The receptive field shown in Figure 10.8(a) indicates that the firing rate of the cortical cell increases (+) when light falls on the left-hand side of its receptive field on the retina but is inhibited (−) when the light is moved to the right-hand side.

SAQ 3    Describe the firing patterns of the three other cortical cells in response to light falling on their receptive fields as shown in Figure 10.8(b), (c) and (d).

These experiments provide evidence that cortical cells respond to bars of light falling on specific locations of the retina. The patterns of light which excite and inhibit these cells provide information corresponding to edges between slit-shaped areas of light and dark. Cells which are able to detect patterns of light falling on the retina which reflect changes between light and dark edges are helpful in indicating the boundaries of objects in the environment. For instance, at the edge of an object like a table there will be a sharp contrast in the amount of light reflected by the shiny top and the legs underneath. Cortical cells like those shown in Figure 10.8 are able to pick up information of this kind. Cells like this are called **feature detector cells** because they respond to particular features (e.g. edges) in the environment.

The visual system is organized as a *hierarchy*. Each layer of cells provides the information necessary for the next layer of cells to respond. When light receptors are stimulated they trigger responses in a particular ganglion cell. Acting together, ganglion cells transmit information to cells higher up in the visual system, which eventually stimulate the firing rate of cortical cells. In this way, information about spots of light picked up by specific ganglion cells can be integrated so that cortical cells can respond to more complex patterns of light like bars and edges.

One point that it is *essential* to remember is that light itself can only be picked up by specialized light receptors (rods and cones) in the retina at the back of the eye. From the eye, all information transmitted up to the cortex is in the form of electrical impulses as cells fire in response to patterns of light falling on specific areas of the retina. So the interpretation of sensory visual information is represented as electrical activity within the visual system. There are no little 'pictures' in the brain.

## 2.4  What have we learnt so far?

This line of physiological research raised great hopes of being able to explain the recognition of objects in terms of a hierarchy of feature detector cells in the visual system, which respond to corners, edges and even more complex shapes. As we shall see in Section 5, many psychological theories of perception have been based on the notion that recognition of objects can be built up from the detection of physical features. For instance, it has been claimed that there are single cells in the cortex of a monkey's brain which respond most strongly to patterns of light reflected from objects with the shape of a monkey's paw (Gross, Rocha-Miranda and Bender, 1972). As shown in Figure 10.9, the cell fired most strongly to paw-shaped objects (objects 5 and 6 in the figure); much less to the other objects. This would seem to imply that there are single cells capable of responding to outstandingly important features in the environment; for example, to distinguish the paws of other monkeys from other kinds of stimulus. It is easy to imagine that this would be adaptive if, as a result of evolution, the ability to detect the presence of crucial objects was built into the physiology of an animal's sensory system. The adaptive advantage of species-specific predispositions to respond to certain classes of objects was discussed in Chapters 5 and 6.

1     1     1     2     3     3     4     4     5     6

**Figure 10.9** The stimuli are arranged from left to right in order of increased firing rate of a specific cell in the monkey's cortex
(Source: Gross *et al.*, 1972, p. 104, Fig. 6)

Unfortunately, it has not proved possible to identify cells in the human brain which respond to particular objects. In fact, if you think of all the multitude and variety of objects and events humans can perceive, it is hard to imagine that recognition of an object would depend on the stimulation of a single cell. For one thing, all the mugs we encounter are likely to look so different that a 'mug' detector cell would have to be capable of recognizing many different patterns of light. One can imagine that the monkey's brain might be 'innately' programmed to recognize monkey paws. But the neurons in the human infant's visual system are unlikely to have included a special 'mug' cell. It seems much more likely that we have *learnt* that certain light patterns indicate the presence of a mug-like object.

To sum up, physiological research has provided fascinating insights into the operation of visual systems in animals. However, one question which still remains unanswered is how all the electrical activity from the retina in the eye to the cortex in the brain comes to be interpreted as corresponding to objects in the environment. This is a crucial issue for psychological theories of perception and, as we shall see, it is not at all easy to arrive at a definitive answer.

## Summary of Section 2

- Sensory receptors are stimulated by inputs of energy from the environment.

- In vision, the retina at the back of the eye contains sensory receptor cells (rods and cones) which are stimulated by light from the environment. The retina also contains layers of other cells, notably ganglion cells.

- Micro-electrodes have been used to record firing rates in single cells in response to patterns of light stimulation on the retina. This technique can be used to map the receptive field of a single cell; that is, that area of the retina which, when stimulated by light, changes the firing activity of the cell.

- At different levels of the visual system, cells respond to different light patterns: ganglion cells in the retina respond to light falling within on–off circular receptive fields; cells in the visual cortex respond to more complex features like bars and light/dark edges falling within on–off slit-shaped receptive fields.

- The visual system is organized so that information is transmitted upwards, each layer of cells responding to the firing of lower cells. In this way, information about the presence of complex patterns of light falling on the retina can be passed on to the cortex in the form of electrical activity.

# 3 | Psychological studies of perceptual experiences

Like the physiologists, with their emphasis on how information is transmitted from one layer of cells to the next, the psychologists who first studied perception also tried to break down perception into component processes. Their aim was to isolate particular aspects of perception in order to study them. However, there is one great difference between physiological research, which was mainly carried out on the visual systems of animals, and psychological investigations of *human vision*. The human species is the only one whose members can be asked to give verbal reports about what they see, hear, smell, taste or feel. One way of exploiting the possibility of communication between human experimenter and human perceiver is for the experimenter to present various visual inputs and ask the people acting as 'observers' to describe their experiences. The methodology used in the earliest studies was to ask people to introspect about the quality of their experiences. The data in this type of research took the form of verbal reports of observers in response to quite subtle changes in the visual stimuli presented to them.

## 3.1 Psychophysics: the study of sensations

Early experimental investigations of perception took place in one of the world's first psychological laboratories, run by Wilhelm Wundt in the last half of the nineteenth century. His method, which built on earlier work by Weber, Fechner and others, was known as **psychophysics** because it investigated *psychological* responses to variations in *physical* stimuli. Rather than ask people to recognize every-day objects, the aim was to investigate **elementary sensations**, such as responses to tones and lights.

These psychologists believed that perception is built up from associations between elementary sensations. Their analogy was with the 'atoms' of the physical scientists, the atoms in this case being individual sensations. In fact, Wundt and his colleagues prided themselves on their scientific approach. They presented observers with carefully graduated physical stimuli measured precisely—for example, in decibels for the loudness of tones—and kept a systematic record of the observers' responses. Nevertheless, because of their reliance on verbal reports of people's sensations, later psychologists tended to emphasize the *subjective* nature of their data. You will have come across this attitude in the discussion of the origins of behaviourism in Chapter 6.

The psychophysicists used their methods to chart the *limits* of sensation. For instance, they investigated how soft a tone people can hear or, if the intensity of light changes by a tiny amount, will observers notice any difference? One strength of this line of research was the extension of psychophysical methods to study sensations in every sense modality, including sight, hearing and touch. One aspect of this, the study of thresholds, is described in Box B.

A **threshold** is defined as the minimum amount of stimulation to which observers will report that they have experienced a sensation. To measure a threshold the experimenter increases the intensity of an undetectable pinpoint of light, or a touch on the skin, until observers report awareness of the physical stimulus.

Technically, an **absolute threshold** is measured by recording when an observer reports the presence of a stimulus on 50 per cent of the occasions on which the stimulus is presented. This 50 per cent criterion of awareness was developed in order to allow for the fact that, when presented with a stimulus at a very low intensity, an observer would sometimes report it, sometimes not. So each level of intensity was tested many times until it elicited 50 per cent 'yes' responses. For example, the loudness of a pure tone would be very gradually increased, a few decibels at a time. Observers' responses would be recorded until they reported the presence of a particular tone a hundred times out of two hundred presentations.

ACTIVITY 2

You might like to try out, with a friend, the procedure for measuring a threshold, described in Box B. You could record a very brief burst of sound on a tape recorder. Turn the volume down very low and then present this 'tone' at a variety of low levels, asking your 'observer' each time whether or not he or she heard the tone. In order to check your observer's absolute threshold, note the loudness of the tone at which a sound is detected five times out of ten.

In addition to their experiments measuring absolute thresholds, the psychophysicists also studied thresholds for detecting minute *differences* between two stimuli, known as **just noticeable differences (JNDs)**. One early study tested the 'two-point threshold' by gently touching the skin with two points, very gradually increasing the distance between the points until observers reported the sensation of feeling two distinct points rather than just one. A fascinating result was that on some less sensitive parts of the skin, like the back of the neck, the points could be placed quite far apart before two separate points were felt. On more sensitive parts of the skin, like the finger tips, a gap of only 2 millimetres would be noticed as two different points of contact. It is adaptive for humans to respond to fine differences in touch sensations on the fingers which are constantly used for handling objects.

The psychophysicists also carried out experiments testing people's ability to notice whether one of two tones was louder than another or whether two lights were of the same or different brightness. On the basis of many such experiments, a psychophysical regularity was noticed. For a just noticeable difference to be reported, the difference in intensity between two stimuli has to be proportionately the same. This is known as **Weber's Law**. As early as the mid-nineteenth century, Weber carried out a long series of experiments on people's judgements of whether objects they held in their hands were the same or different weights. From this he worked out the differences in weights necessary for someone to report a just noticeable difference.

Taking as an example light intensities, suppose that a just noticeable difference is reported between the light of ten candles and the light of eleven candles. This means that adding an extra one-tenth of illumination makes a noticeable difference; that is, the addition of one candle to ten. Weber's Law would predict that one-tenth of extra illumination would always need to be added. So adding an extra three candles to thirty would result in a difference being noticed. Taking an extreme example, you can imagine that in a dark room lighting one candle would have a dramatic effect, whereas in a room lit by 100 candles, lighting one more candle would scarcely be noticed.

SAQ 4   (a) Following the 'one-tenth candle power' rule, how many candles would need to be added to make a just noticeable difference to (i) forty candles; (ii) 500 candles?

(b) Which would be likely to be detected more easily: an identical coughing noise at a pop concert or at a piano recital?

(c) Imagine holding three 10p coins in one hand and four in the other hand. Now imagine holding six in one hand and seven in the other. In which case should you be more likely to notice a difference in weight?

The development of psychophysics is an interesting methodological case study. In the first place, it introduced the notion that sensations can be studied in a controlled manner, varying stimuli precisely on physical dimensions and recording verbal responses. Secondly, it is a good example of how experiments can lead to theoretical laws, like Weber's Law, being proposed and then tested. It has also led to interesting new ways of thinking about what is involved in the detection of stimulus inputs.

For instance, the 50 per cent criterion for absolute thresholds for detecting the presence of a very low stimulus has been given a new theoretical explanation (Gregory, 1972). You will remember from Section 2.2 that there is always a certain amount of background firing activity in cells. The suggestion is that the reason why observers sometimes report the presence of a stimulus and sometimes fail to report it, is due to the existence of this fluctuating amount of background activity in the nervous system. The task for the observer is to distinguish the stimulation actually caused by very low sounds or lights against a background of fluctuating activity in nerve cells. In other words, the observer has to detect a **signal**, the low intensity stimulus presented by the experimenter, from background neural 'noise'. For this reason, the approach is known as **signal detection theory**. A whole new method for analysing the ability to detect stimuli has evolved from this idea.

In general, psychophysical *methods* have had a lot of success in predicting the way observers respond to sensory inputs. It is easy enough to carry out the same experiments today and obtain the same results. The psychophysical method of gradually varying stimuli and measuring responses is still used to test theories about perceptual judgements. But, as a *theoretical* approach attempting to explain perception in terms of individual sensations, it led to a general feeling of disenchantment. In everyday life, people are not often asked to concentrate on detecting tiny changes in pure tones or flashing lights. How could all these elementary sensations provide the basis for perceptions of whole objects? In the next section we shall be introducing an approach which radically challenged the emphasis on studying elementary sensations.

## 3.2  Gestalt psychology: global properties

Both the physiological studies of single cell activity, described in Section 2, and the psychophysical investigations of sensations, just described in Section 3.1, concentrated on the 'atoms' from which perceptions can be built up. This implies that the richness of the visual world can be broken down into its constituent parts. Information derived from spots of light falling on the retina, the analysis of elementary sensations, can somehow all be put together to produce complete perceptions of the whole environment.

In contrast to this, the German group of **gestalt psychologists**, working in the 1920s and 1930s, believed that psychologists should study the perception of *whole* figures rather than the elementary sense experiences that were the stock-in-trade of psychophysics. The gestalt psychologists (**gestalt** from the German word for 'shape' or 'figure') believed that no study of individual sensory elements can add up to an adequate account of perceptual experience. This is because the 'whole' (perception) is more than the sum of its 'parts' (elementary sensations). Because they were interested in the perception of whole figures, the gestalt psychologists wanted to discover what makes us see whole figures standing out against a background. In gestalt terminology this is known as the distinction between **figure** and **ground**.

Wertheimer, a noted gestalt psychologist, compiled a list of gestalt **laws of perceptual organization**, four of which are illustrated in Box C. He believed that these laws represent the **perceptual grouping principles** which result in groups of elements being seen as wholes against a background. The gestalt psychologists used the patterns shown in Figure 10.10 to demonstrate some of the factors which encourage the perception of groups, rather than of individual elements.

There is one overriding law of organization to which all the grouping principles contribute. This is the concept of a **good figure**. A figure is more likely to stand out as a good figure from its background if its elements are similar and close together and it is bounded by a continuous line. It also matters if all the elements in a figure cohere and move around together, known as the principle of a 'common fate'. We would indeed be very surprised if parts of an object moved separately; imagine the ears of a dog, for example, moving in one direction and its legs drifting off in some other direction—rather like the disembodied smile of the Cheshire cat in *Alice in Wonderland*.

The method used to test the effects of perceptual grouping principles was to present observers with figures like those in Figure 10.10 and ask them to describe what they saw; for example, vertical or horizontal rows, squares and circles.

## BOX C  Gestalt laws of perceptual organization

### Proximity
Elements that are close together tend to be seen as forming a group. If you look at Figure 10.10(a), in (i) you can see either horizontal rows or vertical columns with equal ease. When some of the rows of dots are in closer proximity, they appear as groups of dots, forming horizontal rows, as in (ii), or vertical columns, as in (iii).

### Similarity
Similar elements tend to appear together as organized groups: you tend to see columns rather than rows in Figure 10.10(b).

### Closure
One of the best known gestalt laws is the way in which incomplete lines are 'closed up' to produce 'good' figures like squares or circles even when there are only four isolated points, as shown in Figure 10.10(c).

### Continuation
Figures tend to stand out against a background when they appear to be defined by a single unbroken line. Figure 10.10(d) tends to be seen as two overlapping rings, each with a continuous boundary, rather than as three separate areas.

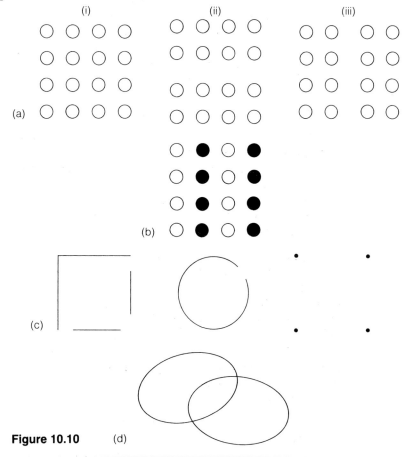

**Figure 10.10**

Most people reported much the same perceptions, which the gestalt psychologists claimed as evidence for their grouping principles. The gestalt psychologists also used **ambiguous figures** to demonstrate the compelling effects which force us to see whole figures. When looking at Figure 10.11, most people alternate between seeing a white vase against a black background or two black faces against a white background. The point is that it is impossible to perceive both figures at the same time. The brain has to select one figure–background interpretation or the other.

**Figure 10.11**

SAQ 5   Identify one *theoretical* aspect in which gestalt psychology differs from psychophysics, and one *methodological* aspect in which the two are similar.

The gestalt psychologists certainly did not believe that people are free to choose which groupings to see. The rationale given by the gestalt school for the operation of the 'laws of organization' was based on a theory of how the brain works. They believed that the brain contains electrical fields which are responsible for the laws of perceptual organization. When sensory receptors are stimulated, sensory information is organized into electrical fields. This property of the human brain was thought to result in automatic perception of 'good' figures. In the case of ambiguous figures, electrical fields in the brain presumably switch from one possible figure–ground configuration to another. There is no room in the theory for interpretations by the observer.

There is no direct evidence to support the gestalt hypothesis about global electrical fields. The physiological evidence outlined in Section 2 demonstrated the importance of electrical activity in the visual system. Cortical cells were shown to respond to patterns such as bars and edges. However, it is not at all easy to reconcile these feature detector cells with the existence of the global electrical fields proposed by the gestalt psychologists. At present, not enough is known to specify the precise way in which neural information might be integrated into perceptions of whole figures.

One of the major problems with the gestalt demonstrations was that some of the perceptual grouping principles were rather vague, as were the responses of the observers. What exactly makes a circle or a square a 'good' figure? Suppose one observer reports perceiving a whole circle while another observer interprets a drawing as a curved line with a small gap in it. Such responses are likely to depend on how observers interpret instructions. For instance, should they be looking for overall patterns or do they think it would be cleverer to notice any imperfections?

In recent years, there has been a revival of interest in whether perceptions are organized according to gestalt grouping principles. Instead of relying on verbal reports, experiments have been designed to test whether people respond to figures in the ways predicted by the gestalt laws of organization. According to the grouping principles, some figures should look 'better' than others. The question at issue was whether people would recognize good figures when they saw them. The experiments described in Box D provided an empirical test of this.

## BOX D   Experiments to test gestalt laws

In one experiment Garner and Clement (1963) asked subjects to rate on a 'goodness' scale the A, B and C figures shown on the left of Figure 10.12. In general, subjects rated A as being 'better' than B and B as 'better' than C.

Pomerantz (1981) reported a later experiment designed to test subjects' behaviour in relation to predictions about the goodness of figures. Subjects were shown dots which they could join up just as they liked, like the dots to be joined up in children's drawing books. The prediction was that, when presented with patterns of dots which suggested simple 'good' figures, nearly all subjects would join them up in the same way. Figure 10.12 shows that this was the case with the figures in A and B. Presented with the 'non-good' pattern in C, subjects varied in the way in which they joined the dots because there was no obvious good figure.

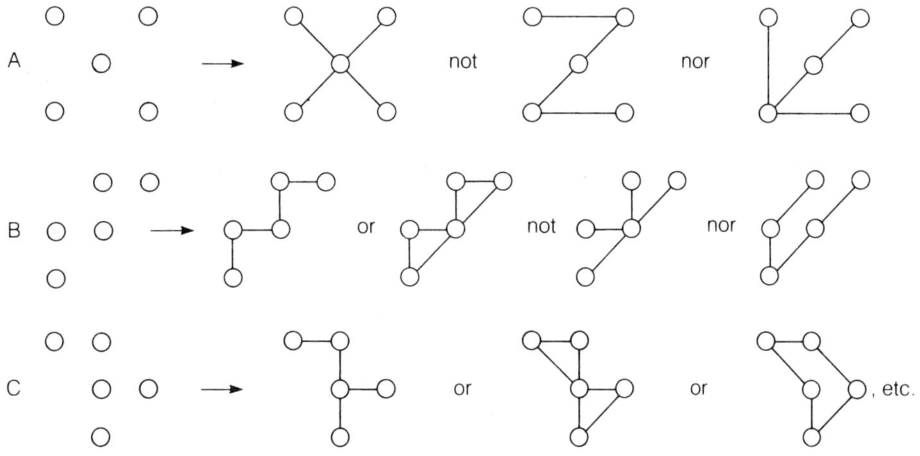

**Figure 10.12**
(Source: Pomerantz, 1981)

Experiments like those described in Box D, and indeed the original gestalt demonstrations, show that certain factors like proximity, similarity and 'goodness' do affect the way individual stimuli are organized into figures. Without these grouping principles, we would see nothing but individual dots of light rather than whole figures. So the gestalt laws of organization may go some way to explaining how elementary sensations are automatically grouped into perceived organized figures which are 'greater than their parts'. Such groups may correspond to patterns of light which we see standing out from their background; for instance, the shiny surfaces of a mug against the background of a table. However, there is still a long way to go in explaining how the abstract patterns which were used in gestalt demonstrations can be integrated into perceptions of recognizable objects in the environment.

## Summary of Section 3

- Psychophysics is the study of elementary psychological sensations which observers report in response to physical sensory inputs.

- An absolute sensory threshold is defined as the intensity of a stimulus at which it is reported as being present on 50 per cent of presentations. Psychophysical thresholds have been reinterpreted as requiring the detection of a signal (stimulus) from background neural activity, a theory known as signal detection theory.

- According to Weber's Law, a constant proportion has to be added to a stimulus for detection of a just noticeable difference (JND).

- The gestalt psychologists proposed that stimuli are perceived as organized figures as a result of grouping principles such as proximity, similarity, closure and continuation, all of which operate to produce perceptions of good figures against background; that is, the distinction between figure and ground.

# 4 | Basic perceptual processes

The theories and research discussed in Section 3 were concerned with aspects of the environment which influence people's perceptual *experiences*. People can report their perceptions of individual tones and lights and of overall patterns as figures. The next step is to explain how these experiences are derived from the sensory inputs of light to the eye. The physiological studies reported in Section 2 indicated that information about patterns of light falling on the retina is transmitted to the brain. Psychologists studying visual perception are interested in the *perceptual processes* which interpret these sensory inputs to the visual system.

One influential approach to perception, which first emerged in the 1950s and 1960s, is to consider the perceptual processes by which information can be extracted from the light falling on the retina to provide sensory cues about the environment. The question is often posed in terms of the **retinal image**, referring to the pattern of light falling on a specific area of the retina. Each object is thought of as *projecting* an image on the retina by stimulating light receptors. As Figure 10.2 showed, light rays enter through the lens in the front of the eye and are focused on a particular area of the retina at the back of the eye. How can the brain interpret the light image on the retina in order to arrive at an accurate perception of the external environment?

The research of psychologists working on this problem is well described in Gregory (1972). One particular concern was to explain how perceivers see objects as a constant size even when they are at quite a distance away from us. It may seem so obvious that objects normally remain the same size that you may be wondering why there is anything here that needs explaining. But remember that all the visual system has to go on is the patterns of light falling on the retinal image.

## 4.1 Size constancy

As Figure 10.13 shows, the rays of light reflected off a tennis ball when it is near to the eye stimulate a relatively large area of the retina. The light rays reflected off a more distant ball stimulate a much smaller area of the retina. The situation is that the very same ball projects *different size* retinal images depending on how far it is away.

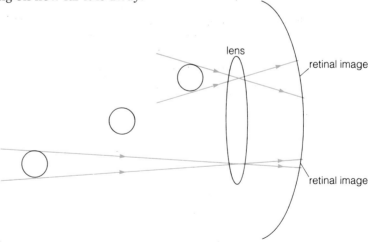

**Figure 10.13** A schematic diagram to show the different sizes of retinal images projected by the same-sized object at different distances

SAQ 6    On Figure 10.13, draw in the light rays from the tennis ball at the middle distance from the eye. What is the relative size of this retinal image compared with those of the ball at the nearest and furthest distances?

The question which struck psychologists was this, 'how can the human visual system cope with all this ambiguous information about the "real" size of the ball?' When we see a tennis ball hurtling towards us, it does not appear to get larger and larger as it approaches. Yet Figure 10.13 shows that its *retinal image* is getting larger and larger. If an actual tennis ball 'grew' as large as its retinal image would indicate, you might be tempted to opt out of the game and run for cover. So it is rather convenient that the visual system perceives the ball as remaining a *constant* size, despite its changing retinal size.

Gregory (1972) suggests an easy way of demonstrating that objects project different-sized retinal images. Hold your left hand out at arms length and your right hand at half the distance away. You will find that both hands look roughly the same size. But, if you move your right hand over to overlap the left hand, you should find to your amazement that the right hand not only overlaps the left hand but is large enough to swamp it completely. The point of this demonstration is to show that your two hands were actually stimulating *different-sized* images on the retina, the image for the more distant left hand being smaller than the image for the nearer right hand. Nevertheless, to start with, both hands were perceived as being roughly the same size, despite the disparity in their retinal sizes. How can **perceived size** be explained in relation to such large differences in **retinal size**? The name for this phenomenon is **size constancy**, referring to the fact that objects are perceived as a *constant* size despite alterations in the size of the retinal image.

**Figure 10.14**

Look briefly at Figure 10.14 and then decide in as natural a way as you can which, if either, of the two women in the picture looks the larger. Most people's response to this picture is to say that the figures look more or less the same size. Now take a look at Figure 10.15 overleaf. Exactly the same figures appear but with their positions in the scene changed. This time the answer to the question is ludicrously obvious. In both photographs the retinal sizes of the images projected by each of the two women are the same. In Figure 10.14 one of the women looks further away and so appears to be roughly normal size. In Figure 10.15 the two women appear to be sitting side by side at the same distance. Why does the size of the woman on the right look so different in the two photographs?

As you can see from looking back to Figure 10.13, the visual system is set to expect objects which are further away to project smaller retinal images. So when you look at Figure 10.14, the fact that the woman on the right appears to be further away 'makes sense' of the small retinal image. In Figure 10.15 the visual system is unable to reconcile the small retinal image of the woman on the right with her apparently nearer position, so it resolves the paradox by perceiving her as a miniature woman. You may think that, even in Figure 10.14, the apparently more distant woman looks *somewhat* smaller than the nearer one. Nevertheless, I am sure you did not see the 'distant' woman as small as she appears in Figure 10.15.

## 4.2 Distance cues

The simplest account of size constancy is that sensory inputs to the retina include information both about the size of the retinal image and the distance of the object. The assumption is that the visual system is *automatically* able to make allowances for the fact that an object is far away. Even though the retinal image of a distant object is tiny, distance cues that it is far away would 'explain' its small retinal size. Instead of seeing a tiny round sphere, the visual system would take into account both size *and* distance and so would 'see' a medium-sized tennis ball far away. In order for this to happen, the visual system must have available sensory cues which allow it to estimate distance, in order to compensate for size.

Several cues for estimating the distance of objects have been identified, of which we shall mention only one or two here. One distance cue is called **retinal disparity**. This depends on the existence of two eyes, each with a retina. The retina in each eye receives a slightly different image, as you can see for yourself if you hold up a finger close to your eyes and then further away. Shut one eye and then the other. The fact that the finger appears to 'jump' further in space when it is closer to your eye demonstrates that the two eyes receive slightly different sensory inputs. When both eyes are open, the visual system is able to calculate how far away the finger is by combining information from the differences between the images on the retinas in the two eyes, depending on the distance from the eyes.

Another distance cue is **motion parallax** which refers to the fact that to a moving observer distant objects appear to move more slowly than nearer objects. When you look out of a train window you will notice that nearer objects like trees 'flash by' faster than trees further away. The visual system can use this information to estimate how far away the trees are. There are other **perspective cues** to distance. One example is the fact that parallel lines—for example, railway lines—appear to converge in the distance.

**Figure 10.15**

## 4.3  Illusions and conflicting cues

Normally, the visual system receives accurate information about the size and distance of objects. Distance cues indicate the correct distance of an object and this can be taken into account when interpreting the retinal size of an object. Because the visual system is usually a fail-safe device, psychologists have been especially interested in cases in which there is conflicting information. Such conflicting information is not easy for the visual system to resolve. In Figure 10.15, the visual system is confronted with a small retinal size that does not match with the apparently close distance of the woman. This is an example of a perceptual illusion. **Perceptual illusions** occur when conflicting sensory cues can be shown to 'trick' the eye. One of the most famous perceptual illusions is known as the **Ponzo illusion** (see Figure 10.16). When subjects are asked to judge the length of the horizontal lines, most people indicate that the upper line is perceived as longer than the bottom line. The question is, 'why?'

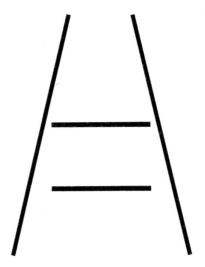

**Figure 10.16**
The Ponzo illusion

Gregory (1972) proposed an explanation based on *over-compensation* by size constancy mechanisms. He suggests that in the Ponzo illusion the long lines on each side look like parallel railway lines or the edges of a road apparently converging in the distance, as shown in Figure 10.17. This acts as a *perspective cue* to distance. You will remember that an object which is further away produces a smaller retinal image than one which is nearer. So why is it that the line which is apparently further away looks longer? The paradox is

**Figure 10.17**
(Source: Gregory and Gombrich, 1973, p. 77)

that the illusion is drawn as a two-dimensional line drawing on a piece of paper. The two lines are exactly the *same* distance from the eye and so project the *same*-sized retinal image. Check this for yourself by measuring the top and bottom lines in Figures 10.16 and 10.17 to convince yourself that they really are the same length. Why, then, do they not *look* the same length?

This is a typical case in which there are conflicting cues. The *retinal size* of the top line is the same as that of the bottom line. However, there is an illusion of depth provided by misleading *distance cues*. The eye is tricked into thinking that the top line is further away. The visual system overcompensates for these distance cues and so the top line looks like a 'bigger' object further away.

There is another very famous illusion called the **Ames room**. A whole life-sized room was designed and built by Ames, a psychologist who started out as a painter. Observers were able to peer through a peephole at people standing and moving around the room. As you can see in Figure 10.18, people standing at different corners of the room look completely different sizes. They also appear to change size as they walk around the room.

**Figure 10.18** The Ames room
(Source: Eastern Counties Newspapers Ltd)

But the shape of the room is another trick. Figure 10.19 shows that the corners at the back of the room are at different distances although the walls are painted to give the perspective appearance of a normal room. You should by now appreciate that the fact that one person looks so enormous and the other so tiny is caused by an illusion of apparent distance. As shown in Figure 10.19, in the Ames room the two people are actually at *different* distances and consequently produce retinal images of different sizes. But the room erroneously gives the impression that both women are standing at the same distance away. The right-hand woman is in fact nearer to the observer's eye and so produces a relatively large retinal image. Because the left-hand woman is further away than she looks, she projects a relatively small image. The visual system interprets this as representing a small object at a relatively close distance. Even in a two-dimensional photograph the illusion is maintained. However, if observers are allowed to look at the odd shape of the room, the size illusion fades away.

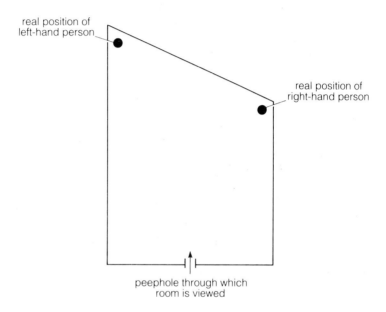

**Figure 10.19** Explanation of the Ames room

## 4.4 Perceptual hypotheses

Gregory (1972) argues that, when perceptual cues conflict, the visual system has to 'bet' on one or other outcome. For example, when the visual system is faced with ambiguous sensory inputs as in the Ponzo illusion, it can either accept the equal lengths of the lines drawn on the page or overcompensate for distance cues, which makes the top line look larger. It can bet on the Ames room being a normal room or it can 'see' the room as distorted and two same-sized people at different distances. To quote Gregory, 'perhaps the most interesting feature of the Ames distorted room is its implication that perception is a matter of making the best bet on available evidence' (Gregory, 1972).

The available evidence includes retinal size and distance cues, and it is on the basis of this that the visual system makes inferences about what is 'really' there. According to Gregory, this process involves formulating a perceptual hypothesis. A **perceptual hypothesis** represents a 'first guess' or bet which is then tested against information from sensory inputs. For instance, faced with the evidence of the apparently normally shaped Ames room, the visual system operates on the hypothesis that the women are different sizes, and this is what is perceived. If further evidence about the distorted nature of the room is available, the perceptual hypothesis is revised. As Gregory puts it, 'perception is an active process of using information to suggest and test hypotheses' (Gregory, 1972).

The assumption underlying this approach is that the visual information derived from the retinal image tends to be sketchy and ambiguous. Gregory's argument is that the visual system has to 'go beyond' this retinal image in order to test hypotheses which fill in the 'gaps', rather like the gestalt principle of closure which results in perceptions of 'good figures' (see Figure 10.10). In order to make sense of the various sensory inputs to the retina, the visual system has to draw on all kinds of evidence, including distance cues, information from other senses, and expectations based on prior knowledge of normal room shapes and the normal size of tennis balls.

The major problem with the perceptual hypothesis approach to perception is that it sounds as if perceivers are making *conscious* decisions about what they see. To caricature this view, it is as if the perceiver says, 'I hypothesize that the room is normal, therefore that the woman on the left is the same distance away, so I conclude that the small retinal image must be caused by a very tiny woman, so that is what I see'. But if perception really requires all this hypothesizing, how can perceptions take place so quickly?

Gregory and other researchers believe that the visual system makes perceptual hypotheses unconsciously and instantaneously. When faced with the Ponzo illusion, everyone sees the top line as longer. There is no question of the perceiver making a *conscious* choice. The radically different size of the women in the Ames room actually goes *against* preconceptions that people are generally the same size. In this case, 'false' distance cues override our expectations about the constant size of human beings. This would argue in favour of automatic built-in perceptual hypotheses.

However, Gregory himself also drew attention to the importance of knowledge about objects in influencing perceptual hypotheses, such as the normal shapes of rooms. Even the basic processes involved in perceiving the size and relative distance of objects can be affected by knowledge about familiar objects.

SAQ 7   In the illustrations in Figure 10.20:

(a)  Which looks nearer, circle or square?

(b)  Which looks nearer, pencil or van?

(c)  Which looks nearer, square or triangle?

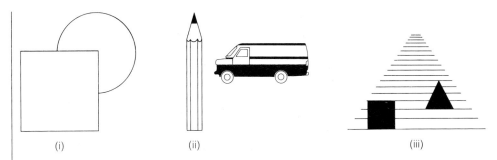

(i)                                    (ii)                                    (iii)

**Figure 10.20**

The importance of knowledge about objects seems to be indisputable. Nevertheless, this still leaves us with some perceptual dilemmas. It seems as if we must have prior knowledge about objects in order to estimate their size and distance. This raises the question about how we come to perceive objects like rooms, pencils and vans in the first place. It seems as if inputs to the retina provide us simultaneously with information about objects and about their size and distance. In the next section, some theories about how objects are perceived will be discussed.

## Summary of Section 4

- Size constancy is defined as the perception of an object as a constant size, regardless of its changing retinal image.

- Size constancy depends on perceptual processes which allow distance cues to be taken into account to produce an appropriate perceived size.

- Gregory suggests that some illusions are caused by misleading distance cues in two-dimensional drawings, leading to over-compensation of size in relation to apparent distance.

- Gregory's conclusion is that the visual system relies on perceptual hypotheses, which enable the visual system to 'go beyond' ambiguous sensory cues provided by the retinal image.

- Knowledge about objects can influence perceptual hypotheses about the size and distance of objects.

# 5 | Theories of object recognition

What has been missing so far is a discussion of how we recognize things in the environment as being particular objects. In the Ames room in Figure 10.18, for instance, it was the perceived *size* of the women that was at issue. But how does the perceiver *recognize* in the first place that the photograph shows a room and that the two objects in the corners are women? What features in the environment act as cues that a flat surface might be a table rather than a bed? The aim of this section is to present theories about how people recognize and identify objects. These are generally known as theories of **object recognition**.

One difficulty about appreciating the need for psychological theories about object recognition is that recognizing objects is something people are doing naturally all the time. Picking up a pen, making a cup of coffee, dressing and undressing, borrowing books from the library, all these activities depend on responding to recognizable objects in the environment. Objects occupy a size and space at a certain distance, they move in expected ways, they are classified as safe and unsafe. Above all, it is their meaning that is important, a cup is for holding liquid, books are for reading, or even sometimes for standing on, or using as a doorstop. Psychologists find it difficult to devise experiments to study such every-day behaviour as recognizing and using objects. If you ask someone what a cup is for, they will find it all too easy to tell you. This is one reason why researchers often study children's gradual accumulation of knowledge about objects. Working with adults, experimenters have to devise ingenious experiments in order to develop theories about the perceptual processes necessary for object recognition.

## 5.1 Mental representations and sensory cues

In Section 1, reference was made to the need to know what things are, or at least what they are used for, in order to perceive them as recognizable objects. Without **mental representations**—stored in the brain—of tables and trees, of rooms and people, our visual systems would be operating in a vacuum. Sensory information could not be interpreted as indicating the presence of a familiar object.

The other basic assumption of theories about object recognition is that sensory inputs provide **sensory cues** for recognizing objects. These perceptual cues provide information about the features of objects. For instance, a certain pattern of dark/light edges picked up by cells in the visual system may provide cues that a table has four legs. The fact that chairs, tables and many animals share the feature of having four legs demonstrates the need for other more subtle cues which provide information about the presence of wooden surfaces or a furry tail, in order to identify a particular array of features as a table or a cat.

Several theories have been formulated since the 1970s to describe how people perceive objects. The basic assumption is that object perception consists of a

**matching process**. Sensory cues picked up by the visual system have to be *matched* against stored mental representations of objects. Object recognition is successful when a set of features is matched unambiguously to a known object. For instance, if the visual system responds to patterns of light which match the features of a table on the other side of the room, that is the object which will be perceived.

It seems obvious that mental representations of what objects look like depend on past experience. It is the many encounters with tables, and all the other objects in the environment, that enable us to recognize them, and indeed to use them appropriately. The question for psychological theories of perception is to explain the processes which enable the visual system to match features in the environment with the known features of a recognizable object.

## 5.2 Feature detection theories of object recognition

The basis for **feature detection theories** is that objects are recognized by extracting cues about features from patterns of sensory inputs. The task of such a theory is to specify the types of processing required to extract from sensory inputs just those cues that are relevant to identifying a particular object. Feature detection as a model for object recognition was developed in an influential computer program, picturesquely styled 'Pandemonium' by Selfridge (1959), which was originally designed to recognize patterns of dots and dashes in Morse code. Lindsay and Norman (1972) applied the same principles to develop a model of how the human brain can recognize letters. The brain was already assumed to have a store of letters, equivalent to stored knowledge of the letters in the English alphabet. The task of the model was to explain how sensory cues about the features of letters can be matched in order to identify a particular letter.

The **pandemonium model** makes use of the term **demon**, a colourful word used by Selfridge to describe a feature detector which is set to identify single features present in the input. Figure 10.21 shows a feature detection model based on Lindsay and Norman's rather joky representations of demons. Each demon detector is portrayed as 'shrieking' to indicate the presence of its particular feature.

The situation in Figure 10.21 is that the letter B is represented by the image demon as a pattern of light falling on the retina. Each demon at the first level of analysis is programmed to search for a particular 'line' feature: vertical, sloping, curved etc. Each of these demons responds by shouting according to whether its feature is present in the input letter B. An important concept is that the strength of the shrieks represents the weighting to be attributed to each feature. If a feature is definitely present, like the vertical line in a B, the vertical 'line' demon detector will 'shout' very loudly (shown by a thick black arrow). The evidence for an oblique line is less in the B input, so the oblique 'line' demon will shout softly, if at all (shown by a thin arrow).

The next step is for the 'angle' demon detectors to put together information from the 'line' demons to see if the particular angle they have been programmed to search for is present. The topmost 'angle' demon responds, and

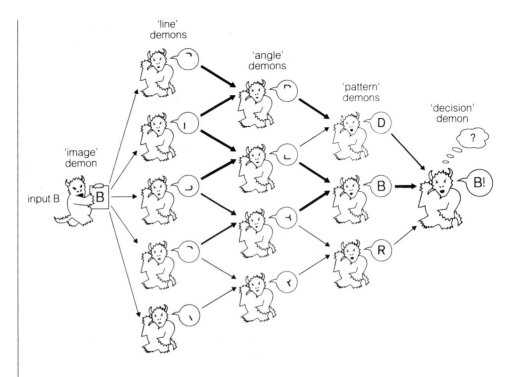

**Figure 10.21** Pandemonium

starts shouting, because the lines reported by the two top 'line' demons can form its required angle. At the next level up the 'pattern' demons analyse the information from the 'angle' demons. The angle recognized by the top 'angle' demon makes the identification of certain letters more probable than others but the angle is still compatible with a D or a B or an R. However, the accumulated information from all the demons in favour of 'B' features makes the B 'pattern' demon shout loudest to the 'decision' demon, and so it wins the day.

The term 'pandemonium' is used to represent the uncertainty inherent in feature processing. Since many features of letters are similar, they may set off many detectors, resulting in a pandemonium of shrieking. It is only at higher levels in the system that the shrieks become more focused on the detection of a particular pattern of features. One point to notice is that the way pandemonium is presented makes it sound as if there are a lot of little demons in our heads all shrieking away while the decision demon listens and makes decisions. This is exactly the picturesque terminology used by Lindsay and Norman. However, the whole system is meant to be a colourful metaphor for automatic processes which are triggered by the presence of certain 'line' features in the image on the retina.

SAQ 8   In Figure 10.21, suppose the input letter had been an R.

(a) Which of the 'line' demon detectors would have shrieked more loudly? (Number the demons from the top downwards.)

(b)  Which of the 'angle' demons would have shrieked more loudly?

(c)  Which of the 'pattern' demons would have shrieked more loudly?

(d)  How would the demons have responded to a lower case 'r'?

(e)  Given a recognition system like pandemonium, which other letters with similar features would be likely to cause confusion when recognizing a C?

It should have struck you, while reading about the pandemonium feature detectors, that this is very like the account of neural processes described in Section 2. Substitute for demons the groups of neurons acting as feature detectors, substitute for the pandemonium of shouts the firing rates of cells and we have a hierarchical model of perception which could be tested by reference to neurophysiological findings. It is a fascinating coincidence of dates that Selfridge's pandemonium article and Hubel and Wiesel's article on cortical cell detectors in the cat appeared in the same year, in 1959. When Lindsay and Norman presented the pandemonium model in 1972, they referred to evidence from Hubel and Wiesel's discovery of cells which respond to bars and edges at certain orientations, and claimed that this fits in well with psychological feature detection theories.

The aim of the pandemonium model is to integrate information from various feature detectors in order to achieve recognition of a whole object, a letter B for example. This parallels the integration of information passed from neuron to neuron in the visual system. What psychological processes are necessary for information from one or more features to be combined? Treisman and Gelade (1980) proposed a theory of feature integration and carried out some experiments in which they compared the performance of subjects when they had to pick out individual letters from a display and when they had to pick out combined features such as the letter T coloured blue. These experiments are described in Chapter 11, Section 4.2, where the issue is the extent to which special *attention* has to be given to detecting combinations of individual features. The question to be discussed in the rest of this section is how combinations of features are recognized as objects in their natural contexts.

## 5.3  The influence of context in object recognition

So far, the discussion has been concerned with recognizing objects in isolation, an R or a blue T. But in ordinary life, objects occur in the **context** of many other objects. If there is a table there are likely to be chairs as well. When recognizing letters, it is easier to recognize that there must have been an R in the word RAT than recognizing an R on its own. Look at Figure 10.22, for example, in which an identical input is more likely to be recognized as the letter H in THE and as the letter A in CAT.

THE CAT

**Figure 10.22**

In principle, a feature detection theory like pandemonium could have 'word' demons. These would respond to shrieks from the 'letter' demons. For instance, if the C and A and T demons shout loudest, a 'word-decision' demon would respond with the word CAT. There are in fact word detector models—for example, McClelland and Rumelhart's (1981) computer program—which operate along these lines. These newer models allow for the system to change its mind in the light of context. If a letter would make an obviously impossible word like TREP, the system will backtrack to test whether the features are equally likely to indicate a letter A to fit in with the word TRAP. However, even sophisticated word-recognition computer programs have so far failed to include sentence contexts to help with the recognition of individual words. It would, of course, be much easier to distinguish between *trip* and *trap* in the context of sentences like 'Mind you don't . . .' and 'Beware the . . .' than as individual words. However, it has simply proved too difficult, at least so far, to store in a computer's memory all the possible contexts in which we recognize words and objects.

## 5.4  Bottom-up and top-down processing

A further problem with pandemonium-type models is that, like the physiological processes described in Section 2, all the information is passed from lower levels ('line' demons) up to higher levels ('angle', 'pattern' and finally the 'decision' demon). It is conventional in psychology to make a distinction between bottom-up processing and top-down processing. **Bottom-up processing** is defined as processing which begins with an analysis of sensory inputs. Information derived from sensory inputs is transmitted up to higher levels of perceptual analysis; processing is from the bottom-up. This kind of processing is also called **data-driven processing** because the information (i.e. data), received by sensory receptors, 'drives' perception.

**Top-down processing** is the reverse of bottom-up. It is based on the idea that sensory information from the retina is not enough to explain how we perceive objects and events; also relevant is the knowledge we already have about what things ought to look like. This knowledge is used in top-down processing, so-called because expectations about objects in the world work downwards to influence the way we interpret sensory inputs received by our sense organs. Since mental concepts about what to expect in our environment 'drive' top-down processing, it is also referred to as **concept-driven processing**.

SAQ 9   Does the processing in pandemonium operate in a bottom-up or top-down direction?

One important point you should note is that object recognition theories always assume a matching process between sensory cues and stored mental representations. Mental representations about the known features of objects represent already acquired knowledge about objects. The real question is whether the matching process itself operates in a bottom-up direction until a match is found. Alternatively, is knowledge involved in the matching process itself? Can the visual system recognize a table solely from bottom-up analysis of individual features like four legs, differentiating it from other four-legged objects? Or is knowledge about tables and chairs, and where they are likely to be found, used in a top-down direction to help with recognizing objects?

## 5.5 Neisser's cyclic model of perception

As indicated in the previous section, feature detector theories like pandemonium start by analysing sensory inputs in order to match them against stored mental representations of objects. It is important to note that the analysis starts without any *prior* indication of what the object is likely to turn out to be. It is not until a feature is matched at the highest level that the system 'realizes' that the input is an A or a B. However, it has also been pointed out that objects are more likely to be recognized in a given context. If we had to interpret patterns of sensory inputs from scratch each time, life would be extremely complex. In reality, perceptions flow easily if all we need to do is to exploit expectations we already have about objects we are likely to see.

Neisser (1976) proposed a theory which assumes that perceivers start with expectations about objects that they are likely to encounter in a given context. On the basis of a preliminary analysis of sensory cues, expectations are used to construct a perceptual model of probable objects. By a **perceptual model** Neisser means mental representations of likely objects or events. According to Neisser, a perceptual model needs to be tested against sensory cues available in the environment. Perceivers use perceptual models to initiate an *active* search for just those kinds of cues that will be likely to confirm, or disconfirm, the current perceptual model.

Neisser's **cyclic model of perception** involves a *continuous* process of checking and rechecking. The perceiver constructs a perceptual model, which guides a search for cues in a top-down direction. If sensory features are found in the environment which *confirm* the presence of the features specified in the perceptual model, then this perceptual model is accepted as a perception. If other different features are discovered in a bottom-up analysis of sensory cues, the perceptual model will have to be revised. Neisser's cyclic model of perception is shown in Figure 10.23, and demonstrates the *interaction* between top-down processing and bottom-up processing. As a result of this interaction, a perceptual model becomes a fully fledged perception.

Neisser calls his model an **analysis-by-synthesis** theory of perception. This is because perception arises from generating a perceptual model (synthesis) and extracting information about features from the environment (analysis). This synthesis–analysis process is a cycle which continuously monitors the environment in the light of expectations arising from previous experiences.

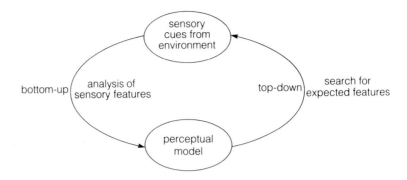

**Figure 10.23** Neisser's cyclic model of perception

SAQ 10 In Neisser's model, which type of processing is top-down and which is bottom up: (a) synthesis; (b) analysis?

A nice example of analysis-by-synthesis can be demonstrated by looking at Figure 10.24. Without any perceptual model based on context, what can you make of it from a bottom-up analysis of its sensory features? Now turn to Figure 10.25 on page 514. Is your perception of the object changed as a result of looking at it in the light of a perceptual expectation based on context? Your original response to Figure 10.24 might have been an abstract gestalt figure defined by three circles, probably not as a perception of a recognizable and meaningful object as in Figure 10.25.

**Figure 10.24**

The great advantage of Neisser's theory of perception is that it combines hypotheses based on knowledge of objects in context with the extraction of features (sensory cues) from the environment. A perceptual model is constantly being revised in line with experience, and the matching process involves an active search for cues. For Neisser, perception is a continuous *active* interaction between top-down processing, driven by expectations, and bottom-up processing, driven by sensory data.

There are, however, some problems with this attractive theory. The first question to ask is where perception actually occurs in the long drawn-out analysis-by-synthesis cycle. As an example of Neisser's cyclic model, imagine I walk into a dimly lit room and see a shadow against the sofa. My perceptual model, generated from past experiences, might be that this is a cat. I search in the half-light for further cat-like features such as ears and a tail. None is present so I discard the cat perceptual model and I generate a new perceptual model of some shoes left about by my daughter. This leads to a search for shoe features, and heels and laces are found which confirm my second perceptual model. Did I 'see' the shadow as a cat first and then as a pair of shoes, or did I only see the shoes when that perceptual model was confirmed? Of course, all this perceptual processing may be unconscious, but the question still remains of what counts as a perception. If we take Neisser's statements too seriously, it sounds as if we only see what we expect to see. If we have to start with a perceptual model which stimulates an active search for clues, how can humans cope with the totally unexpected?

Neisser's theory has quite a lot in common with Gregory's concept of perceptual hypotheses which was explained in Section 4.4. The perceptual model gives rise to expectations and hypotheses about what must be there. However, one of the points Neisser stresses is that 'perception is hypothesis testing only in a very general sense' (Neisser, 1976). By this he means that perceivers do not formulate very specific hypotheses which are only discarded if they fail to fit. Instead, expectations are constantly changing, sometimes being directed to the small detail, sometimes to larger meanings. A smile can be perceived as a movement of the lips, as the loving smile of a friend or the cynical smile of an enemy. Absence of an expected object or the presence of an unexpected object will be picked up from the environment and initiate further exploration.

Both Neisser and Gregory stress what the *perceiver* actively brings to perception. The light falling on the retina may be the same. But different perceivers will be aware of different aspects of the environment. The Eskimo people recognize a hundred different kinds of snow; the expert chess player will 'see' chess pieces on a board quite differently from a novice. Interaction with the environment is a truly continuous cycle. Rather than setting out to recognize objects as such, we are continually applying our knowledge to the environment and at the same time learning about new aspects of the environment which add to our store of knowledge of the world.

There is no doubt that Neisser's model provides a plausible account of how perceivers integrate information from sensory cues and their own knowledge. But how can theories of recognition like this be tested? In the study of psychophysics described in Section 3.1, it was possible to ask observers to report whether they could hear or feel stimuli at low intensities (thresholds) and whether they were aware of just noticeable differences. The gestalt psychologists required subjects to respond to unusual combinations of dots, lines and figures (Section 3.2). Size constancy and the effects of illusions can be measured by getting subjects to match the length of lines in carefully constructed line drawings. All these investigations present people with novel tasks which can be tested in experiments. Using examples, like those in Figures 10.24 and 10.25, it is possible to demonstrate the effects of contextual information on making objects easier to recognize. But it is not an easy matter to investigate the precise processes involved in perception of objects in the natural environment. Nor does Neisser address the whole question of what kind of neural activity would underlie interactions between perceptual models and sensory cues.

**Figure 10.25**
(Source: Beaumont, 1988, p. 50)

## Summary of Section 5

- Object recognition is the process of matching sensory inputs against stored mental representations of objects.

- In feature detection models, features detected at each level are combined to produce more complex features at higher levels, as in the pandemonium model.

- Bottom-up processing refers to the transmission of sensory information up from lower-level feature detectors, driven by sensory data. Top-down processing refers to the application of prior knowledge, driven by concepts based on previous experiences.

- Neisser's cyclic model combines generating perceptual models based on expectations with an active search for cues in sensory inputs.

# 6 | Perceiving the natural environment: an overview

You will have gathered by now that the purpose of perception is not to be able to perform tasks in a laboratory. Its function is to monitor the environment, using all our senses: vision, hearing, smell, and the sensation of our own body movements. By becoming aware of features of the environment, we can learn from our experiences and develop ways of interacting with objects, including other people. In the course of this chapter, a variety of approaches to perception have been introduced. At this point we can ask how much they have contributed to our knowledge of how perceivers recognize objects, and their place and space in the environment as a whole.

## 6.1  Bottom-up models

The description of the physiology of the visual system in Section 2 demonstrated that the sense organs receive sensory inputs which are integrated and transmitted to the brain. This seems an important first step in understanding how perception works. The psychological research described in Section 3 charted people's reports of individual sensations in response to low-level inputs such as tones and spots of light. The gestalt psychologists were interested in the identification of good figures against a background. The pandemonium feature detection model described in Section 5.2 was based on processes for integrating sensory analysis of individual features to provide more complex patterns of features higher up in the system.

All these models involve bottom-up processing, in which information extracted from sensory inputs is transmitted to higher levels where it can be combined and integrated. The main problem is how to bridge the gap between analysis of features, sensations and good figures, on the one hand, and the perception of recognizable objects, on the other. How are sensory cues in the environment analysed to enable us to recognize the features which define particular objects? One possible approach is that perceivers need to have perceptual models which guide their analysis of sensory cues.

## 6.2  Perceptual hypotheses and perceptual models

You may have noticed that the idea of perceptual hypotheses covers quite a wide range of perceptual phenomena. They were introduced by Gregory to explain the way that the visual system 'bets' on conflicting cues in the environment (see Section 4). Information derived from the retinal image may be compatible with several possible interpretations, a large object further away or a nearer small object. These kind of size and distance adjustments seem to occur automatically in the visual system, so that everyone sees one line as longer in an illusion like that of the Ponzo (Figure 10.16).

Other hypotheses are based on a perceiver's knowledge about expected events. In a context of teacups, any vaguely round object will be interpreted as a cup. On the basis of expectations, sensory cues are analysed to see if they fit a perceptual model. Neisser's cyclic model of perception incorporates both bottom-up and top-down processing (see Section 5). Rather than being analysed from scratch, sensory cues are sampled to see if they conform to the current perceptual model.

The implication is that different perceivers may generate slightly different perceptual models depending on past experiences. For someone who has never used a library before, it may be quite difficult to recognize the loan desk for what it is. Wine connoisseurs can easily distinguish wines which might all taste the same to the rest of us. Except in moments of puzzlement, perceptions are instantaneous, even when they require knowledge. The hypotheses derived from perceptual models are normally unconscious and automatic.

It is interesting, though, to note the theoretical shift from automatic adjustments in the visual system, emphasized by Gregory, to Neisser's references to the *perceiver* as an active explorer. The distinction is between hypotheses which can be thought of as being resolved *within* the visual system itself, as opposed to perceptual hypotheses which depend on knowledge of past experiences. In a theory which evokes an integration of both sensory cues and knowledge, it is more natural to think of the perceiver being actively involved in interpreting the environment.

## 6.3  Gibson's theory of direct perception

One characteristic of all the approaches discussed so far is that they imply that there are *processing stages* in perception. Feature detection models are explicit about stages of analysis from initial reception of inputs, each level of analysis providing information for the next stage. Gregory's and Neisser's theories also assume that there are stages during which perceptual hypotheses are tested. Neisser's cyclic model proposes a continuous process of checking and testing. However unconscious and instantaneous these processes are, they still involve the notion that perception is *indirect*, in the sense that information has to be processed in the visual system before it can be perceived.

A totally different approach to perception is known as *direct* perception. Gibson, one of the best known researchers who takes this position, has been developing his theory of perception over the past 30 years. Gibson (1986) has argued vigorously that there is sufficient sensory information available in the visual system from the whole environment to reflect *directly* those aspects of the environment, notably size, shape, distance and movement, which are necessary for action.

Gibson defines **direct perception** as meaning that there are no intermediate stages between light falling on the retina and an animal's actions. There are no sensations to be interpreted, not even a retinal image which is transmitted to the brain. It is not surprising that Gibson dismisses the need for hypotheses which 'go beyond' retinal information. In his theory, perception does not involve matching inputs against a mental representation. In particular, he opposes the notion that perception depends on individual sensory stimuli acting as sensory cues. Instead, Gibson suggests that light rays from the *whole* environment provide sufficient information on the retina for animals to interact directly with the environment.

Gibson points to the fact that vision is not a *static* representation of individual sensory inputs; rather, it is a function of observers moving around in a visual environment. Animals are surrounded by what Gibson calls the **ambient optic array**, consisting of all the transmitted and reflected light rays from the environment converging on observers as they move around. Figure 10.26 shows the changes in the ambient optic array as an observer moves from a sitting position to a standing position. The black lines show the light rays impinging on the eye of the seated person. As the person stands up the changes in light rays are shown by the blue lines. The standing observer can now see behind the stool, for instance. As animals move, the inputs on the retina provide them with new information about the environment.

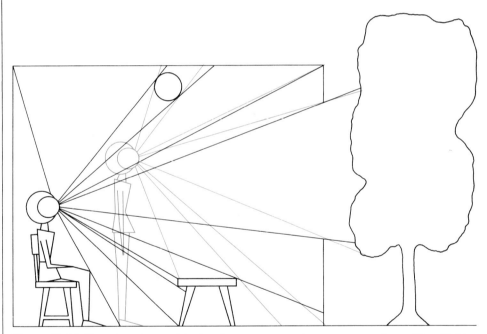

**Figure 10.26** The changing ambient optic array as an observer moves from sitting (light rays shown by black lines) to standing (light rays shown by blue lines)
(Source: Gibson, 1986, p. 72)

Gibson calls his theory an **ecological approach** to visual perception to emphasize the direct contact between an animal and the meaningful characteristics of its environment. These include relatively unchanging aspects of the earth and water, the potentiality of objects for shelter and tools, and the constantly changing positions of other animals. All these enable animals to adapt to their ecological environment. In Gibson's theory, perception cannot be divorced from action in the environment.

Gibson's theory is very attractive because it stresses the *function* of perception as providing the information required for interacting with the environment. He is also right to point to the richness of information provided by light falling on the retina. The implication is that perceptions are less ambiguous than might have been thought by researchers like Gregory. Rather than having to compensate for retinal size by reference to distance cues, Gibson emphasizes the natural gradients and textures in the environment which are responsible for objects appearing at different distances. If you look out of the window, the whole scene is spread out in front of you. Gibson considers that the notion of separate objects, each with a retinal image and an estimated distance, does not do justice to the perceived environment. Objects are always embedded in scenes and so cannot be treated in isolation.

One drawback of Gibson's theory is that he tends to ignore the visual processing which transforms environmental inputs into perceptions. Because of Gibson's emphasis on the directness of perception, he concentrates on the activation of the visual system as a whole. He presumably accepts the role of neural activity to process the rich array of stimulation on the retina, but in his theory it is not clear how this information is transmitted to the brain. He is more interested in the role of the perceived environment in regulating the action of animals.

The other main problem with Gibson's theory is that it works best for innately programmed reactions to aspects of the natural environment, as when a bee finds its way back to the hive or a fish swims in water. Birds migrating for the first time use the stars in the southern hemisphere to guide them, although they can never have seen these stars before. The trouble with these kinds of interactions with the environment is that they are *stereotyped*. Just one example is the extremely annoying habit of a fly that continually buzzes against a windowpane without even noticing the window which has helpfully been left open for it to fly out. The fly never seems to learn but continues to react to the environment of an apparently clear field of light through the transparent window pane.

## 6.4  Do we learn to perceive?

Many animals do learn to change their ways in response to the environment. But the question of whether we have to learn to see in the first place has given rise to a lot of acrimonious argument. It all really comes down to what one means by perception. It is generally agreed that the basic cells and neural connections in the visual system are there at birth. On the other hand, perceptual experience is necessary for infants to learn about the objects in their world. As discussed in Chapter 2, very young children appear to have a predisposition to react to their mothers, or other caretakers, who in turn react to the baby as if it intends to communicate. Nevertheless, learning about physical objects and the intentions of other people is something that takes a considerable time, as charted in Piaget's theory outlined in Chapter 3.

Some researchers have emphasized the innate abilities of young children. One well-known experiment is the **visual cliff** devised by Gibson and Walk (1960) to test whether young babies are aware of depth cues. As shown in Figure 10.27, the baby would be quite safe if it crawled across the glass. However, the visual depth cues indicating that there is a deep drop under the glass override the feel of the glass to such an extent that the majority of babies refuse to crawl over the 'cliff' even when called by their mothers.

**Figure 10.27** The visual cliff
(Source: Gibson and Walk, 1960)

The young of other species, when placed on the visual cliff, show exactly the same reaction. This research supports the hypothesis that basic perceptual processes like depth perception are present at birth. It is, however, typical of research in this area that the babies cannot be tested until they are old enough to crawl around. So it cannot be ruled out that they have already had experiences of falling off chairs and climbing, from which they have learned about depth cues. However, it can be argued that, if children were not equipped with some inborn, at least very rapidly maturing, perceptual mechanisms, how would they ever get started on learning about the environment?

## 6.5  Lack of visual experience: a case study

One type of evidence which is often quoted in relation to the issue of whether we need to learn to see is the comparatively rare case of someone who has been blind since birth and then has their sight restored. If they can see as well as anybody else, this is evidence that no learning is necessary. On the other hand, if their ability to see is still impaired, this demonstrates the need for experience in order to see objects in the environment.

Gregory and Wallace (1963) give an account of a person, whom they called S.B., who had been blind since birth but had his sight restored by an operation at the age of 52. Having been a very active man while blind, he was at first delighted at the opportunity of seeing all the brightly coloured objects he had only known by touch before. When Gregory and Wallace took him around after his operation he was able to recognize many objects, such as animals and cars, as long as he had had experience of them by touch. He could recognize capital letters, which he had been taught to read by touch, but not lower case letters which he had not previously experienced. Figure 10.28 is a picture of a bus drawn by S.B. after he had had some experience of sighted travel. In general it shows the parts he knew by touch, omitting the bonnet in front of the bus. However, by this time he had obviously perceived the bright colours of the advertisement on the side of the bus.

**Figure 10.28**
(Source: Gregory and Wallace, 1963)

As the months passed by, though, it became clear that S.B. was in some ways like a newborn baby when it came to recognizing objects and events by sight alone. Gregory and Wallace report that S.B. found it impossible to judge distances by sight alone. For instance, he knew what windows were from touching them both from inside a room and from outside standing on the ground. However, never having been able to look out from a top-floor window, he thought 'he would be able to touch the ground below the window with his feet if he lowered himself by his hands' (Gregory and Wallace, 1963), although the window of his hospital room was actually 40 feet above the ground.

This rather leaves open the question as to whether such basic mechanisms as depth cues have to be learned or whether they are automatically mediated by the visual system. The infants in the Gibson and Walk (1960) study were able to judge depth by visual cues. An alternative explanation is that S.B. had passed the critical age for picking up distance cues. Or, as Gregory and Wallace suggest, S.B.'s prolonged reliance on touch cues may have interfered with the development of normal visual mechanisms.

Another interesting observation was that S.B. never learnt to interpret facial expressions like smiles and frowns, although he could read a person's mood from the sound of a voice. Unfortunately, experiences like this depressed S.B. and, like other tragic cases of this kind, he often reverted to sitting in darkness, and eventually died 3 years later. The sad case of S.B. provides a timely reminder that the emphasis on vision in this chapter, and in many other psychology textbooks, ignores the importance of other senses such as touch and hearing.

This consideration of whether we 'learn to see' raises again the important question of the role of past experience in perception. It seems indisputable that normal infants are born with sense organs, physiological mechanisms necessary for processing sensory information, and a brain which can interpret information it receives. Nevertheless, evidence also shows that human perceptions depend on the integration of past experiences with current sensory inputs. These issues are of crucial importance in defining human perception.

## 6.6  What is perception?

I have given this last section the same title as the very first section to give us the opportunity to reconsider the three basic questions about perception posed in Section 1.

The first question asked how information is extracted from the multitude of inputs received by sensory receptors. Relevant physiological evidence was presented in Section 2 suggesting that information derived from patterns of light falling on sensory receptors in the retina is transmitted to the visual cortex in the brain in the form of electrical activity in nerve cells at all levels in the visual system. Psychophysical judgements of elementary sensations and the gestalt laws explaining perceptual experiences of figures were described in Section 3. Section 4 considered evidence about basic perceptual processes for extracting information from the retinal image about the size and distance of objects in the environment.

The second question asked how sensory information is processed to provide a representation of the environment. The theories outlined in Section 5 defined object recognition as the matching of sensory cues against stored mental representations of objects. Feature detection theories like pandemonium concentrated on bottom-up extraction of features from sensory images. Neisser points out the need for a continual cycle of interaction between analysis of sensory cues in the environment and expectations based on prior knowledge. This is a plausible description of what goes on in perception, but it needs a more precise specification of the mechanisms involved.

In this section, we have seen that Gibson also addresses the problem of how perceivers interact with the environment. However, Gibson emphasizes the complex structure in the light rays which impinge on the eye. Gibson's theory is at its strongest when explaining innate stereotyped reactions to the overall 'optical flow' of the environment. Neisser accepts the importance of the information in the optic array but makes the point that Gibson's theory says 'nothing about what is in the perceiver's head' (Neisser, 1976). From this point of view, Gibson's is a bottom-up theory with its stress on information picked up directly from the environment. In contrast, Neisser's main concern is with the prior knowledge which is employed in a top-down direction to generate the perceptual models which underwrite perception.

This raises important issues in connection with the third question about the role of past experience in perception. What indeed would our perceptions be like if we knew nothing about the environment? The evidence presented in Sections 6.4 and 6.5 about the development of perception in infants and recently sighted adults was rather equivocal. However, when it comes to recognizing objects, children have to learn what tables and trees are, how to use an object such as a spoon even if they do not yet know what it is called. Adults, too, are constantly exposed to new experiences. Despite television pictures about events all over the world, it is impossible to imagine the feel of snow or the heat of a tropical sun until you have experienced them. It is even more difficult to grasp what a baby, or someone with restored sight, actually 'sees'. The same light rays shine on the eye of a baby as on the eye of an adult. What we perceive are ordered representations of a room with furniture, curtains at the window and pictures on the wall. It is almost impossible to visualize perceptions of the environment by an infant lacking such knowledge.

These are deep and difficult issues. Psychologists certainly do not claim that all the physiological and psychological theories of perception add up to a complete explanation of the complex interaction between knowledge and perceptual experience. We exploit our perceptions to gain experience and knowledge about the world. We use current expectations to explain apparent contradictions in the environment. At the same time, we have to pay attention to what is actually happening. Survival would be difficult if animals moved around in a haze of top-down expectations, without the ability to react instantaneously and directly to bottom-up stimulation of sensory receptors. It is not at all easy to strike the right balance between representations of prior knowledge and the analysis of sensory inputs by sensory systems. Perception can be thought of as a 'conflation of what one remembers and what one sees'. This is indeed a crucial issue both for perceivers in general and for psychologists who study perception, although, as perceivers ourselves, it normally causes us very little bother.

# Summary of Section 6

- According to feature detection models, feature detectors operate in a bottom-up direction, analysing sensory inputs and combining them at higher levels.

- Perceptual hypotheses and perceptual models involve the testing of hypotheses based on past experiences against sensory cues, incorporating both top-down and bottom-up processing.

- Gibson's theory of direct perception emphasizes the total array of light stimulation which he claims is sufficient for perceptual interactions with the environment, without the need for intermediate processing stages.

- Basic sensory processes like depth perception are innate in most species and develop at a very early stage of infancy in humans. Without some basic perceptual mechanisms, human infants would not have the equipment necessary to learn about the environment.

- Evidence from the restoration of sight to people born blind indicates that some learning is required for fully effective perception.

- For perception to provide a basis for adaptable behaviour in humans, there needs to be an interaction between analysis of sensory information and interpretations based on learned knowledge and expectations about the environment.

### Personal acknowledgements

I would like to thank Ilona Roth and John Pickering whose work in an earlier Open University psychology course has been helpful in the writing of this chapter.

# Further reading

GREGORY, R.L. (1972) *Eye and brain*, 2nd edn, London: Weidenfeld and Nicolson.
This little book is a delightful introduction to all aspects of visual perception, including optics and physiology, illusions and hypotheses, perspective and painting. It gives many interesting examples, including the case study of S.B., the man whose sight was restored (see Section 6.5). It is packed with well-chosen illustrations.

Other interesting books by Gregory include:
GREGORY, R.L. (1970) *The intelligent eye*, New York: McGraw Hill.
GREGORY, R.L. and GOMBRICH, E.H. (eds) (1973) *Illusion in nature and art*, London: Duckworth.

NEISSER, U. (1976) *Cognition and reality*, San Francisco: Freeman.
Neisser's readable book presents his own cyclic model of perception. Chapter 2 compares this with the perceptual hypotheses approach and comments on the advantages and disadvantages of Gibson's theory of direct vision.

BEAUMONT, J.G. (1988) *Understanding neuropsychology*, Oxford: Basil Blackwell.
This is a short introductory textbook which nevertheless gives a thorough account of the physiology of the nervous system. Chapter 2 goes into some detail about the visual system, including theories of colour vision.

BRUCE, V. and GREEN, P.R. (1985) *Physiology, psychology and ecology: visual perception*, London: Lawrence Erlbaum Associates.
This is a considerably more advanced textbook which includes a wide range of physiological theories, as well as an extended account of Gibson's ecological approach to perception.

GIBSON, J.J. (1986) *The ecological approach to visual perception* (reprint of 1979 edition), Hillsdale, NJ: Lawrence Erlbaum Associates.
Gibson's book presents his own theory of direct perception from a personal point of view. It also gives a fascinating account of many byways of perception, everything from the flight of birds to speculations about the psychology of film splicing to the development of children's drawings.

## References

BEAUMONT, J.G. (1988) *Understanding neuropsychology*, Oxford: Basil Blackwell.

BRUCE, V. and GREEN, P.R. (1985) *Physiology, psychology and ecology: visual perception*, London: Lawrence Erlbaum Associates.

GARNER, W.R. and CLEMENT, D.E. (1963) 'Goodness of pattern and pattern redundancy', *Journal of Verbal Learning and Verbal Behaviour*, vol. 2, pp. 446–52.

GIBSON, E.J. and WALK, R.D. (1960) 'The visual cliff', *Scientific American*, vol. 202, pp. 64–71. Hillsdale, NJ: Lawrence Erlbaum Associates.

GIBSON, J.J. (1986) *The ecological approach to visual perception* (reprint of 1979 edition), Hillsdale, NJ: Lawrence Erlbaum Associates.

GREGORY, R.L. (1972) *Eye and brain*, 2nd edn, London: Weidenfeld and Nicolson.

GREGORY, R.L. and GOMBRICH, E.H. (eds) (1973) *Illusion in nature and art*, London: Duckworth.

GREGORY, R.L. and WALLACE, J.G. (1963) 'Recovery from early blindness', *Experimental Psychology Society Monograph*, no. 2.

GROSS, C.G., ROCHA-MIRANDA, E.E. and BENDER, D.B. (1972) 'Visual properties of neurons in inferotemporal cortex of the macaque', *Journal of Neurophysiology*, vol. 35, pp. 96–111.

HUBEL, D.H. and WIESEL, T.N. (1959) 'Receptive fieldings of single neurons in the cat's cortex', *Journal of Physiology*, vol. 160, pp. 106–54.

KUFFLER, S.W. (1953) 'Discharge patterns and functional organisation of mammalian retina', *Journal of Neurophysiology*, vol. 16, pp. 37–68.

LE FRANCOIS, G.R. (1980) *Psychology*, Belmont, CA: Wadsworth.

LINDSAY, P.H. and NORMAN, D.A. (1972) *Human information processing; an introduction to psychology*, New York: Academic Press.

McCLELLAND, J.L. and RUMELHART, D.E. (1981) 'An interactive activation model of the effect of context in perception: Part I An account of basic findings', *Psychology Review*, vol. 88, pp. 355–407.

NEISSER, U. (1976) *Cognition and reality*, San Francisco: Freeman.

POMERANTZ, J. (1981) 'Perceptual organization in information processing', in Kubovy, M. and Pomerantz, J. (eds) *Perceptual organization*, Hillsdale, NJ: Lawrence Erlbaum Associates.

SELFRIDGE, O.G. (1959) 'Pandemonium: a paradigm for learning', in *Symposium on the mechanisation of thought processes*, London: HMSO.

TREISMAN, A. and GELADE, G. (1980) 'A feature integration theory of attention', *Cognitive Psychology*, vol. 12, pp. 97–136.

## Answers to SAQs

### SAQ 1

Among the many examples you may have thought of are dreams and hallucinations. One very famous case is when the guilty Macbeth in Shakespeare's play asks, 'Is this a dagger which I see before me?' and goes on to question, 'or art thou but a dagger of the mind, a false creation, proceeding from the heat-oppressed brain?'

### SAQ 2

Figure 10.7(a) is a centre-on cell because light stimulation of the centre of its receptive field on the retina increases its firing rate and stimulation of its surround inhibits its firing rate. Figure 10.7(b) is a centre-off cell because stimulation of the centre of its receptive field inhibits firing rate and stimulation of its surround increases firing rate.

### SAQ 3

For the cell in Figure 10.8(b), firing rate is increased when a bar of light falls on the right-hand side of its receptive field on the retina but is inhibited by light on the left-hand side; for cell (c) firing rate is increased when a bar of light is focused on the centre of its receptive field but is inhibited by light on either side; for cell (d) firing rate is increased by bars of light falling on either side of its receptive field but is inhibited by light falling on the centre.

### SAQ 4

(a) Four candles would have to be added to forty candles and fifty to 500 candles, one-tenth in each case.

(b) A cough would be more likely to be heard at a piano recital. This is because the piano has a lower level of noise and so a cough is equivalent to a larger proportion of noise. At the pop concert, the cough would add only a proportionately tiny increase in noise.

(c) You would have been more likely to report a just noticeable difference between three and four coins because the fourth extra coin adds an extra third to the weight of the three. In the case of six and seven coins, the extra seventh coin only adds one-sixth to the weight.

## SAQ 5

*Theoretically*, the gestalt psychology emphasis on whole figures rather than individual elements was the exact opposite of psychophysical investigations into elementary sensations. *Methodologically*, both approaches used the same technique of asking people to report what they see or hear. This is known as a *phenomenological method of introspection* because people introspect about the phenomena they see.

## SAQ 6

The retinal image for the tennis ball at the middle distance is shown in Figure 10.29. The size of its retinal image is intermediate between the largest retinal image projected by the near ball and the smallest retinal image projected by the distant ball.

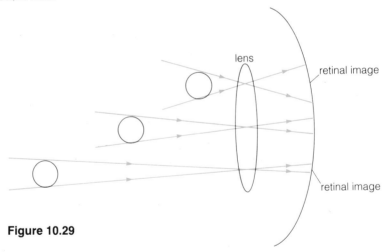

**Figure 10.29**

## SAQ 7

(a) In Figure 10.20(i) the square looks nearer than the circle. This is due to the fact that the square looks as if it is in *front* of the circle, known as an *interposition cue*. It is debatable whether the distance cue of interposition is due to an automatic adjustment of the visual system, or whether it is based on prior knowledge that objects which partly hide other objects are normally nearer to the perceiver. (b) In (ii) the pencil looks nearer than the van. This depends on our knowledge that pencils are smaller than vans. If a pencil and a van produce the *same* size retinal image (from flat drawings on a page), the visual system infers that the pencil is nearer to 'explain' its relatively large retinal image. (c) In (iii) the square looks nearer than the triangle due to the illusion of perspective lines which automatically give the impression of distance.

## SAQ 8

(a) The top two 'line' demons and the bottom 'line' demon would have shrieked more loudly.

(b) The top and bottom 'angle' demons would have shrieked more loudly.

(c) The 'R' pattern demon would have shrieked more loudly.

(d) In order for pandemonium to recognize capital letters and lower case letters as both representing the same letter 'R', the system of demons would have to be much more complex. The features of a lower case 'r' could easily be confused with features of many other letters. The problem would be even greater if the letter recognition model had to be extended to recognize letters in different people's handwriting, rather than printed letters.

(e) Letters like G, O and Q might be confused with C because they share some of the same features, such as curves. This means that the 'line' and 'angle' demons looking for curved lines would respond to all these letters, making it difficult for the C 'pattern' demons to sort out which letter was being signalled. The letter recognition system might learn that some features are more informative, like the 'tail' of a Q which distinguishes it from an O.

## SAQ 9

The processing of features operates in a bottom-up direction, with the 'line' demons passing information up to the 'angle' demons, then to the 'pattern' demons and finally to the 'decision' demon.

## SAQ 10

(a) Synthesis involves generating a perceptual model, based on past experiences, which guides perception in a top-down direction.

(b) Analysis involves analysing sensory cues to extract information about features from the environment, which is passed up in a bottom-up direction.

chapter **11** **ATTENTION**

Jon Slack

## Contents

# 1 | Introduction: what is attention?

It may seem obvious that sometimes we find it easy to attend to objects and events in the environment, and that sometimes we are able to attend to many *different* things without losing concentration. At other times, we feel that our attention is constantly being distracted and that we are unable to concentrate at all. This chapter will be looking at all these aspects, but, first of all, to give you an idea of what attention is all about, you might like to try the following activity.

### ACTIVITY 1

You can do this activity wherever you are studying; it should take you about 5 minutes. For just a moment, turn your attention to what you can hear going on around you. If you are at home, this might include the sound of a radio or television in an adjoining room, the tick of a clock, the low hiss of a gas fire, or whatever. You should be aware when you do this of many noises of which you were previously quite oblivious. Now list as many sounds as you can which went unnoticed when you started reading this chapter but of which you have now become aware through directing your attention to them.

If you have a radio or tape cassette handy, tune to some singing. Try selectively to pick out the voice singing the words. Now try ignoring the voice and focus your attention on the background instruments. Do you notice that, although the piece of music does not alter in any essential way, your *experience* of the music takes on a different quality each time you attend to a different aspect of it?

Re-tune the radio to a station which is not playing music, and try to listen to the radio programme while at the same time attempting to solve a couple of crossword clues from a newspaper. How well can you concentrate on the crossword problems without the task affecting your ability to listen to the radio?

## 1.1 Focused and divided attention

The purpose of Activity 1 is to demonstrate that people have the ability to attend selectively to different aspects of the flood of incoming information from their senses. You should have noticed that, when you attend to one sensory input, you inevitably ignore others. For example, when you are performing a task such as reading, the degree of attention required to concentrate upon it is typically very high. So much so that, when reading, you are usually quite oblivious of most of the other things going on around you. This ability to focus on a particular aspect of a sensory input is known as **focused attention**. It is also known as **selective attention** because we *select* what to attend to. Picking out the voice from a recording of a piece of singing provides an even more striking example of **focused attention**. On first hearing the music, we perceive it as a single continuous sound but, once we focus on the sound of the voice, or the background instruments, our perception of the music changes. It is as if we can tease out the music into its component parts, highlighting some of the sounds and largely ignoring others.

By way of contrast, there are other activities that allow us to attend to something else at the same time. For instance, when driving a car you can easily hold a conversation with a passenger, listen to the radio, or plan the menu for a dinner party. This example suggests that, as well as being able to focus our attention, we can also *divide* our attention across more than one task. This ability to attend to two tasks at once is known as **divided attention**. However, it probably became apparent in performing the last part of Activity 1 that there are constraints on the ability to divide your attention across different tasks. Solving crossword puzzles is a difficult task and it is almost impossible to concentrate adequately on the clues and at the same time give your attention to the radio programme.

The distinction between selective and divided attention is not completely clear-cut. Even when you are trying to focus your attention selectively, unexpected events can impinge upon your concentration on the task in hand. When reading, the sound of children squabbling in the next room will break through. Similarly, while driving, any sudden change in the situation (such as somebody unexpectedly changing lanes in front of you) will make you rapidly switch from your divided attention to focus on the driving.

Why is it that we have this ability to focus and to divide our attention? The simple answer is that our mental capacities are limited. Our perceptual systems provide us with a lot of information about the nature of the external world (see Chapter 10) but our ability to *respond* to aspects of our environment is much more limited. The common wisdom is that 'you *can only do one thing at a time*'. If this is the case, then it is obviously necessary to be able to *select* those perceptual inputs relevant to the task in hand and to ignore other inputs. In reading this chapter, many aspects of your present environment are not relevant to the task, and much sensory information can therefore be blocked out. Section 2 explores the nature of the limitations that underlie *doing one thing at a time*, and investigates the means by which we focus our attention on a particular task or sensory input.

The motorway driving example, given above, suggests that the common wisdom about doing one thing at a time does not always reflect the limits on our mental abilities. Certain tasks can be performed at the same time. When the driving situation is easy you can divide your attention across a number of tasks, but when the driving becomes difficult you are forced to focus your attention solely on it. Why is it that certain tasks force us to the limits of our mental capacity, whereas others make much lower demands? Section 3 of this chapter examines our ability to divide our attention across two or more tasks, *doing more than one thing at a time*, and considers how such tasks can be accommodated within our limited mental capacity.

## 1.2 Information-processing models

In order to explain how selective attention works and how divided attention is possible under certain conditions but not others, we require a theoretical framework as a foundation for thinking about mental events. To illustrate this point, consider the idea of *limited mental capacity* which I touched on briefly in Section 1.1. It is difficult to divide your attention across two tasks such as solving a crossword puzzle and listening to the radio. To perform either task adequately you have to focus your attention on one of them, to the exclusion of the other. Intuitively, it seems that, together, the two tasks require you to process more information than you can cope with at any one instance. That is, the joint mental demands of the tasks exceed your mental capacity. At this point, you need to know how to describe this notion of 'mental capacity'. You could think of mental capacity as the maximum amount of mental work one can perform at any particular instant. However, you now need to explain the concept of 'mental work'. What we need, therefore, are some theoretical concepts which can be used as an accepted foundation from which to build an explanation of mental events. To describe and explain ideas like 'mental capacity' and 'mental work', we require as a starting point theoretical frameworks which can be used to talk about the types of mental events that mediate between the sensory analysis of a stimulus and the behavioural response that the stimulus evokes.

The work of psychologists such as Broadbent (1958) in the study of attention (to be discussed in Section 2) and Neisser (1963) in the investigation of visual search (to be discussed in Section 4) has led to the view of the brain as an **information-processing system**. That is, mental events can be explained in terms of a model of the brain in which information is transmitted (as in a telephone system) and processed (as in a computer). Broadbent and Neisser argue, along with many other psychologists, that *information processing* provides a suitable framework for explaining notions such as 'mental work' and, thus, can be used as a basis for explaining our attentional abilities. In applying the information-processing framework to the understanding of mental events, psychologists began with a very simple model of how information flows through the brain. Such a model is illustrated in Figure 11.1.

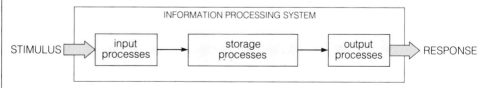

**Figure 11.1** The information-processing model

In Figure 11.1 three stages of processing have been distinguished: **input processes** concerned with the perception and sensory registration of stimuli; **storage processes** concerned with elaborating, manipulating, selecting and storing this information; and **output processes** which produce the appropriate responses. The basic idea underlying the system depicted in Figure 11.1 is that mental processes are conceived of as processing information in the brain, analogous to the way information is processed by a computer. External stimuli impinge on the different senses which then convert the various forms of energy (light, sound, etc.) into information about the nature of the external environment (see Chapter 10). Using the example of driving, the *input processes* transform the light and sound received by the eyes and ears into visual and auditory information about the driving situation.

The information supplied by the input processes is then passed to the next stage of processing, the *storage processes*. It is at this stage that the system must *select* from the wide range of sensory information those aspects that will receive further processing. We cannot attend to *every* aspect of the driving situation, so we focus on those sensory cues that are important for safe driving. One special set of processes that operate at this stage is concerned with the storage and retrieval of information in memory. In driving, we constantly draw on the information stored in our memories, to perform activities such as interpreting traffic signs, remembering where we are going, and deciding on the most appropriate driving action for the conditions. One of the main goals of this stage of processing is to create the information necessary for producing an appropriate response. This information is passed to the last stage of processing, the *output processes*. The output processes retrieve from memory appropriate motor patterns (that is, patterns of activity in the brain that control the activity of muscles or glands). These are manifest as behavioural responses. For example, these output processes are responsible for creating an appropriate sequence of driving actions, such as steering and changing gear.

Figure 11.1 illustrates two important notions. First, mental activity is conceptualized as the processing of information by the brain. Second, mental activity can be broken down into different **stages of processing**, the sequence of stages defining the overall flow of information in the brain. The information-processing framework allows us to examine each stage of processing in detail, identifying sub-stages and sub-processes with precision. Within such a framework, we can now start to think about how we can explain human attention.

Psychologists began by looking at attention as a problem of information transmission. The central stage of processing in Figure 11.1 cannot cope with the whole flood of information passed from the input processes. Some form of **attentional process** is necessary to *select* certain inputs for processing at later stages. That is, certain inputs are transmitted through the system and evoke appropriate responses, while others are discarded and fail to get beyond the input-processing stage. Psychologists adopted the more specific information-processing analogy of the brain as a **communication channel** to emphasize the **flow of information** through the system.

This idea can be made clearer by considering the example of a radio channel. A large number of channels are simultaneously available on the radio wavebands, but all radios are fitted with a *tuning mechanism* which allows you to *select* just one of the channels to which to listen. In selecting a channel, you set up a flow of information from the transmitter of the radio station to you via the radio waves. Similarly, we can view the input processes in Figure 11.1 as generating a number of simultaneously available **channels of**

**information**. By selecting *one* particular channel for further processing, the 'tuned-in' information is allowed to flow through the rest of the system.

This analogy for information processing enables us to capture the notion of **limited mental capacity**. Mental capacity can be thought of as the *amount of information* that can be processed by the system at one time. To bring this analogy to life, consider the performance of air traffic controllers. One of the main jobs of these controllers is to keep track of the different locations of a number of aircraft (depicted as 'blips' on a radar screen) in order to co-ordinate their movements, and this is done through communication with the pilots. Optimal performance in this task requires the controllers both to *divide* their attention across several simultaneous radar signals and aircraft communications, and to *select* the crucial signals to which to attend at any one moment. Controllers typically find that they can deal effectively with only one communication at a time. If a controller receives two radio messages simultaneously, he or she has to choose (and quickly!) which is most important and *focus* on the selected channel of communication. In this situation, the controller's mental capacity seems to be limited to processing one spoken message at a time.

However, the situation is not quite that simple. Although controllers can only focus on one spoken message at a time, the job requires them to monitor the different radar signals at the same time as dealing with the selected message. This implies that controllers can either process more than one type of information at a time, or, at the very least, switch rapidly between the two.

In the next section, I begin with the communication channel analogy and show how it has been used to explain our ability to focus our attention on certain sensory inputs and to block out others. The chapter then goes on to trace the development of more complex models of human attention, and highlights the crucial role of experimental work in guiding the building of information-processing models of human processes.

## Summary of Section 1

- There are two facets of human attention: focused (selective) attention and divided attention. Focused attention refers to the ability to focus our attention on a particular stimulus or task. Divided attention refers to the ability to divide our attention across two or more tasks.
- Information-processing models provide an explanatory framework for describing and explaining mental activity, in terms of the transmission and manipulation of information.
- The information-processing approach analyses mental activity as a sequence of processing stages, and distinguishes between three main categories of processes: input processes, storage processes and output processes.
- Attention is necessary for selecting those sensory inputs, or communication channels, which are to be transmitted to later stages of processing.

# 2 | Bottleneck theories of selective attention

The first theories of human attention were based on the *communication channel* model. According to this view, the **sensory organs** transform sensory inputs through channels of information. In the simplest version of this model, each independent sense organ is regarded as a separate information channel. The information processed by each ear is regarded as constituting two *separate* channels. However, the information provided by the eyes corresponds to a *single* channel because one can never distinguish the inputs to the separate eyes, except in the trivial case of closing one eye.

The later stages of processing cannot cope all at once with all the channels of information generated by the sense organs. A *bottleneck* occurs at the point where the input processes feed their information into the next stage. The simplest model assumes that only *one* channel of information at a time can be processed by the later stages. To overcome this bottleneck, some form of **selection mechanism** is required which allows through only one channel at a time for further processing. The class of theories based on the communication channel analogy are referred to as **bottleneck theories** because they all assume the presence of a bottleneck somewhere in the flow of information. One of the earliest bottleneck theories was developed by Broadbent (1958).

## 2.1 Broadbent's filter theory

Donald Broadbent, a British psychologist, is recognized as one of the major originators of the information-processing approach. Since his work was originally directed towards the study of selective attention, I will begin with a review of his ideas and experiments. Broadbent's research grew out of the practical problems created by the growth of aviation during the Second World War. He was especially concerned with the difficulties which confront air traffic controllers when they need to *select* one message from many competing simultaneous messages from pilots. In this situation, failures in attention can be catastrophic, so the need to understand how human attention works is vital.

In 1958, Broadbent published *Perception and communication*, in which he described his research. Although the original studies stemmed from practical problems, this book was of enormous importance to academic psychology. First, it renewed interest in the study of attention as a mental event. Secondly, as a result of his work, Broadbent was among the first to liken the brain to an information-processing system. The successful marriage of renewed interest in the topic of attention, and a new theoretical framework in which to conceive it, yielded a whole new approach to research.

To develop his model, Broadbent needed to identify the exact properties of focused attention. Because of the complexity of their job, it is difficult to form a precise picture of the attentional abilities of air traffic controllers by observing and measuring their performance in real-life situations. Broadbent therefore decided to investigate attention in the laboratory in order to isolate attentional processes from other complex mental activities. He claimed that it is possible to test theories of selective attention by careful measurement of people's responses in situations where they have to process more material than they can attend to at any one time. Accordingly, Broadbent devised a number of simple tasks designed to ensure that the mental capacity of the subjects taking part in the experiment would be overloaded. The most important of these tasks is known as **dichotic listening**. The word *dichotic* in this context refers to a situation in which the two ears are independently stimulated. In dichotic listening, subjects are required to listen to two different messages simultaneously, each message presented to a different ear. Broadbent (1954) developed a dichotic listening experiment which he called the **split-span procedure**, of which Box A describes a typical experiment.

## BOX A  Broadbent's split-span experiment

The typical experiment required subjects to listen to series of digits (i.e. numbers) through headphones. Three pairs of digits were presented in such a way that one digit of a pair was presented to one ear, while at the same time the other ear heard the other digit. Between the presentation of each pair of digits there was a half-second interval. Figure 11.2 illustrates this split-span procedure.

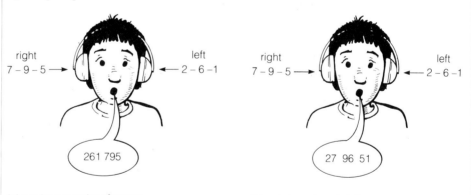

(a) ear-by-ear order of report

(b) pair-by-pair order of report

**Figure 11.2** Broadbent's split-span procedure

Following the presentation of the six digits, subjects were asked to recall them in either of two ways: (i) pair-by-pair, in which they had to repeat the first pair presented, followed by the second pair, and then the third pair; or (ii) ear-by-ear, in which they had to repeat the three digits heard by one ear followed by the three digits heard by the other ear. Broadbent found that the ear-by-ear report was much easier for subjects and also produced more accurate recall.

At first sight, the results of Broadbent's experiments, described in Box A, seem rather odd because they show that recalling the simultaneous digit pairs is more difficult than having to group the three digits heard by one ear and the three digits heard by the other ear. What could be happening to produce this result? If you try to imagine what the task might be like, you will probably conclude that you cannot focus your attention on the two digits in each pair *simultaneously*. Instead, you would have to process one digit and then rapidly switch to the other ear in order to process the other digit. In fact, subjects often report trying to use this strategy in the pair-by-pair recall condition. However, because the pairs of digits follow each other in fairly quick succession, there is not enough time constantly to switch attention from one ear to the other.

In contrast, subjects in the ear-by-ear recall condition report that they deal with the digits presented to one ear first, and only then switch to the digits coming in to the other ear. On the basis of subjects' impressions of how they perform the task, it seems that the level of difficulty they experience is determined by the extent to which it is necessary to switch between ears in the limited time available between stimulus presentations. In the ear-by-ear condition, subjects only have to switch from ear to ear once; that is, after grouping the three digits from the first ear.

SAQ 1    (SAQ answers are given at the end of the chapter) According to Broadbent's findings, which response should be easier to give in the following dichotic listening task?

| Presentation | Digits to left ear: | 8 5 7 |
| | Digits to right ear: | 4 7 3 |

(a) *Response* pair-by-pair          4 8 7 5 7 3

or

(b) *Response* ear-by-ear            4 7 3 8 5 7

Such statements do not constitute an *explanation* of task performance; we have merely concluded that rapid switching of attention from ear to ear is difficult. To understand why this should be the case, we need to consider the stages of information processing that underlie the task. To account for his findings, Broadbent (1958) proposed the type of explanation shown in Figure 11.3.

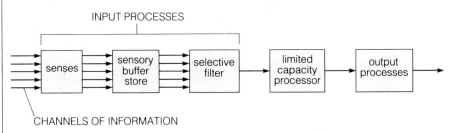

**Figure 11.3** Broadbent's filter model of selective attention

If you compare Figure 11.3 with the basic information-processing framework shown in Figure 11.1, you will notice that Broadbent's model is a more specific version of the information-processing framework, applied to selective attention. There are two important assumptions which are the 'keystones' of his model. First, the two ears act like independent input *channels* of information. Second, the system *as a whole* can only deal with *one* channel of information at a time. These two ideas led Broadbent to propose the notion of a **selective filter** which selects just one input channel for attention. Notice in Figure 11.3 that all the input channels feed into the selective filter, but only one channel is allowed through from there to the next stage of processing. For this reason, Broadbent's model is known as a **single-channel theory of attention**.

Broadbent argued that the selective filter selects a single channel on the basis of the *physical* characteristics of the information. For example, it is possible to select the information arriving at the left ear as opposed to the right ear because the spatial localization of the information—left or right ear—is a physical characteristic. Similarly, if one ear received a message spoken in a male voice, and the other ear a message spoken in a female voice, the filter could use the timbre of the voice to select one message rather than the other, as this is also a physical characteristic of the information. What Broadbent's filter *cannot* do is select an information channel on the basis of the meaning of the message it carries, as *meaning* is not a physical property of a message. I will examine this notion of meaning in greater detail in Section 2.2.

---

SAQ 2   According to Broadbent's model of selective attention, which of the following channels of information can the selective filter discriminate between:

(a) Channel 1: a spoken text about forms of transport.
Channel 2: a spoken text concerning Open University courses.

(b) Channel 1: a spoken text in a high voice.
Channel 2: a spoken text in a low voice.

(c) Channel 1: a random list of words.
Channel 2: a random list of digits.

---

To explain the differences in recall performance in his dichotic listening task, Broadbent suggests that the selective filter requires a certain amount of time to switch from one channel to another. The pair-by-pair order of report requires subjects to switch continually between channels (that is, between the two ears) as each pair of digits is presented. Many of the digits cannot be reported because, by the time the subject has switched channels, the digit on the new channel has been replaced by the next digit presented to that ear. Subjects found the ear-by-ear order of report much more effective because it requires only *one* switch of attention, from one ear channel to the other ear channel.

However, the question remains as to what happens to the digits input to the *second* ear, while the digits in the first ear are being processed. Broadbent observed that, even when subjects are asked to attend to only one ear, they can still successfully report some of the items presented to the other ear. The ability to hold some information while attending to something else suggests that some kind of brief-duration memory store exists, depicted as the **sensory buffer store** in Figure 11.3. In the ear-by-ear recall condition, as the digits presented to the first ear are being processed, the digits arriving at the second ear are held in the sensory buffer store until they can be processed. However, if the information is held in the store too long, it will begin to decay and will eventually disappear.

In Broadbent's model, the selective filter reduces the amount of information that is passed through the system by selecting some sensory inputs and rejecting others. In this way, we can attend to the limited amount of information that we can deal with at any one time. Information from rejected, unattended channels, which does not manage to pass through the selective filter, is simply left to decay in the sensory buffer store. If attention can be switched back fast enough to the unattended channel then one or two items may still be retrieved from the buffer.

## 2.2 Channels and meaning

The notion of a 'channel' in Broadbent's model seems quite straightforward, at least when applied to a dichotic listening task. Each ear is supposed to represent a separate channel. However, this notion of a channel is not so easily applied to the tasks in Activity 1 which you did at the beginning of the chapter. You may not have found it too difficult to pick out the singer's voice from a piece of music. You could probably also focus your attention on the background instruments and switch your attention between them and the voice of the singer. Does this mean that the voice and the instruments are separate channels in this task? One of the drawbacks of Broadbent's original conception of attention is that it is very difficult to define precisely what constitutes a channel.

Another problem with Broadbent's model relates to his concept of the selective filter. In calling the mechanism a selective filter, Broadbent wanted to suggest that selection can be made on the basis of different physical properties of a message, such as spatial location (i.e. right or left ear), loudness, voice timbre or pitch. Just as the light filter fitted to a camera lens works by allowing through certain frequencies of light and blocking other frequencies, so Broadbent's filter would allow through that information channel with the selected physical property (for example, the left ear, or the male voice) and block the others. But, as noted in the last section, his filter mechanism cannot select a channel on the basis of the *meaning* of the information it carries. A light filter cannot block out the light reflected by particular objects in the camera's image because it is unable to distinguish between objects, only between frequencies of light. Similarly, Broadbent's filter mechanism does not have access to the meanings of messages on different channels; it can only recognize the physical properties of messages. However, it seems that meaning can be an important factor in determining which information you focus your attention on, as, for example, when your attention is drawn from reading this chapter by something said on television.

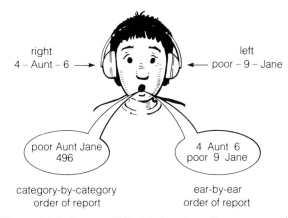

right
4 – Aunt – 6 →

left
← poor – 9 – Jane

poor Aunt Jane
496

4  Aunt  6
poor  9  Jane

category-by-category
order of report

ear-by-ear
order of report

**Figure 11.4** Gray and Wedderburn's split-span procedure

The importance of meaning as a basis for selection was demonstrated in a study carried out by Gray and Wedderburn (1960), two undergraduates at Oxford University. They made a very slight modification to Broadbent's split-span task by presenting, simultaneously, pairs of stimuli drawn from two different categories of items, digits and words. These were presented to the two ears as shown in Figure 11.4.

The subjects were asked to report the items in one of two ways, either (i) an ear-by-ear report, identical to Broadbent's condition; or (ii) a category-by-category order of report, in which the items from one category—say, words—have to be reported before the items from the other category, digits. What prediction would Broadbent's model make concerning the relative performance in the two conditions? Like the pair-by-pair report, recalling items by category requires subjects to switch continually between ears, and should result in lower performance relative to the ear-by-ear condition. In fact, Broadbent's model goes further than this and predicts that the category-by-category order of report should be *impossible* because the selective filter cannot distinguish the meaningful categories.

Gray and Wedderburn showed that subjects *were* able to report, in category-by-category order, the phrases 'poor Aunt Jane' and '496' just as easily as the ear-by-ear order of report (see Figure 11.4). This implies that constant switching between ear channels does not necessarily present difficulties. More importantly, subjects find it as easy to select items in terms of their category—that is, words or digits—as by ear, which strongly suggests that items can be selected for processing on the basis of their meaning. To report by category, the subject has to group the three words and the three digits separately. This means that the items must be recognized and categorized as words or digits before the selective filter chooses between them.

These findings are a serious problem for Broadbent's model as they call into question his assumption that items are filtered on the basis of their physical properties alone. The Gray and Wedderburn result indicates that the filter also seems to be able to distinguish items in terms of their meanings. For this reason, it is better to talk about a selection mechanism as this term does not carry the misleading connotations of a *physical* filter which can only select between physical properties.

## 2.3 Treisman's attenuation theory

Another young researcher at Oxford called Anne Treisman (1960, 1964a, 1964b) set out to investigate how the meaning of items in sensory channels might affect the selection mechanism. She employed an experimental technique, originally developed by Cherry (1953), known as shadowing. This technique is described in Box B.

---

### BOX B    Shadowing technique

In this experimental technique, subjects were played two passages of prose over headphones, one passage to one ear and the other passage to the other ear, simultaneously (i.e. dichotically). The subject's task was to attend to *one* passage (say, for example, the one coming in to the left ear), referred to as the **attended message**. Subjects had to repeat the attended passage out loud continuously as they heard it—a technique Cherry called **shadowing**. The passage played to the other ear, the **unattended message**, was meant to be ignored. When questioned subsequently, Cherry's subjects could tell him nothing about the verbal content of the *unattended* message, but were aware of its general physical characteristics. For example, they did notice if the unattended message had been spoken by a man's or woman's voice, or if it changed from a voice to a pure tone, but they could not detect a change in the use of language from English to French. This was taken as evidence in support of Broadbent's assumption that an input channel can be recognized in terms of its *physical* properties, but not in terms of the meaning of the information.

---

Treisman extended Cherry's technique by varying both the kind of material input to the unattended ear, and its relationship to the material input to the attended ear. Her aim was to discover in which circumstances shadowing was disrupted, indicating that attention had shifted from the attended to the unattended ear. She also asked subjects what they had noticed about the unattended message.

Treisman's experiments, described in Box C, show that, under certain circumstances, **intrusions** can occur from the unattended ear into the attended message, as when a word in the unattended message is repeated as part of the shadowing of the attended message. It seems that a subject who is instructed to attend to one ear may nevertheless hear items from the unattended ear if these fit the context of the message to which the subject has previously been attending. This means that the subject must have been unconsciously monitoring the unattended channel for its meaning. This contradicts Broadbent's assumption that unattended channels (i.e. those blocked by the selective filter in his theory) cannot be processed for meaning. Like Gray and Wedderburn's finding, Treisman's results strongly suggest that the meaning of a message can be recognized *prior* to the processing stage at which focused attention has its effect.

## BOX C    Treisman's shadowing experiments

In one experiment, Treisman used bilingual subjects. The attended message was presented in English, and the unattended message was a French translation of the same message. When the French version, which was meant to be ignored, lagged slightly behind the English version, the majority of subjects noticed that both messages had the same meaning. Quite clearly, the meaningful content of the unattended channel was not being completely ignored, otherwise subjects would not have noticed the similarities between the two channels. Some analysis of the meaning of the unattended message was clearly being carried out. It would be very difficult to explain these results if the selection mechanism controlling access to the limited-capacity processing stage worked in a way in which only the physical characteristics of the unattended messages were analysed.

Treisman conducted two further experiments to shed light on this issue. In one study she presented different strings of words to the left and right ears, but both strings had only a rough correspondence to well-formed English sentences. The following is a sample of two example messages:

Attended (shadowed) ear:    '. . . I saw the girl song was wishing . . .'
Unattended ear:          '. . . me that bird jumping in the street . . .'

The listener was asked to shadow the message given on the first line. The second line is a sample of the unattended message that was presented simultaneously with the first. The actual verbal response made by the subjects was:

'. . . I saw the girl *jumping* wishing . . .'

where the word in italics is an intrusion from the unattended message. Notice that the intruding word extends the meaning of the phrase 'I saw the girl' better than the words on the attended channel. However, if the word strings on the shadowed channel are structured to resemble better-formed English prose (e.g. '. . . I saw the girl wishing for . . .'), intrusions from the unattended channel do not occur.

In another experiment, Treisman presented subjects with a normal prose message to be shadowed, while the other, unattended ear received a string of words that only approximately resembled the structure of an English sentence. At a certain point during the task the two messages were changed over from one ear to the other without warning. What subjects did was to 'follow' the normal prose by switching suddenly to shadowing the other ear, often apparently unaware that they had done this. It is clearly difficult to ignore the so-called 'unattended channel' when it continues the meaningful content of the attended message.

Another piece of evidence supporting the idea that the meaning of an unattended message can be recognized is provided by the **cocktail party phenomenon**, first described by Cherry (1953). To understand this, imagine that you are at a party, and that a number of conversations are going on all around you. Even though you may be giving your full attention to the conversation with the person nearest you, you might still hear your name if it was mentioned in one of the unattended conversations. Using the same shadowing technique, Moray (1959) demonstrated this phenomenon experimentally by showing that one's own name can be recognized even when it is presented in the supposedly unattended channel of a shadowing task.

Findings such as these led Treisman to propose a revision of Broadbent's original model. This revised model is shown in Figure 11.5. In Figure 11.5(a) a selective filter still selects one attended channel on the basis of its physical features. But Treisman suggested that it does not block the unattended channels completely. Rather, the filter attenuates them so that it passes on information from the unattended channels, but only in a depleted or weakened form. Treisman's theory is thus known as an **attenuation theory**.

Treisman argued that the *attenuation process* occurs at the early filter stage in which stimulus items are analysed in terms of their *physical* features, similar to Broadbent's model. The difference between the two models, as noted above, is that Treisman proposed that, although one channel, the main attended channel, is fully selected for further processing, other unattended channels are not blocked completely. Thus, Broadbent's 'all-or-nothing' mechanism is replaced by one which focuses on one input and weakens, or attenuates, others. This implies that there needs to be a second stage in which decisions can be made about the information carried by the attenuated channels. It is important to note that the second stage of selection operates on the *meanings* of the attenuated messages.

The mechanism proposed by Treisman for the *second* stage of selection is depicted in Figure 11.5(b) which is an enlargement of the limited capacity semantic processor shown in Figure 11.5(a). You will remember that, in Treisman's model, information from more than one channel is transmitted, though in weakened form, as far as the limited capacity processor stage. In Figure 11.5(a), a number of channels feed into the filter mechanism (shown by solid lines), and the main selected channel (shown as a heavier line) passes on to the next stage. The other channels (shown by dashed lines) are also passed on, but in an attenuated form. The attenuation of a channel in some way reduces the intensity of the information carried by the channel.

In Figure 11.5(b), the intensity of a channel is shown by the length of the corresponding arrow emanating from the filter mechanism. The selected channel is depicted by the longest arrow, showing that its intensity is highest. The unattended channels are represented by much shorter arrows, indicating that the intensity of their information has been reduced. However, the attenuated messages do reach the second stage of selection. This stage of processing carries out an analysis of the information in the attenuated channels in terms of its meaning, known as **semantic analysis**.

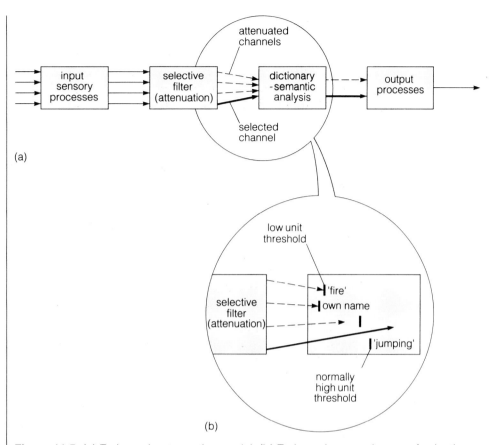

**Figure 11.5** (a) Treisman's attenuation model; (b) Treisman's second stage of selection

The semantic analysis stage consists of a **dictionary** which lists words and meanings. These representations of words are called **dictionary units**. Recognition of a word occurs if a word comes in on one of the channels with sufficient intensity to exceed the threshold of a dictionary unit. The **threshold** of a dictionary unit represents the minimum intensity a word needs in order to trigger that particular unit in the dictionary: the lower the threshold, the more easily a word will be recognized in the semantic analysis stage.

Dictionary units have different thresholds. Dictionary units for some words have permanently low thresholds and thus are always more easily recognized. For example, the units for important words, such as your own name, and words like 'fire', have very low thresholds. This means that recognition of these words will be triggered even by a very attenuated input, as shown in Figure 11.5(b). However, dictionary unit thresholds can also be momentarily lowered by the listener's expectations. For instance, if the words 'I saw the athlete' are heard, the threshold for dictionary units like 'jumping' may be temporarily lowered, making recognition of that word more likely.

SAQ 3 (a) Which of the following words should be easy to recognize—that is, have low dictionary unit thresholds?

pullover     help     cow     look-out     food.

(b) On hearing the phrase 'I've been to the greengrocer and bought some . . .', which of the following word(s) might have their dictionary unit thresholds temporarily lowered?

bicycles     oranges     vegetables     units     food.

As reported in Box C, Treisman found that, in shadowing experiments, subjects sometimes shadowed words that were input on the unattended channel. To explain her results, Treisman argued that the attenuation of words on the unattended channel means that they will be less intense than words on the attended channel. Generally, they will not be intense enough to exceed their unit threshold in the dictionary, unless their threshold is momentarily lowered, or unless, for reasons of importance, they have a permanently low threshold. In Figure 11.5(b), higher thresholds (i.e. those further to the right in the diagram) require more intense signals for the corresponding word to be recognized. Since important words like 'fire', or your own name, have permanently lower thresholds, they can often be heard even on the unattended channel. A word like 'jumping' generally has a high threshold, but this can be momentarily lowered by expectations generated by the semantic context (i.e. the meaning) of the attended message. This accounts for Treisman's finding that words on the unattended channel were sometimes incorporated into the shadowed message if they were compatible with its context. Treisman's model is also able to account for our ability to recognize our own names in an unattended channel.

**Table 11.1** A comparison of Broadbent's and Treisman's models of selective attention

| Information-processing stages | | Broadbent model | Treisman model |
|---|---|---|---|
| Input processes | Sensory processing | All input channels initially processed at the same time | Same as the Broadbent model |
| | | Only physical properties of inputs processed, such as pitch, voice timbre etc. | |
| | Selection mechanism | Selective filter selects one channel on the basis of physical features, and blocks the others | Attenuation filter selects one channel on the basis of physical features, and attenuates the others |
| Limited capacity processor | Main functions | Recognition of stimuli to extract meaning | Same as the Broadbent model |
| | Capacity | Single input channel | Single attended channel plus semantic analysis of attenuated channels |
| Output processes | | Production of response from a single channel | Production of response which can incorporate items from unattended channels |

Unlike Broadbent's model, Treisman's is really a **two-stage selection model**. To recap, the first stage is a selective filter which processes all channels and selects one on the basis of physical characteristics. The second semantic stage consists of threshold settings for words (i.e. dictionary units). The similarities and differences between Broadbent's and Treisman's models are summarized in Table 11.1.

There are, however, two main problems with Treisman's theory. First, although the function of the attenuation process is obvious enough, it is not clear what 'attenuation' means. It does not mean that the unattended message becomes quieter. Rather, it means that in some way its information content is reduced. Failure to specify how this process could occur is a major weakness of the model. Secondly, the idea of a filter operating on physical characteristics is easy enough to conceive, but a selection process acting on meaning is much more problematic. The findings of Gray and Wedderburn, and of Treisman, suggest that semantic analysis of unattended channels is carried out. This is necessary in order to explain switching to the unattended channel, to preserve meaning, as in 'poor Aunt Jane' and 'the girl is jumping'. However, recognizing the meaning of a message requires extensive processing. Unfortunately, Treisman's model has not specified clearly enough the exact semantic mechanisms which allow switching between attended and unattended inputs on the basis of their meaningful content.

## Summary of Section 2

- Broadbent's model of selective attention is based on the idea that people can only attend to one physical channel of information at a time, referred to as a single-channel theory of attention.

- Broadbent's model includes a sensory buffer store in which material is held for a second or two, a selective filter which selects the channel of information to be passed through the system and a limited capacity processor.

- Gray and Wedderburn found that people are able to switch their attention between channels on the basis of meaning in addition to the physical properties of input channels. This challenges the view that the selective filter selects inputs for attention only on the basis of their physical features.

- Treisman's shadowing experiments led her to revise Broadbent's model by suggesting that the selective filter selects one main attended channel, but the unattended channels are not completely blocked off. Instead, they are attenuated, leaving them available for a later stage of semantic analysis.

- The semantic analysis stage comprises a dictionary of word units. When an input exceeds a unit threshold, this triggers the recognition of the word even in an unattended channel.

# 3 | Divided attention

The bottleneck models of Broadbent and Treisman both require some form of selection mechanism which chooses between the channels of information simultaneously made available to the sensory processes. In Broadbent's single-channel theory the selective filter allows only one channel of information through to the limited capacity processor. In Treisman's theory the filter selects one channel and attenuates the others rather than blocking them altogether. However, even in this model, attention is focused on one channel even if it is possible to switch temporarily to another unattended channel. Both models provide an account of the ability to focus our attention on particular sensory inputs, emphasizing that our attention is limited to one input channel at a time. But, the concept of single-channel processing has not gone unchallenged. Although the common wisdom is that one can only do one task at a time, a little consideration of our real-world behaviour reveals a different picture. The examples given in Section 1.1 demonstrated that we can often divide our attention across two or more tasks.

Driving a car while holding a conversation is a good example of divided attention because it highlights some of the general factors that determine whether attention can be divided between two tasks performed simultaneously. Driving while talking to a passenger is only possible in certain conditions. If something unexpected arises in the driving situation— for example, a pedestrian stepping out into the road—the conversation comes to an abrupt end whilst full attention is given to deciding what action to take to avoid hitting the pedestrian. Moreover, someone *learning* to drive often finds it difficult to converse with their instructor, and the level of conversation is generally influenced by the difficulty of the driving situation. These two facts tend to suggest that an important factor influencing the simultaneous performance of two tasks is the extent to which one or both of the tasks can be performed *automatically*; that is, without conscious thinking. If you do not have to think about how to perform one of the tasks, then you have *spare capacity* which you can allocate to another task, such as conversing with your passenger.

In the 'talking while driving' example, a number of channels of information have to be processed. Driving involves close co-ordination between the visual input, giving you information about the road situation, and your motor responses, which require constant adjustment to meet the needs of the moment. In addition, the auditory channel carries the conversational interactions. So, another factor which might influence the simultaneous performance of two tasks is whether the tasks use the same or different *modalities*; for example, the **auditory modality** (hearing) and the **visual modality** (vision). Talking and driving operate within different modalities. Doing two things simultaneously may be much more difficult for tasks which make use of the *same* modality, such as driving whilst trying to read a road map, both of which use the visual modality. Part of the difficulty that subjects experience in dichotic listening tasks, such as those used by Broadbent, is that the simultaneous messages to the two ears both use the auditory modality; the subject has to try and listen to two things at once.

The rest of this section looks at these issues in more detail, considering the conditions under which the single-channel, limited-capacity bottleneck does not seem to apply, and also examining the attentional strategies people use to facilitate multiple-task performance.

## 3.1 Doing two tasks at once

The idea that two tasks can be performed concurrently, providing the associated sensory inputs are in different modalities, was supported by the research of Allport, Antonis and Reynolds (1972). The experimental method they used is known as the **dual-task method**, which is commonly used to study people's ability to do two tasks simultaneously. Such simultaneous-performance tasks are often called **concurrent tasks** because they are done concurrently. The rationale underlying the method is that, if subjects can successfully divide their attention between two tasks, they should be able to perform both tasks without detracting from the level of performance on either task. This can be shown by comparing the levels of performance on the two tasks when performed separately with levels of performance when both tasks are performed simultaneously.

If there are no differences in performance in the single-task and simultaneous multi-task conditions, then the two tasks are shown not to interfere with each other. This implies that the tasks draw on *different* processing mechanisms which can operate quite independently of each other. On the other hand, if the two tasks do interfere with each other—that is, if performance on one or both tasks is poorer in the simultaneous multi-task condition—this suggests that the tasks are competing for the *same* processing mechanisms.

The dual-task method has been developed to sort out which input channels and processing mechanisms are required by different tasks. Allport *et al.* conducted a number of studies based on this rationale. They employed the shadowing technique (described in Box B) in which one task was to shadow a message by repeating it aloud, and the experimenters varied the other concurrent task. Their studies are described in Box D overleaf.

On the basis of their findings, Allport *et al.* concluded that the attention demands of a shadowing task do not prevent the processing of other channels. It seems that tasks which centre on different sensory modalities can be performed simultaneously without mutual interference. This result was extended through the research of Shaffer (1975) which is described in Box E.

How can we explain the decreased performance in Shaffer's second study, as opposed to the successful dual-task performance in the other studies? The crucial difference is in the modalities which need to be used in the two concurrent tasks. Shaffer's results indicate that both the input and output modalities of the two tasks are important for efficient dual-task performance. This idea becomes more apparent by inspecting the summary of the dual-task studies shown in Table 11.2. The table indicates the input and output modalities for each of the tasks used in the different dual-task studies. The **input modality** refers to the input channel; that is, whether the materials are presented in a visual or auditory manner. The **output modality** refers to the

---

### BOX D    Allport *et al.'s* dual-task studies

**First Allport study**

In this study, one task required subjects to shadow continuous speech presented to both ears over headphones. The second task required them to study and remember a set of pictures of complex visual scenes unrelated to the content of the shadowed message. Later, the subjects' memories of the scenes were tested by the number of pictures they recognized correctly (recognition task). Subjects' memory scores for the pictures were the same regardless of whether the pictures were presented on their own or simultaneously with the shadowing task. Similarly, the level of performance on the shadowing task was unaffected by the simultaneous presentation of the pictures. These results suggest that processing complex visual material draws on different processing mechanisms from those required for continuous speech.

**Second Allport study**

In a second study, the subjects were all skilled piano players. The first task again involved shadowing continuous speech. The second task required the subjects to sight-read piano music from a score they had not seen before. Like the results of the first experiment, the two tasks did not interfere with each other when performed concurrently. Performance on the sight-reading task was at the same high level with or without the concurrent shadowing task. Equally, the sight-reading task had little or no effect on the accuracy of speech shadowing. These results imply that the analysis and reproduction of speech involves quite separate processing mechanisms from those underlying piano playing by experienced performers.

---

nature of the response mechanisms which produce the task behaviour. For example, the task of copy-typing involves *motor* responses (i.e. movements of the hands and fingers) as an output. The output of a shadowing task, on the other hand, centres on the **articulatory modality** which comprises the response mechanisms associated with the production of speech.

What do you notice from Table 11.2 concerning the influence of input and output modality on dual-task performance? Remember that only the tasks in Shaffer's second study produced interference effects, since all the other studies demonstrated efficient dual-task performance. It seems from these results that two tasks can be performed simultaneously without mutual interference as long as the tasks employ different input modalities and different output modalities. For example, in Shaffer's first study the copy-typing task occupies the visual input modality and the motor output modality, whereas the input for the shadowing task is in the auditory modality and the output is articulatory. However, if the typing task is switched to the auditory input modality, as in audio copy-typing, this does produce interference with a concurrent shadowing task, as shown in Task 2(a) of Shaffer's second study. In this case, both tasks employ the same input modality. This result pinpoints the difficulties experienced in Broadbent's dichotic listening experiments as they involve the concurrent processing of two auditory inputs (Section 2.1).

## BOX E  Shaffer's dual-task studies

### First Shaffer study

Shaffer (1975) demonstrated that a skilled typist could copy-type prose in German (a language she did not understand) presented visually while simultaneously shadowing a prose passage presented over headphones. Both tasks were done almost as accurately together as they could have been when done separately. Although typing was a skilled activity for the subject, the information-processing demand of the experimental task was extremely high because she was having to copy-type a language she did not understand. However, this hardly hindered performance on the shadowing task.

### Second Shaffer study

In a different series of experiments (Shaffer, 1975), the skilled typist performed an audio-typing task which involved listening to the material to be typed, presented over headphones to one ear. Employing the dual-task method, this first task was combined with each of the following concurrent tasks:

*Task 2(a)*: a shadowing task in which the shadowed message is presented to the ear not receiving the audio-typing input;
*Task 2(b)*: a task of reading aloud, where the concurrent message is presented in the visual modality.

In each case, performing the first task, the audio-typing task, at the same time as the second task, led to a significant decrease in performance on one or both of the tasks, compared to the higher level of performance noted when the typing task and the second task were carried out separately.

**Table 11.2** Summary of dual-task studies

|  | Input modality | Output modality | Results |
|---|---|---|---|
| *First Allport study*<br>Task 1 (shadowing)<br>Task 2 (memory for pictures) | Auditory<br>Visual | Articulatory<br>No direct output but later recognition test | No interference |
| *Second Allport study*<br>Task 1 (shadowing)<br>Task 2 (sight-reading piano music) | Auditory<br>Visual | Articulatory<br>Motor | No interference |
| *First Shaffer study*<br>Task 1 (shadowing)<br>Task 2 (copy-typing: visual) | Auditory<br>Visual | Articulatory<br>Motor | Little interference |
| *Second Shaffer Study*<br>Task 1 (copy-typing: audio)<br>Task 2(a) (shadowing)<br>Task 2(b) (reading aloud) | Auditory<br>Auditory<br>Visual | Motor<br>Articulatory<br>Articulatory | Considerable interference |

The rationale of the dual-task method implies that, if two tasks can be performed effectively at the same time, they must draw on different processing mechanisms. Applying this rationale to the studies summarized in Table 11.2 leads to the conclusion that the different input and output modalities comprise quite separate and independent processing mechanisms. Thus, we can process both visual and auditory inputs at the same time because they are analysed by different processing mechanisms. Similarly, we can perform various motor activities and speak at the same time because the output processes underlying the two modalities are different.

If you look again at Table 11.2, you will notice that the results in Shaffer's second study complicate this picture. In this study, as well as shadowing interfering with audio-typing, so too does reading aloud (Task 2b). Reading aloud does not use the same input or output modality as audio-typing, yet the interference effects imply that the tasks *are* competing for the same processing mechanisms. One important factor is that in the case of Task 2(b) the *material* being processed is the same; that is, meaningful language. The typist had to process two sets of meaningful messages: the text coming in through her ears for audio copy-typing and the different written text which had to be read aloud. Ironically, in Shaffer's first study, the fact that the typist was copy-typing German, a language she did not understand, may have actually made her task easier because only one of the messages was meaningful to her.

SAQ 4    Which of the following pairs of tasks do you think would interfere with each other when performed simultaneously?

(a) Task 1: skilled knitting.
    Task 2: listening to a lecture.

(b) Task 1: holding a conversation.
    Task 2: listening to music.

(c) Task 1: watching television.
    Task 2: writing a letter.

To sum up, it seems that we can divide our attention across two or more tasks providing they occupy different input and output modalities and do not compete for the same processing mechanisms. However, this account is not sufficient to cover all aspects of divided attention. For instance, why is it that we can divide our attention across tasks such as driving and talking in normal circumstances, but not when the driving situation becomes difficult? In both cases, the tasks draw on different input and output modalities (driving occupies the visual and motor modalities, and talking the auditory and articulatory modalities), so what changes produce the shift to focused attention on driving?

If you think for a moment about driving behaviour in difficult situations, what makes the driving harder is that we cannot *automatically* respond to external stimuli as we would under normal conditions. Instead, we are forced to think about the road conditions and to be aware of different, and even dangerous, possibilities when deciding on the speed we should be going or on which manoeuvre to make. Instead of continuing to make automatic adjustments, conscious attention has to be focused on the task in hand.

## 3.2 Automatic and attentional processes

The efficient dual-task performance demonstrated in the Allport *et al.* and Shaffer studies required the subjects to be highly skilled at the non-shadowing task. Being a skilled pianist or typist requires many aspects of the skilled behaviour to be performed automatically. The notion of **automated performance** was first introduced by William James (1890) when he referred to task performance which did not require any significant degree of focal awareness. This notion has been made more precise by Posner and Snyder (1975) who proposed three criteria to determine whether performance is automatic. The performance of a task is *automatic* if it: (1) occurs without intention on the part of the performer; (2) does not give rise to conscious awareness; and (3) does not interfere with other mental activities.

Riding a bicycle is a common example of task performance where most of the underlying operations quickly become completely automatic. You may be able to remember when you first learnt, and the difficulties you had trying to balance the bicycle and move forward at the same time. The operation of balancing the bicycle initially required attention on your part; you were conscious of trying to balance it, and the mental effort required prevented you from concentrating on other operations, such as moving the pedals. However, once you had learnt to ride, the task of balancing was never again a problem. If you imagine for a moment riding a bicycle now, you never get on one with any conscious intention of balancing it. Because you have little conscious awareness of the movements involved in balancing, you can focus your attention on other tasks such as checking the road conditions, or observing the scenery.

The fact that certain types of task performance become automatic is very important for the development of every-day skills. However, there is also one serious drawback to automatic processing: it is difficult to undo. There is a famous Victorian fairground amusement based on this in which one is offered a relatively large sum of money if one can ride a bicycle just 10 feet. Initially this is not a problem, until one realizes that the steering mechanism has been adjusted so that in turning the handlebars to the right the bicycle turns to the left, and vice versa. Under these conditions it is impossible to move even 10 feet because one cannot override one's automatic balancing processes which are geared to the steering mechanisms of normal bicycles.

ACTIVITY 2

Read the following sentence once and then read it again counting the 'f's'.

FRENCH FIREWORKS ARE THE
RESULT OF YEARS OF SCIENTIFIC
INVESTIGATION COMBINED WITH
THE DESIRES OF MANY CHILDREN.

In doing Activity 2 you should have counted a total of six 'f's' in the sentence. If you counted fewer than this, please try the activity again. Many people find this task difficult because they do not detect the 'f's' in the word 'of' which occurs three times in the sentence. A possible explanation of why people often miss this particular 'f' is that it is pronounced like the letter 'v'. This is not the whole story, however. Another explanation is that in the process of reading we automatically recognize frequently occurring words like 'of' and 'the' as units, and find it difficult to focus on their component letters. Healy (1976) has provided experimental evidence for this idea. She asked subjects to read a prose passage at normal reading speed but to circle the letter 't' whenever it occurred in the passage. Her findings showed that subjects were more likely to miss the letter when it occurred in common words than when it occurred in rare words. They were particularly poor at detecting the 't' in the word 'the', which is the most common word in the English language. The processes involved in recognizing frequent words become automatic, enabling the words to be processed as whole units rather than by their individual letters. Unfortunately, this means that it is then difficult to override the automatic recognition process and attend to the individual letters as units.

Shiffrin and Schneider (1977) conducted a series of studies to explore the nature of automatic processes. Their investigations led them to characterize two modes of human information processing, attentional processing and automatic processing. They suggested that **attentional processes** have the following general properties:

1   They are limited-capacity and require focused attention.

2   They are usually **serial** in nature; that is, each process has to be dealt with one at a time, as suggested by single-channel theory.

3   Tasks that are attentionally processed can be learnt relatively quickly and modified fairly easily.

4   Attentional processing is often consciously directed to a task.

These properties contrast with those identified for **automatic processes**, which are:

1   Automatic processes are not hindered by capacity limitations.

2   They often seem to operate in **parallel**; that is, more than one process can be active at a time, as in multi-task performance.

3   Tasks only become automatic through considerable training, and they are difficult to modify once learnt.

4   Automatic processing is usually unconscious, at least until difficulties arise.

When applied to task performance, the distinction between attentional and automatic processing is not clear-cut, but should be viewed as a graded continuum. Certain aspects, or sub-processes, of a task may be automatic, while others may be attentional. For example, riding a bicycle generally involves more automatic processing than the task of baking a cake, which requires the average cook to attend to many aspects of the activity, such as monitoring the consistency of the mixture. Overall, most tasks will be neither fully automatic, nor fully attentional, but a mixture of the two; that is, they will lie at some point on the graded continuum between them.

Learning many of the skills we use in our every-day lives involves a transition along this continuum from the initial state of task performance, which is based mainly on attentional processes, to the acquisition of the skill, when performance is dominated by automatic processing. As noted earlier, for example, under normal circumstances skilled driving performance involves a high degree of automatic processing. Many of the actions are performed in parallel, such as steering and changing gear. The basic actions of driving do not draw on the limited capacity of attentional processes, and thus leave the driver spare capacity to use in performing another task, such as holding a conversation. Optimal driving performance requires a lengthy learning period and driving faults which have become automatic are notoriously difficult to rectify. Finally, the skilled driver is generally unaware of his or her driving behaviour. Drivers will often report not being able to recollect particular driving operations, such as going round a roundabout, or even whole stretches of driving.

This contrasts with the trials and tribulations of the learner driver whose performance is mainly dependent on attentional processes. Early driving lessons make the limitations of the learner's processing capacity all too apparent; there is no possibility of holding a conversation as the learner has to give his or her full attention to the task. To learn each driving operation, the learner has to break it down into manageable parts which can be coped with in a serial fashion—first one action and then the next, and so on. The sequence of behaviours required for a particular driving task can be learnt relatively quickly. For example, it would probably not take a learner driver very long to develop a consistent strategy just for changing gear alone. Unfortunately, this has to be done at the same time as pressing the accelerator and monitoring road conditions. Being under conscious control, early driving strategies can also be changed relatively easily. For instance, when learner drivers have to practise an emergency stop, they rapidly adapt the strategy they have developed for doing a controlled stop. Learning to drive is therefore not so much about learning the basic operations; it is learning to perform them in parallel automatically, bypassing the limited capacity of attentional processes.

In the Allport *et al.* and Shaffer studies the subjects needed to be highly skilled at one of the tasks for dual-task performance to be possible. For the typist in Shaffer's experiments, typing was an automatic task requiring minimal attentional processing between sensory analysis of the text and the response of touching the appropriate keys. All the limited-capacity attentional processing could be allocated to the concurrent shadowing task. Similarly, Allport *et al.*'s piano players needed to be at a level of proficiency at which sight-reading music is relatively automatic, freeing attentional processing for the concurrent shadowing of speech.

SAQ 5   Which of the following activities would normally involve mainly automatic processing and which would draw mainly on attentional processing?

(a) brushing your teeth;

(b) skilled tennis playing;

(c) deciding on a dinner menu;

(d) solving a novel problem.

## 3.3 Kahneman's capacity theory

A conclusion that emerges from the distinction drawn between automatic and attentional processes is that some tasks seem to require a greater degree of attention than others. When a number of separate tasks do not require the full capacity of the attention system, they can be dealt with simultaneously, as in the case of driving and holding a conversation. However, there also seems to be an *overall capacity limitation*. No-one can read a book, sew on a button, shadow a message and tap their foot, all at the same time. There is an overall limit on total attention. This implies that there is some sort of limited-capacity **central processor** which co-ordinates and allocates a central pool of attentional resources. The idea of sharing out attentional resources between tasks has led to the concept of **resource allocation**. Instead of a simple single-channel processor coping with one channel at a time, we can think in terms of a central processor controlling an array of processing resources which can be deployed in a flexible manner. This is sometimes known as the 'butter spreading theory': attention can be spread across tasks like butter over bread.

Processing capacity should therefore be viewed as a flexible process, and not an absolutely fixed property of the system. For example, watching television may place great demands on your attention, but it is still possible to do other things at the same time which require much less processing—such as knitting, for instance—mainly because they have become so practised that they are virtually automatic. What emerges is the concept of **mental effort**, which defines how much attentional processing is required. Notice that this is not directly related to the amount of information which must be processed. Automatic tasks may involve the processing of a large amount of information but require little mental effort. Knitting is an intricate, sensory motor skill with a high information load, but skilled performance is almost fully automatic, requiring minimal mental effort. This idea of mental effort captures the extent to which a task draws on the central limited-capacity processor. Tasks which require a lot of mental effort make heavy demands on this processor.

Kahneman (1973) has incorporated the concept of mental effort into his theory of attention which assumes that there is an overall limit to a person's capacity to perform mental work. His theory also embodies the idea that a person has considerable control over how this limited capacity can be allocated to different tasks. Kahneman's capacity model of attention is shown in Figure 11.6.

The major features of Kahneman's capacity model are:

1   Some activities require more mental effort than others.
2   **Arousal** (which refers to the physiological state which determines the degree of mental activity) controls the total amount of processing capacity available. More capacity is available when arousal is moderately high than when it is low.
3   Several activities can be carried out at the same time provided the total effort does not exceed the available processing capacity. When tasks become automatic they take up less mental effort and put fewer demands on total capacity.

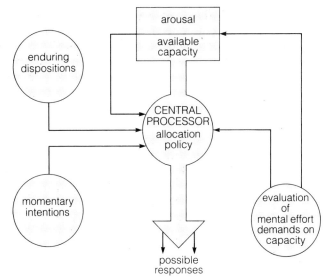

**Figure 11.6** Kahneman's capacity model of attention
(Source: adapted from Kahneman, 1973)

4   The central processor constantly evaluates the level of demand on
    capacity. If this level of mental effort becomes excessive, the **allocation
    policy** must determine whether to concentrate more attention on
    particular tasks.

5   The allocation policy adopted by the central processor can be influenced
    by enduring dispositions, momentary intentions and the general level of
    mental-effort demand on capacity (see Figure 11.6). When a number of
    simultaneous demands are made on limited processing capacity, the
    decision of how best to allocate attention is strongly influenced by
    **momentary intentions**, such that the central processor is likely to allocate
    more attention to activities directly related to current goals. Certain types
    of external stimuli are natural candidates for attention and so are selected
    for further processing. Kahneman referred to these factors as **enduring
    dispositions**.

The picture that emerges from research on attentional capacity is that
attention is a far more flexible system than is suggested by the models of early
theorists like Broadbent. By considering the factors which affect the extent to
which two tasks can be performed simultaneously, it is possible to identify
the various conditions under which the limited-capacity bottleneck does not
apply. It seems that two tasks can be done at once if:

1   One, or both, of the tasks is highly practised and has become automatic
    (Shaffer, 1975).

2   The two tasks use different modalities (Allport *et al.*, 1972).

3   Limited central capacity can be exploited through the use of attentional
    strategies (Kahneman, 1973).

If you think about the way attention works in every-day behaviour, you will
realize that there are a number of other factors that govern the way it shifts

and fluctuates over time. In the absence of explicit experimental instructions about what to attend to, attention is sensitive to both external and internal factors. Your attention can be 'grabbed' by certain external stimuli, such as cries for help, or novel situations or events. Factors such as the novelty, intensity and importance of a stimulus determine the extent to which it can *attract* your attention and override the attentional needs of your current goal. It was factors like these that Kahneman referred to as enduring dispositions. Many of them have a strong biological foundation in that they signal danger, or possibly food. It makes sense, in evolutionary terms, for survival signals to override all ongoing processes and commandeer sufficient attentional resources for appropriate action to be taken. Outside such circumstances, attention is generally at the service of your current goals (Kahneman's momentary intentions). The tasks in hand evoke internal goals which control the allocation of attentional resources to the processing of external stimuli and the integration of behavioural responses.

Accommodating all of these factors in a model of attention requires a conception of attention as a flexible process. In fact, Neisser (1976) has suggested that attention should not be seen as a mechanism or process, but as a *skill*. Neisser quoted the example of two subjects who, after several weeks' practice, were able to write *and understand* dictated words at the same time as reading a different text, *understanding that too*. Allport (1980) has made the proposal that one of the factors involved in determining the demand on attention is the familiarity of a particular task. When a task is novel, the subject does not know what processing resources are needed, so all of them are kept 'on call' in case they are required, and so are unavailable for any other task. Allport claims that one of the reasons why quite complex tasks, such as knitting and reading, or typing and shadowing, can be tackled concurrently, is that practice has enabled the efficient allocation of automatic resources.

## Summary of Section 3

- Two tasks can be performed simultaneously if they use different modalities, or one or both are highly practised.

- A distinction can be made between attentional and automatic processes. Attentional processes put demands on limited-capacity resources, and are usually serial in nature. Automatic processes make minimal demands on the attentional capacity and can operate in parallel.

- Kahneman's capacity theory implies that attention can be flexibly allocated by a central processor, sometimes being divided between several different tasks, sometimes having to be focused on a single task.

- Attention can be viewed as a skill involving the efficient allocation of processing resources. The degree of skill developed by an individual with a particular task can affect the total processing capacity available.

# 4 | The study of visual attention

Most of the research on both selective and divided attention that we have looked at is based on data from auditory tasks where the two ears correspond to different input channels. However, in the case of visual processing there is no equivalent correspondence. You cannot selectively attend to the input from, say, just your right eye (except in the trivial case of closing, or covering your left eye). The process of fusing the images from the two eyes must occur at a stage of processing prior to the stage at which visual attention can operate. This means that, as far as the investigation of visual attention is concerned, the visual system functions as a single input channel.

You cannot switch between alternative visual input channels, but by moving your head, or eyes, you can shift your attention to different parts of the *visual field*. For example, your visual attention is presently focused on the words in this sentence, rather than on the words at the bottom of the paragraph, but both sets of words form part of the current contents of your visual input. The difference is that the words you are reading are at the centre of your visual field whereas the bottom of the paragraph is in your peripheral vision. To read the last word of the paragraph you need to move your eyes down the page so that the word enters your central visual field. The difference between the visual and auditory modalities is that, in vision, the sense organ (the eyes) can be directed to the focus of attention, whereas in the auditory modality the sense organs cannot shut out some sounds and pick up others. Both ears convert all the sound energy they receive regardless of its source. Hence, selective attention in the auditory modality must operate at a later stage of processing.

Many of the important ideas underlying the models of attention we have considered can be carried over to the study of visual attention. However, unlike the auditory modality, it is impossible to define the capacity of visual attention in terms of the number of channels that can be processed simultaneously. Instead, we need to think of capacity in terms of the number of items in the visual input which can be perceived at any one time.

### ACTIVITY 3

To get a feel for this idea of capacity, fix your vision on one of the words on the next page, and while fixing on the word, count the number of words on the page that you can perceive. This measure gives you a rough estimate of the capacity of visual attention at a single fixation of the eyes.

## 4.1 Visual search

The study of human visual attention has centred on research using the **visual search** paradigm. Visual search was originally studied by Neisser (1963) to investigate the factors that influence our ability to process visual information. In a typical visual search experiment, subjects are given a list of items like this:

```
B T N K L
G W Q X Y
U L M X A
T P D F S
O K D S H
I G 8 Y V
K B G E Q
S O F X H
```

They have to search for a particular target (in this case the number 8). The experimenter knows how many letters the subject must look through before reaching the number 8, and so can calculate how long it takes to compare each letter with the number 8, and decide that it is not 8. Neisser did many experiments varying the kinds and number of targets (he might specify the number 8, for example, or just tell the subject to look for 'any number') and the kinds of items to be searched for (the letter Q might be searched for among round letters or straight letters, for instance). These experiments are described in Box F.

Neisser reached the general conclusion that, with sufficient practice, subjects can process many target items at the same time. Presumably each non-target item, when it is scanned, must be compared with some kind of stored memory representation of the target or targets before it can be rejected. If this comparison can be carried out as quickly for ten targets as for one target, then the comparisons must be taking place at the same time. One problem with Neisser's results has since come to light, however. Neisser stressed the need for speed to his subjects, and in consequence they made a high proportion of errors. Neisser's results are therefore complicated by the fact that, although his subjects were as fast in searching for one target as for ten, they made more errors in searching for the ten targets, and so it is difficult to compare overall performance across the two conditions. Nevertheless, his findings and theorization had tremendous impact upon the way psychologists approached the study of attention.

Neisser has suggested that there are different levels of recognition of an item within the framework of visual processing. You can become fully aware of the identity of an item but you can also respond to an item without recognizing it fully. In Neisser's visual search tasks, subjects often reported not being aware of the identity of most of the distractor items in the lists, even though they had correctly identified the target item. The evidence from the feature analysis experiments in Box F indicates that search times are affected by the similarity of features between the target item and the distractor items. The fact that it is easier to pick out a Q from letters like Z and V indicates that the analysis of each item need only go far enough to identify *features* which are inconsistent with it being a target item. In these circumstances, subjects can determine that an item is not a target and make an appropriate response without having to recognize the item fully. This line of thinking led Neisser (1967) to propose the existence of a **pre-attentive stage** of visual processing.

According to Neisser, processes that operate at the pre-attentive stage do not require attention and are evoked automatically by the visual input. One such process is **feature detection** which extracts visual features from the sensory

## BOX F   Neisser's visual search experiments

Neisser's visual search task involved asking subjects to search for a particular **target item** in a display of several rows of letters. Only one target item was present in each display and could occur at any position in the display. The display was presented and a timer was simultaneously started. The subject scanned the display from top to bottom and pressed a response button as soon as the target was located. Over several trials, the position of the target was varied in the display. The time taken to press the button, indicating that the target had been found, was used to estimate the scanning rate of the non-target items in the list.

Neisser was specifically interested in how the scanning rate varied as a result of varying the nature of the background items, known as **distractor items**, and the number of targets being searched for in any trial.

### Feature analysis experiments

In a series of experiments, Neisser found that subjects could scan at a faster rate for the letter Q than for the letter Z. This could be explained by the fact that many of the background non-target items, which were simply other letters chosen at random from the alphabet, were visually more similar to Z than to Q. There are more characters consisting of straight lines, similar to Z (e.g. M, N, W and so on), than characters containing curved segments, similar to Q (e.g. O, P, R etc.). Therefore, it was easier to pick out a Q target from the dissimilar letters.

### Multi-target search experiments

If the subject was given *two* targets to search for in any trial, either of which might be present in the list, then with a little practice the search rate improved so that searching for two targets became as quick as searching for just one target. This latter finding was extended even further in another experiment by asking subjects to search for *ten* targets at once. In each trial, any one of the set of characters A F K U 9 H M P Z 4 might occur as a target in the list. The study lasted for 27 days. At first, the scanning rate for ten targets was much slower than the scanning rate for one target. But by the tenth day the difference in scanning rates for the single-target and multiple-target conditions was negligible.

input. Neisser's findings were interpreted as showing that visual feature detection is an automatic process which operates at the pre-attentive stage. In visual search tasks, if a display item can be distinguished from the target items by single visual features, then these features merely need to be detected for the item to be rejected. Subjects do not have to become fully aware of the identification of each item, but can respond on the basis of the presence of particular features. For example, in searching for the letter O amongst distractors consisting of straight-line characters (e.g. M, H, N etc.), the subject only has to detect a curved-line feature to respond positively to the presence of the O.

To the extent that Neisser's subjects could perform multi-target searches as quickly as a single-target search, this implies that the multiple comparisons are carried out simultaneously; that is, as parallel processing. This is consistent with Neisser's proposal that pre-attentive processes are automatic. Like other automatic processes, feature detection can operate in parallel (see Section 3.2). The comparisons underlying multiple search can be performed in parallel providing they are based solely on pre-attentive processes such as visual feature detection. However, if the display items and target items need to be compared in terms of features other than single visual features, then it may be necessary to go beyond the pre-attentive stage of processing and apply attentional processes to each item. In this case, each item would need to be recognized fully, and it is unlikely that multiple comparisons could be performed in parallel.

## 4.2  Feature integration: an attentional process

Neisser showed that certain aspects of visual processing are automatic and operate at a stage of processing which is prior to the operation of visual attention. However, recognizing an item at the level of full awareness may draw on attentional resources, referred to as **focal attention**. The visual search paradigm has been used extensively to identify the processes involved in visual analysis when it requires focal attention.

In one series of experiments, Treisman and Gelade (1980) used a visual search task in which subjects had to search for target items specified either by a single feature, such as a blue item, or by a conjunction of features, such as a green letter T (i.e. a stimulus item is only a target if it is *both* green and has the visual form of a letter T). The rationale underlying their task was based on the following question: 'If you increase the number of distractor, non-target items in the display, how does this affect feature detection times?'

Their argument was that increasing the number of display items will lead to an increase in the number of comparisons that have to be performed for a target to be detected. If the comparison process operates serially, so that display items are scanned one at a time, then increasing the number of display items will lead to longer detection times. On the other hand, if the comparison process can operate on all the display items in parallel, then the time to detect a target should remain the same, even though the number of display items is increased. In this case, all the items are processed at the same time, so additional stimulus items will not increase the overall processing time.

Treisman and Gelade showed that the detection time for a target identified by a *single feature* is independent of the number of items in the display, illustrating that it involves parallel processing. In contrast, detection times for targets defined by a *conjunction of features* increased as display size increased, which implies that each display item has to be inspected separately. The details of their experimental procedure are given in Box G.

## BOX G   Treisman and Gelade's experiment

The experiment conducted by Treisman and Gelade (1980) consisted of two conditions: the *single-feature* condition and the *conjunction* condition.

In the displays shown in Figure 11.7, the distractor items (non-target items) are the characters T (grey) and X (white).

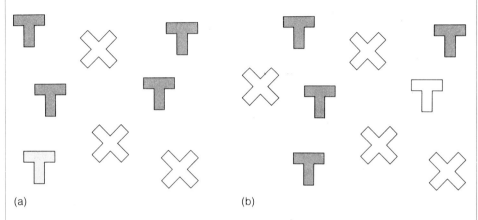

(a)                                                                          (b)

**Figure 11.7** Example displays used in the Treisman and Gelade visual search task. (a) Single-feature condition in which targets are any blue characters (e.g. a blue T or a blue X) *or* the letter S; (b) conjunction condition in which the target letter is, for example, a white letter T

In the single-feature condition, subjects had to detect either of two target items which were (i) any blue character, the particular letter being irrelevant (so a blue T or a blue X would both count as target items), or (ii) an S character, where the colour of the letter is irrelevant. Some displays contained no targets at all, while others contained just *one* of the two targets, either target being equally likely to appear as a display item. Subjects had to search each display for one of the two targets, but they did not know which target item might be present, either a blue letter or a letter S.

In the conjunction condition, subjects were presented with displays containing the same distractor items, but they now had to search for a target defined by a conjunction of features: in Figure 11.7, for example, a white letter T. Only one item in the display could have this particular combination of features.

In both conditions the task required subjects to search for two features, a colour feature and a shape feature. But in the conjunction condition subjects had to check that *both* features were present and belonged to the same item in the display before a positive response could be made. The number of distractor items in the display was varied to investigate how search times in the two conditions were affected by display size.

The findings of Treisman and Gelade showed that search times in the single-feature condition were not affected by the size of the display, implying that the underlying comparisons were performed in parallel. When a target can be detected on the basis of a single feature (either colour or shape), all the display items can be compared with the two possible target items at the same time. This contrasts with the conjunction condition in which search times increased as display size increased. This latter finding suggests that, when it is necessary to integrate two or more features to detect a target, the display items have to be processed serially. This is known as **feature integration**.

This experiment demonstrates that the processing of single features can be carried out in parallel, but that integration of features involves serial processing. Treisman and Gelade's results agree with Neisser's findings in showing that *feature detection* is an automatic process operating at the pre-attentive stage of visual processing. But, in addition, their results show that the process of feature integration can be classified as an attentional process in that it requires focused attention.

This line of research has important implications for understanding how the detection of visual features works. It seems that the extraction of individual visual features occurs automatically and in parallel. In visual search tasks, targets defined in terms of single features, such as a blue item, or a letter S, can be searched for in parallel because the feature detectors can analyse all the display items at the same time. The unique features normally 'pop-out' by *calling attention* to their location in the display. But in the normal course of perception we do not see *individual* features, rather we perceive objects which consist of combinations of visual features. The visual search data might suggest that detecting conjunctions of visual properties requires attention to verify how the features are put together. Treisman (1988) has argued that, in recognizing visual objects, attention is required to ensure error-free feature integration. Her research illustrates how a theory of visual attention can be woven into a more embracing theory of visual processing in general.

There are, however, one or two points which ought to be emphasized here. The first is that the conjunction of features studied by Treisman and Gelade (see Box G) were arbitrary. There is no reason why the letter T should necessarily be written in green or in blue. But objects normally have features which do seem to go *naturally* together. For instance, most kinds of plant life are naturally green; oranges are round and orange-coloured. In other every-day examples, particular combinations of colour and shape are predictable because they are highly overlearned, like the combination of 'red' and 'round' features to define a cricket ball.

A second point is that the subjects in Treisman and Gelade's experiment had to detect the targets from a confusing set of distractor items, such as brown Ts and green Xs. In normal life, objects are not necessarily surrounded by other similar objects. Despite this, it is easy enough to think of some occasions when focal attention directed at distinctive combinations of features might operate in the way suggested by Treisman and Gelade. Looking out for someone in a crowd might be helped by searching a sea of similar-looking faces for a particular combination of red hair, spectacles and a blue scarf, features which identify a person we know.

The final point concerns the *familiarity* of objects. In every-day life we seem to recognize familiar objects without paying any special attention to them. In Chapter 10, many examples are given, including Neisser's cyclic model of perception, when top-down expectations enable us to recognize familiar objects, and to read familiar words, on the basis of fragmentary cues. In all these cases, object recognition appears to be an automatic rather than an attentional process. Automatic monitoring of the environment means that we are not always conscious of what we see or hear, until something occurs which requires us to focus our attention.

## Summary of Section 4

- Neisser has used the visual search paradigm to identify the processes involved in the recognition of visual stimuli.

- Neisser's results led him to propose the existence of a pre-attentive parallel stage of visual processing of features, which occurs before the focal attention required to recognize items.

- Treisman and Gelade used the visual search paradigm to show that the detection of single visual features is carried out automatically and in parallel. The integration of visual features to detect multi-featured targets requires focal attention and involves serial processing.

- Object recognition involves many processes, including feature detection and expectations about familiar objects. Much visual processing is automatic and unconscious, attention being allocated when necessary.

# 5 | Attention: theory and data

In this chapter we have traced the development of theoretical models that underpin our understanding of human attention. This development has to a large extent been shaped by experimental findings. In the laboratory the investigation of attention has given rise to some useful concepts, but the ultimate value of this work is dependent on the extent to which such concepts can be used to explain real-world examples of attention.

## 5.1 Models and experiments

In research on attention, the interplay between theory and data has not been haphazard, but has followed the normal course of scientific progression. The stages of theory development, which typify research in this area, are broadly:

1   *Observation* of phenomena in the real world which pose questions to be answered. Good examples of this include the way in which Broadbent observed the problems experienced by air traffic controllers (Section 2.1), and Cherry noticed that at cocktail parties people can direct their attention from one conversation to another (Section 2.3).

2   *The construction of a model.* In general terms, a model acts as a 'conceptual framework' to suggest ways of formulating problems and to generalize (in the way that Broadbent's model allowed him to think of attention in general terms, not just in terms of the specific example of the air traffic controllers).

3   *The derivation of a theory.* In Section 2.1 you saw how Broadbent's single-channel theory of attention was derived from the information-processing model. A theory is a set of interconnected *axioms* (underlying assumptions) which are intended to describe and explain how things happen. Some theories are very specific, intended only to relate to particular topics or issues. Notice that theories of selective attention are limited in their range. They attempt to describe and explain how salient information is selected for selective attention, while other less important information is rejected. But they give no account of, for example, *why* some information is 'important' and other information is 'unimportant'. They touch on the issue of consciousness, but do not attempt to explain the relationship between conscious attention and unconscious automatic processing. Contrast this with more ambitious theories such as Freud's theory of psychodynamics (see Chapter 4), which, although difficult to test, was intended to explain human behaviour and experience, from child development to adult sexuality, from extremely bizarre mental illness to universal experiences like dreaming and slips of the tongue.

4   *Prediction.* From a theory, it is possible to make *predictions* and in this way test the validity of the theory. For example, Gray and Wedderburn argued that alternation of a set of connected words from one ear to the other would facilitate a words/numbers order of report only if Broadbent's model was *wrong*. This prediction allowed them to test, and potentially refute, Broadbent's theory (Section 2.2). This is called a *refutation model of enquiry*, and philosophers of science agree that it is the only unequivocal method by which theories can be tested.

5   *Experiments.* Predictions from a theory can be used to *design an experiment*. Recall the case of Gray and Wedderburn discussed in Section 2.2. They presumably looked at Broadbent's theory and the results he used to support it. Switching channels would, of course, be difficult if there was no discernible difference between them, but perhaps it could be made easier by switching a *meaningful* message from one ear to the other. They therefore designed an experiment to test the hypothesis that different categories of items would make it significantly easier to switch from one channel to the other. They carefully chose two convenient categories (words and numbers) that were quite different, and made up several three-word phrases and three-digit numbers.

The next stage in the experiment is to perform it, monitor the results, and see how they match up to the experimental hypothesis. Gray and Wedderburn found that the recall of the categorized stimulus material was significantly better in the words/numbers order, even though subjects had to switch continually between the channels. This result means that their experimental hypothesis was confirmed. They concluded that Broadbent's proposal that channels are selected only on an ear-by-ear basis is false. So his theory of attention, which assumes a selection stage operating solely on physical characteristics, must clearly be reformulated.

6   On the basis of results like these, Treisman constructed a new model, a new theory, and a new set of predictions (Section 2.3). This led to new experiments with new hypotheses to be tested.

In any topic area, models and theories are progressively tested, modified and reformulated, becoming ever more complex and sophisticated. In one sense they become more accurate. The theories of attention discussed in Section 3, for instance, generate better accounts of selective and divided attention that Broadbent's original model could not explain. However, as models become more complex they can quickly become conceptually unwieldy, in that they comprise so many components that it is difficult to understand fully how they work. The aim of the theorist is, on the one hand, to account for an increasing range of data and phenomena, and on the other, to create theories which are as simple as possible, and always conceptually manageable. As research areas within psychology develop, these twin goals are generally only reached through the occurrence of a fundamental shift in the way the area is conceptualized. An example of this in attention research is Kahneman's capacity model of resource allocation which explains the continual interplay between total demands and total attentional capacity. On the other hand, the ambitious framework of Kahneman's model means that it is difficult to test experimentally many aspects such as goals, intentions and attentional strategies.

## 5.2  A theoretical framework

As research on attention has developed over the years, certain ideas have become accepted as useful for explaining the way we select specific aspects of our environment to attend to. First and foremost is the idea that mental operations such as attention are best explained within the information-processing framework. That is, the workings of the mind are conceptualized as processes that operate on information which is delivered by the senses or stored in memory. As the human information-processing system is of limited capacity, not all the information supplied by the senses can be fully processed. We have to select actively from the wealth of sensory data what we will attend to, and concentrate processing on the material that is, at any particular moment, most relevant to our goals.

Originally, limited-processing capacity was explained as a 'bottleneck' identified with a particular stage in the human information-processing sequence. For example, Broadbent formulated the single-channel notion of attention which assumes that the selective filter is the source of the limitation. However, the work done by Treisman and Neisser showed that recognition cannot be considered as an all-or-nothing bottleneck. Theories of attention must allow for varying degrees of attention. Research into dual-task performance and skilled behaviour has shown that certain types of behaviour are not restricted by the limited-capacity bottleneck. The notion of a limited-capacity mechanism has been replaced in modern theories of attention with the idea of limited processing resources. Different processes make different demands on central resources, which are limited within the human information-processing system. Attention is seen as a mechanism which deploys an array of processing resources in a flexible manner as a form of resource allocation. This allows us to view selective attention as a skill which can be improved through practice. The proficiency of the skill increases as the allocation policy reaches an optimal level in coping with constantly varying processing demands.

Another important idea in understanding our ability to process information selectively is to distinguish between automatic processes, which make minimal demands on the limited processing resources, and attentional processes which draw more heavily on attentional resources. Tied in with this distinction is the distinction between parallel and serial processing. Automatic processes are independent of each other as long as they do not draw on the same input and can thus operate in parallel. Attentional processes, on the other hand, draw on a common pool of limited processing resources. If two or more processes require the full capacity of some particular resource, they will interfere with each other, necessitating some form of allocation policy.

Collectively, these ideas provide a rich, theoretical framework within which we can attempt to explain the range of phenomena encompassed by human attention. The framework supports a range of models and theories at different levels of specificity. For example, the notion of a *limited-capacity bottleneck* embraces Broadbent's and Treisman's theories of selective attention which are relatively specific, in that they try to account for a specific set of data: findings from dichotic listening tasks and shadowing experiments. This contrasts with Kahneman's capacity model of attention which, by emphasizing the capacity and resource allocation aspects of attention, attempts to integrate a more diverse set of phenomena. Neither theory tells the whole story; rather, they draw out different aspects of our attentional abilities.

One reason why no comprehensive theory of attention exists is that we do not fully understand the function of attention within human cognition as a whole. Early research tended to view attention as a self-contained mental function, operating relatively independently of other functions such as perception and memory. However, as researchers explored a wider range of attentional phenomena, the shortcomings of this view quickly became apparent. It was realized that it is very difficult to tease apart the attentional aspects of a task from the other mental processes underlying its performance. This has led to the modern research trend of identifying the role of attention within the wider context of understanding human information processing. The ultimate goal of this approach is not merely a definitive model of attention, but an explanation of attentional abilities set in the context of a more complete understanding of mental functions and processes.

# Summary of Section 5

- Models of attention generate hypotheses which can be tested experimentally. Experimental findings can lead to new theories and models which, in turn, create new hypotheses to be tested.

- The notions of limited-processing resources, resource allocation, automatic and attentional processes, and parallel-versus-serial processing, provide a theoretical framework within which models of attention can be specified.

- One of the major trends in attention research is to treat it as just one component of a more general explanation of human information processing.

**Personal acknowledgement**

I would like to thank David Hiles whose work in an earlier Open University psychology course has been helpful in the writing of this chapter.

# Further reading

A useful account of attention is given in Chapter 3 of:

EYSENCK, M.W. (1984) *A handbook of cognitive psychology*, Hillsdale, NJ/ Hove: Lawrence Erlbaum Associates.

# References

ALLPORT, D.A., (1980) 'Attention and performance', in Claxton, G. (ed.) *Cognitive psychology: new directions*, London: Routledge and Kegan Paul.

ALLPORT, D.A., ANTONIS, B. and REYNOLDS, P. (1972) 'On the division of attention: a disproof of the single channel hypothesis', *Quarterly Journal of Experimental Psychology*, vol. 24, pp. 225–35.

BROADBENT, D. (1954) 'The role of auditory localization in attention and memory span', *Journal of Experimental Psychology*, vol. 47, pp. 191–6.

BROADBENT, D. (1958) *Perception and communication*, Oxford: Pergamon.

CHERRY, E.C. (1953) 'Some experiments on the recognition of speech, with one and two ears', *Journal of the Acoustical Society of America*, vol. 25, pp. 975–9.

GRAY, J.A. and WEDDERBURN, A.A.I. (1960) 'Grouping strategies with simultaneous stimuli', *Quarterly Journal of Experimental Psychology*, vol. 12, pp. 180–4.

HEALY, A.F. (1976) 'Detection errors on the word *the*: evidence for reading units larger than letters', *Journal of Experimental Psychology: Human Perception and Performance*, vol. 2, pp. 235–42.

JAMES, W. (1890) *The principles of psychology*, vol. 1, New York: Henry Holt.

KAHNEMAN, D. (1973) *Attention and effort*, Englewood Cliffs, NJ: Prentice-Hall.

MORAY, D. (1959) 'Attention in dichotic listening: effective cues and the influence of instructions', *Quarterly Journal of Experimental Psychology*, vol. 11, pp. 56–60.

NEISSER, U. (1963) 'Decision-time without reaction time: experiments in visual scanning', *American Journal of Psychology*, vol. 76, pp. 374–85.

NEISSER, U. (1967) *Cognitive psychology*, New York: Appleton-Century-Crofts.

NEISSER, U. (1976) *Cognition and reality*, San Francisco: Freeman.

POSNER, M.I. and SNYDER, C.R.R. (1975) 'Facilitation and inhibition in the processing of signals', in Rabbitt, P.M.A. and Dornic, S. (eds) *Attention and performance: V*, London: Academic Press.

SHAFFER, L.H. (1975) 'Multiple attention in continuous verbal tasks', in Rabbitt, P.M.A. and Dornic, S. (eds) *Attention and performance: V*, London: Academic Press.

SHIFFRIN, R.M. and SCHNEIDER, W. (1977) 'Controlled and automatic human information processing: II Perceptual learning, automatic attending and a general theory', *Psychological Review*, vol. 84, pp. 127–90.

TREISMAN, A. (1960) 'Contextual cues in selective listening', *Quarterly Journal of Experimental Psychology*, vol. 12, pp. 242–8.

TREISMAN, A. (1964a) 'Verbal cues, language and meaning in selective attention', *American Journal of Psychology*, vol. 77, pp. 206–19.

TREISMAN, A. (1964b) 'Monitoring and storage of irrelevant messages in selective attention', *Journal of Verbal Learning and Verbal Behaviour*, vol. 3, pp. 449–59.

TREISMAN, A. (1988) 'Features and objects', *Quarterly Journal of Experimental Psychology*, vol. 40A, pp. 201–37.

TREISMAN, A. and GELADE, G. (1980) 'A feature integration theory of attention', *Cognitive Psychology*, vol. 12, pp. 97–136.

## Answers to SAQs

### SAQ 1

The ear-by-ear order of recall in response (b) is easier because it involves fewer switches between channels.

### SAQ 2

Broadbent's selective filter can only discriminate between the channels in option (b), as these are distinguishable in terms of physical characteristics (i.e. pitch of voice). The channels given in the other two options can only be distinguished in terms of meaning.

### SAQ 3

(a)  The words 'help' and 'look-out' should have relatively low unit thresholds in the dictionary and, thus, always be easy to recognize. These words have an important survival value and so should have permanently low thresholds. The word 'food' may also have a temporarily lowered unit threshold for a hungry person.

(b)  'Oranges', 'vegetables' and, to a lesser extent, 'food'. All of these words provide a natural extension to the meaning of the phrase and so would result in temporarily lowered thresholds. These words would therefore be more easily recognized at the semantic analysis stage.

### SAQ 4

The tasks listed in (b) and (c) would interfere with each other when performed simultaneously. In (b) both tasks draw on the same input modality, the auditory modality. In (c) both tasks make use of the visual modality. The tasks in (a) should *not* interfere with each other, as skilled knitting draws on a motor input modality, and a motor output modality, whereas listening to a lecture draws on the auditory input modality.

### SAQ 5

Activities (a) and (b) should normally involve mainly automatic processing. By contrast, activities (c) and (d) will draw heavily on attentional processes.

chapter **12**

# MEMORY

Gillian Cohen

## Contents

# 1 | Introduction

A good way to begin studying memory is to spend a few minutes reflecting about your own experience. Introspecting like this does not reveal how memory works, but it does remind us what memory is for, and this is a useful starting point.

## 1.1 Memory experience

In everyday life, memory is continually at work guiding our actions, informing our thoughts and enabling us to interpret our experiences. Let us illustrate this claim with an example from a typical day. Before leaving for work this morning I *remembered* to feed the cats. I *remembered* to leave money for the milkman—I used *remembered* rules of arithmetic to calculate the correct amount, but *forgot* to order an extra pint. I phoned a friend, *remembering* the number, and we made an arrangement to meet one evening later in the week which I wrote in my diary in case I *failed to remember*. I *recalled* my work schedule for the day and *remembered* to put the papers I would need into my bag. I *recognized* my neighbour as I got into the car and waved to her. I switched the car radio to the *Today* programme, *remembering* the wave-length. The knowledge which I had acquired previously, and *stored* in my memory, enabled me to understand a news item about the crisis in the national health service.

Do Activity 1 now to get some idea of how *your* memory works in your daily life.

### ACTIVITY 1

Consider a short stretch of about 5 minutes from your own day. Make a list of all the different uses of memory during this period. My list above is far from complete. Notice, for example, that you also need memory to recognize and identify objects like telephones and milk bottles and to know what they are for.

The purpose of Activity 1 is to make you aware of just how great a role memory plays in our experience of the world. You have probably realized by now that the contents of memory include new, recently acquired information as well as the 'old' information which is stored in memory in the form of permanent knowledge. You may also have become aware that without memory you would be virtually helpless; each action would have to be learned anew and each experience would be incomprehensible and surprising. You would have no personal history, no skills, no language, no relationships. To a considerable extent you *are* your memories, so that, when someone suffers very severe memory loss as a result of injury or dementia, the person's friends and relatives may feel that he or she is no longer the same person.

We are usually more aware of forgetting things than remembering them, and sometimes we do not realize just how frequently, accurately and efficiently our memory works. Whatever we do and whatever we experience involves a contribution from memory. Every time we react to something in the present, we interpret it by drawing on past experience. Whether the current input is a sensation coming in from the external world, or whether it arises from an internal thought or feeling, we can only understand what it means by reference to what we already know.

But memory is not perfect. Nobody can remember all the information he or she receives. We forget names and faces, places, past events, conversations, dates and times. We forget facts, jokes and stories, and we forget to carry out our intentions. Modern living overloads the human memory system. In the past, when people lived more simple, repetitive lives in small communities, travelling only short distances, meeting few strangers, and reading only a few books in a lifetime, the demands on memory were much less severe. Today, our complicated lives are filled with new experiences in changing surroundings, and we are bombarded with information in every waking hour, so the inadequacies of our memories are more apparent. We cannot remember all the information we receive, so, to be efficient, memory must be selective. We make decisions about what we want or need to remember, and try to filter out or discard the rest. The operations of selective attention, described in Chapter 11, enable us to focus on the selected information and so reduce the input to the memory system. Even so, these strategies are not one hundred per cent effective. We cannot remember all we want to remember, and, paradoxically, we remember many things that seem useless. In the modern world, many of us are increasingly reliant on memory aids like Filofax to supplement our overloaded memories.

SAQ 1    (*SAQ answers are given at the end of the chapter*) Filofax is an external memory aid. What other external memory aids can you think of that are in common use?

## 1.2 Memory processes

Because memory pervades everything we do, and works in such a variety of ways, it is difficult to construct a theory that will explain all the different aspects of how memory functions. In order to make this problem more manageable, psychologists have tried to *decompose* this complex system into a set of component processes, and to discover the underlying principles that govern their operations.

We can identify three different kinds of basic memory processes that form a sequence of stages.

1    **Acquisition processes**   These are the *input processes* which receive information from the outside world and create some form of internal representation of the information which can be stored in memory.

2   **Retention processes**   These are the *storage processes* used to maintain information that is already in memory.

3   **Retrieval processes**   These are concerned with getting information out of the memory store and include recognition and recall. **Recognition** involves matching a currently perceived item, such as a face or a piece of music, to a previous experience of that same item stored in memory. (You recognize that the face is one you have seen before.) **Recall** involves summoning up something that is stored in memory and bringing it into consciousness, as when you recall a conversation or a telephone number. (You recall the telephone number in response to a question or because you need to use it.)

You may have been puzzled by the way psychologists seem to talk about memory and learning as if they are different. When you read psychology textbooks it seems as if animals *learn* and humans *remember*. Why are learning and memory processes treated separately in this way? The difference is mainly one of emphasis. Learning theories focus on the acquisition processes and are concerned with how information gets into the system. The study of memory encompasses retention and retrieval processes as well as input processes. Memory research is primarily concerned with questions like: How is information represented, retained and retrieved? What are the limits to the amount of information that can be handled? How long can it be retained? And, how is storage organized so that information can be found when it is required?

To get a feel for how memory processes work, and how recognition differs from recall, try the mini-experiment in Activity 2.

ACTIVITY 2

You will need several pieces of paper and a pencil. Follow these instructions step by step:

1   Cover up List 2 overleaf with one piece of paper.

2   Read through the list of words in List 1 once only, trying to remember them.

    Read at a steady rate of about 2 seconds per word; this is the *acquisition* stage.

    *List 1*

| | | | | |
|---|---|---|---|---|
| dollar | jade | nurse | cabbage | word |
| ladle | air | camel | ant | iron |
| golf | berry | nut | trout | boat |
| hour | leaflet | mirror | board | queen |
| beer | scissors | cello | sand | canvas |

3   Now cover up List 1, and *rehearse* all the words you can remember by going through them in your head (this is the *retention* stage).

4   Now do the sums: $7 \times 271 =$     ; $8 \times 196 =$     ; $3 \times 482 =$
    This is an **interpolated task**, or filler task, designed to prevent any further rehearsal.

5    Now write down all the words you can remember from the list; this is
the *recall* stage.

6    When you have recalled as many words as you can, uncover List 2
(leaving List 1 covered). In List 2 the twenty-five words from the
original list (called *targets* or *old* items) are mixed up with twenty-five
*new* words (called *distractors*). Go through the list and put a tick
beside each of the target words you recognize as coming from the
original list, and put a cross against the words you think were not on
the original list. This is the *recognition* stage.

*List 2*

| | | | | |
|---|---|---|---|---|
| lake | queen | stick | camel | entrance |
| berry | boat | air | hour | scissors |
| pipe | cello | board | doll | church |
| ginger | tooth | cabbage | dollar | nurse |
| sand | golf | worm | mirror | novel |
| sack | nylon | aunt | roof | leaflet |
| tulip | belt | pink | pigeon | iron |
| word | trout | sergeant | canvas | mile |
| cottage | jade | ladle | milk | ant |
| nut | melon | coal | hammer | beer |

7    Finally, check List 1 and count up how many words you *recalled*
correctly, and how many you *recognized* correctly in List 2. Note your
scores. Did you recognize more words that you were able to recall?
Did you tick any words that were *not* in the original list by mistake?
Sometimes people make this kind of false recognition error.

When you have finished Activity 2, try to analyse what you did at each stage.
In the *acquisition stage* you may have said the words aloud so you could
remember what they sounded like; or you may have tried to imprint visual
images of the words on your mind; or you may have tried to link or group
words together and remember groups. In the *retention stage* you may have
rehearsed the words by repeating them aloud or by visualizing them. In the
*recognition test* you probably found that you could pick out the original
words because they seemed familiar and acted as cues to jog your memory. In
the *recall test* you probably had to engage in active search processes and
dredge up the words without any cues to help you. You may have tried to
recall the first or last part of the list first and then tried to fill in the middle
items. Although recognition and recall are both retrieval processes,
recognition is usually easier and you probably recognized more words than
you had been able to recall. You should now be getting a feel for the different
processes involved in memory.

Dividing memory up into logically distinct stages helps us to understand that
forgetting can arise at any stage. Memory failures can be due to faulty
acquisition, poor retention, or not using the right retrieval processes. When
you fail to remember the name of a person you met recently, this may be
because you did not pay attention properly when you were introduced
(acquisition failure); or because, although stored initially, the memory
decayed or was overlaid and confused with other names (retention failure); or

because you failed to hit on the appropriate strategy to retrieve the name (retrieval failure). If you succeed in remembering the name later, this shows that it must have been acquired and retained, so your previous inability to remember the name must have been a retrieval failure.

Experimental psychologists work rather like plumbers, testing different parts of the system to isolate the faulty stage. They use this method in experiments that aim to reveal the operating principles of each stage. To do this, they devise memory tasks that are designed so as to increase or decrease the pressure on a particular stage, and then observe the results. Some examples of the kind of manipulations used are:

1 varying the study time or number of repetitions of items allowed in the acquisition phase;

2 varying the length of the retention period; permitting or preventing rehearsal during the retention period;

3 making retrieval easier by giving hints or cues.

Observations from such experiments are fed back into the theories that attempt to model the memory system so that it can be modified, or specified in greater detail.

SAQ 2 Do you think the following manipulations would tend to increase or decrease the number of words correctly recalled in Activity 2?

(a) making the list shorter,

(b) allowing more time to read the list;

(c) increasing the number of sums to be done in the interpolated task during the retention period.

## 1.3 Memory representations

In trying to describe the memory system, we need to specify the *contents* of memory as well as the processes that act on these contents. When you did Activity 1, you will have realized that a huge variety of different things need to be stored in memory. What form does all this information take once it gets inside your head?

The first point to note is that a memory representation does not necessarily correspond exactly with the original experience. During the acquisition phase the information is encoded. The internal memory representation is a product of these **encoding processes**. Encoding may involve converting or transforming the information so that the internal memory representation is in a different form from the original input. When you studied the words in Activity 2 there are several ways in which you could have encoded them in memory.

1 As a **visual representation**: this could take the form of a visual image of the printed words on the page, or images of the objects named (a pair of scissors, an electric iron etc.). Or visual images may be used to link pairs of items; for example, a nurse sitting on a camel.

2    As an **acoustic representation** or **articulatory representation**: saying the written words aloud, or sub-vocalizing them silently in your head, converts written words to a **speech code** or **verbal code**. This may be acoustic, representing words in terms of their sounds, so that you 'hear' them in your head, or it may be articulatory, representing them in terms of the muscle movements of the mouth necessary to articulate them. Note that auditory inputs, like spoken words or other sounds, can be directly represented in an acoustic code. Visual inputs, like written words or objects have to be recognized and named first. Then the names and verbal labels can be stored in an acoustic or articulatory form. Rhythm, and rhyme can also be used to link words into groups; for example, jade–ladle, camel–cabbage.

3    As a **semantic representation**: this represents words (and objects) in terms of their meaning. Meaning-based representations can rest on knowledge of definitions or characteristics (e.g. dollar = money, US currency), or be based on previous experiences (using dollars on a holiday trip). Semantically related words, such as the animal words (ant, camel, trout) or the food words (berry, cabbage, beer, trout), can be grouped together.

The study of human memory has concentrated on memory for verbal, visual and semantic information, but these are not the only forms of information represented in memory. Skills like riding a bicycle or skiing are represented in a **motor code** which carries information about the type and sequence of movements that are involved. When it comes to memory for other kinds of sensory information like smell and taste, music, pain and emotions, psychologists know very little about how these are represented.

How can we find out what kinds of internal representations people use? We cannot rely on asking people to introspect because memory processes are often unconscious. For example, you may be quite unable to say how you solved a crossword clue or what caused you suddenly to think of an old friend. However, more objective evidence can be obtained. A major source of evidence about internal representations comes from the kinds of mistake people make. **Substitution errors** are very revealing. For example, if you were supposed to recall the word 'hare' and you recalled 'hair' instead this substitution error would reflect an acoustic or articulatory code. You must have represented 'hare' in a speech-based code and, at recall, confused it with something which sounds the same.

SAQ 3    What kinds of internal representations are revealed by the following substitution errors?

(a)  *Rabbit* for *hare*      (b)  *Lemon* for *demon*

# 1.4 Some misconceptions about memory representations

The issue of memory representation is extremely complex, and in some ways Activity 2 was misleading because lists of words are not typical of what we usually need to remember. It is important to bear in mind the following points about memory representations.

1   The input to the memory system does *not* normally consist of single discrete items or sets of unrelated items like lists of numbers or words. In normal circumstances, we more often need to remember large chunks of coherently related facts or events. We remember stories or articles or conversations, not single words or single sentences. We remember experiences which happen to us as a sequence of connected events. Memory representations therefore need to be complex, global and interconnected, not single entities.

2   New information is *not* stored separately but is integrated with knowledge already stored in memory. There is a two-way relationship in the memory system between new inputs and stored knowledge. Old knowledge is used to interpret, label, and make sense of the new input. So, for example, I may use prior knowledge to interpret my current experience of a discussion at a committee meeting. New information is also used to update or modify the stored knowledge. So new information about, say, a political scandal, may cause me to revise my previously acquired opinions of cabinet ministers.

3   We have talked so far about memory representations almost as if actual words or sounds or pictures are stored in memory. However, this is misleading. At a biological level memory representations consist of **neural excitations** in the brain, or patterns of connections between neurons which somehow have the potential to regenerate the original information. It is this relationship between the underlying brain processes, and the mental representations we are consciously aware of, which is the real heart of the mystery.

4   The memory system is not a stand-alone system, but is part of a larger cognitive system. Other cognitive processes, such as perception and attention, are intimately bound up with remembering. Inputs to the memory system are the products of what we perceive and perception is governed by attention. The form of the input may also be transformed by language and reasoning while it is in store. In the example of my memory of a committee meeting, I may have missed some of the discussion because I could not hear the speaker, I may have not attended to points that did not interest me, and I may remember the gist and the implications of what was being said rather than the exact words uttered; I would have interpreted what the speakers meant and what were their motives and intentions. So memory of the meeting is affected by perception, attention and reasoning. Finally, it is important to bear in mind that memory is not just designed for information storage, but for information *use*, so it must also be linked to a response system which can initiate actions.

## Summary of Section 1

- Memory is involved in all our activities and experiences. Memory is an overloaded system and remembering is selective.

- Memory processes can be divided into those concerned with acquisition, retention and retrieval. Information can be lost from the system at any of these stages.

- Inputs from the outside world are encoded into internal memory representations. These may be visual, acoustic or articulatory, or semantic.

- New inputs are integrated with previously acquired knowledge and old knowledge is used to interpret new experiences.

# 2 | Approaches to memory

In this section we will consider a number of different approaches to the study of human memory and discuss different theoretical explanations of the known facts about memory. Which, you may ask, is the right one? Why are you not told which approach is the best and which theory is correct? The reason is that no one theory can be identified as *the* definitive account of how memory works. Some theories seem to account for some kinds of memory, but do not satisfactorily explain other aspects of memory function. So we cannot point to one single 'right' answer.

What we can do is to try to evaluate the different approaches, and pick out the strengths and weaknesses of each. We can try to judge how well a theory fits the experimental findings and what further tests would help to prove or disprove it. Much of the interest and excitement of doing psychology arises because many aspects of the subject are still controversial. Psychologists and students are both part of an on-going investigation and as you read about the various theories outlined below, you should use your own critical judgement to assess them.

The different approaches to memory we will consider represent major landmarks in the historical development of memory research. Their popularity has ebbed and flowed, but none of them has been completely discarded, and each has produced valid findings and added to our pool of knowledge about memory.

## 2.1 The associationist approach

Early ideas about memory arose out of the assumption that all learning and memory is based on the **association of ideas** or sensations that occur close together in time. These views were developed in the seventeenth and eighteenth centuries by the British Empiricist philosophers, in particular Locke, Berkeley and Hume. Relying on their own introspections, they observed that when experiences occur together (e.g. 'snow' and 'whiteness') they become associated and are remembered together. The strength of the learned association is determined by the frequency with which the experiences occur together and by the vividness of the sensations.

These views later formed the basis for the first experimental investigations of human memory, and of the stimulus–response (S–R) learning theories, described in Chapter 6, whereby learning was thought to consist of forming an S–R association. This theory dominated the study of learning and memory from the time of Pavlov in 1902 until the 1960s. According to this view, the process of learning a list of words or numbers consists of forming associations between the items, the strength of the association increasing with the frequency of repetition. Note that the formation of an association is regarded as a passive process which is not affected by any special effort the learner might make.

In the late nineteenth century, a German psychologist, Hermann Ebbinghaus, used the **associationist approach** to study memory by means of rigorously controlled laboratory experiments. Ebbinghaus set out to study as objectively as possible the way *new* associations are formed and remembered. In order to do this, he needed to use stimulus material which did not already have any associations. This requirement ruled out the use of familiar, meaningful words because these are already part of a complex web of associated ideas. So Ebbinghaus created **nonsense syllables**—consisting of consonant–vowel–consonant (CVC) trigrams like FAZ, BUX, HEJ—because these are novel stimuli devoid of any pre-existing associations. He generated many thousands of CVCs and made up hundreds of lists to use as the to-be-remembered material in his experiments. Thus, he was able to study the formation of completely new associations between each nonsense syllable and the next one in the list. These experiments were standardized and controlled as carefully as possible. Ebbinghaus acted as his own subject and read each list out loud to himself, over and over again. He systematically varied the number of times he read a list, or the delay between learning a list and trying to recall it. In this way, he was able to measure the influence of the variables of *repetition* and *delay* on the processes of remembering and forgetting. Some of his experiments are shown in Box A and Box B overleaf.

## BOX A   An Ebbinghaus experiment: the effects of repetition

Ebbinghaus prepared several sets of six lists, each list consisting of sixteen CVCs. He read through each set of lists 8, 16, 24, 32, 42, 53 or 64 times. Exactly 24 hours later he tested himself by seeing how much time it took him to re-learn each set of six lists until he could repeat them correctly without hesitation. His results are shown in Figure 12.1. The more times Ebbinghaus had repeated the lists when he originally learned them (shown at the bottom of the graph), the less time he needed to re-learn them (shown on the vertical axis of the graph). The time needed to re-learn is a measure of memory, because the better something is remembered the easier it is to re-learn. The downward slope of the line in Figure 12.1 shows that the more times a list was repeated, the less time it took to re-learn.

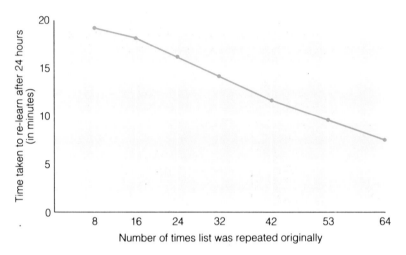

**Figure 12.1** Ebbinghaus' results showing how the number of repetitions of learning trials affects retention
(Source: Ebbinghaus, 1885)

SAQ 4   Read Box B and study the graph in Figure 12.2.

(a)  What was the percentage of re-learning trials needed after 8 hours retention?

(b)  What was this percentage after 48 hours?

(c)  Look at the slope of the line for retention intervals of *less* than 8 hours and the slope of the line for retention intervals of *more* than 8 hours. What does this tell you about the rate of forgetting?

## BOX B  An Ebbinghaus experiment: the effects of delay

Ebbinghaus used sets of eight lists each consisting of thirteen CVCs, reading them through again and again until he reached the stage where he could repeat them accurately without hesitation. He then tested himself on the sets of lists after delays varying from 20 minutes to 31 days. After each of these delays he found out how many times he had to go through a list in order to re-learn it.

The vertical axis of the graph in Figure 12.2 shows the number of trials needed to re-learn expressed as a percentage of the number of trials needed originally. For example, if it takes ten trials to learn a list originally and five trials to re-learn it then the amount of re-learning required is 50 per cent. Another way of putting this is that there is a 50 per cent saving in re-learning, so this is known as the *savings* method of measuring memory. The greater the percentage of re-learning required, the smaller the savings so this means that more has been forgotten.

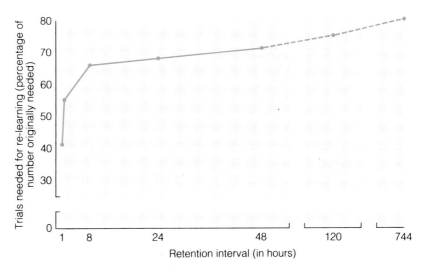

**Figure 12.2** Ebbinghaus' results showing how delay before recall can influence forgetting
(Source: Ebbinghaus, 1885)

Figure 12.2 shows that the longer the retention interval, that is, the delay between original learning and testing, the more re-learning was required. A greater percentage of re-learning trials was required after a delay of 120 hours compared with shorter delays. Notice that forgetting was at first very rapid, most of it happening in the first hour after learning. After that, forgetting slowed down, as shown by the fact that the percentage of re-learning trials required was much the same after delays of 24 hours and after 48 hours.

A century later, Ebbinghaus' results are still recognized as valid. His general approach, with its rigorous methodology and its emphasis on measurement and control, is still employed in many studies, although today computers are usually used to display the lists and to control and measure timing.

## 2.2  The constructivist approach

The associationist account characterizes memory as a *passive* process whereby if lists of items are simply repeated enough times they are automatically stored in memory. This contrasts sharply with a **constructivist approach** to memory which sees people as employing *active* strategies to memorize and to retrieve their memories. Instead of considering a memory representation as a *copy* of the stimulus, constructivists emphasize that the memory representation is a *construction* which integrates past experience with the new input. The idea is that, when we remember something in real life, the memory is rarely, if ever, an exact copy of the original event. Instead, it is a reconstruction which is partly based on our general knowledge and previous experience.

This approach focuses on meaningful material rather than lists of nonsense syllables and seeks to study the operation of memory in more natural situations. However, when psychologists try to study the processes involved in remembering more natural and meaningful material, it becomes difficult to achieve hard, objective evidence. Remembering meaningful material involves general knowledge and past experience which vary from one individual to another, so different people may construct quite different memories of the same input. These individual differences make it extremely difficult to formulate general principles about how people remember.

The earliest exponent of the constructivist approach was Sir Frederick Bartlett who wrote *Remembering*, one of the classic books on psychology, in 1932. Bartlett was interested in studying memory in situations that were much closer to real life than learning lists of nonsense syllables. Before we look at his ideas in detail, you should try one of his investigations for yourself in Activity 3.

### ACTIVITY 3

This activity will take about 30 minutes. Get a sheet of paper, a pen or pencil and a watch or alarm clock. Then read the story below in Extract A: take as long as you like, but read it through only once. Do not backtrack or re-read some sections. When you have read it through once, do something else for a period of 15 minutes. You may read the paper, or watch television, but you should not try to recall the story. When the 15 minutes is up, write down as full an account as you can of the story. Spend about 5 minutes doing this, but do not labour over it once you have done all you can. This is not a test of ability or intelligence. You are doing it to experience some of the factors which influence memory.

EXTRACT A 'The war of the ghosts'

One night two young men from Egulac went down to the river to hunt seals, and while they were there it became foggy and calm. Then they heard war-cries, and they thought 'Maybe this is a war-party'. They escaped to the shore, and hid behind a log. Now canoes came up, and they heard the noise of paddles, and saw one canoe coming up to them. There were five men in the canoe, and they said, 'What do you think? We wish to take you along. We are going up the river to make war on the people.'

One of the young men said, 'I have no arrows'. 'Arrows are in the canoe,' they said. 'I will not go along. I might be killed. My relatives do not know where I have gone. But you,' he said, turning to the other, 'may go with them'. So one of the young men went, but the other returned home. And the warriors went on up the river to a town on the other side of Kalama. The people came down to the water, and they began to fight, and many were killed. But presently the young man heard one of the warriors say, 'Quick, let us go home: that Indian has been hit.' Now he thought, 'Oh they are ghosts'. He did not feel sick, but they said he had been shot.

So the canoes went back to Egulac, and the young man went ashore to his house, and made a fire. And he told everybody and said, 'Behold I accompanied the ghosts, and we went to fight. Many of our fellows were killed, and many of those who attacked us were killed. They said I was hit, and I did not feel sick.'

He told it all and then became quiet. When the sun rose he fell down. Something black came out of his mouth. His face became contorted. The people jumped up and cried. He was dead.

(Bartlett, 1932, p. 65)

Bartlett gave stories like 'The war of the ghosts' to people to study. After 15 minutes he asked them to write down as good a recall of it as they could manage, just as you were asked to in Activity 3. At this stage, compare your own recall of 'The war of the ghosts' with the original. I expect you will find, as Bartlett did, that your recall is much shorter, contains distortions and mistakes, and misses out large areas altogether. See if you can note in your own recall the same kinds of errors that Bartlett found. These are listed in Box C overleaf.

Bartlett tested people's memory for 'The war of the ghosts' story several times at gradually increasing intervals of time. The longest interval was ten years. Bartlett described what happened:

The subject read the story in 1917. In 1919 she unexpectedly saw me pass her on a bicycle and immediately afterwards found herself murmuring 'Egulac', 'Kalama'. She then recognized me, and remembered reading the story and that these names were part of the story. In the summer of 1927 she agreed to try definitely to remember the tale. She wrote down at once 'Egulac' and 'Calama' but then stopped and said that she could do no more. Then she said she had a visual image of a sandy bank and of two men going down the river in a boat. There, however, she stopped.

(Bartlett, 1932, p. 70)

## BOX C    Bartlett: typical errors in story recall

- *Omission* of details, particularly those which are inconsistent with subjects' understanding of the story.

- *Rationalizations*, sometimes introducing new material, to make the remembered story more logical; for example, giving a reason for the fighting.

- *Alterations in importance*, where subjects tend to use one aspect of the story as a central theme, and often make it more central and dominant than it was in the original; for example, emphasizing the ghost element.

- *Transformations of order*, where events are changed around; this is much less common with a structured story than an unstructured descriptive passage.

- *Affect* (i.e. *emotional* or *attitudinal*) *distortions*, where subjects construct their recall around their own attitudes and reactions to the story; for example, remembering that 'something horrible came out of his mouth'.

Bartlett carried out numerous experiments to find out how people remember a wide range of different kinds of material. He studied memory of faces, pictures, passages of texts, inkblots and drawings like the ones shown in Figure 12.3. One of Bartlett's experiments is outlined in Box D.

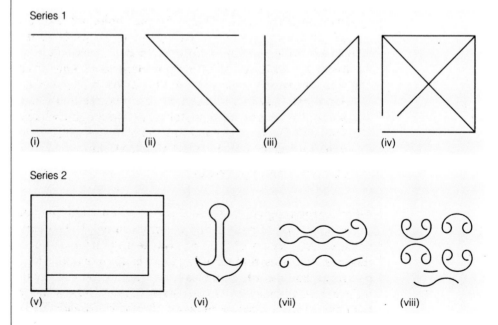

**Figure 12.3** Figures used by Bartlett to study memory for drawings (Source: Bartlett, 1932)

## BOX D   Bartlett: memory for line drawings

Bartlett showed subjects simple drawings (see Figure 12.3) drawn in ink on postcard-sized cards. After the drawings had been taken away, subjects were asked to draw them from memory. Bartlett did not cross-examine his subjects, but they often provided a commentary for him while they were drawing, so he was able to analyse the memory processes.

With the simple drawings (Series 1) shown in Figure 12.3 Bartlett commented:

> Each design was looked at as a whole and was reproduced without hesitation. . . Even with very simple figures names were commonly used. Thus (i) was often called a 'square with one of its sides gone'; (ii) was said to be 'Z upside down'; (iii) was called 'N'; and (iv) was 'a square with diagonals'. . . . Although there was no specific effort of analysis, yet even simply constructed material of perception, such as this, had its dominant features. For example, a gap, such as illustrated in (iv) was almost always noticed and reproduced, though as often as not it was assigned the wrong position. This is one case of the carrying over into an experiment of a characteristic of everyday observation. We readily notice any unfamiliar feature in familiar objects, or anything unmeaningful in figures that carry common meaning. The familiar is readily accepted: the unfamiliar may hold us.

> (Bartlett, 1932, pp. 18–19)

With designs from Series 2, Bartlett noted that:

> Naming occupied a position of great importance . . . [it] helped to shape [the subject's] representation. For example, (vi) was once called a 'pick-axe' and was represented with pointed prongs. Once it was termed 'turf-cutter' and made with a rounded blade. It was called in part a key (the handle), and in part a shovel (the blade) and changed accordingly in the representation . . . Now in all these cases the name was given immediately and unreflectingly; for the presented visual pattern seemed at once to 'fit into' or to 'match' some preformed scheme or setting. I shall call this fundamental process of connecting a given pattern with some setting or scheme: effort after meaning.

> (Bartlett, 1932, pp. 19–20)

When Bartlett argued that one of the most important determinants of human memory is what he called 'effort after meaning', he was putting forward the constructivist theory of memory. He meant that we do not passively record pictures or stories; remembering them is not like taking a photograph, or making a tape-recording. Instead, we actively reconstruct them so as to make more sense, associating new inputs with knowledge already stored, and fitting the new material into a framework of what we already know and comprehend. As a result, what is remembered is not the original stimulus but a constructed representation which emphasizes some aspects, and ignores others.

When the Ebbinghaus approach and the Bartlett approach are compared, it is clear that neither can provide all the answers. Experiments like those conducted by Ebbinghaus are scientifically rigorous but they are not representative of real-life situations. Because of this they have sometimes been criticized as 'dust-bowl empiricism'. Bartlett's work is more representative of memory in real life, but there are many unsolved difficulties in measuring recall of this kind. You may have been aware, for example, when you looked at your own recall in Activity 3, how difficult it is to decide if something should be counted as a rationalization or as an affect distortion. Until recently, experimental research following in the Ebbinghaus tradition has dominated memory research (see Section 2.3), but Bartlett's ideas still have great intuitive appeal, and his influence is reflected in current attempts to study memory in everyday life as outlined in Section 2.4. Modern versions of both approaches to memory continue and coexist today.

SAQ 5   Does each of the following statements describe the Ebbinghaus approach or the Bartlett approach or both? Write E, B or E and B after each statement.

(a)  What matters most is to obtain objective measurements of memory.

(b)  What matters most is to study memory in real-life situations.

(c)  Memory depends upon the number of times material is experienced.

(d)  Memory depends upon 'effort after meaning'.

(e)  Material is lost from memory when time elapses.

## 2.3  Modern approaches, 1: information processing

The information processing approach follows the Ebbinghaus tradition in using formal laboratory experiments. However, its theoretical framework has been derived from communication science. The idea that cognitive processes, including memory, could be understood as **information processing** gained ground in the years after the Second World War. This view originally arose out of developments in communication science which characterized information processing devices as 'channels' with a maximum 'channel capacity' defined as the number of 'bits' of information that can be processed per second. Models of selective attention, described in Chapter 11, adopted the terminology and concepts of information theory. When information processing theories were applied to memory, the technical definition of 'bits' was dropped in favour of the vaguer term 'items'. However, the key concept derived from the information processing approach was that processing is limited by the processing capacity of the system. Psychologists working in the Ebbinghaus tradition of formal laboratory experiments sought to measure and define the upper limits of memory capacity.

The **stage model of memory** shown in Figure 12.4 is essentially an information processing model showing the different stages of memory processing, and this general framework still underpins most of the research on memory today. This is a very simplified version of the model. We will add

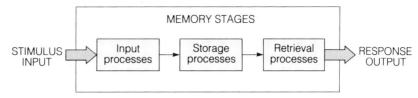

**Figure 12.4** The information flow model of memory

more detail to it as we progress through this chapter. The essential ideas of the information processing approach are shown in Box E.

---

**BOX E    The information processing approach to memory**

1    Memory can be characterized as a flow of information through a system.

2    The system is divided into separate stages or sub-systems.

3    Information enters the system and passes through each stage in a fixed sequence.

4    Each stage has a limited **capacity** and a limited **duration**, i.e. the amount of information it can handle and the length of time it can hold the information are both limited.

5    At each stage the information is coded. Transfer to the next stage may involve recoding. (Look back to Section 1.3 for examples of forms of coding.)

6    Laboratory experiments similar to those devised by Ebbinghaus are used to investigate the mechanism of each stage.

7    Information processing models are sometimes known as **box and arrow** models because this is a convenient way to represent the flow of information through the system.

---

## 2.4  Modern approaches, 2: the cognitive approach

The **cognitive approach** follows in the Bartlett tradition. It recognizes that memory is not just a simple mechanism, but is influenced by many factors, such as the individual person's intentions, state of mind and prior knowledge; the context in which the to-be-remembered material is encountered; and the kind of strategies that are used. The cognitive approach tries to take account of all these factors. It employs experimental methods in the laboratory, but, since the 1970s, more naturalistic methods have also been developed. In 1976, Ulric Neisser gave a very influential talk in which he claimed that rigorous experimental methodology of the type pioneered by Ebbinghaus has yielded very little understanding of how memory functions in everyday life. He pointed out that many important practical questions about memory remain unanswered and suggested that psychologists should turn their attention to these issues (see Neisser, 1978). Since then there has been a resurgence of research within the Bartlett tradition, which is investigating **everyday memory**. This research examines memory for the kind of material which is part of everyday life (like names, faces, birthdays, appointments and childhood experiences). Considerable progress has been made in devising methods for studying memory in the natural context. Psychologists have collected observations of memory in real-life situations, and have also designed experiments which reflect everyday life.

The study of everyday memory has brought with it a more *functional* approach. Psychologists are looking again at the mechanisms revealed by experiments, asking what purpose the mechanisms serve in everyday life and why the memory system should have developed in this way. They are also more interested now in the ways that individuals differ in how their memories work. Another characteristic feature of the cognitive approach to memory is that memory is no longer treated as a stand-alone system but as part of the whole cognitive system. So interest now focuses on the role of memory in vision, in language and in thinking rather than on memory for its own sake. The naturalistic approach embodies many of the ideas that Bartlett put forward forty years before.

## Summary of Section 2

- Psychologists borrowed from philosophy the idea that memorizing consists of forming associations between items.

- Associationists like Ebbinghaus conducted controlled experiments showing that the strength of these passively formed associations depended on factors like repetition and the time delay before recall.

- Bartlett studied people's memory of meaningful material like stories and drawings under more natural conditions. He claimed that memories are actively constructed.

- Both approaches are still discernible in contemporary research. The Ebbinghaus approach evolved into the stage models of information processing. The Bartlett tradition is evident in the cognitive approach and in naturalistic research on everyday memory.

# 3 | Short-term memory processes

All the work on short-term memory described in this section exemplifies the information processing approach. Within the information processing framework a basic distinction, which is widely accepted, can be made between short-term memory and long-term memory. Consider two examples from everyday experience. In the first, I look up a telephone number and remember it while I pick up the phone and dial. Immediately afterwards it is forgotten. In the second example, I remember the route I take when I drive home from work. I have known this route for some years and can remember it reliably whenever I want to. The phone number was held temporarily in short-term memory, which stores recent inputs for a brief period. The route is stored in long-term memory and may be retained more or less indefinitely. Because these two parts of the memory system seem to differ in many ways, they are commonly treated as separate sub-systems when a model of memory is constructed, but not everybody agrees with this point of view. We shall have more to say about the arguments for and against this distinction between short and long-term memory in Section 4.3. Here we start by considering how information gets into short-term memory.

## 3.1 Input processes: sensory registration

Before anything can be remembered, information has to get into the system. As was emphasized in the discussion of perception in Chapter 10, inputs from the environment have to be registered by the senses, and perceived and recognized for what they are. From the whole array of information in the environment, some items are selected for processing in the memory system. These early stages are sometimes known as **sensory registration**. During the few seconds needed for perception and recognition, inputs are very briefly maintained in **sensory buffers**, but these buffer stores are more properly regarded as part of the perceptual process than as part of the memory system.

Nevertheless, the sensory buffer store for visual information has been called iconic memory and the sensory buffer store for auditory inputs is known as echoic memory. **Iconic memory** has been demonstrated in experiments by Sperling (1960) who showed that, when subjects viewed a display of letters, visual information persisted in the sensory buffer for up to a second after the display itself had terminated. Baddeley (1988) has suggested that one function of iconic storage is to allow information from successive eye fixations to persist long enough to be assembled and to give continuity to the visual scene when we blink our eyes or shift our gaze.

There is also evidence for brief sensory storage of auditory inputs in echoic memory. **Echoic memory** has been demonstrated using a technique called *shadowing* described in Chapter 11. Subjects wear earphones and two different inputs, such as lists of words or digits, are presented, one to each ear. The subjects are asked to repeat aloud (i.e. to shadow) the message entering one ear (the attended message) and to ignore the message concurrently presented to the other ear (the unattended message). In some conditions the two messages are identical, but the attended message lags behind the other. Because the ignored, non-shadowed message persists in echoic memory for up to 2 seconds, subjects notice that the two messages are identical when the lag is less than 2 seconds. However, if the lag between the messages is greater than 2 seconds the non-shadowed, unattended message is lost from echoic memory before the identity can be recognized.

What is the function of echoic storage? It allows auditory inputs to persist just long enough to be picked up and transferred into memory, but not long enough to get in the way of further incoming information. You are sometimes aware of echoic memory operating if somebody speaks to you when you are not listening, but reading a book or watching television. Just as you are about to ask 'What did you say?', you realize you can 'play back' the words that are still echoing in your head.

Both the iconic and the echoic sensory buffers store incoming information in a raw uncoded form for a brief moment *before* the processes of selective attention and recognition operate on it. We can now add the evidence about sensory registration to the information flow model of memory as shown in Figure 12.5.

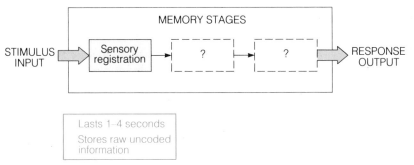

**Figure 12.5** The information flow model of memory: sensory registration

## 3.2 Short-term memory

What happens when information is selected and recognized and enters into the short-term store? An example of **short-term memory (STM)**, introduced at the beginning of Section 3, was looking up a phone number. Try Activity 4 to get some idea of how your short-term memory works.

ACTIVITY 4

Read through the following list of digits once quickly. Then cover them and try to write down the sequence in the correct order.

5 7 4 8 3 1 9 6 2

How many did you recall in the correct order? This is a rough measure of your **immediate memory span.**

The technique of measuring memory span usually involves presenting spoken sequences of numbers, and requiring the subject to repeat them in the correct order. The sequences begin with two or three numbers and gradually increase in length. The number of items that a subject can correctly repeat on 50 per cent of attempts is designated as his or her memory span. The average memory span for most normal adults is seven items plus or minus two. This finding holds good for lists of numbers, letters, or larger chunks of information such as words or phrases, and has given rise to the expression 'the magic number seven' (Miller, 1956).

Although you may be able to repeat back seven or eight items correctly immediately after hearing or reading them, after a few minutes they will be forgotten unless you keep repeating them either silently or out loud. Experience confirms that, without this process of rehearsal, short-term memory has only a short duration. Normally we use **rehearsal** to extend the duration of STM. You can think of it as a loop within STM which continually recirculates information to keep it established there. Notice, though, that rehearsal itself is limited by the capacity of STM; it is impossible to rehearse more than about seven items without losing track of them.

The finding that, without rehearsal, material soon disappears from STM led Peterson and Peterson (1959) to measure the *duration* of STM; see the description of their experiment in Box F overleaf. They presented their results as evidence that material in STM is forgotten within a period of 6 to 12 seconds. Their view of how forgetting occurs is that STM consists of a memory trace (of neural activity) which gradually decays; this is called the **trace decay theory of forgetting**. Rehearsal, it is argued, prevents forgetting because it keeps replenishing the trace before it decays completely, but Peterson and Peterson prevented rehearsal by making subjects count backwards. They concluded, therefore, that the memory trace for each trigram gradually decayed.

However, there are other ways of explaining forgetting in the Petersons' experiment. When other psychologists repeated the experiment they noticed that the first trigram was very rarely forgotten. Forgetting only occurred when subjects had been tested on several trigrams and began to mix them up. This led them to explain the Petersons' result in terms of the **interference theory of forgetting**. Memory for the later trigrams suffered from interference from the earlier trigrams. We will look at this theory in more detail in Section 5.1, because evidence for interference is more readily obtained in long-term memory. But it is worth remembering that many memory theorists believe that interference as well as trace decay occurs in STM.

A further question about short-term memory concerns *coding*. At the sensory registration stage, visual or auditory information is still in its original **modality** and has not been recoded. Visual inputs are in the visual modality; auditory inputs are in the auditory modality. What happens when information reaches STM? Conrad (1964) carried out an experiment, summarized in Box G on page 593, which investigated this. The technique he used involved analysing substitution errors. Substitution errors, when one item is confused with another, reveal the code that is being used (see Section 1.3). If letters that *sound* alike are confused, this indicates acoustic coding. If letters that *look* alike are confused, this indicates visual coding.

## BOX F    Peterson and Peterson's (1959) trigram experiment

Peterson and Peterson wanted to study the rate of forgetting for items that are well within the memory span, so they chose *trigrams* which were nonsense syllables consisting of three consonants like XPJ. On each trial, subjects were given a single trigram to remember. In normal circumstances people can easily remember a single trigram by repeating it over and over to themselves. In order to prevent this kind of rehearsal subjects were given an interpolated task to do in between hearing a trigram and recalling it. In this experiment, the interpolated task consisted of asking subjects to count backwards out loud in threes, which was designed to prevent them from rehearsing. After retention intervals of either 0, 3, 6, 9, 12, 15 or 18 seconds of counting backwards, a tone was sounded as a signal for the subjects to stop counting and try to recall the trigram. The sequence for each trial was: receive trigram; count backwards; recall trigram.

Peterson and Peterson scored subjects' recalls as correct only when all three letters of the trigram were reported in the correct order. The percentage of trigrams recalled correctly after each of the different retention intervals was calculated; Figure 12.6 shows the results they obtained. The average percentage of trigrams recalled correctly is high after short delays of 3 or 6 seconds but falls as the delay period increases. After 18 seconds delay, subjects were correctly recalling only 10 per cent of the trigrams.

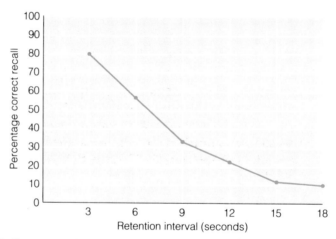

**Figure 12.6**  Percentage frequency of correct recall of three-consonant trigrams (Source: Peterson and Peterson, 1959)

SAQ 6    Read Box G and study the matrix of substitution errors shown in Figure 12.7. Some of the squares have been filled in with Conrad's data. In each of the empty squares put a plus sign if you think there would be *many* substitution errors confusing this pair of letters and put a minus sign if you think there would be *few* substitution errors of this kind. Base your judgements on Conrad's findings about which type of errors were most frequent.

## BOX G   Conrad's substitution error experiment

Conrad showed 387 subjects sequences of six letters (selected from the consonants B, C, F, M, N, P, S, T, V, X). The six letters appeared on a screen one at a time, and subjects had to write them down as they appeared. The rate of presentation was too fast for subjects to keep up, so the sequence of letters had to be partly held in memory. Conrad then examined the response sequences which contained a single error, as shown in Figure 12.7.

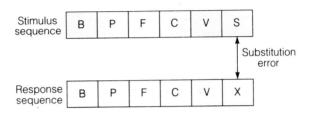

| | Stimulus letters | | | | | |
|---|---|---|---|---|---|---|
| Response letters | | B | P | V | S | X | T |
| B | | | + | + | − | − | + |
| P | 62 | | | + | − | − | + |
| V | 83 | + | | | − | − | + |
| S | 12 | − | − | | | 59 | − |
| X | − | − | − | + | | | |
| T | + | + | + | − | 2 | | |

**Figure 12.7** Conrad's stimulus sequence, a typical response sequence and a simplified matrix showing the number of substitution errors for some of the pairs of letters

He collected together all the data from all the trials from the 387 subjects, and constructed a matrix of substitution errors. Figure 12.7 shows part of the matrix. The B column shows the response letters that subjects produced instead of the correct letter B: in sixty-two cases P had been substituted, in eighty-three cases V had been substituted; but in only twelve cases had S been substituted. With X as the stimulus letter, there were only two cases of T being substituted, but fifty-nine cases where S had been substituted. The results showed that substituted letters are ones which *sound* like the actual letters. Substitution errors based on sound are called acoustic confusions. In Conrad's experiment, subjects seemed to be making **acoustic confusion errors**. These results provided firm evidence for acoustic coding in STM, even when the original stimulus is presented visually.

Conrad concluded that STM uses an acoustic code. Other experimental evidence for an acoustic code shows that it is more difficult to recall in the correct order lists of items which are acoustically similar (like B, C, P, T, or map, cap, lap) than lists of acoustically dissimilar items like (A, B, L, Z, or dog, tree, cup). Similar sounding items are confused in memory so that it is hard to remember which one came in which list position.

The evidence suggests that information which is presented visually is coded verbally in acoustic form in STM. This means that visual inputs must be recoded from a visual to an acoustic (sound-based) code when they pass from sensory registration. This suggests that there is a recoding mechanism between sensory registration and STM which carries out the translation. By the time items such as letters, words or objects are in STM, they have been recognized for what they are. They are no longer just visual patterns but have been identified and named, and it is their names which are represented in the verbal acoustic code.

Studies which provide evidence for acoustic coding in STM tend to be ones which examine recall for verbal items (like words, letters or numbers). However, if memory for other kinds of material is tested, there is evidence that visual or visuospatial coding may occur in STM. Den Heyer and Barrett (1971) used a technique based on **modality specific interference effects** to

## BOX H   Den Heyer and Barrett: modality specific interference

Den Heyer and Barrett showed subjects letters in a grid array like the one illustrated in Figure 12.8. Just after the display had terminated, subjects had to perform either a verbal task (counting backwards aloud) or a visual task (matching patterns) for a few seconds.

|   |   |   |   |   |
|---|---|---|---|---|
| T |   | A |   | E |   |
|   | K |   |   |   |   |
|   |   |   | H |   | N |
|   | R |   | Y |   |   |

**Figure 12.8** One of the stimulus arrays used by Den Heyer and Barrett

Den Heyer and Barrett scored subjects' recall in two ways: recall of the letters in the array, and recall of the grid positions in which the letters had occurred. They found that letter recall was most disrupted by the intevening verbal task, whereas position recall was most disrupted by the intervening visual task. Den Heyer and Barrett concluded, therefore, that the letters were encoded verbally, because letter recall was affected by the intervening verbal task. Their relative positions on the grid must have been encoded visually, because position recall was affected by the intervening visual task.

demonstrate visuospatial coding. This technique involves presenting target material to be remembered and then introducing a secondary interfering task. The assumption is that if the interfering task is in the same modality as the modality of the code used to store the target material, they will interfere with each other, and memory for the target material will suffer. If the secondary task uses a different modality, it will not interfere, showing that interference is modality specific. Therefore a visual secondary task would disrupt visually coded material but *not* verbally coded material, and vice versa. By studying the pattern of disruption it should be possible to work out which code is being used to memorize the material.

Den Heyer and Barrett's experiment, described in Box H, demonstrates that STM does code visual information as well as verbal information. We can now extend the information flow model of memory to incorporate the results of these studies as shown in Figure 12.9.

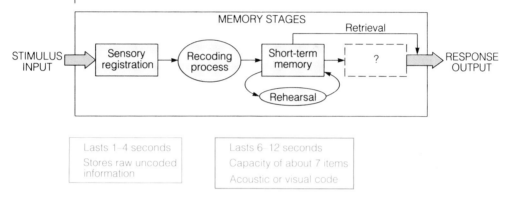

**Figure 12.9** The information flow model of memory: short-term memory

## Summary of Section 3

- At the input stage, information is briefly held in sensory buffer stores. The visual buffer store is known as iconic memory; the auditory buffer store is called echoic memory.

- Information is selected out of the sensory buffer stores and transferred to short-term memory.

- STM holds about seven items. Unless maintained by rehearsal, the duration of memories is about 6–12 seconds.

- Items in STM have been recognized and named and are stored in an acoustic or verbal code. STM can also store visual information.

# 4 | The modal model: criticisms and new interpretations

The experimental investigation of STM using an information processing approach has focused on capacity, duration and code as the important characteristics of each processing stage. As part of this approach, a distinction has traditionally been made between short-term memory and long-term memory. According to the information flow model, information passes from the short-term store into a long-term store. This long-term store has different characteristics. The most obvious difference is that in long-term memory (LTM) the amount of information that can be stored and the length of time it can be maintained have no known limits. The differences between short and long-term memory are reflected in multi-store models of the memory system like the one shown in Figure 12.10.

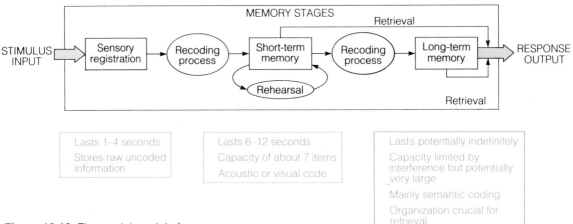

**Figure 12.10** The modal model of memory

This version has been called the **modal model** of memory (modal means most frequently occurring), because it represents the features common to a number of very similar models. It is a multi-store model designed to show how information is acquired, stored and retrieved. The modal model characterizes memory as a sequence of discrete stages. Information flows through the system with recoding processes operating at each stage. However, the modal model has been criticized as over-rigid and over-simplified.

## 4.1 Criticisms of the modal model and the information processing approach

One way in which the model is inaccurate is that it implies that information flows in only one direction—from sensory registration to STM and from there to LTM. But notice that, for information to enter STM from sensory registration, it needs to be recoded and this recoding requires the use of previously stored knowledge. For example, visually presented letters need to be translated into letter names. The visual pattern of the letter F will be recoded in STM and represented as the sound *eff*. To translate F to *eff* requires knowledge about letter shapes and names stored in LTM. So, as well as information passing from STM to LTM, it must flow from LTM to the recoding stage prior to STM. Similarly, information about meaning is required from LTM in order to recode information into a semantic code when it passes from STM to LTM. Information flows through the system in *both* directions. Another way to state this is to say that the stages are *interactive*, not sequential.

A weakness of the information processing approach is its emphasis on *amount* of information. Many psychologists no longer believe that memory capacity can be measured purely in terms of the quantity of information (whether this is measured as the number of bits or the number of items). Many experimental results confirm our intuitive opinion that the *nature* of the to-be-remembered material is a critical factor. Some things are easier to remember than others because they are familiar, or funny, or distinctive, or interesting, or associated with something else. You may be able to remember no more than seven unrelated numbers, but the whole of the *Ancient Mariner*. You may be a whiz at remembering football scores or stock market prices, but not French vocabulary. So a theory which seeks to treat everything alike, as some abstract neutral thing called 'information' which may vary in quantity but not in quality, has to be wrong. Most current research has retained the idea of multiple stages, and of control processes such as recoding or rehearsal acting on the input, but it is recognized that the nature of the input is crucially important in determining what can be remembered.

The information processing approach can also be criticized because the mechanism that is proposed seems too simple and too inflexible. When people try to memorize something they do not always do it in exactly the same way. They may make more or less effort or use different kinds of strategies. The information processing approach does not take account of these variations in the way people tackle memory tasks.

Another shortcoming of the information processing approach is its failure to consider the question of function. As well as asking what each stage of the system does and how it works, Baddeley (1981) believes that we should be asking *what memory is used for*. According to this functional approach, we should be thinking about the role of each memory stage in the sort of tasks and activities that are carried out in everyday life.

Some psychologists have also questioned whether it is valid to make a distinction between STM and LTM and treat them as anatomically and functionally separate structures. However, clinical evidence from cases of amnesia following head injury, or occurring in the **Korsakov syndrome** (dementia and amnesia produced by the brain damage which results from chronic alcoholism), tends to support the distinction. STM can be severely impaired while LTM remains relatively intact. At some fundamental biological level it is likely that the brain uses different mechanisms for holding information for just a short time, and for storing it more or less permanently. However, not everybody accepts the STM/LTM distinction and an alternative point of view is outlined in Section 4.3.

The criticisms of the information processing approach are summarized in Box I. The new interpretations of STM, which are described in Sections 4.2 and 4.3, attempt to meet these objections. And, looking forward to Section 5, we will see that the information processing approach and the modal model fail to do justice to the great complexity and flexibility of LTM. Long-term memory is far more than just a repository for material passed on from STM, and it cannot be characterized simply in terms of features like capacity and duration.

---

**BOX I   Criticisms of the modal model and the information processing approach**

1   Information is described as flowing through the system in only one direction and so cannot account for interactive processes.

2   It ignores qualitative differences in the nature of the to-be-remembered information.

3   It fails to consider functional issues about what memory is used for.

4   It is too fixed and invariant and ignores factors such as effort and strategy.

5   There may not be a clear distinction between STM and LTM, although the clinical evidence favours the possibility that different neural mechanisms are involved.

6   Long-term memory cannot be characterized in terms of capacity, duration or simple forms of coding.

---

## 4.2 New interpretations, 1: working memory

Adopting a functional approach, Baddeley and Hitch (1974) have argued that we can get a far better impression of what STM *is* by considering what it is *for*. In other words, it is better to characterize it in terms of the particular functions it carries out, rather than just as a staging post on the route to long-term memory. They propose that STM should be reformulated as a **working memory** which can perform a number of different functions. One of these functions is dealing with stimulus inputs as they arrive, rehearsing them or coding them into a form suitable for entry into LTM. However, working memory can also perform other tasks. For example, it can hold information arising from sub-stages in processing; a typical example arises in doing mental arithmetic.

ACTIVITY 5

Try adding 443 and 659 in your head. You will find, whatever method you adopt, that sub-totals have to be stored while you work on the rest of the problem.

The concept of the short-term store as a *working* memory store emphasizes that it is an *active* store used to hold information which is being manipulated. Working memory is the focus of *consciousness*—it holds the information you are consciously thinking about now. Processes like adding and subtracting, reasoning or solving problems, or thinking about the meaning of what you hear or read, or carrying out a sequence of operations like making a cake, all involve carrying out operations on information while it is currently held in working memory. Note that working memory holds information that is derived from sensory inputs *and* information that has been retrieved from LTM. New inputs (such as the amount of butter you have just weighed for your cake) and old stored knowledge (such as the recipe you have stored in LTM) come together in working memory.

On the basis of their experiments, Baddeley and his colleagues have suggested that working memory consists of several components (Baddeley, 1981). These components include three modality-based stores and a **central executive** which controls them. The three stores consist of an **articulatory loop** which stores verbal information represented in an articulatory (speech-based) code and is used for verbal rehearsal. The **visuospatial scratchpad** holds visuospatial information of the kind demonstrated in Den Heyer and Barrett's experiment. The **primary acoustic store** holds auditory inputs coded in terms of acoustic features. The working memory system is illustrated in Figure 12.11.

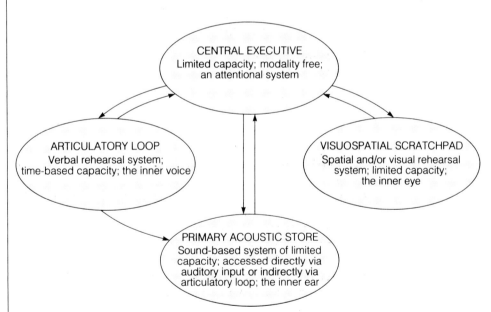

**Figure 12.11** The working memory model showing the different components (Source: Cohen *et al.*, 1986)

You can try out one of the experimental techniques Baddeley and his colleagues used in Activity 6 below. They demonstrated the role of the articulatory loop in working memory by examining the effects of **articulatory suppression**. If people are made to mutter repeatedly some phrase or words, this will occupy and suppress the articulatory loop so that it cannot be used very efficiently to hold information in working memory at the same time. The experimental technique involves asking subjects to repeat a phrase continuously while simultaneously performing a task such as learning a list of words or reading. This is known as **concurrent verbalization**. When performance on a task is impaired by concurrent verbalization it shows that the task is one that utilizes the articulatory loop. Activity 6 demonstrates the important part played by the articulatory loop in language comprehension.

### ACTIVITY 6

Open a book or magazine and read silently through half a page of the text at your normal reading speed. At the same time repeat aloud, 'Coca Cola, Coca Cola', rapidly and continuously. When you finish reading, test yourself to see how much of the text you have taken in. You will probably find you do not remember much, but this depends on how difficult the text is. Concurrent verbalization has more effect if the material is difficult to understand.

The working memory model is similar in many ways to the earlier version of STM described in Section 3, but it is more detailed. The articulatory loop is used for rehearsal and holds about seven items. Both the primary acoustic store and the articulatory loop are speech-based stores, where information is encoded in a verbal code, and the visuospatial scratchpad stores visual information. The main differences are that working memory is *active*; its *function* is to carry out on-going tasks, not just to hold information passively; it has several *components*; and its operations are *flexibly controlled* by the central executive.

## 4.3  New interpretations, 2: levels of processing

The modal model shown in Figure 12.10 divides the memory system into different *structures* that correspond to the different stores, each of which is characterized by a typical form of coding. An alternative argument claims that we do not need to postulate these different structures at all, and proposes a **process model**. According to this model, different stages correspond to different processes. There is a continuum of processing so there is no need to make a sharp distinction between STM and LTM.

Craik and Lockhart (1972) proposed that stimulus inputs undergo successive processing operations. The early stages of processing are 'shallow' and involve coding the stimulus in terms of its physical characteristics (e.g. the visual characteristics of the letters and typeface in which a word is printed, or the acoustic features of its sound). 'Deep' processing involves coding the stimulus more abstractly in terms of its meaning. So visual and acoustic coding are shallow, but semantic coding is deep. Rehearsing material by simple rote repetition is called **maintenance rehearsal** and is classified as shallow. Rehearsing material by exploring its meaning and linking it to semantically associated words is called **elaborative rehearsal** and is classified as deep. The crucial assumption of this **levels of processing theory** is that retention of an item is dependent on the level or depth of processing carried out on to-be-remembered material. Superficial processing leads only to shallow, short-term retention; deep processing leads to efficient, durable retention.

Elias and Perfetti (1973) gave subjects a number of different tasks to perform on each word in a list, such as finding another word that rhymes or finding a synonym. The subjects were not told they would be asked to recall the words, but nevertheless they did remember some of the words when subsequently tested. (This is called **incidental learning** as opposed to **intentional** or **deliberate learning**.) They recalled significantly more words following the deep synonym task (involving semantic processing) than following the shallow rhyming task (involving only acoustic coding), a result which supports the depth of processing hypothesis.

ACTIVITY 7

Work through the following list of words at a steady pace, thinking of a rhyming word for each word marked (R), or a meaning-related word for each of those marked (M). For example a rhyme for 'bread' could be 'head', a meaning-related word for 'tree' might be 'leaf'.

| boy | (M) | | flower | (M) |
| ship | (R) | | lake | (R) |
| house | (R) | | milk | (M) |
| book | (M) | | sand | (R) |
| arm | (M) | | gate | (M) |
| cow | (M) | | ink | (R) |
| sky | (R) | | ball | (R) |
| bell | (R) | | map | (M) |
| face | (R) | | hill | (M) |

Now cover up the list and write down as many words as you can recall. Then check your answers and total up the number of M (meaning) words and the number of R (rhyming) words you remembered.

According to the levels of processing theory you should have remembered more of the deeply processed M words than the shallow processed R words. Did you find this?

Although the predicted result usually emerges, there is now an argument about whether it is *depth* of processing or processing *effort* that produces the result. Tyler *et al.* (1979) gave subjects two sets of anagrams to solve—easy ones (like DOCTRO) or difficult ones (like OCDRTO). Afterwards, subjects were given an unexpected test for recall of the anagrams. Although the processing level was the same, subjects remembered more of the difficult anagram words than the easy ones. So Tyler *et al.* concluded that retention is a function of processing effort, not processing depth.

Another problem is that subjects typically spend a longer time processing the deeper or more difficult tasks. So it could be that the results are partly due to more time being spent on the material. The type of processing, the amount of effort and the length of time spent on processing tend to be *confounded*. Deeper processing goes with more effort and more time, so it is difficult to know which factor influences the results. Another objection to the levels of processing theory is that it does not really explain *why* deeper processing is more effective. However, recent studies have clarified this point. It appears that deeper coding produces better retention because it is more elaborate. **Elaborative encoding** enriches the memory representation of an item by activating many aspects of its meaning and linking it into the pre-existing network of semantic associations. Deep level semantic coding tends to be more elaborated than shallow physical coding and this is probably why it works better. This view fits well with the constructivist approach which emphasizes the importance of integrating new information with existing knowledge.

The levels of processing theory replaces the multi-*store* model with a multi-*process* model. Shallow processing occurs at the early stages, and information is processed more deeply as it passes on through the system. There are no clear distinctions between separate stores.

## Summary of Section 4

- The modal model of memory has been criticized on the grounds that it is too inflexible and too passive, that it neglects functional issues and cannot account for the richness and complexity of knowledge in LTM.

- STM has been reformulated as working memory, an active store which is used to hold and manipulate information while thinking, speaking and reading.

- The levels of processing theory claims that only different types of processing and not separate STM and LTM structures can be distinguished.

- Deep processing produces better recall but also involves more time and effort, and elaboration of the input.

# 5 | Long-term memory

As indicated in the previous section, long-term memory does not fit into the information flow model so readily as STM because it cannot be characterized in terms of factors like capacity, duration or simple codes. LTM has no known limits on capacity, or on duration of storage, and in addition to semantic coding it also uses a variety of different forms of organization. The most important point to note about LTM is the great diversity of information it stores. All kinds of knowledge and beliefs—including language and music, objects and events, people and places, plans and skills—are stored in LTM. Once we start to study LTM, the focus shifts from mechanism to strategy. Instead of fixed mechanical characteristics like capacity and duration, the important factors turn out to be the flexible and highly individual strategies employed in organization and retrieval. The cognitive approach (see Section 2.4) is therefore more appropriate.

Traditional experimental research on LTM has not reflected its richness and complexity because it has concentrated on material which has been stored for minutes or hours rather than for months or years, and many studies have looked at memory for lists of words learned specially for the experiment. However, the cognitive approach is apparent in some studies of LTM, especially in the last decade or so. Recent work (e.g. Neisser, 1982) has focused on naturally acquired memories for things like current events, television shows, school-days or town plans. These are much more representative of the kind of material stored in LTM.

Many of our long-term memories are not even accessible to consciousness, or only become conscious with professional help such as psychoanalysis. Unlike the highly artificial lists of words used in experiments, naturally acquired memories often have great personal and emotional significance. It is also important to realize that LTM is not just a storehouse but a *dynamic* system in which knowledge is being continually updated, revised and modified in the light of new experiences or fresh information. And LTM is also an *interconnected* system in which items of information are related together in a huge and complex web of interconnections; they are not represented as single discrete entities.

Tulving (1972) proposed that there are two different systems within LTM. **Episodic memory** consists of memory of personal experiences. These are specific events which occurred at a particular time and place. They include important episodes of your past life, such as births, and weddings; public events like assassinations or disasters; and more humdrum events like going shopping and the current experience of just reading this page. **Semantic memory** consists of general knowledge, including knowledge about the meanings of words and concepts, and general knowledge about the world. Your knowledge of history, geography, science and other subjects forms part of your semantic memory. Information in semantic memory is not related to time or place or any particular occasions. You may find it helpful to think of episodic memory as being like a diary, whereas semantic memory is like an encyclopaedia-cum-dictionary.

The distinction is not always clear-cut because information in semantic memory is often acquired in the course of personal experiences. Information that is originally part of episodic memory may pass into semantic memory if it is recognized as being generally true. When I learn that daffodils are always yellow and $2 \times 3 = 6$, these episodes gradually become part of my general knowledge in semantic memory. I can no longer remember where or when I first learned these facts. Moreover, episodic memories for specific events, like, for example, a train journey, are mixed up with general semantic knowledge about trains and travelling. For these reasons, the two systems cannot be viewed as completely separate; it must be possible to transmit information from the episodic system to the semantic system and vice versa. In some of the experimental tasks described in the following sections both episodic and semantic memories are involved.

## 5.1 Forgetting in LTM

Even if there are no discernible limits to the capacity of LTM, everyday experience confirms that all too often we forget things. How does forgetting in LTM occur? Section 3.2 introduced two theories of forgetting in STM—trace decay and interference. Although it is plausible that memories in LTM are also lost because of decay over time, there is no real evidence that this is so. In late old age, people can still recall events from their childhood, although memories which have lain dormant and disused for a long time may be very difficult to retrieve. Interference theory, however, is supported by experimental evidence and by subjective experience.

Psychologists have identified two categories of interference. One type is when the material you learn first interferes with material you learn subsequently. This is called **proactive interference**, since its effects operate forwards in time. The other kind is when material you learn later interferes with material you learned previously. This is called **retroactive interference**, since its effects operate backwards in time (Figure 12.12). It has been suggested that interference tends to be worst when items are most similar. This assumption was used as the basis for an experiment to discover the kind of code used in LTM, see Box J.

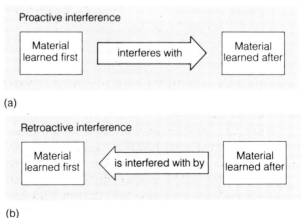

(a)

(b)

**Figure 12.12** Proactive and retroactive interference

## BOX J   McGeoch and Macdonald (1931): retroactive interference

McGeoch and Macdonald divided their subjects into five experimental
groups and a control group, and gave each group a list of words to learn.
When they had learned the list, the five experimental groups were each
given a different intervening task. Each of these groups spent ten minutes
learning either numbers, or nonsense syllables, or words that were unrelated
to the original list, or words of opposite meaning to those in the original list,
or words of the same meaning as the original list. The control group had a
ten minute rest with no intervening task. Recall of the original list was then
tested. Comparison of the number of words recalled by each of the
experimental groups with the number recalled by the control group shows
how much interference was caused by each of the intervening tasks. As
Figure 12.13 shows, subjects who had learned lists of numbers as an
intervening task suffered least retroactive interference; subjects who learned
lists of synonyms suffered most retroactive interference.

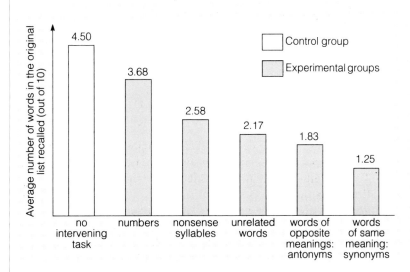

**Figure 12.13** McGeoch and Macdonald's results, showing the effect of similarity of
material upon amount of interference deficit in recall
(Source: McGeoch and Macdonald, 1931)

From this experiment, we can conclude something about how words are
coded in LTM. It is usually assumed that, if items are similar to each other,
there is greater potential for confusion and therefore more interference. In
what way was the intervening list which caused the most interference similar
to the original list? It was *meaning* that mattered—the closer the lists were to
each other in terms of meaning, the greater the interference effect. This
suggests that LTM uses a code based on word meanings, called a semantic
code. Note, therefore, that as information passes from STM to LTM a further
recoding process is involved. Semantic coding predominates in LTM,
especially for verbal material. However, other codes may also be used; for

example, scenes and faces may be visually coded and voices and music can be retained in LTM in an acoustic code.

## 5.2  Organization in LTM

The problem in LTM is not so much forgetting as being unable to retrieve. We often know we have the information that is required, but we cannot recall it on demand. To make it accessible, some order must be imposed on the complex mass of information stored in LTM. It must be labelled, sorted and organized in some way. There is evidence that a dominant form of organization in LTM is **categorical clustering**, with items being grouped according to the semantic category to which they belong. Some of this evidence comes from studies which examine free recall, like those described in Box K. Note that in **free recall** subjects are allowed to recall the items in any order they wish. Free recall allows the experimenter to study the way subjects naturally order and group the items for output when they are free to do so. The observed order of output reflects memory organization.

---

### BOX K   Free recall experiments on organization in memory

Bousfield (1953) gave subjects a list of sixty items to learn. Within this list were fifteen names of animals, fifteen names of people, fifteen professions, and fifteen vegetables, all mixed up together. Subjects were asked to recall as many of the words as possible in any order they liked. Despite the fact that the categories had all been jumbled up together when originally presented, subjects tended to remember them in clusters of words all belonging to the same category. For instance, once they had recalled 'dog', then other animals were likely to follow—'cat', 'mouse', 'rat', 'horse', 'donkey'. Bousfield concluded that such category clusters are indicative of semantic organization in memory.

As well as items being grouped into semantic categories, the categories themselves can be organized and arranged in hierarchies. Bower et al. (1969) asked two groups of subjects to learn a list of 112 words. For one group, the words belonged to four different **conceptual hierarchies** (one of these, the mineral hierarchy, is shown in Figure 12.14) and the words were presented already organized into the hierarchies as shown. The other group received the same number of words arranged in the same patterns, but the words themselves were randomly selected and unrelated. After only one trial, the group who received the conceptual hierarchies remembered 65 per cent of the words, whereas the group who received the random words remembered 18 per cent. After three trials, recall of the conceptually related words was 100 per cent compared with 47 per cent for the unrelated set. These results strikingly demonstrate that a hierarchical organization is a powerful aid to recall and may be a fundamental principle of the way material is stored in LTM.

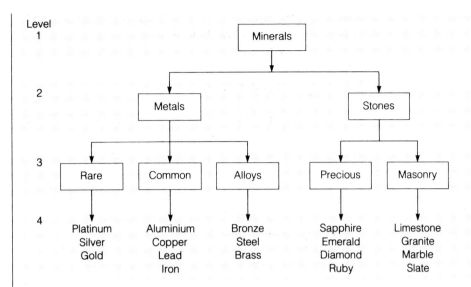

**Figure 12.14** The minerals hierarchy
(Source: Adapted from Bower *et al.*, 1969)

These experiments, as well as McGeoch and Macdonald's demonstration of retroactive interference effects, were carried out long before the episodic–semantic distinction was thought of. However, they can be interpreted as showing how an episodic memory (the specific experience of learning a list of words at a specific time and place) is influenced by permanent knowledge about word meanings and categories stored in semantic memory. Both systems interact in these tasks.

A hierarchical model of the way factual knowledge is organized in semantic memory was constructed by Collins and Quillian (1969) and this is summarized in Box L overleaf. This is an example of a **network model** of semantic memory. A network is a structure consisting of a set of *nodes* with *links* or paths interconnecting them. Network models are in the associationist tradition (see Section 2.1) because the links represent associations between items. The knowledge that an ostrich is an animal or that a fish can swim is represented in a network like the one shown in Figure 12.15. These models generate quite definite predictions about the time it should take to retrieve information from store and these predictions can be tested experimentally. One experimental technique involves presenting subjects with statements which have to be judged true or false (e.g. 'a fish can swim' or 'an ostrich is an animal'), and measuring response times. If semantic memory is organized in such a way that the two concepts ('fish' and 'swim') mentioned in the statement are closely linked, then responses are fast. If the concepts are not closely associated (as in 'ostrich' and 'animal'), then responses are slower. Box L shows how Collins and Quillian used this technique to test their model of semantic memory organization.

They proposed a hierarchical model of memory organization as shown in Figure 12.15. At the highest level there are a small number of general concepts, at the bottom many specific concepts. General facts about a high

## BOX L    Experimental testing of the Collins and Quillian model

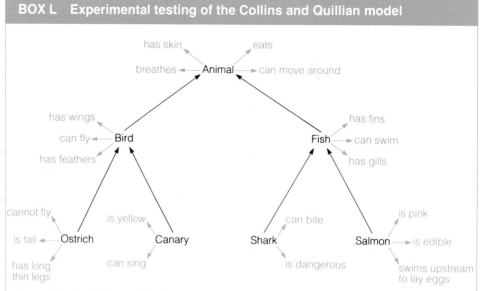

**Figure 12.15**  Collins and Quillian's hierarchical organization model
(Source: Collins and Quillian, 1969)

If memory is organized into a hierarchy of levels as shown in Figure 12.15, Collins and Quillian predicted that, as a person searches for information, the more levels the search has to pass through, the longer it will take to make judgements about the relationship between the concepts. To test their model, Collins and Quillian generated statements which linked concepts at different levels. For example:

A canary can sing    0–level search through the hierarchy (i.e. both concepts are at the same level)

A canary can fly     1–level search (via 'canary is a bird' and 'birds can fly')

A canary has skin    2–level search (via 'canary is a bird', 'a bird is an animal', and 'animals have skin')

Subjects were shown statements like these in a visual display, together with other statements like 'a shark can sing' and 'a canary has gills'. Subjects were asked to verify each statement as 'true' or 'false', and they were timed from the onset of the display to the point at which they pressed either a 'true' or a 'false' button. As you can see from Figure 12.16, reaction times conformed to the prediction and were longer as the number of levels to be traversed increased.

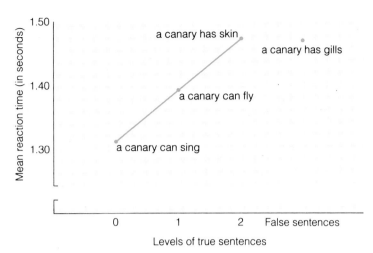

**Figure 12.16** Collins and Quillian's results, showing that response time is increased when search through the hierarchy involves more levels
(Source: Collins and Quillian, 1969)

level category like 'animals' (e.g. 'an animal has skin') are to be found at the top of the hierarchy; detailed facts about specific animals (e.g. 'a canary is yellow') are to be found at the bottom.

SAQ 7 Study Collins and Quillian's hierarchical network in Figure 12.15. Which of the following sentences should be verified fastest? Which should be slowest?

(a) A shark can bite.

(b) A salmon can move.

(c) An ostrich has feathers.

Although Collins and Quillian's model seems intuitively plausible, some observations do not fit the model very well. For example, people can verify a statement about a very *typical* member of a category (such as a 'robin is a bird') faster than a statement about an *untypical* member of the category (like 'a penguin is a bird'), even though the search distance is the same in both cases. This finding, known as the **typicality effect**, cannot be explained by Collins and Quillian's model. According to their model, in which all birds are at the same level in the hierarchy, whether they are typical like robins and sparrows, or untypical like ostriches and penguins, response times should not vary with typicality.

**The spreading activation model**

Difficulties like this led Collins and Loftus (1975) to revise their views and propose a different kind of network model in which related concepts are grouped into interconnected clusters, as shown in Figure 12.17. This model of how knowledge is represented is not hierarchical in structure. Instead, concepts that are closely related share many links, and lie close together, so that the paths connecting them are short. In Figure 12.17, for example, 'car',

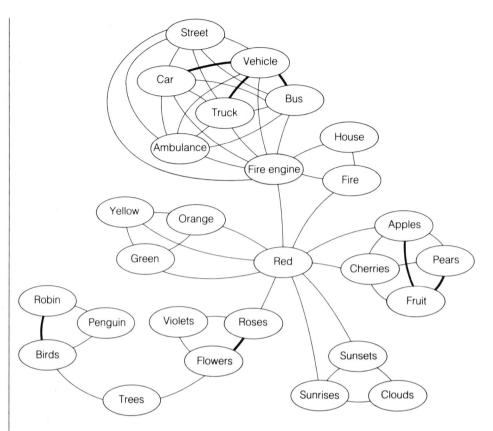

**Figure 12.17** The spreading activation model
(Source: Adapted from Collins and Loftus, 1975)

'truck' and 'bus' are closely connected by many short links. In the Collins and Quillian model, response time is determined solely by the number of levels or *distance*, but Collins and Loftus introduced an additional variable by allowing that links could also vary in *strength*. Links that are frequently used become stronger and faster than links that are seldom used. This assumption then explains why statements about very typical category members, like 'an apple is a fruit' or 'a robin is a bird', can be judged 'true' faster than statements about untypical ones, like 'a penguin is a bird'. The robin–bird link is stronger and faster because a robin is a typical bird so we more frequently think of robins as birds. In Figure 12.17, strong, frequently used links of this kind are shown as thicker connecting lines.

The key features of the **spreading activation model** are:

1   Speed of access depends on the length *and* the strength of the linking paths.

2   Frequently used links are stronger (so the robin-to-bird path would be stronger than the penguin-to-bird path).

3   Activation of a given concept spreads outwards to adjacent concepts; for example, thinking about fire-engines would automatically activate related concepts like 'fire' 'red' and 'ambulance'.

4    The strength of activation decreases as the distance increases so it does not spread indefinitely. Thinking about roses is unlikely to lead you to think about penguins. These concepts are only connected by a long, indirect pathway.

This network model has no difficulty in handling the typicality effect. Another advantage is that it readily maps on to what we know about how information is represented in the brain as a pattern of neural activity. Current activation of a concept can be thought of as corresponding to excitation of a neuron, with activation spreading to other neurons and producing a pattern of excitation across sets of neurons. Such patterns are transitory, so that they can only represent information briefly, but long-term changes in synaptic connections, which facilitate or inhibit particular links making them easier or harder to excite, are thought to underlie long-term representation of information.

So far, we have only considered organization in semantic memory, where items appear to be grouped according to the categories to which they belong and the properties they share. What about the organization of *episodic* memories? How do people group the episodes of their past lives in memory? Studies of autobiographical memory have revealed the organization of episodic memory by getting people to 'think aloud' while they are trying to retrieve particular memories. Typical responses are:

'I remember having a car accident—that was about ten years ago—I was in my first job—we had just moved to London'.

'I remember the Coronation—I was about sixteen at the time—still at school—it was the first time I saw television'.

Notice how episodic memories are stored in terms of time and place and personal landmarks. Although episodic memories may also be organized in categories (holidays, friends, jobs) the typical forms of organization are *spatial* and *temporal*; where and when the events occurred.

## 5.3  Retrieval from LTM

In Section 1, when you carried out Activity 2, you experienced two different ways of retrieving information—recall and recognition. You probably found that recall is more demanding than recognition. The fact that you sometimes recognized a word which you were unable to recall shows that the word was actually stored in memory, although you could not produce it when you tried to recall it. Tulving (1968) has characterized this situation by stating that a word may be *available* in memory but not *accessible*. There are some impressive examples of forgetting which vividly illustrate the distinction between availability and accessibility. One of these is known as the tip-of-tongue state (TOT).

The **tip-of-tongue** state occurs when you are temporarily unable to retrieve a word or name which you know quite well. The subjective feeling is that the word is 'on the tip of your tongue' because you can almost, but not quite,

## BOX M   Brown and McNeill (1966): the TOT state

Brown and McNeill induced 233 TOT states by reading definitions of rare words such as: 'a small boat used in the river and harbour traffic of China and Japan'. The subject was asked to produce a single word that fits this definition; (the answer is 'sampan'). A TOT state was identified when subjects felt sure they knew the target word and were on the verge of retrieving it but did not succeed, although they could recognize the sought-for word when given some alternatives to choose from.

Two main findings emerge from analysis of the TOT states:

1   *Partial recall:* while unable to recall the target word, people can often recall partial information about it such as the first letter, the number of syllables and the location of stress. Subjects trying to retrieve 'sampan' may know it begins with 's' and has two syllables equally stressed.

2   *Recall of related words:* these come to mind while searching for the target word but are recognized as being wrong. These related words usually resemble the target either in sound (e.g. 'sarong', 'Siam' instead of 'sampan') or in meaning (e.g. 'junk', 'barge').

produce it. Brown and McNeill (1966) used this phenomenon to explore retrieval in a classic experiment; see Box M.

Retrieval strategies reflect the way information is organized in memory. These results show that retrieval processes home in on storage locations within semantic memory, where words are grouped and associated on the basis of either similarity of sound or similarity of meaning. The search may succeed in locating the correct group, but fail to retrieve the correct item within the group, resulting, therefore, in near-miss responses and the subjective feeling of almost-but-not-quite remembering something. Next time you experience a TOT state yourself and find you cannot recall a word, or a person's name, notice whether your retrieval attempts conform to Brown and McNeill's findings.

People search by sound or by meaning when trying to retrieve words from semantic memory, but when they are trying to retrieve episodic memories, people use quite different tactics. They often try to reconstruct the context of the target event. For example, to recall the names of schoolmates, people mentally reconstruct scenes of particular classes or activities in particular locations, and then try to fill in details of the participants (Williams and Hollan, 1982).

How do these findings about retrieval strategies fit in with the network models described in Section 5.2? In the network models, retrieval occurs automatically as a result of activation spreading along the linking pathways. This kind of automatic retrieval is known as *direct access*. The kind of retrieval strategies involved in TOT states, or in the recall of autobiographical episodes, are conscious searches and this kind of active effortful retrieval is known as *indirect access*.

## Summary of Section 5

- The cognitive approach has proved most appropriate for studying LTM. LTM stores many different kinds of information. There are no known limits on capacity, but interference from similar items is the main cause of forgetting.

- Memory for general knowledge (semantic memory) can be distinguished from memory for personal experiences (episodic memory). Semantic memory is organized in categories. Episodic memory is organized along the dimensions of time and place. Organization is a powerful aid to retrieval.

- In network models of semantic memory, related concepts are linked by interconnecting pathways and may be arranged in hierarchies. Retrieval time depends on the position of an item in the hierarchy.

- In spreading activation models, semantically related concepts lie close together in the network. Retrieval time is influenced by the length and strength of the pathway. Strength is determined by the frequency with which it is used.

- Information may be available in LTM but not accessible. Direct automatic retrieval is distinguished from indirect effortful search. Different kinds of strategy are used to search LTM when retrieval is difficult. Search strategies reflect the way information is organized.

# 6 | Individual differences in memory

We have talked so far as if everybody's memory works in the same way, yet we all know from our own experience that there are very considerable individual differences in memory ability. The modal model described in Section 4 implies that everybody's memory is the same. However, this is misleading, because, even if everybody is equipped with the same basic neural mechanisms, people have different experiences and different knowledge. It is a strength of Bartlett's approach that he recognizes how reconstructed memories depend on knowledge and so differ from person to person. A lot of psychological research has tended to emphasize the limitations and failures of memory but some people have exceptionally good memories. And even ordinary people are capable of surprising feats of memory. An educated person remembers 40 000 to 60 000 words. Elderly people retain detailed memories of events that occurred seventy years ago. You may pick up the telephone and instantly recognize a voice you have not heard for decades. Human memory is a remarkably effective information storage system.

# 6.1 Studies of exceptional memory

Luria, a Russian neuropsychologist, studied a mnemonist (a memory expert)
he calls 'S' who came to him asking to have his memory tested. S was a
journalist and had been sent to Luria by his editor who had noticed his
amazing ability to remember. S performed quite differently on memory tests
from other people. For example, he could recall perfectly lists of seventy or
more items (words, numbers or letters) instead of showing the normal
memory span of seven plus or minus two items. He was given a matrix of fifty
numbers and took 3 minutes to study it. He could not only remember all the
numbers, but could start from any specified line as though he were reading
from a page. He was tested a few days later, and his performance remained
perfect. What is perhaps most surprising was his ability to remember material
which was meaningless to him—poems in languages he did not know,
chemical formulae, and so on.

When asked how he managed these memory feats, S reported to Luria that he
could call up an enormous range of physical images for each item. For
example, with a number he would describe his image like this: 'Take the
number one. This is a proud well-built man. Two is a high spirited woman,
three, a gloomy person (why, I don't know); six a man with a swollen foot.' He
said of one of the psychologists: 'What a crumbly yellow voice you have.' He
described a musical sound as: 'It looks something like fireworks tinged with a
pink-red hue. The strip of colour feels rough and unpleasant, and it has an
ugly taste—rather like that of a briny pickle. . . . you could hurt your hand on
this' (Luria, 1968, pp. 23–5). Such reconstructions of a stimulus into many
physical images in other modalities is called **synesthesia**, a not uncommon
phenomenon, but shown by S to an unusually marked degree.

One technique S used to remember a list of items was to imagine a familiar
street in Moscow, and then mentally place the items along the street. When he
forgot any item, it was usually because he misperceived the images, either
because he had placed them in 'dark corners', or because they blended into
the background (he lost an egg because he had imagined it against a white
wall). Although the images he used were synesthetic (i.e. in many modalities)
he relied most on visual images.

You might expect that a memory like this was a tremendous asset to S. He did
in fact become a professional mnemonist, and gave stage shows. But the way
his memory worked had its disadvantages. He was very poor at semantic
coding, and he did not cluster items of a particular category in a list. Normal
subjects take advantage of the structure and redundancy in the matrix shown
below, and find it easy to remember. But S found it no easier than an
unstructured matrix.

| | | | |
|---|---|---|---|
| 1 | 2 | 3 | 4 |
| 2 | 3 | 4 | 5 |
| 3 | 4 | 5 | 6 |
| 4 | 5 | 6 | 7 |

In other words, S was poor at using those memory strategies which the rest of us find most effective. He did not categorize or recognize patterns or meaning. He said that, if he were asked to remember the alphabet in order, he would be unlikely to recognize it for what it was, and treat it just like any string of unpredictable letters. Further, his synesthesia made simple skills like reading very difficult for him. He said, 'Each word calls up images; they collide with one another, and the results is chaos, I can't make anything out of this' (Luria, 1968, p. 53). When he read the phrase 'the work got under way normally', he gave this account of his impressions:

As for 'work', I see that work is going on . . . there's a factory . . . but there's the word 'normally'. What I see is a big, ruddy-cheeked woman, a normal woman . . . then the expression to 'get under way': Who? What is all this? You have industry . . . that is a factory, and this is a normal woman—now how does all this fit together? How much I have to get rid of just to get the simple idea of the thing!

(Luria, 1968, p. 98)

You can see from this account that remembering too much can be a disadvantage. The ability to forget is useful as a means of 'clearing the decks'.

More recently Hunt and Love (1972) studied another mnemonist they called 'VP'. Strangely, VP was born not far away from S in Latvia. Hunt and Love were more systematic in the way they studied VP; Table 12.1 shows how he scored in some of the experiments you have read about.

**Table 12.1** Comparisons of exceptional and normal memory

|                                                                                      | VP's score                  | Normal subjects' scores |
| ------------------------------------------------------------------------------------ | --------------------------- | ----------------------- |
| Remembering a random string of digits in the correct order (memory span)             | 17                          | 7–9                     |
| Peterson and Peterson paradigm: retention of a trigram after 18 seconds backwards counting | 90%                         | 5–10%                   |
| Retention of Bartlett's 'The war of the ghosts' after six weeks                       | virtually word perfect      | very poor               |

As you can see, VP had an exceptional memory. However, when Hunt and Love asked him to describe how it worked, his replies made it evident that he was working in a way quite different from S. VP relied mainly on semantic associations rather than visual imagery. Because he was fluent in several languages, he found it relatively easy to form semantic associations. One of Hunt and Love's tasks demonstrated this semantic mnemonism. They showed VP a large number of outline drawings of objects like a shoe, a cup, and so on, and then asked him to recall them. The items were drawn in such a way that they could be clustered either visually (according to their orientation) or semantically (according to their meaning). VP's use of highly developed semantic coding was confirmed by the fact that he only used semantic categories.

Another case was investigated by Coltheart and Glick (1974). A college student, referred to as Sue d'Onim, had an exceptionally good visual memory. This was demonstrated most strikingly by her ability to spell sentences backwards. With sentences of five or six words she could spell backwards rapidly and accurately, working from a clear image. Because the ends of longer sentences tended to 'fall off the edge' of the image, she visualized these as several short rows of words. You can get some idea of her ability by testing yourself or a friend.

### ACTIVITY 8

Read the following sentence, then cover it up and try to spell it backwards as fast as you can. If you have a digital watch you can time yourself.

'The furniture was highly polished'

Coltheart and Glick tested Sue d'Onim's iconic memory capacity. They found that when she was shown a row of eight letters for 100 milliseconds she could, on average, correctly report 7.44. Most people average about 4.5, so her performance was far superior.

You may wonder what the study of people like Sue d'Onim, S and VP has to offer for an understanding of normal human memory. Such people provide evidence of what memory *can* do and show that limits and constraints are not nearly as fixed as the modal model would lead us to believe. These detailed investigations of a single person demonstrate that the limits assumed by the modal model can be overcome, sometimes to a spectacular degree. Of course, such cases are exceptional, but the results of memory training suggest that we all have the potential to make our memories work more efficiently.

## 6.2 Mnemonic strategies

In discussing different forms of coding, and the exceptional abilities of the mnemonists, we have already indicated some of the **mnemonic strategies** which lead to enhanced performance. Some of these can be adopted by anybody seeking to improve their memories, or to memorize some particular material. If you ever do experiments in memory, you will probably be very surprised at the range of difference in scores. For example, if you ask people to recall a twenty word list, it is not unusual to find that some people remember about sixteen correctly and others only five or six. The main reason for such differences is that learning and remembering are skills. People who are practised at remembering acquire strategies which can greatly extend any built-in capacity limitations.

Chase and Ericsson (1982) reported a study of a subject who started with a normal memory span of seven digits. After training for nearly 300 hours he eventually achieved a digit span of eighty-two. That is, he could repeat back a list of eighty-two numbers in the correct order. During the long hours of practice he developed strategies for coding the numbers as times for running various distances (e.g. 3492 = near world record mile time), as dates (e.g. 1943 = near end of Second World War), or as people's ages. Chase and Ericsson concluded that STM *capacity* was unchanged because none of the coded groups ever exceeded six numbers. The subject had used his strategies to group the numbers and had transferred the mnemonically coded groups into LTM.

Of course, this is an exceptional case showing great dedication on the subject's part. However, most people can learn to use grouping, labelling, imagery or rules to improve performance on memory tasks. Below are listed some common mnemonic strategies. All of them involve making the material more meaningful, fitting new material to already learned frameworks, or elaborating it by images or associations.

1 *Method of loci:* This can be traced back to Greek and Roman orators who used the method to remember the order of the topics they intended to cover in a long speech. The method consists of mentally placing each one of a list of to-be-remembered items in a well known *locus* (a place) such as the rooms of a familiar house, or, like S did, the buildings along a street. A 'mental walk' then serves to retrieve the items in the correct order. This method, which can be demonstrated in the classroom, reliably produces much improved recall. The trick consists in learning a new ordered series of items by relating it to an already known ordered series of locations.

2 *Peg words:* This method of learning a word list entails first learning a peg list of rhyming pairs:

| | |
|---|---|
| one is a bun | six is a stick |
| two is a shoe | seven is heaven |
| three is a tree | eight is a gate |
| four is a door | nine is a line |
| five is a hive | ten is a hen |

The to-be-remembered list of words is then hung on the pegs by means of interactive imagery. If the first word is 'cigar' you imagine a cigar stuck in a bun; if the next is 'cat', you imagine a cat wearing shoes, then a 'chair' in a tree, and so on.

3 *Story linkage:* Lists of words can be linked together by incorporating them into a story. You can make up a story about how a cigar was given in exchange for a cat which went and sat in a chair, etc.

4 *Initial letters mnemonics:* A sentence with the same initial letters, like 'Richard Of York Gains Battles In Vain' can be used to remember the order of the spectral colours Red, Orange, Yellow, Green, Blue, Indigo and Violet. The sentence is easier to remember than the list because the sequence is meaningful.

5 *The PQRS method:* It is appropriate to conclude this chapter on memory with some advice which may actually be helpful to you in studying course material. The mnemonic techniques described above do work for short lists, like shopping lists, but do not offer much help with mastering a whole body of knowledge. But PQRS is a study technique which has been tested by students. It consists of four stages:

(a) *Preview*—examine the chapter looking at headings to grasp what topics are covered and get a general idea of what it is about.

(b) *Question*—formulate questions so you know what information you are aiming to extract.

(c) *Read*—read the material, actively seeking the answers.

(d) *Summarize*—summarize what you have read.

You will probably realize that the SAQs and section summaries in this text are designed to induce a PQRS type of studying. The main feature of this technique is that it firmly links remembering to understanding, and this is a theme which has been running through much of this chapter. Short lists, songs and poems may be learned by rote repetition. But long-term retention of a large body of information is only achieved by understanding and elaborating the meaning of whatever you are trying to remember, and organizing the material so that it can be readily retrieved when required.

## Summary of Section 6

- Some individuals have exceptional memory capacity, but inability to forget can be a handicap.

- People with normal memory capacity can extend it and make their memory more efficient by using appropriate mnemonic strategies.

## Further reading

WINGFIELD, A. and BYRNES, D. *The psychology of human memory*, New York: Academic Press, 1981.

This book gives comprehensive coverage and is very clear and readable.

COHEN, G., EYSENCK, M. and LE VOI, M. *Memory: a cognitive approach*, The Open University, 1986.

This is one of the course books for the Open University course D309 *Cognitive psychology*. The first part gives an account of reseach on everyday memory and the second part is about working memory. Its treatment of these topics is more detailed than in this chapter.

# References

BADDELEY, A.D. (1976) *The psychology of memory*, New York: Harper and Row.

BADDELEY, A.D. (1981) 'The concept of working memory: a view of its current state and probable future development', *Cognition*, vol. 10, pp. 17–23.

BADDELEY, A.D. (1988) 'But what the hell is it for?', in M.M. Gruneberg, P.E. Morris and R.N. Sykes (eds), *Practical aspects of memory: current research and issues*, vol. 1, Chichester: John Wiley and Sons.

BADDELEY, A.D. and HITCH, G. (1974) 'Working memory', in Bower, G.H. (ed.), *The psychology of learning and motivation*, vol. 8, pp. 47–90.

BARTLETT, F.C. (1932) *Remembering*, Cambridge: Cambridge University Press (paperback version, 1967).

BOUSFIELD, W.A. (1953) 'The occurrence of clustering in recall of randomly arranged associates', *Journal of General Psychology*, vol. 49, pp. 229–40.

BOWER, G.H., CLARK, M.C., WINZENZ, D. and LESGOLD, A.M. (1969) 'Hierarchical retrieval schemes in recall of categorized word lists', *Journal of Verbal Learning and Verbal Behaviour*, vol. 8, pp. 323–43.

BROWN, R. and McNEILL, D. (1966) 'The "tip of the tongue" phenomenon', *Journal of Verbal Learning and Verbal Behaviour*, vol. 5, pp. 325–37.

CHASE, W.G. and ERICSSON, K.A. (1982) 'Skill and working memory', in G.H. Bower (ed.), *The psychology of learning and motivation: advances in research and theory*, vol. 16, New York: Academic Press.

COHEN, G., EYSENCK, M. and LE VOI, M. (1986) *Memory: a cognitive approach*, Milton Keynes: The Open University Press.

COLLINS, A.M. and LOFTUS, E.F. (1975) 'A spreading activation theory of semantic processing', *Psychological Review*, vol. 82, pp. 407–28.

COLLINS, A.M. and QUILLIAN, M.R. (1969) 'Retrieval time from semantic memory', *Journal of Verbal Learning and Verbal Behaviour*, vol. 8, p. 244.

COLTHEART, M. and GLICK, M.J. (1974) 'Visual imagery: a case study', *Quarterly Journal of Experimental Psychology*, vol. 26, pp. 438–53.

CONRAD, R. (1964) 'Acoustic confusion in immediate memory', *British Journal of Psychology*, vol. 55, pp. 75–84.

CRAIK, F.I. and LOCKHART, R.S. (1972) 'Levels of processing: a framework for memory research', *Journal of Verbal Learning and Verbal Behaviour*, vol. 11, pp. 671–84.

DEN HEYER, K. and BARRETT, B. (1971) 'Selective loss of visual and verbal information in short-term memory by means of visual and verbal interpolated tasks', *Psychonomic Science*, vol. 25, pp. 100–2.

EBBINGHAUS, H. (1885) *Uber das Gedachtnis*, Leipzig: Dunber, H. Ruyer and C. E. Bussenius. Published in translation (1913) as *Memory*, New York: Teacher's College Press.

ELIAS, C.S. and PERFETTI, C.A. (1973) 'Encoding task and recognition memory: the importance of semantic coding', *Journal of Experimental Psychology*, vol. 99(2), pp. 151–7.

HUNT, E. and LOVE, T. (1972) 'How good can memory be?', in Melton, A.W. and Martin, E. (eds), *Coding process in human memory*, Washington, DC: Winston/Wiley.

LURIA, A.R. (1968) *The mind of mnemonist*, New York: Basic Books.

McGEOCH, J.A. and MACDONALD, W.T. (1931) 'Meaningful relations and retroactive inhibition', *American Journal of Psychology*, vol. 43, pp. 579–88.

MILLER, G.A. (1956) 'The magical number seven plus or minus two', *Psychological Review*, vol. 63, pp. 81–97.

NEISSER, U. (1978) 'Memory: what are the important questions?', in M.M. Gruneberg, P.E. Morris and R.N. Sykes (eds), *Practical applications of memory*, London: Academic Press.

NEISSER, U. (1982) *Memory observed*, San Francisco: W.H. Freeman and Co.

PETERSON, L.R. and PETERSON, M.J. (1959) 'Short-term retention of individual items', *Journal of Experimental Psychology*, vol. 58, pp. 193–8.

SPERLING, G. (1960) 'The information available in brief visual presentation', *Psychological Monographs*, vol. 74, no. 498.

TULVING, E. (1968) Theoretical issues in free recall', in T.R. Dixon and D.L. Horton (eds), *Verbal behaviour and general behaviour*, Englewood Cliffs, NJ: Prentice Hall.

TULVING, E. (1972) 'Episodic and semantic memory', in Tulving, E. and Donaldson, W. (eds), *Organization of memory*, New York: Academic Press, pp. 381–403.

TYLER, S.W., HERTEL, P.T., McCALLUM, M.C. and ELLIS, H.C. (1979) 'Cognitive effort and memory', *Journal of Experimental Psychology (Human Learning and Memory)*, vol. 5(b), pp. 607–17.

WILLIAMS, M.D. and HOLLAN, J.D. (1982) 'The process of retrieval from very long term memory', *Cognitive Science*, vol. 5, pp. 87–119.

## Answers to SAQs

### SAQ 1

Some examples are diary, shopping list, wall chart, knot in handkerchief, reference books, computer files.

### SAQ 2

(a) A shorter list would lead to more items being recalled.

(b) Increasing the study time would also improve recall.

(c) Increasing the number of sums to do in the retention period would make recall poorer. Doing sums prevents rehearsal of the items to be remembered and damages retention.

## SAQ 3

(a) *Rabbit* and *hare* are semantically related and the two animals are also visually similar, so this error could reflect *either* a semantic encoding *or* a visual representation process.

(b) *Lemon* and *demon* are visually similar words, but sound different and have no semantic relationship. This error looks as if visual images of the printed words are being stored in memory.

## SAQ 4

(a)  65 per cent

(b)  70 per cent approximately

(c)  Forgetting is very rapid in the first 8 hours after learning. After 8 hours the rate of forgetting levels out, and over the next 40 hours not much more is lost from memory.

## SAQ 5

(a)  What matters most of all is to obtain objective measurements of memory—E

(b)  What matters most of all is to study memory in real-life situations—B

(c)  Memory depends on the number of times material is experienced—E

(d)  Memory depends on 'effort after meaning'—B

(e)  Material is lost from memory when time elapses—E and B

(E = consistent with Ebbinghaus' approach; B = consistent with Bartlett's approach)

## SAQ 6

|  |  | Stimulus letters | | | | | |
|---|---|---|---|---|---|---|---|
|  |  | B | P | V | S | X | T |
| Response letters | B |  | + | + | − | − | + |
|  | P | 62 |  | + | − | − | + |
|  | V | 83 | + |  | − | − | + |
|  | S | 12 | − | − |  | 59 | − |
|  | X | − | − | − | + |  | − |
|  | T | + | + | + | − | 2 |  |

Acoustically confusable pairs would generate many errors (+ cells); pairs that are not acoustically confusable would generate few errors (− cells).

## SAQ 7

To verify (a) should be fastest because all the information is at the same level; (b) should be slowest because a 2-level search is required up from shark to animal; (c) requires only a 1-level move from ostrich to bird.

# Overview of Part V

One striking point which emerges from all the chapters in Part V is the extent to which the processes involved in perception, attention and memory are intertwined. The discussion in Chapter 10 demonstrates that it is impossible to recognize objects without any memory for past experiences of these objects. Conversely, if no sensory inputs are processed, there will be no experiences for people to remember. Equally, attention is necessary for both perception and memory, and, in turn, attention is allocated according to the knowledge and motivations stored in memory.

**Information-processing models**

One concept that underpins much of the research on cognitive processes is that of an information-processing model consisting of a series of separate stages. The suggestion is that information flows in a linear direction; that is, through each stage to the next in one direction only. Figures 11.1, 11.3 and 11.5 in Chapter 11 and Figures 12.4, 12.5, 12.9 and 12.10 in Chapter 12 all show information flowing from sensory inputs through separate stages to a final response output.

These models assume that a great deal of information processing is going on. Inputs from the senses have to be selected and perceived and passed on to a limited-capacity short-term memory. At the next stage, information is categorized and stored in long-term memory. The final stage is one in which information is retrieved and output in the form of a response. This represents the linear information-processing model based on Broadbent's original formulation, as shown in Figure 11.1 in Chapter 11.

However, there are other characteristics of perception, attention and memory which do not fit into a strictly linear information-processing model. Instead, they support the notion that there is constant *feedback* between the various stages. This implies that, at each stage, information has to be fed in from other processes. Neisser's cyclical model, shown in Figure 10.23 in Chapter 10, with its continual feedback between sensory cues and perceptual models, represents a radical departure from the linear information-processing model. In Treisman's theory, described in Chapter 11, Section 2.3, incoming information from both attended and attenuated channels is subjected to semantic analysis by dictionary units representing words. This in turn affects the interpretation of inputs, which means, for instance, that we can give special attention to hearing our own name. Processes interact with each other to direct attention to what is important or what is expected.

Models which emphasize the role of *central processes* in allocating attention and selecting responses also contradict the classic information-processing model. In Kahneman's capacity theory of attention, described in Chapter 11, Section 3.3, a central processor assesses mental effort requirements and allocates the amount of motivational and attentional capacity available at any one time. The ability to perform dual tasks, as long as they are well learned and automatic, fits in with Neisser's visual search experiments which demonstrate people's ability to scan for several targets at once. These experiments imply that several kinds of processes are going on in *parallel*, requiring a continual interaction between a preliminary analysis of sensory demands and knowledge stored in long-term memory to guide responses.

The constructivist approach to memory, stemming from Bartlett's early work, is another approach which assumes that past experiences stored in long-term memory affect the way people reconstruct memories of stories and objects. The way in which memories are organized has a direct effect on the ability to remember, as shown in the studies of free recall in Chapter 12, Section 5.2. Equally important is the *content* of what has to be remembered: for example, lists of numbers in a psychology experiment versus lists of stock market prices. People's motivations and interests make all the difference to what is likely to be retained in memory.

## Mental representations: the cognitive shift

As indicated above, the original notion of the information-processing model implies that information flows from input to output in a linear direction. From this point of view, the basic information-processing model has much in common with the classic version of the stimulus–response (S–R) model described in Chapter 6. As explained in Chapter 6, early behaviourists viewed learning as a process of forming direct stimulus–response links. However, Tolman's exploration of the purposive and flexible nature of rats' behaviour initiated the idea that there may be *mental* events going on inside the animal's brain. Tolman spoke of a rat's cognitive map of the environment, representing, for example, the knowledge that food is near the window; in other words, a mental representation, a cognition which may guide behaviour. This is very different from the notion of direct links between stimuli and responses, which is the hallmark of S–R psychology. The 'cognitive shift' represents an elaboration of Tolman's ideas, suggesting that rats can have cognitions about events which are likely to lead to more or less satisfying events, and even that animals search for something which can act as a predictor for a novel event.

When it comes to human beings, arguments in favour of mental representations (i.e. cognitions) become even stronger. Evidence has already been quoted showing that interpretations of events are the result of an interaction between sensory analysis and knowledge of past experiences. This knowledge of the world is mentally represented as cognitions in long-term memory. Chapter 12, Sections 1.3 and 1.4, describe some of the forms these mental representations might take: visual images, speech or motor codes or, most commonly of all, semantic representations of meanings. It is semantic representations that influence perception and recognition of objects, and the way new inputs will be stored in memory.

It is the crucial role of mental representations that defines the cognitive approach. Cognitions are implicated in all human actions. But does this imply that cognitions are always conscious? Are we always aware of our mental representations of objects and events? What about over-learned automatic responses, like riding a bicycle, which appear to be run off directly without the intervention of any conscious thinking? As demonstrated in the dual-task experiments described in Chapter 11, Section 3, it is the ability to perform routine tasks automatically which enables us to cope with several different tasks in parallel. Nevertheless, even the most automatic actions are mentally represented, perhaps as a motor code. Furthermore, conscious attention can usually be directed to an automatic task if necessary.

It is the recognition that cognitions of all kinds affect the way information is processed that has led to a cognitive shift within the psychology of perception, attention and memory. While still acknowledging the importance of information *processing* as a general framework, the new emphasis is on mental representations of knowledge, the *cognitions* which are pervasive in human functioning. It is in the spirit of both these considerations that the title of Part V is 'Cognitive Processes'.

### Ecological validity

In the chapters you have read so far, you have been introduced to several different methods for studying psychology. These include experiments, observational studies, psychometric analysis of scores and asking people to describe their perceptions, feelings and emotions. The relative advantages and disadvantages of different methodological approaches will be taken up in detail in later chapters, notably Chapter 14 and Chapter 17. Here the concern is the extent to which the chapters in Part V offer an account of human perception, attention and memory as they occur naturally in everyday life. The question is whether the experimental methods typically used to study cognitive processes are ecologically valid, in the sense that they reflect behaviour in the natural habitat.

As explained in Chapter 10, Section 6.3, Gibson called his theory of direct perception an ecological approach to vision because it emphasizes direct interactions between animals and their habitat. However, it was also argued that Gibson made little attempt to explain the processing mechanisms involved. Physiological studies of neural activity within visual systems, and the systematic recording of people's responses to tones and lights, described in Chapter 10, Sections 2 and 3, have revealed interesting properties of the transmission of information within visual systems of mammals. But the complexities of human perception, especially the influence of mental representations based on past experiences, have proved much more difficult to investigate experimentally.

In the field of attention, many experiments have been carried out to test bottleneck theories of attention. However, you might well feel that feeding pairs of digits into people's ears through headphones, and getting people to search lists of letters to find a blue T, are rather far removed from the demands of ordinary life. The dual-task experiments described in Chapter 11, Section 3, can be considered more ecologically valid in that they studied people doing tasks, such as typing, that they were used to doing in everyday life. Chapter 12 covers a range of psychological approaches to memory, many of which bring out a tension between experiments designed to test the ability to learn artificially constructed word lists, and other—perhaps more ecologically valid—studies exploring the strategies used by individuals with exceptional memories.

It is important to appreciate the disadvantages as well as the advantages of ecologically valid experiments. In a naturalistic setting it is not easy to measure and control for all the variables which may be affecting people's behaviour. Experiments use simple materials and artificial settings in order to achieve objective measures and to eliminate irrelevant factors which may be obscuring a specific process. The aim must be to carry over the rigour of the experimental method into more naturalistic studies. There is certainly no simple answer to debates about the 'best' method for psychologists to describe and explain the varied nature of human behaviour and experience.

# PART VI
# THE SOCIAL DIMENSION

# Introduction to Part VI

Part V described the cognitive processes involved in perceiving, attending and remembering. Most of the studies assume that everyone perceives the environment, allocates attention and stores items in memory using basically the same kinds of processing. Furthermore, there was relatively little emphasis on the influence of social context. In earlier chapters, especially those in Part II, a great deal of attention was paid to the importance of social interactions with other people in cognitive and social development. The two chapters in Part VI take up again the crucial role of the social dimension in explaining human behaviour.

Chapter 13 introduces the dual nature of language and communication. Language can be used by each individual to formulate ideas and to reflect on private feelings and thoughts. At the same time, language exists as a means of communicating shared meanings accepted by all members of a society. Without some form of language it is hard to imagine how a human society could survive.

Chapter 14 is concerned specifically with social issues and takes aggressive behaviour as a case study. Because aggression is usually considered to be an undesirable phenomenon, a great deal of research has been carried out to discover the causes of aggressive behaviour. As indicated in Chapter 1, psychological approaches to this topic have varied from accounts of innate aggressive tendencies to theories which take the view that aggression arises from conformity to social expectations, as represented, for example, in the media.

Both chapters in Part VI reflect a tension between psychological approaches which study people at the level of individuals and those which pay special attention to the social world in which individuals live. Is it possible to view the use of language and aggressive behaviour simply in terms of the individuals taking part? Or is it essential to consider the role of other people and social institutions in determining whether people follow expected conventions for expressing their thoughts and emotions?

# TOPICS IN LANGUAGE AND COMMUNICATION

Judith Greene

## Contents

# 1 | Introduction: what is language?

Many psychology textbooks start chapters on language with an introduction pointing out the crucial importance of language in human affairs. There is no doubt that most of us talk a lot. Even people who lead relatively solitary lives are exposed to language through television, radio, books and newspapers. What is the point of all this chatter? Think back over the chapters you have read so far. How many of them take for granted the human ability to use language?

All the chapters in Part II assume that, as children develop, they acquire the use of language. Right from the beginning children start *communicating*, progressing from crying, gestures and babbling to the use of words and sentences. This allows them to interact socially, to reflect on events and to learn from others. In Part IV, methods of studying intelligence and personality rely on people's use of language to *reflect* on their own thoughts and feelings in order to answer questions in IQ tests and to fill in written responses to questionnaires. The more idiographic approaches, like those of Allport and the humanistic psychologists, analyse writings and speech in order to explore characteristic modes of thinking, feeling and acting. It is interesting to note that the same is true of the experimental research into cognitive processes described in Part V. Work on visual perception is largely based on subjects' verbal reports of what they see. Theories of attention are often tested using verbal materials such as letters, words and texts. Memory relies even more heavily on recall of words and stories.

The only apparent omission in this catalogue are the two chapters in Part III on biological and learning mechanisms. Studies of animals obviously do not involve the use of language. Indeed, it is usually claimed that the ability to use language is *the* critical difference between humans and other animals. However, there is still much debate about how human language emerged from the process of evolution. Certainly most animal species have some means of communicating with each other. The 'bee dances' which bees perform on arriving back at a hive provide precise information about where pollen can be found ranging over long distances. Particularly relevant are studies of **primates**, the name for the apes who are nearest to humans in the evolutionary scale. Observations of chimpanzees and gorillas in the wild have identified intricate social interactions between male and female, young and old, mediated by well-understood calls and gestures.

Language as used by humans differs in crucial ways from other animal communications. It appears that animal signals are direct responses to cues in the immediate environment. In contrast to this, humans are not confined to responding to their immediate environment. In fact, it is the use of language which frees them from the here and now. In some miraculous way, the grunts of prehistoric men came to take on meanings which developed into words and utterances. Human language uses **symbols** to refer to past, present and future events, to cabbages and kings, lions and unicorns, and to abstract ideas like the existence of God. The use of language to convey the whole range of human ideas constitutes an invaluable biological advantage which has (so far) ensured the survival of the human species.

It is hard to imagine a human society which lacks the ability to transmit traditions, laws and customs from generation to generation. With the advent of writing and written records, many years of education are deemed necessary for children to be made aware of the accumulated history, cultural traditions and scientific discoveries of past generations. One of the main themes of this chapter will be the extent to which learning to use language in social contexts is necessary for communicating meanings understood within a whole speech community.

## 1.1 Definitions of language

Conventionally, language is defined as having two main functions: *external* communication with other people and *internal* representation of our own thoughts. In the light of this, it may seem a trivial matter to define language and communication. However, you may be surprised to hear that whole books have been written to try to answer the questions 'what is language?' and 'what is communication?'

ACTIVITY 1

Consider what is implied by the following statements about, and examples of, language:

1   Language distinguishes humans from animals.
2   English has a rich and flexible grammar.
3   The English language is derived from Latin and Anglo-Saxon roots.
4   John knows English but can't speak Turkish.
5   John speaks English particularly well.
6   John can't find the right words to express what he is thinking.
7   John said, 'I'm going home'.
8   John said, 'Peter's home is over there'.
9   John said, 'It's chilly'.

Let us go through each of the statements and examples of language, given in Activity 1, in turn. The first statement categorizes language as an ability which is distinctive to humans. Statement number two refers to one of the many hundreds, if not thousands, of human languages, the one which happens to be spoken by members of English-speaking societies, and by many other people as a second language. The third statement suggests that a language 'exists' as an entity in its own right with a history of change over the centuries.

The next three statements are concerned with an individual's knowledge of a language. The fourth statement emphasizes the need for knowledge of a language in order to be able to speak that language. It implies that John has knowledge of English but not of Turkish. Statement five indicates that there can be variations in the way individuals use a particular language. This raises questions about what is defined as 'good' English and the way in which cultural factors may affect the way language is used. The sixth statement points to the relationship between thought and language, which is not always obvious or easy.

Finally, there are three typical examples of language use. 'I'm going home' is an utterance which can be understood by any competent speaker of the English language. The utterances in statements eight and nine are also, of course, acceptable English sentences. But 'Peter's home is over there' can only be fully understood in a context in which it is obvious where 'over there' is. 'It's chilly' can be interpreted as a straightforward comment about the weather or as an indirect request to close a window. Even a silent shiver and pointing to a window can communicate the same request.

The examples in Activity 1 demonstrate that language is a complex business. In the rest of this section, each of the nine statements in Activity 1 will be examined in order to indicate the many ways in which researchers have approached the study of language and communication.

## 1.2  The structure of language

The first three statements in Activity 1 are concerned with definitions of what constitutes a human language. The focus is on describing the structure of language regardless of how particular individuals use it.

The first statement in Activity 1 defines human language as having a unique structure when compared to animal communication systems. However, there are two features of human language which are of pre-eminent importance. The first is the ability to develop *arbitrary* relations between symbols and their meanings. For instance, there is no reason why the sound 'basket' should mean a receptacle made of cane to people who speak English, rather than the sound 'panier' to French speakers or the sound 'serpet' to Turkish speakers. Yet to English speakers the sound 'basket' has an obvious meaning and is not merely a combination of random sounds. This example illustrates how arbitrary is the relation between sounds and their meanings. In fact, if you want to learn a new language, you have to start by learning these essentially arbitrary connections between sounds and meanings in the vocabulary of that language.

The second crucial feature of human language is the ability to string together words into arbitrary *patterns* which make sense. In English, for example, word order is very important. For instance, 'Tom tickles Tim' means something different from 'Tim tickles Tom'. In contrast to this, attempts have been made to teach human sign languages to chimpanzees: the famous case of Washoe is one example (Gardner and Gardner, 1969). Washoe and other chimpanzees were able to put together signs such as 'Drink fridge' and 'More tickle', very reminiscent of the utterances of very young children. However, the chimpanzees tended to use words in any order; for example, 'fridge drink' or 'drink fridge'. As we shall see in Section 3, young children very soon pick up rules for uttering words in particular orders.

The next two statements in Activity 1 are largely the concern of **linguists** who study the *structure* of languages. While it is admitted that languages cannot exist without a community of speakers, linguists tend to treat them as self-contained systems. Latin, for instance, is termed a 'dead' language as it is generally no longer used. But this does not prevent linguists from studying the vocabulary and grammar of Latin, and other 'dead' languages, in order to examine the way in which borrowings from these languages have affected the development of modern languages such as Italian, French and English.

In general, linguists describe the structure of languages in terms of grammar, known technically in linguistics as the **syntax** of a language. Syntax specifies how words can be put together to make grammatical sentences. It involves the use of the correct inflections which are added to words, such as the addition of 'ly' to a word which turns the adjective 'beautiful', for example, into the adverb 'beautifully'. As I pointed out earlier, word order is an important aspect of syntax in English: 'the cat sat on the mat' is a grammatical sentence, but 'sat mat cat the on' is not.

Linguists also pay attention to the meanings of words in a language which make up its vocabulary, technically known in linguistics as the **lexicon** of a language. Finally, words have to be combined to make sentences which are both grammatical *and* meaningful. The stringing together of words to make up meaningful sentences is technically known in linguistics as the **semantics** of a language. In Section 3, we will be returning to these important aspects of language when we consider how children learn to speak a language.

SAQ 1   (*SAQ answers are given at the end of the chapter*) Categorize each of the following examples of English utterances as correct or incorrect according to whether they conform to (i) English vocabulary (the lexicon); (ii) English grammar (syntax); (iii) acceptable meanings in English (semantics):

(a)  Twas brillig and the slithy toves did gyre and gimble in the wabe.

(b)  Colourless green ideas sleep furiously.

(c)  The cat sat on the mat.

# 1.3 Knowing a language

Statements four to six in Activity 1 focus on the personal knowledge of the individual language speaker. In order to use a language, a person obviously needs to know that language. For example, I am able to communicate in English, to a lesser extent in French, and can order a meal in Greek. However, there are many hundreds of languages I do not know at all and therefore cannot use for social communication.

It is an interesting fact that it is not at all easy to 'hear' a language you know well in the same way that you hear the sounds of other languages. For instance, you can describe what a foreign language 'sounds like': soft and sibilant or harsh and angular, for example. You have only to listen to speakers of a language you are not familiar with to realize the difficulty of even beginning to pick out from the stream of sounds where one word begins and another ends. But it is virtually impossible to stand back and consider what

English sounds like (Fodor, 1983). The sounds of your own language are transparent. The meaning leaps out directly from what people say; combinations of words are immediately recognized as meaningful sentences.

The implication is that children must have the opportunity to learn the meanings of the words and sentences in the languages to which they are exposed. Without that linguistic experience, they will not be equipped to use a language for communicative purposes. It is essential for children to learn the basic vocabulary, syntax and semantics of a particular language if they are to become functioning members of their society. The rare cases in which children are deprived of language point to this. One famous example is Ittard's eighteenth-century account of a 'wolf-boy' who had no language when he was found at the age of about eight. Although he appeared to be intelligent, the boy only gradually learnt to speak a few words.

Children like the wolf-boy, and others who do not acquire normal language—autistic children, for instance—are at a great disadvantage in social interactions. I should make it clear, though, that the sign languages used by those who are deaf constitute fully developed languages which can be used symbolically to refer to past, present and future events. It was the inability of Washoe and her fellow chimpanzees to use human sign languages in this way that emphasized the crucial difference between animal communication and the complex languages used as effective means of communication by human signers.

Statement six in Activity 1 specifically refers to the dual nature of languages for internal reflection and external communication. Language can be used to reflect on our innermost thoughts. Our inner mental representations consist of floating ideas, often beyond our conscious control. As they reach consciousness, many thoughts are expressed using words as symbols to represent situations to ourselves. Chapter 2 drew attention to the importance of symbols for representing social concepts, as exemplified in the writings of Mead and Vygotsky. It is because of the close links between thinking and language that questions have been raised about how much influence language has on the way we think and communicate.

Sometimes we may wish to keep our private thoughts to ourselves. At other times, we struggle to find the right words to convey to another person what we feel, and occasionally we think, 'I didn't know I thought that until I said it'. People will sometimes borrow a word or phrase from another language because there is no suitable word in their own language to convey their exact meaning. An example would be the French phrase 'savoir faire', meaning to know exactly what to do in a situation, corrupted in English to 'savvy', a concept now perhaps more colloquially represented as 'streetwise'. The French borrowed the English 'weekend' when their lifestyle of working on Saturday changed.

## 1.4 Communication in social contexts

Finally, statements seven to nine in Activity 1 focus on an aspect of language of primary concern to social psychologists. This is the use of language to communicate thoughts and feelings to other people. The point is that the use of language to communicate never occurs in a vacuum. Communication always has a social context, either face-to-face or with an unseen audience. Even when writing in a room on my own, as I am doing now, the aim is always to communicate to an audience, in this case to you, the readers of this chapter. This use of language to communicate in particular contexts is technically known in linguistics as **pragmatics**. Pragmatics is concerned with the factors which affect the use of language to achieve communication in a social context.

As the examples in Activity 1 made clear, the selection of what to say has to be tailored to allow for the listener or the reader's existing knowledge of the social context. Unless the listener already knows where 'over there' is, the utterance 'Peter's home is over there' will be ambiguous. It could mean 'over the hill' or 'over in America'. Perhaps an accompanying non-verbal gesture like pointing might make the meaning clearer. Sharing some basic knowledge about the topic being discussed is essential for successful communication.

Equally important is a common understanding between people about the nature and purpose of any social interaction which involves language. Conversations between close friends, for example, are expected to take a different form from the format of a formal lecture. Appreciating the speech patterns appropriate in specific social settings is part of being a skilled language user. It is not enough to be able to produce grammatical meaningful utterances. We all need to be able to adjust our utterances in response to the demands of social situations. If one participant is joking and the other deadly serious, misunderstandings are inevitable. Examples of the kinds of 'knots' into which people can tie themselves were described in the conversations noted by Laing, in Chapter 9, Section 5.2. Failure to respect social conventions and social roles can lead to unexpected confrontations.

The next two sections will look at more individual aspects of language. These include the relationship between language and thought and the processes involved in a child's acquisition of the ability to use a particular language. As children inevitably learn language in order to communicate in a social context, later sections will consider the social factors necessary for communication, and the use of language to further the purposes of social interaction.

## Summary of Section 1

- The term 'language' can be used to refer to:
  a universal human ability;
  a particular language understood by communities of language speakers;
  the fact that an individual knows a particular language;
  the use of language to communicate in social contexts.

- Linguists describe the structure of language, including grammar (syntax), word meanings (the lexicon) and the production of meaningful utterances (semantics).

- People must know a language in order to use it for communication. Children therefore need to learn the meanings of the words and sentences in the particular language used in their society.

- Language has a dual nature: *internal* reflection about thoughts, feelings and situations, and *external* communication with other people.

- For language to be used for successful communication, some basic knowledge about the topic being discussed must be shared between speakers and listeners. Account must also be taken of the purpose of the communication and of the social settings in which it takes place (pragmatics).

# 2 | Language and thinking

In the 1920s and 1930s, two individuals challenged the commonly held notion that all human beings think in similar ways. One was an anthropologist and linguist, Edward Sapir. The other was Benjamin Lee Whorf (a fire prevention engineer for an insurance company who spent his non-business hours working in linguistics). The theory which they independently put forward has come to bear their names: the Sapir–Whorf hypothesis. This is also known as the **linguistic relativity hypothesis**. The term means that thought is *relative*, depending on the way concepts are expressed *linguistically* in a particular language. It asserts that individuals around the world do not 'see' or think about the world in the same way. Rather, people's native languages constrain them to certain modes of perception and thought.

## 2.1 Whorf's linguistic relativity hypothesis

Whorf produced many examples to support his view that language affects the way we view the world. For instance, he pointed out that European languages (which he grouped together as Standard Average European, abbreviated to SAE) use tenses to indicate past, present and future time. He claimed that this leads SAE speakers to treat time as an objective entity, as if it were a tape with spaces marked off. By contrast, the Hopi Indian language of North America has no words, grammatical forms, constructions or expressions that refer directly to what we call 'time'. The consequences of these kinds of linguistic differences have been nicely summarized by Stuart Chase in his foreword to the selected writings of Whorf (edited by Carroll, 1956):

'The light flashed', we say in English. Something has to be there to make the flash; 'light' is the subject, 'flash' the predicate. The trend of modern physics, however, with its emphasis on the *field*, is away from subject–predicate propositions. Thus a Hopi

Indian is the better physicist when he says *Reh-pi* – 'flash' – one word for the whole performance, no subject, no predicate, no time element. We frequently read into nature ghostly entities which flash and perform other miracles. Do we supply them because some of our verbs require substantives in front of them?

(Carroll, 1956)

The Sapir–Whorf hypothesis claims that other linguistic aspects of the particular language we speak also restrict the way we view the world. An example which is often quoted is that of the Eskimo people who have many more words to describe different kinds of snow than we have in English. You will remember from Chapter 10, Section 5.5, that different perceivers will be aware of different aspects of the environment. In the context of language, the question arises as to whether the wide choice of words for naming different kinds of snow means that the Eskimo people actually perceive differences between snow suitable for making igloos and snow suitable for sledging on. Is there any evidence that people perceive and remember different categories of objects as a result of the names used to label them?

One rather clear example of the effects of labels on the way people categorize objects is provided by a classic experiment carried out by Carmichael, Hogan and Walter (1932). In this experiment, Carmichael *et al.* presented simple line drawings which subjects were later asked to reproduce. One group of subjects was shown one set of labels with the drawings, a second group was shown a different set of labels and a control group saw the drawings without any labels. The dramatic effects of the verbal labels are shown in Figure 13.1 overleaf. As you can see, subjects produced very different drawings of the first picture, depending on whether they had originally seen the label 'curtains in a window' or the label 'diamond in a rectangle'.

SAQ 2    What was the purpose of including a control group of subjects who saw the drawings with no labels?

The experiment carried out by Carmichael *et al.* provides a simple demonstration of the effects of verbal labelling when people are presented with neutral drawings which could be interpreted in different ways. It is interesting, too, to note that Bartlett's work on memory, which was carried out at about the same date as Carmichael *et al.*'s experiment (1932), also drew attention to the importance of context and names in the way people reconstruct memories (see Chapter 12, Section 2.2). But is this the same as Whorf's claim that a whole world view is influenced by the particular language people speak? The fact that it is possible to translate Hopi into English and vice versa implies that there must be some universally shared knowledge of the physical world, regardless of how it may be expressed in different languages. In all parts of the world, plants grow, the sky is blue, some man-made objects are hard and rigid, some can be picked up easily and carried, others are rooted to the ground.

It is possible, too, that some of the apparent differences in categorizing the world may be due to too great a reliance on *literal* translations of the Hopi language. The Hopi use the same word for an insect, an aeroplane and a pilot.

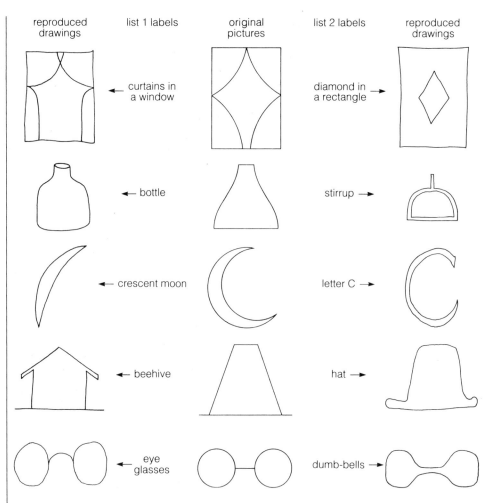

**Figure 13.1** Drawings and labels used in the experiment by Carmichael *et al.* (1932)
(Source: Carmichael *et al.*, 1932)

But can this possibly mean that the Hopi cannot perceive any difference between a bee and a pilot? Imagine a Hopi linguist carrying out a Whorfian analysis of English. Would she think, from a literal translation of the phrase, 'the foot of a mountain with its head in the clouds', that we have 'primitive' beliefs that mountains wear shoes and hats?

One further problem which undermines Whorf's linguistic relativity hypothesis is that it may in fact be cultural differences which influence language in the first place. Whorf assumes that a language exists and it is this which determines how people perceive the world. But it could equally well be argued that the Eskimos *need* to perceive many different kinds of snow and so have invented words to represent them. Expert skiers also develop a special 'snow' vocabulary which may mean nothing to non-experts. So it is not always clear whether it is language which influences thinking or whether it is the various categories of objects in the environment that determine the terms used in a language.

How, then, does this leave Whorf's theory? As far as perception is concerned, the models of perception described in Chapter 10 indicate that some basic physical aspects of the environment may be directly and automatically perceived by everyone, such as the distance and size of objects. On the other hand, recognition and categorization of objects depend largely on past experiences, which in turn will be influenced by our cultural background. The experience of having different kinds of snow pointed out to them, for example, must help young Eskimo children to learn to perceive the distinctions between the different kinds of snow, knowledge of which is essential to their way of life.

If this is true in the case of perceiving and recognizing physical objects, it is even more likely that subtle linguistic distinctions influence the interpretation of *social* categories, which are remote from basic physical features. Labelling the perpetrator of an act as a 'freedom fighter', as opposed to a 'terrorist', will influence the way that act is perceived even within one language community. The main problem in this area is that it is difficult, if not impossible, to find objective methods for separating out universal, linguistic and cultural influences.

To summarize, the evidence seems to show that, as far as basic perceptions go, most people see the world in much the same way. In so far as we can read and understand what Whorf says about the Hopi, therefore, it is possible for us to understand other people's particular views of the world. On the other hand, differences in the way we conceive objects and ideas depend on linguistic distinctions which draw attention to particular aspects of the environment. Originally the language of the Eskimos probably merely reflected their need to distinguish between snows for different purposes. But for each new generation, ways of categorizing the environment are transmitted through the language children hear. These linguistic influences are even stronger when they are applied, not just to obvious physical features, which every community is likely to describe in a roughly equivalent way, but to social conventions of which we are mostly unaware.

### ACTIVITY 2

One gain from considering the linguistic relativity hypothesis is that it forces us to look more critically at some of the taken-for-granted assumptions underlying the use of the English language.

Below, you will see a list of words which commonly occur in English. Go through them and indicate which ones you think are related to universal categories of the world, and which are imposed by the culture of a particular society.

| | | |
|---|---|---|
| male and female | child and adult | teenager |
| student | weekend | morning |
| afternoon | teatime | mother |
| housewife | chair | magazine |
| book | treat | reward |

## 2.2 Piaget's views on thinking and language

In this chapter, I cannot give more than the briefest outline of Piaget's attitude to the relationship between language and thought. In general, he took more or less the opposite view to Whorf's linguistic relativity theory. For one thing, he was concerned with the *universal* stages of development that occur in all children's thought, rather than with any differences that might result from children speaking particular languages. Moreover, Piaget opposed the idea that language in general is responsible for thought. In his earliest work he tended to use language as a direct reflection of what children were thinking, asking them questions such as, 'What makes the clouds move?' or, 'Why do some things float?' Later, in an article considering the role that language might play in the development of thought (Piaget, 1968), he pointed out that language is only one type of symbolic function, which also includes the earliest forms of symbolic play and symbolic imagery. Although Piaget acknowledges that language has an enormously facilitating effect on the range of symbolic thinking, his position is that intelligence has deeper roots in actions which have become internalized as mental operations (see Chapter 3).

Piaget and his supporters make the point that it is impossible for children to understand the expression of a concept in language until they have mastered the underlying concept. We have probably all had experiences when words and sentences are simply not understood by children until they grasp what is meant by concepts such as 'next week', 'money', 'gratitude', 'rules of a game', and so on. Nevertheless, the question remains as to what extent exposure to language itself helps the child to grasp new concepts. Piaget sums it up thus: 'language and thought are linked in a genetic circle . . . In the last analysis, both depend on intelligence itself, which antedates language and is independent of it' (Piaget, 1968).

## 2.3 Vygotsky's theory: the roots of thinking and language

In his seminal book, *Thought and language*, originally published in Russia in the early 1930s but only translated into English in 1962, Vygotsky was one of the first people to stress the double aspect of language, both as a reflection of our own private thoughts (**inner speech**) and as a code for communicating with others (**external speech**). Vygotsky believed that in infancy the development of thinking and language are independent. He describes the infant's first attempts to use words to communicate purely *social* speech, suggesting that it occurs without internal thought. At the same time, infants are developing primitive ways of thinking and reasoning about objects and events in their environment which do not involve the use of language. At this stage, speech fulfils merely social functions and thinking occurs without language.

It is only at the age of about 2 years that social speech without thought and thought without language come together. Words begin to act as symbols for thoughts and it is only at this stage that truly social development can blossom.

Children can start using language to explore their own and other people's thoughts and feelings. At the same time, they begin to imbibe the social and cultural norms of society. From then on, thinking and language interpenetrate in both directions.

Vygotsky agrees with Piaget that the very earliest development of thought is independent of language, depending on sensations and actions in the sensori-motor stage. Where he differs from Piaget is that Vygotsky believes that, from the age of two, language itself comes to play an essential part in the child's further intellectual development, which for Vygotsky is inextricably bound up with social development. Vygotsky's example of two girls playing at being sisters, referred to in Chapter 2, Section 4.1, demonstrates his belief that language helps to indoctrinate children into the social rules and norms of their society. Similarly, in Chapter 3, Section 5, studies were described which showed that children's interpretations of what an experimenter is asking them to do have a striking effect on performance on Piagetian tasks. This line of research has been much influenced by Vygotsky's concern with the role of symbolic language in intellectual and social development.

## 2.4 Comparison of theories

When comparing these different theories, it is clear that each puts a slightly different emphasis on the interrelation between language and thought. In general, these represent three possible views of the relationship between language and thinking:

1   Language determines thinking.

2   Thinking determines linguistic development.

3   Language and thinking have independent roots but together they determine intellectual and social development.

Whorf's theory takes the extreme line that thought is determined by language and that many of society's distinctions are transmitted to new generations by the linguistic concepts enshrined in particular languages. Whorf's position, therefore, is that language dominates the internal function of thought. In contrast, Piaget, far from giving language a dominating role, sees it as a symbolic tool, which may greatly facilitate, but is not sufficient on its own to bring about the stages of cognitive development. Vygotsky concentrates on the interaction between the internal and external functions of language. Once the fusion between internal thinking and external social language has occurred, Vygotsky stresses the role of language in the social, as well as the intellectual, development of the child.

SAQ 3   Indicate which of the three possible views of the relationship between language and thinking listed above (1, 2, 3) best typifies the theory of:

(a)  Whorf;

(b)  Vygotsky;

(c)  Piaget.

## Summary of Section 2

● Whorf claimed that particular languages affect the way a speech community perceives and thinks about events in the environment.

● There is some evidence that verbal labels can influence the way objects are perceived and remembered.

● Piaget admitted that linguistic development is important but he stressed that the use of language is dependent on the child's ability to think and understand.

● Vygotsky described the separate roots of internal thinking and the external social use of language for communication. Truly social development begins when the symbolic and social functions of language are integrated to produce a two-way process of social and intellectual development.

# 3 | Learning a language

In Section 2, three different approaches—Whorf's, Piaget's and Vygotsky's—were discussed in terms of language in general. It was assumed that all children learn both to think and to speak. But how does each child manage to become a native speaker of a particular language? What is needed for children to join a community of speakers who understand each other?

Before discussing the stages in which children acquire language, it has to be pointed out that there has been a lot of disagreement about the kinds of knowledge necessary to master a language. Depending on their theoretical view of the learning process, psychologists will emphasize different aspects of the learning process. For instance, Skinner, whose theory you read about in Chapter 6, believes that learning a language is exactly the same as learning any other responses.

## 3.1 Learning verbal responses

Skinner's book *Verbal behaviour* (1957) was a virtuoso attempt to explain language without taking into account any 'mentalistic' events such as ideas, meanings or grammatical rules. From Skinner's point of view, a child's first verbal utterances consist of combinations of random sounds. These first sounds that a child happens to produce can then be shaped by reinforcement to ripen into the full range of utterances exhibited by an adult. Verbal responses are conditioned solely in terms of the function of the response–reinforcement contingencies in operation when they happen to occur.

Skinner's aim was to identify the stimulus situations in which verbal responses might be emitted and reinforced, as a result of which particular responses would become more likely to reoccur. Some examples from Skinner's book are given in Table 13.1, showing the development of two types of responses he called mands and tacts. What he calls a 'mand' is the result of a need stimulus. The example given in the table is a need for salt, to which a response 'Pass the salt' might happen to be emitted, followed by the reinforcement of the person needing the salt being handed some. A 'tact' occurs when the stimulus input is an object like, say, an iceberg, to which the response 'That's an iceberg' is followed by the reinforcement 'That's right.' The motivation in this case, Skinner suggests, is the usefulness for parents of having 'tacting' children rushing around telling them what things are!

**Table 13.1** Skinner's analysis of verbal responses

| Stimulus situation | Emitted verbal response | Reinforcement |
| --- | --- | --- |
| Need for salt | 'Pass the salt' (MAND) | Salt |
| Iceberg | 'That's an iceberg' (TACT) | 'That's right' |

Skinner goes on to apply this type of analysis to a bewildering variety of linguistic behaviour, the flavour of which you can get only by reading *Verbal behaviour*. Skinner's analysis carries you along in an extremely plausible manner, stretching to such delightful flights of fancy as explaining Robert Browning's *Home-Thoughts, from Abroad*. 'Oh, to be in England, Now that April's there' is described as a 'magical mand', presumably based on the success of 'Oh, to be' statements in obtaining rewards in the past.

It is only when you stop to consider the theory that several points occur to you. First, it is only for the very simplest cases that Skinner spells out precise response–reinforcement contingencies. Second, only a limited proportion of verbal behaviour takes the form of mands and tacts, on which Skinner spends so much space. Most utterances are examples of what Skinner called 'intraverbal responses', as in the case when one person says something and another replies. Perhaps it is not surprising that Skinner skates rather quickly over this type of response since there are enormous difficulties in explaining all the thousands of verbal responses that might happen to be uttered in different situations. It is indeed an uphill task to explain people's utterances as if they were equivalent to a rat pressing a lever to obtain a food reward, ignoring totally the meanings of the sounds being uttered.

Relevant to Skinner's account is some research reported by Brown, Cazden and Bellugi (1969). Brown *et al.* found that mothers very rarely correct their children's utterances, responding much more often to the child's intended meaning. They quote a nice example of an instance when a child said, 'He a girl' and the mother answered, 'That's right'. According to Skinner, the mother would be reinforcing an incorrect response and so would be hindering her child's progress. However, as we shall see in Sections 3.3 and 3.4, it appears to be far more important to engage in mutual exchanges of meanings than to carry out a strict regime of using reinforcement to shape correct verbal responses.

While Skinner's account is inadequate as a general explanation of language learning, there are undoubtedly some instances in which specific verbal responses are reinforced; for instance, 'say goodbye to Granny nicely and you can have an ice-cream later'. There are other cases in which stereotyped patterns of speaking are maintained by reinforcing conditions. For example, many 'destructive' verbal interactions of the kind, 'It was your fault', 'No it wasn't', may be deeply reinforcing to both parties concerned.

## 3.2  Learning syntactic rules

Other researchers have emphasized the creative use of language. The well-known linguist, Noam Chomsky (1957) made the point that most utterances are novel rather than being learned responses. Apart from a few ritual greetings, most utterances are made up on the spot and may never have been uttered before. Chomsky was interested in specifying the linguistic knowledge necessary for producing an infinite number of possible novel sentences. His term for this knowledge is **linguistic competence**.

Chomsky defined linguistic competence as consisting of grammatical rules, known as **syntactic rules**, constituting the syntactic structure of language. It is important to realize that Chomsky is a linguist, not a psychologist. As a linguist, he set out to describe the syntactic rules which define the structure of a language. These rules specify **competence**; that is, the knowledge which all speakers need in order to speak a language. This linguistic description defines the grammar of a language, the syntactic rules which define all possible *grammatical* sentences.

But what about all the non-grammatical utterances we are constantly making? A psychologist attending a conference noted down the actual utterances made by the speakers, who were all professional psychologists. There were many 'ums' and 'ers', stops and starts, and incomplete and ungrammatical utterances. Surely this is even more true of children's first utterances. Chomsky relegates all these slip-ups to errors in **performance**. He believes that, underlying the performance of incomplete utterances, there must be 'true' linguistic competence. Without this shared knowledge of the 'ideal' grammar of a language, the audience would not be able to recognize that the conference speakers were producing understandable English, even if it was not completely grammatical.

During the 1960s, research into children's speech was greatly influenced by Chomsky's analysis of the structure of language in terms of syntactic rules. Researchers looked for syntactic rules that children might be using and which could explain the utterances made by young children. Braine (1963) was one of the first to provide a systematic grammatical description of children's early language. His aim was to provide an account of the rules underlying a young child's speech. His method was to look at a set of children's utterances, purely in terms of their grammar, ignoring the meanings of the utterances and the circumstances in which they were produced.

Braine took recordings of his young child Stephen's two-word utterances in order to look for any rules which explained the order of the two words in each utterance. He found that Stephen's vocabulary could be divided into two classes of words. First, there was a small set of words which always occurred in a particular position in the utterance; that is, first but never second or second but never first. Braine called these words that always occurred in a fixed position the *pivot class* of words. He identified a second type of word which could occur in any position, which he called the *open class* of words. As shown in Table 13.2, examples of pivot words are 'allgone', which only occurred at the beginning of a sentence, and 'pretty' which only occurred in the second position. Open class words, such as 'boy', 'sock', 'milk', 'mummy', could occur either in first or second position. Two open words could occur together but no utterance could contain two pivot words. Braine called his system of rules to explain the form of two-word utterances a **pivot/open grammar**.

**Table 13.2** Examples from Braine's pivot/open grammar for two-word utterances

| Pivot words in first position only | Pivot words in second position only | Open words |
| --- | --- | --- |
| 'Allgone' | 'Pretty' | 'Mummy' |
| 'Big' | 'Bye-bye' | 'Boy' |
| | | 'Sock' |
| | | 'Milk' |

· SAQ 4   Which of the following two-word utterances conform to pivot/open grammar and which do not?

(a) 'Allgone' sock';

(b) 'Mummy sock';

(c) 'Allgone pretty';

(d) 'Boy allgone'.

Braine's strategy may seem unduly sterile. However, it must be remembered that this whole area of research was very much inspired by Chomsky's new theory which was exclusively concerned with explaining the grammatical rules of language. It is not surprising that researchers studying child language followed suit and neglected the semantic and pragmatic aspects of speech. Nevertheless, Braine's analysis of children's speech represented an important advance in exploring the rules children themselves might be using to generate what at first sight appear to be ungrammatical utterances, such as 'Allgone milk'. It is particularly interesting, too, that even in these early two-word utterances, children adhered to simple word-order rules, unlike the attempts of Washoe and other chimpanzees (see Section 1.2). However, pivot/open grammars are not without their problems. For one thing, they relate only to the production of two-word utterances. Moreover, the terms 'pivot' and 'open' are arbitrary and not at all related to what the child's utterances might mean. For instance, 'Allgone milk' may make more sense than 'Allgone boy' and yet both utterances are equally likely according to the pivot/open grammar.

## 3.3 Learning semantic rules

Braine's approach explicitly rejected taking into consideration either the possible meaning of a child's utterance or the context in which it was made. Bloom (1970), on the other hand, argued that it is impossible to identify the rules the child is using unless the meaning of the utterance is taken into account. Bloom's work represented a shift in emphasis because she looked at the *semantic* rules a child uses to produce meaningful utterances. Instead of merely looking for regularities in the way that children structure their two-word utterances, Bloom took into account the meanings children were trying to convey in these utterances. For instance, one of the children Bloom studied, a child called Kathryn, produced the two-word utterance 'Mummy sock', in two different contexts. In one case, Kathryn uttered 'Mummy sock' whilst her mother was putting a sock on Kathryn's foot. Bloom interpreted the child's utterance as meaning 'Mummy is putting my sock on'. The other context in which 'Mummy sock' was uttered was while Kathryn was picking up her mother's sock. Bloom interpreted the utterance on this occasion as meaning 'That's Mummy's sock'. In contrast to Braine's analysis, Bloom provided a more meaningful account of the child's utterances. For example, Braine's pivot/open grammar would assign the *same* rule for producing both occurrences of 'Mummy sock'; that is, two open class words put together.

On the basis of interpretations of children's intended meanings, Bloom and other researchers (notably Brown, 1973) drew up lists of semantic relations that the children were trying to convey. Brown and his co-workers noticed that the child's early two-word utterances seem to encode a restricted set of semantic relations. A summary of these relations and some examples are given in Table 13.3.

**Table 13.3** Semantic relations in two-word utterances

| | Relation | Example |
|---|---|---|
| 1 | Agent–action | 'Mummy fix' |
| 2 | Action–object | 'Hit ball' |
| 3 | Agent–object | 'Mummy pumpkin' (is cutting up) |
| 4 | Action–location | 'Put floor' |
| 5 | Object–location | 'Baby table' |
| 6 | Possessor–possessed | 'Adam ball' |
| 7 | Attribute–object | 'Big dog' |
| 8 | Demonstrative–object | 'This house' |

(Source: adapted from Brown, 1973)

SAQ 5    Categorize the following utterances in terms of the semantic relations 1 to 8 given in Table 13.3:

(a) 'Car go';

(b) 'Mummy sock';

(c) 'Put light'.

These semantic relations can be thought of as semantic rules for producing two-word utterances. They are very different from the purely syntactic rules of pivot/open grammar. The argument is that semantic rules are necessary to explain why some combinations of words are more likely to occur than others and why the same utterance can be used to express different meanings. Although many two-word utterances may at first sight appear to be random combinations of pivot and open words, if you also take into account the context of an utterance the correct semantic rule becomes obvious.

Bloom's approach is concerned with the production of individual utterances with a particular meaning. But how do children learn when a particular utterance is *appropriate*? Comments like 'Mummy sock' may seem meaningful enough, but why did the child choose to make a comment about her mother's sock at that particular moment? The expression 'Allgone milk' is likely to be a request for more milk. The semantic approach explains the semantic content of utterances and the semantic rules for producing them, but it leaves out of account what children intend their communications to achieve. To become really skilful speakers, children have to renounce the constant chatter of a 2 year old in favour of more comprehensible conversations.

## 3.4 Pragmatics: learning conversational rules

The one year old does not come to language learning unprepared. Even before infants start to babble, they smile, cry and contact people's eyes, a type of primitive conversation. A number of researchers (for instance, Snow, 1977) have argued that these '**proto-conversations**' without words tend to have a one-sided quality, that they are dependent upon a generous adult attributing some kind of intended meaning to the child's behaviour. From this perspective, the infant is pictured as an inadequate conversational partner continually supported by the adult who gives meaning and structure to the dialogue.

Bruner (1975) has pointed out that these proto-conversations may provide the context for infants to discover that people interpret their actions in different ways. In typical interactions between parent and child, the adult and infant manage to work together to create an exchange which is satisfying for both partners. Bruner argues that adult–child interactions help the child to discover the social function of communication. Other ritual exchanges such as 'peek-a-boo' emphasize the need for turn-taking when interacting with another. In this way, children begin to appreciate themselves as autonomous, communicative individuals. Bruner's emphasis on the role of early interactions in the development of a child's social self is described in Chapter 3, Section 6.

Bates, Camaioni and Volterra (1975) have documented how an Italian child, Carlotta, gradually exploited her communicative skills to master two distinct communicative acts. The following excerpt was recorded when Carlotta was 13 months and 2 days:

Carlotta (C) is seated in a corridor in front of the kitchen door. She looks towards her mother and calls with an acute sound 'ha'. Mother comes over to her, and C looks towards the kitchen twisting her shoulders and upper body to do so. Mother carries her into the kitchen and C points towards the sink. Mother gives her a glass of water and C drinks it eagerly.

(Bates *et al.*, 1975, p. 217)

This description leaves one in no doubt that the mother understands what Carlotta intends by her actions. Carlotta is signalling to her mother that she wants a glass of water and that she wants her mother to get it for her. Bates *et al.* call this kind of communication act a **proto-imperative**, thus identifying it as a precursor of the use of imperative commands, such as 'Close the door'. Bates *et al.* describe another communicative act in which Carlotta attempts to gain the attention of an adult by drawing the adult's attention to an object. Typically, the child will point at an object whilst looking back and forth between object and adult. Bates *et al.* label this act a **proto-declarative**, again identifying it as a precursor of the later ability to make statements such as 'There's a ball'. The importance of Bates *et al.*'s analysis lies in the demonstration that the child is already using communicative skills to perform two distinct acts, the proto-imperative and the proto-declarative, *before* the emergence of spoken language.

The next stage occurs when the child begins to learn words that aid understanding in the conversations which take place between child and adult. The child's first phrases can be interpreted, not just in terms of their meaning, but also from the point of view of their pragmatic role in a conversation. Table 13.4 shows how children might use different utterances to indicate pragmatic functions, such as getting what they want and obtaining new information. These can be thought of as **pragmatic rules** for carrying on meaningful conversations.

**Table 13.4** Pragmatic categories of utterances

| Request/demand | Question | Statement |
|---|---|---|
| Give me a drink | Where doggy gone? | Doggy in garden |
| Look at doggy | What dat? | Doll got blue dress |
| Put dolly pram | Come doggy back? | Food allgone |
| Don't want it | Coming nanny today? | TV not work |

SAQ 6   Categorize the following utterances in terms of the pragmatic categories listed in Table 13.4. Looking back to Table 13.3, how would they be categorized as semantic relations?

(a) 'Baby table';
(b) 'Put light';
(c) 'Mummy sock';
(d) 'The cat sat on the mat'.

One interesting point is that not all children learn pragmatic rules in quite the same way. Child language researchers, notably Nelson (1981), have uncovered some enlightening differences between children's use of language at a number of stages of development. Nelson particularly refers to 'referential' children and 'expressive' children. **Referential children** conform most closely to the traditional picture of language development. These children's early vocabulary consists of a large proportion of object names (nouns with some verbs, proper names and adjectives). However, according to Nelson, there is another group of children whose vocabularies contain a large number of social formulas (such as 'Stop it', 'I want it', 'Don't do it'). Nelson calls these children **expressive children**.

These differences in communicative style have suggested that the expressive mode of language might have a different pragmatic function from the referential mode. It certainly appears to be the case that expressive children tend to use language more often for social purposes than referential children. There is also some evidence that referential children tend to use their language for more cognitive purposes such as making statements.

SAQ 7   Look at Table 13.4. List the pragmatic categories—that is, requests, questions and statements—which are most likely to be made by:

(a)  expressive children;
(b)  referential children.

One point that needs explaining is how children make the jump from wordless proto-conversations to using recognizable utterances. If parents can understand every gesture of their children's intended meanings, why should children ever bother to learn the complex rules necessary for using language? One answer is that, as they grow older, children have to communicate with other people, like playschool and kindergarten teachers, for example, who will not recognize the idiosyncratic gestures of proto-conversations. It seems likely, too, that children will want to be able to join in the more complex conversations that go on between adults and older children. But it is certainly a problem to explain how children come to understand the rules of language from the often ungrammatical conversations they hear around them. It would seem an almost impossible task.

One line of research concentrated on the type of speech adults actually use when talking to very young children. Snow (1972) found that adult speech to children is much simpler in structure than in adult-to-adult conversations. Adults avoid complex sentences and tend to use the simplest syntactical word orders; for example, subject–verb–object, as in 'Mary watered the flowers', rather than 'The flowers were watered by Mary'. Utterances to children contain simple concrete words and usually refer to here-and-now events. Reference has already been made to the tendency of parents not to correct their children's speech but to respond to what they think their children mean by their earliest words and two-word utterances.

The simplification of adult-speech to children has been called **motherese**. However, to indicate that the child may have other caretakers than its mother, the more neutral term **baby talk register** is sometimes used. A *register* is a special mode of speech appropriate to a social situation, in this case talking to babies. Caretakers descend to baby talk in order to achieve a mutual understanding with children who have not yet mastered the full complexity of language. In fact, long after children can speak grammatically, adults carrying on conversations with a child still need to tailor their speech to concepts and situations familiar to the child. Sensitivity to a child's vocabulary and intellectual and social knowledge is just another example of a pragmatic rule for ensuring a degree of shared understanding.

Despite the help given by adult use of baby talk, learning a language involves many skills. If you look back to Table 13.4, you will see that, by the age of around three, most children have acquired all the linguistic rules we have discussed in this chapter. These include *syntactic rules* for word order for different kinds of utterances; for instance, the reversal of words in questions. The utterances obey *semantic rules* so that the combinations of word meanings make sense; for instance, drinks can be 'given', people can 'come', TV sets break down. Utterances like 'Drink not work' or 'Colourless green ideas sleep furiously' would break semantic rules, although the utterances are grammatically well formed. Finally, there are the *pragmatic rules* necessary to carry out conversations. If an adult asks, 'Where doggy gone?', 'Doggy in garden' is an appropriate answer to the question. An inappropriate response, such as 'Coming nanny today?' or 'The cat sat on the mat', does not conform to the pragmatic rules necessary for carrying on conversations.

No psychologist would claim that language learning is fully understood. However, research has demonstrated that children acquire the syntactic rules, an extended vocabulary (the lexicon) and the semantic rules of a particular language. As they learn to communicate, these rules become increasingly automatic and implicit. All these abilities underpin the child's gradual mastery of pragmatic rules for using language to communicate. Learning all the niceties of conversation is a slow and time-consuming business, as anyone who has tried to keep a telephone conversation going with a young child knows only too well. In the next section I shall explore some of the assumptions about communicative intentions which are necessary to keep the conversational merry-go-round turning smoothly.

## Summary of Section 3

- Language learning has been described by Skinner in terms of conditioning verbal responses. However, the learning of precise verbal responses in this way normally only applies to stereotyped phrases.

- Chomsky's theory of syntactic rules led to the analysis of the structure of children's two-word utterances in terms of a pivot/open grammar.

- Other researchers emphasized the importance of analysing the semantic rules which specify the meanings of children's utterances in context.

- Research has shown that children learn to use pragmatic rules as they develop from proto-conversations to using language appropriately in conversations.

- The use of a baby talk register enables conversation skills to develop gradually.

# 4 | Communicative functions of language

The importance of respecting the pragmatic use of language was emphasized in Section 3. The first rule of linguistic communication is to bear in mind the knowledge and expectations of your listeners or readers. If you flout these too much, your prospective audience will fail to understand you. On the other hand, if you only stick to things they already know, there is not much point to the conversation either. The issue is to explain how participants in a conversation ensure that just the right balance of knowledge is available for the conversation to be understood.

## 4.1 The given-new contract

Clark (1977) introduced the idea of a **given-new contract** which holds between a speaker and a listener, or a writer and a reader. According to the contract, it is the duty of a speaker or writer to indicate the given information by making it clear who or what is being referred to when providing *new* information. An example would be, 'Mary Brown was feeling ill at the party, so she left to go home'. Clark analyses 'Mary was feeling ill' as the *given* information. Without this reference to Mary and her illness, the second part of the utterance would make no sense to the listener. In other words, the given information is necessary in order to understand the *new* information that 'Mary left to go home'. Without knowing that the speaker is referring to an illness at a party, the significance of Mary's departure would be totally unclear. If there was more than one Mary at the party, the 'given' information might have to indicate that it was Mary Brown who was taken ill. Sometimes it is not necessary to spell out the given information as explicitly as this, since the speaker may correctly assume that the listener *already* knows some or even all of the given information. For instance, if both the speaker and the listener had actually witnessed Mary Brown looking ill at a party, the speaker could just say, 'She's left to go home'.

What is the role of the listener in the given-new contract? The listener has to act on the assumption that the speaker is attempting to provide the appropriate given information on which to base plausible interpretations. Suppose someone says, 'I walked into John's room. The chandeliers sparkled brightly'. In this case the listener can be expected to infer—that is, to make the expected inference—that the chandeliers are hanging in the same room as the one the speaker walked into. Clark calls this a **bridging inference** because it 'goes beyond' the literal meaning of sentences in order to make a 'bridge' between what is actually said and the inference; in our example, the bridging inference is that the second sentence referred to the chandeliers in John's room.

The point about a bridging inference is that there is not enough given information to make explicit the intended meaning. For instance, the speaker could have said, 'I walked into John's room in which there were several chandeliers. These chandeliers sparkled brilliantly'. This would indeed spell out the intended meaning clearly. But conversations that take nothing for granted would not only be rather boring but also tediously long-winded. Instead of saying, 'Dinner's ready', one would have to say something like, 'I've cooked the food and I know you're hungry and I'm going to bring in the food and put it on the table so you can eat it'.

The given-new contract ensures that speakers and listeners can understand each other as long as the speaker gives a minimum amount of given information necessary to make any required bridging inferences.

SAQ 8  'John was murdered yesterday. The knife was found in the kitchen.'

(a) What bridging inferences might the speaker expect the listener to make?

(b) What would be the 'given' information and what would be the 'new' information in the second sentence? (*Hint*: the 'given' information may not be explicitly mentioned but depend instead on a bridging inference.)

Clark and Murphy (1982) have extended the notion of the given-new contract by introducing the more general term **audience design**. This refers to the fact that we always design our utterances to be understood by the particular audience to whom they are addressed. Understanding is always based on the assumption that speaker and listener share some mutual 'given' knowledge and beliefs. For instance, you may have noticed that I have been assuming that you have read the earlier chapters in this book and so have already acquired some shared knowledge about psychological approaches. I therefore expect you as readers to make any necessary inferences in order to understand what I am trying to say. Readers and listeners are expected to make the assumption that writers and speakers have good reason to expect them to make inferences on the basis of shared knowledge. It is this which leads readers and listeners to make bridging inferences in order to understand the meanings of utterances.

Most linguistic communications proceed smoothly without our even noticing any bridging inferences we may be making. A good conversationalist makes sure that a listener has, or can reasonably be expected to infer, the required given information. Sperber and Wilson (1986) quote an exchange they overheard as an example of the difficulties that can arise when a speaker makes a statement requiring too many inferences on the part of the listener:

*Flag seller* 'Would you like to buy a flag for the Royal National Lifeboat Institution?'
*Passer-by* 'No thanks. I always spend my holidays with my sister in Birmingham.'

(Sperber and Wilson, 1986)

SAQ 9  List a chain of bridging inferences you think might be needed to make sense of this conversation. (*Hint*: In what circumstances might someone never need the services of a lifeboat?)

The point about cases like this is that very little is 'given' to provide the necessary information for the exchange to be understood. The bridging inferences depend on general knowledge about the likely circumstances and motivations of the speakers. But, when so little information is given, the listener has to cast about to decide which inferences are *relevant* to understanding the conversational exchange. Sperber and Wilson (1986) assume that people adhere to the principle of optimal relevance. **Optimal relevance** is achieved when just the right amount of information is given to justify inferences necessary for understanding; that is, when these necessary inferences are sufficiently relevant to warrant extra processing effort. If a listener expects a communication to be relevant, any inferences required will be worth the extra processing effort. For instance, people are eager to grasp the point of a joke or to learn something new. But the principle of optimal relevance can also be broken. If a new topic is introduced too abruptly, the listener will simply fail to see its relevance. If the gap between speaker and listener is too wide, the principle of optimal relevance predicts a failure in understanding. Sometimes, communicators—writers of textbooks, for example—may believe that they are adhering to the principle of optimal relevance when in fact the amount of extra processing required is far too onerous for readers to grasp the assumptions taken for granted by the writer. On the other hand, the principle of optimal relevance can also be broken by giving too much detail, as in the laboured example explaining the presence of food on the table.

So far, the emphasis has been on the way in which speakers assume that listeners will draw on their general knowledge in order to understand the meaning of utterances. But speakers also use different types of utterances to convey different pragmatic intentions. For instance, we may understand sentences like, 'I walked into John's room. The chandeliers sparkled brightly' or 'The cat sat on the mat'. But *why* did the speakers make these statements? What was the intention of their communications? In the next section I will be looking at approaches which analyse the appropriate use of utterances to convey a speaker's intentions.

## 4.2  Speech acts

Speech act theory originated from the work of philosophers, such as Austin and Searle, who were interested in analysing the uses to which language can be put. They identified ways in which language can be used to perform various kinds of speech acts. The term **speech acts** arose from the observation that certain utterances can be used to perform acts. The utterance, 'With this ring I thee wed' in itself performs the act of marriage. 'I promise to visit you' performs the act of promising. Austin (1962) called these **performative utterances** because the actual words used—for example, 'promise'—are necessary to *perform* the act. Of course, it is not just the words that are necessary but also the appropriate conditions. 'With this ring I thee wed' has to occur in a proper setting and someone who makes a promise has to intend to keep it.

Searle (1969) listed other types of speech acts which, rather than performing one particular act, signal speakers' intentions about the purpose of their utterances. For instance, a speaker might intend an utterance to perform the speech act of commanding someone to do something, of making a request, or of asking a question or making a statement. If you look back to Section 3, you will come across many examples of speech acts. The proto-imperatives and proto-declaratives described by Bates *et al.* (1975) are the first wordless attempts of a child to convey requests, commands and statement speech acts. Even Skinner's mands and tacts can be thought of as learning to demand things (mands) and to make descriptive statements (tacts). Finally, the utterances in Table 13.4 in Section 3.4 represent early versions of speech acts which aim to communicate the child's intention to demand or request something, or to ask a question or make a statement.

Searle goes on to point out that many speech acts are *indirect*. For instance, the words, 'It's chilly in here' could be interpreted as a plain statement when they are really intended to express a request speech act such as, 'Can you close the window?' Even this question is a polite form of an indirect request. If some joker interprets the request literally, as a genuine question about their ability, and answers, 'Yes I can', the speaker will doubtless be annoyed.

One of Searle's important contributions was to outline the contextual conditions, which he called 'felicity' conditions, necessary for the interpretation of speech acts. For instance, the felicity conditions for making a request depend on the speaker wishing to change the situation and the listener being in a position to do something about it. So, faced with the utterance of the words 'I'm chilly', the listener has to work out whether the situation conforms to Searle's felicity conditions for a request. If the listener believes that the speaker likes being cold, and/or there is no feasible action the listener can take to alter the situation, the 'request' meaning will fail. The listener will then have to consider other speech act interpretations of 'I'm chilly'. If someone had just asked the speaker how he felt, this might incline the listener to interpret the speaker's intended speech act as a statement about the temperature in the room.

Searle's analysis of intended speech acts is very plausible. However, it does have some limitations. The first point is that, if one particular utterance, such as 'I'm chilly', can be interpreted as performing several different indirect speech acts, the literal meaning of an utterance seems almost irrelevant. It is easy to accept that the word 'promise' should imply the intention to perform a promise. But indirect speech acts can only be identified by taking into account everything else that is happening: whether people want windows closed or open, for instance.

A more serious limitation is that the majority of utterances do not fall into the relatively small class of specified speech acts, such as demanding, requesting and so on. A great many utterances take the form of statements, which are categorized as a single kind of speech act. Yet statements can be used in many ways. They can be used to comment, to make jokes, to carry on an argument, and to show one understands something, as well as for the usual 'speech act' definition of conveying information. The following extract from a play by Samuel Beckett demonstrates the subtle differences in meaning that utterances can convey depending on the context:

MR ROONEY: I hear something behind us. [*Pause.*]

MRS ROONEY: It looks like Jerry [*Pause.*] It is Jerry.

[*Sound of* JERRY'S *running steps approaching. He halts beside them, panting.*]

JERRY: [*Panting.*] You dropped—

MRS ROONEY: Take your time, my little man, you will burst a blood-vessel.

JERRY: [*Panting.*] You dropped something, sir. Mr Barrell told me to run after you.

MRS ROONEY: Show. [*She takes the object.*] What is it? [*She examines it.*] What is this thing, Dan?

MR ROONEY: Perhaps it is not mine at all.

JERRY: Mr Barrell said it was, sir.

MRS ROONEY: It looks like a kind of ball. And yet it is not a ball.

MR ROONEY: Give it to me.

MRS ROONEY: [*Giving it.*] What *is* it, Dan?

MR ROONEY: It is a thing I carry about with me.

MRS ROONEY: Yes, but what—

MR ROONEY: [*Violently.*] It is a thing I carry about with me!

[*Silence.*]

(Beckett, 1957)

As can be seen from this extract, individual utterances are not produced in isolation, each to be interpreted as a single speech act, according to its social context. Instead, they are combined into whole conversational episodes. Conversations can be almost thought of as having a life of their own, over and above the intended utterances of the individual participants.

## 4.3 Understanding conversational episodes

The following exchange from Winograd (1980) gives an amusing example of a conversational episode which can hardly be regarded as successful:

A: I'm thirsty.

B: There's some water in the fridge.

A: Where? I don't see it.

B: In the cells of the tomato.

What is wrong with this conversation? Let us start by considering what is right about it. First, the words are all meaningful English words. Second, the sentences are perfectly grammatical. Third, each sentence has an acceptable meaning. Fourth, the speech acts, such as questions and statements, are clearly specified.

SAQ 10    List the technical linguistic terms for the four aspects of language listed in the above paragraph. (*Hint:* Look back to Section 1.)

Despite the fact that there are four well-formed English sentences in A and B's conversation, there is something distinctly odd about the conversation as a whole. A's first remark is obviously quite all right; as is B's first rejoinder and A's second remark. But B's final answer somehow shows a total lack of understanding about the intention of A's first statement, which was to express a request for some water to quench his thirst. B's answer might, or course, be perfectly appropriate in another context, such as a scientific discussion about the properties of cells, or a joke.

This simple example reinforces some important characteristics of pragmatic language use. It reinforces the crucial role of context. This covers both the **linguistic context**; that is, what has been said before, and the **social context**, including the intentions of the participants. In the first place, why do we—and B—infer that A's first remark, although couched in the form of a statement, really indicates an indirect request? How do we know from A's second remark that A must have opened the fridge and looked inside? How do we know that 'it' refers to water and not to the fridge itself, which is after all the last object referred to in B's first remark? All these are bridging inferences which participants are likely to make in order to achieve mutual understanding (see Section 4.1). The problem with this 'joke' conversation is that B ignored the given-new contract, setting up A to believe the given information that there is some water in the fridge.

In their book, *Understanding computers and cognition*, Winograd and Flores (1986) widened the stage to look at the overall structure of whole conversations rather than concentrating on the understanding of individual utterances. They suggest that a conversation should be thought of as a 'dance' in which speech acts follow one another in a 'mutual coupling' between language users. After each commitment to a speech act by a speaker—for example, to make a request—there are various options for the other participant, such as to promise to carry out the request, to reject it or make a counter request. In turn, the first participant can accept, withdraw, and so on. Figure 13.2 shows an example of a **conversational dance** giving all the options from which each participant can select. Participant A starts by making a request. B can either promise to do what is asked; or reject the request, or make a counter request, in which case A may withdraw, or make a counter request. B then has several options and the conversational dance continues.

The point Winograd and Flores are making is that conversations are carried on against a background of joint social purposes. If people ignore reasonable expectations, communication will break down and may leave a residue of mistrust which will affect future social interactions. Winograd (1980) gives several examples of what happens when a speaker ignores the implicit commitments of a speech act and so confuses potential listeners. One of Winograd's examples is the oddity, indeed the 'bad faith', of a speaker using the statement, 'Joan has never failed a student in her linguistics class' to express the fact that Joan has never taught a linguistics class. It is strictly

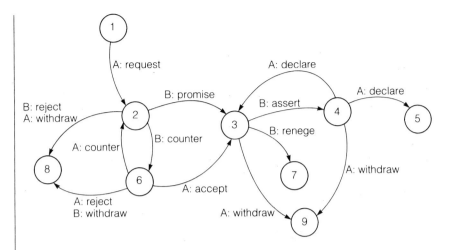

**Figure 13.2** A conversational 'dance'
(Source: adapted from Winograd and Flores, 1986)

possible that one reason why Joan has never failed any students is that she never took the class at all. But the normal interpretation would be that the 'given' information is that Joan certainly *had* taught a linguistics class and that the 'new' information is that she never failed a student. The point that is being made here is that conversations do not make sense except in the context of the whole communication episode in which they are embedded.

## 4.4 Communication in social encounters

The concept of **communication episodes** has been developed by a number of investigators. The main concern of these writers is in the role of language in social interactions in general. Goffman (1971) describes social encounters as if they are part of an ongoing play. People 'act' so as to convey impressions. This includes a full range of possible 'acts' such as behaviour, choice of dress, speech and gestures. The situations in which these acts occur include every possible situation in which people find themselves: applying for a job, joking with friends, asking for a loan, saying goodbye. Goffman describes many fascinating examples of social rituals. For example, people use special acts when making farewells. Goffman draws attention to the embarrassment people feel when, after bidding emotional farewells to their nearest and dearest, and preparing to wave goodbye, the train firmly refuses to go. The descent into small talk covers a social unease.

Goffman's **dramaturgical theory** was first introduced in Chapter 2, Section 6.2, with its emphasis on people as actors in an ongoing drama. However, you may be wondering what all this has to do with language as such. The point is that a great deal of what goes on in a social encounter is expressed as speech communications. These may be embedded in all sorts of other, non-verbal behaviours which emit important signals. But speech is nevertheless one of the major channels of communication.

ACTIVITY 3

Imagine you are going to two job interviews, one to work in a bank (job 1) and the other to join a co-operative running a vegetarian restaurant (job 2). Based on any expectations you might have, how would you wish to present yourself at the interview?

|  | Job 1 | Job 2 |
|---|---|---|
| (a) What would you wear? | | |
| (b) How would you expect the interviewer to address you? | | |
| (c) What would you plan to say if you were asked why you wanted the job? | | |

The examples in Activity 3 emphasize the importance of selecting appropriate speech and behaviour in particular situations. People often unconsciously adjust their speech behaviour depending on perceived social requirements. And, of course, people are continually judging other people on the basis of what they say and how they say it.

The study of interrelations between the use of language and social and cultural factors is known as **sociolinguistics**. One topic that has attracted a lot of research by sociolinguists is the use of different forms of language depending on the status of the participants. For instance, English speakers learning French find the 'tu/vous' distinction very complicated ('tu' is the informal way to say 'you' and 'vous' is the more formal word for addressing people). First, you have to decide whether to use 'tu' without sounding either patronizing (as to children or to inferiors) or too intimate (as with friends or lovers). In fact, this is not always an easy choice for French speakers themselves. Then there is the added syntactic difficulty of having to use quite different verb endings depending on whether you are using 'tu' or 'vous'. However, the switches in syntax all seem to come naturally to native speakers who switch from one code to another as occasion demands, so much so that they are probably quite unconscious of the rules for using the different speech forms until asked to explain them to enquiring linguists.

Tanner (1967) describes a particularly complex set of multilingual choices used by a group of Indonesian students and their families in an American university town. The variables which affect the languages and dialects they use in conversation include the status of the participants and their intimacy, social settings and topics of conversation. Quite apart from this particular group, Javanese is a language in which 'it is nearly impossible to say anything without indicating the social relationship between the speaker and the listener in terms of status and familiarity' (Geetz, 1960).

ACTIVITY 4

Just to make yourself aware of some of the different sociolinguistic variants you use yourself, try writing a brief holiday postcard to:

(a)  your best friend;

(b)  an elderly aunt;

(c) a small child.

Did you find that your style of language changed as you switched from writing a postcard to one person to writing a postcard to another?

Of course, it would not be surprising if some people were better at selecting appropriate styles than others—witness the serious academic who is hopeless at making small talk at a cocktail party or can never feel at ease in the local pub. The ability to use language styles appropriately is the hallmark of a skilled communicator. It also has an important effect on the success of communications and the way in which the participants regard each other.

## Summary of Section 4

● For communication to be successful it is essential to take into account the listener's prior knowledge (given-new contract) and to tailor language for a particular audience (audience design). This is essential for the listener to make the appropriate bridging inferences.

● According to speech act theory, the intentions of utterances are more important than their literal meaning. Context is necessary for identifying indirect speech acts.

● Conversations can be considered as communication episodes which are embedded in social encounters.

● Language styles vary in accordance with the social status of participants and the requirements of the social setting.

# 5 | The social dimension: an overview

As this chapter has progressed, the aim has been to emphasize the role of language in social communication. The social dimension is so dominant that it is impossible to think of language existing without speakers. It is equally impossible to visualize a human society without the ability to communicate with others. However, running through this chapter has been a tension between the internal aspects of language and its social functions. This was first raised in Section 2 in connection with the question as to whether the way people think is determined by the language used by their community. The question at issue is the relationship between private thoughts and the role of language in maintaining a particular society's conventions and norms. As Vygotsky (1962) pointed out, it is extremely important that people use the same language for private thinking and for public social communication. Only by doing so will they be able to pass on the fruits of their thinking to other people, and to internalize and reflect on communications from other people.

The reason why language is so crucial in mediating the way people view the world is that language has a peculiar advantage compared with other types of experience. Linguistic symbols are at *one remove* from perceptions of the here and now. If you actually see someone sitting on a tree stump, you may categorize that tree stump as acting as a chair for that occasion. But you do not tell yourself that you have actually seen a chair with legs and arms. The special nature of language is that it can be used to describe something 'as if' it is a chair. Using language, people can discuss future plans, alternative constructions of what is going on, hypothetical events, entities which may never have existed, philosophical speculations and so on, with no apparent limit. Yet, at the same time, the constraints of a shared language can confine debate and discussion within accepted frames of thought.

A tension also arises between the knowledge involved in learning to speak a language and the social contexts in which language is actually used. In order to use a language to communicate, individual speakers each have to learn that language. When two people share no common language, inferences based on mutual knowledge of the situation may give some hints about what each person intends to communicate. But this can lead to frustration and misunderstandings which could rapidly be dispelled if one person knew how to say in the other person's language, 'Can you tell me the way to the railway station?' or, 'Does God exist?'

When reading about the role of inferences based on shared knowledge and intentions in order to understand conversations, it may sometimes sound as if the literal meanings of utterances like 'I'm chilly' are almost irrelevant, since they can be interpreted very differently in different situations. Yet the literal meanings of words must impose some limits on what utterances can mean. Otherwise, one might end up with Humpty Dumpty's claim in *Alice through the Looking Glass*:

'When I use a word,' Humpty Dumpty said in rather a scornful tone, 'it means just what I choose it to mean—neither more nor less.'

'The question is,' said Alice, 'whether you can make words mean so many different things.'

'The question is,' said Humpty Dumpty, 'which is to be master—that's all.'

(Carroll, 1872, p. 124)

In the conversation about the water in the fridge in Section 4.3, speaker A would have been even more taken aback if B had replied volubly in a foreign language. Although the word 'water' can apply to many things, it cannot be used to refer to a piano. It is our knowledge of the usual meaning of the word 'water' that makes us smile at the fridge example. If someone wishes to use a word to mean something quite different from its usual meaning, it is up to the speaker to explain the new usage to potential listeners, as we have tried to do in this book whenever a new psychological term is introduced. So the lexicon, the syntactic rules and the semantic rules of a language are important in helping us to achieve communication with other people who speak the same language. On the other hand, a lack of awareness about the social situation and the intentions of a communication would result in an exchange of formal language with no exchange of understanding.

Language undoubtedly has two faces: one is turned towards the internal cognitive processes involved in learning to use a language, the other towards external communication in a social context. The use of language to articulate thoughts, and the emphasis on each individual's ability to speak a language, represent the cognitive aspects of language. The role of shared knowledge and intentions in understanding conversations, and the use of language to promote social encounters within accepted cultural conventions, represent the social aspects of language. The dual function of language ensures a constant interaction between internal reflection and socially constructed meanings, without which communication would be impossible. In this sense, language can be defined as a truly social activity.

**Personal acknowledgement**

I would like to thank Kim Plunkett whose work in an earlier Open University psychology course has been helpful in the writing of this chapter.

# Further reading

An interesting book which covers many aspects of communication is:
ELLIS, A. and BEATTIE, G. (1986) *The psychology of language and communication*, London: Lawrence Erlbaum Associates.

The range of topics covered includes the diversity of human languages, the structure of language, the use of dialects and other styles of speech, analysis of conversations, and language acquisition.

# References

AUSTIN, J.L. (1962) *How to do things with words*, Oxford: Oxford University Press.

BATES, E., CAMAIONI, L. and VOLTERRA, V. (1975) 'The acquisition of performatives prior to speech', *Merrill-Palmer Quarterly*, vol. 21, no. 3.

BECKETT, S. (1957) *All that fall*, London: Faber and Faber.

BLOOM, L. (1970) *Language development: form and function in emerging grammars*, Cambridge, MA: MIT Press.

BRAINE, M.D.S. (1963) 'The ontogeny of English phrase structure: the first phase', *Language*, vol. 39, pp. 1–14.

BROWN, R. (1973) *A first language: the early stages*, Cambridge, MA: Harvard University Press.

BROWN, R., CAZDEN, C.B. and BELLUGI, U. (1969) 'The child's grammar from 1 to 111', in Hill, J.P. (ed.) *Minnesota symposia on child psychology*, vol. 2, Minneapolis: University of Minnesota Press.

BRUNER, J.S. (1975) 'From communication to language: a psychological perspective', *Cognition*, vol. 3, pp. 255–87.

CARMICHAEL, L., HOGAN, H.P. and WALTER, A.A. (1932) 'An experimental study of the effect of language on the reproduction of visually perceived forms', *Journal of Experimental Psychology*, vol. 15, pp. 73–86.

CARROLL, J.B. (ed.) (1956) *Language, thought and reality: selected writings of Benjamin Lee Whorf*, New York: MIT Press and Wiley.

CARROLL, L. (1872) *Alice through the looking glass, and what Alice found there*, London: Macmillan.

CHOMSKY, N. (1957) *Syntactic structures*, The Hague: Mouton.

CLARK, H.H. (1977) 'Bridging', in Johnson-Laird, P.N. and Wason, P.C. (eds) *Thinking: readings in cognitive science*, Cambridge: Cambridge University Press.

CLARK, H.H. and MURPHY, G.L. (1982) 'Audience design in meaning and reference', in Le Ny, J.F. and Kintsch, W. (eds) *Language and comprehension*, Amsterdam: North-Holland.

FODOR, J.A. (1983) *The modularity of mind*, Cambridge, MA: MIT Press.

GARDNER, R.A. and GARDNER, B.T. (1969) 'Teaching sign language to a chimpanzee', *Science*, vol. 165, pp. 664–72.

GEETZ, C. (1960) *The religion of Java*, New York: Free Press.

GOFFMAN, E. (1971) *Relations in public*, Harmondsworth: Penguin.

NELSON, K. (1981) 'Individual differences in language development: implications for development and language', *Developmental Psychology*, vol. 17, pp. 170–87.

PIAGET, J. (1968) 'Language and thought from the genetic point of view', in Piaget, J. *Six psychological studies*, London: University of London Press.

SEARLE, J.R. (1969) *Speech acts*, Cambridge: Cambridge University Press.

SKINNER, B.F. (1957) *Verbal behaviour*, New York: Appleton-Century-Crofts.

SNOW, C.E. (1972) 'Mothers' speech to children learning language', *Child Development*, vol. 43, pp. 549–65.

SNOW, C.E. (1977) 'The development of conversation between mothers and children', *Journal of Child Language*, vol. 4, pp. 1–22.

SPERBER, D. and WILSON, D. (1986) *Relevance: communication and cognition*, Oxford: Blackwell.

TANNER, N. (1967) 'Speech and society among the Indonesian elite: a case study of a multilingual community', *Anthropological Linguistics*, vol. 9, pp. 15–39.

VYGOTSKY, L.S. (1962) *Thought and language*, Cambridge, MA: MIT Press.

WINOGRAD, T. (1980) 'What does it mean to understand language?', *Cognitive Science*, vol. 4, pp. 209–41.

WINOGRAD, T. and FLORES, F. (1986) *Understanding computers and cognition*, Norwood, NJ: Ablex.

# Answers to SAQs

## SAQ 1

(a) This example is from a nonsense poem by Lewis Carroll in *Alice through the Looking Glass*: (i) the words are not in the lexicon of the English language; (ii) nevertheless, the structure of the sentence conforms to the syntax of English. It is obvious that 'slithy' is an adjective, 'toves' is a noun, and that 'gyre' and 'gimble' are verbs; and (iii) it is debatable whether the meaning of this sentence conforms to the semantics of English but most people feel that nonsense poems like this do make some meaningful sense.

(b) This is a famous sentence invented by the linguist Noam Chomsky and designed to show that sentences can be grammatical although not meaningful: (i) the vocabulary is correct; (ii) the syntax is correct; but (iii) the sentence has no meaning (semantics): it is impossible for an object to be both 'green' and 'colourless'.

(c) This example conforms to all three requirements for an acceptable sentence in English. The words are in the lexicon and the syntax and semantics are correct. The fact that it is an exceedingly dull sentence is quite another matter.

## SAQ 2

The purpose of the control group was to provide a check on the way subjects might have perceived and remembered the neutral drawings. For instance, even without a label, subjects might remember the first drawing as a window with curtains.

## SAQ 3

(a) Whorf's theory is best represented by view no. 1.

(b) Vygotsky's theory is best represented by view no. 3.

(c) Piaget's theory is best represented by view no. 2.

## SAQ 4

(a) This utterance conforms because 'allgone' is a pivot word which can only be in first position and 'sock', being an open word, can occur anywhere.

(b) This also conforms because two open words can occur together.

(c) This does not conform because, although the pivot 'allgone' occurs first and the pivot 'pretty' occurs second, two pivot words cannot occur together.

(d) This also does not conform because 'allgone' cannot occur in second position.

## SAQ 5

(a) This is likely to be an example of relation no. 1 agent–action, although adults would probably not think of a car as an agent.

(b) This could be either relation no. 1 agent–action, meaning that Mummy is putting a sock on Kathryn, or relation no. 6 possessor–possessed, meaning the sock that belongs to Mummy.

(c) Strictly speaking, this is relation no. 2 action–object, but it also probably means 'put light in a certain location' (relation no.4 action–location).

You can see from these answers that it is not at all easy to assign utterances to categories without knowing the exact purpose of the communication.

## SAQ 6

(a) 'Baby table' appears to be a statement about an object–location relation. However, in other circumstances it could be interpreted as a request for the child to be lifted on to a table.

(b) This is almost certainly a demand for an action to be taken with regard to an object (action–object) with an implied location (action–location).

(c) If spoken with a question intonation, this is probably a question about whether it is Mummy's sock (possessor–possessed). Otherwise it could be either a statement (that it is Mummy's sock) or a request that Mummy put the sock on Kathryn's foot.

(d) Obviously a statement about agent–action–location—if you think cats are agents! But the purpose of this statement is more problematical.

## SAQ 7

(a) Expressive children are most likely to make requests and ask questions as part of ongoing social interactions.

(b) Referential children will, of course, also request things but they are also likely to make a lot of statements and to ask questions to gain new information.

## SAQ 8

(a) The expected inference would be that the knife was a murder weapon. It would be a *bridging* inference because it is not stated explicitly that the knife was the murder weapon. The victim might have been poisoned and the detective wanted a knife to make himself a sandwich.

(b) The given information is that the knife was the murder weapon and the new information was that it was found in the kitchen. If the speaker had meant to refer to some other knife, he or she would have broken the given-new contract by not providing any alternative given information about which knife was being referred to.

## SAQ 9

The main chain of bridging inferences is that this passer-by always spends his holidays inland. He is therefore never likely to drown in the sea, and so will never need a lifeboat to save him. He thus does not want to contribute to any lifeboat funds. Perhaps you also thought of other incidental stereotypical inferences including that the passer-by is probably a *man* who lives on his own.

## SAQ 10

(i)   Meaningful English words: the lexicon;

(ii)  Grammatical sentences: syntax;

(iii) Sentence meanings: semantics;

(iv)  Speech acts: pragmatics.

# ISSUES IN SOCIAL PSYCHOLOGY

Dorothy Miell

## Contents

# 1 | Introduction

The previous chapter stressed the importance of social context. We saw that only by studying the social context can we fully understand what language is, how it functions and why it has a central place in human life. It is only within a social frame that we see language as *communication* between people. This chapter looks further at the implications for psychology of emphasizing the social context, an emphasis which is the distinctive contribution of social psychology. In the chapter a number of key issues in social psychology will be set out through the discussion of a case study. The study of aggression was chosen for this purpose because, in many ways, it is representative of the dialogues and debates in social psychology. It provides a good vehicle for picking out crucial issues in psychology's study of social topics, giving an idea of how social psychologists think about such topics and conduct research. It is also a relevant example to use since the incidence of aggression is of wide concern. Although there are daily reports of apparently diverse forms of aggression in the media, there does seem to be some common core to the reports which make us feel that an explanation and ultimately a solution for the problem should exist. Aggression has become a major topic in social psychology because such explanations are eagerly sought and psychologists are seen as holding the key to understanding this 'common core'. In this chapter we will explore whether any such core exists and what it might be. .

## 1.1 Introducing the issues

The main issue in social psychology which the case study of aggression will raise is which **level of analysis** it is appropriate to use to account for human behaviour. In seeking to explain an aggressive incident, psychologists can attempt an explanation at one of a number of levels. Some may suggest that aggression is caused by the genetic make-up of the people involved, others by their 'instincts', their upbringing, their personality, their relationship with the victim or the social, economic and historical circumstances in which they feel trapped. Social psychologists continue to debate which is the most appropriate level of analysis to adopt when studying aggression, but characteristically place an emphasis on the factors involved in *interactions* between people and groups, rather than examining the individual alone. Each of these levels of analysis has different implications for, amongst other things, the types of data that are seen as appropriate, the methods that are used, and the ways in which research and theories are applied.

The case study will also highlight the issue of the appropriate methodology to be used when studying complex social phenomena. Can aggression be recreated in the laboratory, or can it only be studied when it occurs in real life? Some social psychologists believe valuable insights about aggression can be achieved by systematic investigations in the laboratory. Others believe that aggression cannot, indeed should not, be studied away from the social context in which it normally occurs. As a result, they set up field experiments in a real-life setting, observe naturally occurring incidents of aggression or examine the way that our beliefs about aggression, and ultimately our behaviour, are influenced by factors such as the media. This chapter discusses both laboratory methods and more naturalistic methods and evaluates their respective contributions.

Finally, the way social psychology can be applied to real life is an important issue. To what extent does social psychology investigate problems which are found in real life, and how are the findings of various studies fed back to those in society who are concerned with these problems? These issues are clearly illustrated in our aggression case study since it is such a problem in many societies. Are social psychologists providing any answers?

## 1.2 Defining aggression

Before we begin to look at theories and studies of aggression, we must define what we mean by aggression. At first it seems obvious: we all know an aggressive action when we see one—or do we? As Tedeschi *et al.* (1984) have pointed out, part of the problem is that 'aggression' is a word from ordinary language which is used to refer to a wide range of behaviours and on to which psychologists have tried to impose scientific clarity. This is a problem that besets much of social psychology, since it so often seeks to define and explain issues that have commonsense meanings, like love, attitudes and opinions.

### ACTIVITY 1

Look at the list below and indicate whether or not aggression is involved in each of the cases listed (put a tick for aggression and a cross for non-aggression). Where you are not sure, put some notes alongside, such as 'an aggressive thought but no harm actually done'.

1   A soldier shoots an enemy soldier on the front line.
2   The warden of a prison executes a condemned prisoner.
3   Someone knocks over a window box which falls and injures a passer-by.
4   A child kicks a chair.
5   A couple are seen tussling with each other. The 'victim' laughs.
6   A person mentally rehearses a planned murder.
7   A driver gets drunk and knocks someone over when driving home.
8   A young child tries with all her might to punch an older child, but is laughed at.
9   A driver kills a pedestrian when the car mounts the kerb after a tyre bursts.
10   A person at a party gossips in a disparaging way about someone (who may or may not know about this).
11   A father attacks someone who has abused his child.
12   A dentist drills into a patient's nerve when working on a filling.
13   A lion brings down a gazelle.

(Based on Kaufmann, 1970)

The most striking thing about this activity is the difficulty of arriving at a precise definition. In almost every case, there is some ambiguity, some qualification needed to the 'yes' or 'no' response asked for. This difficulty highlights the fact that our understanding and use of the word 'aggression' alters with the context in which the 'aggression' occurs. In seeking for working definitions we need to be aware that the choice we make is somewhat arbitrary, and may need to be changed in different circumstances.

It is clear from Activity 1 that aggression is a *social* act. Few people would claim that a person can be truly aggressive alone, although someone can be angry or destructive alone (e.g. item 4). Aggressive actions seem necessarily to involve more than one person, and thus social psychological explanations will inevitably look first and mainly to social factors to explain them. This is also true of most other topics which social psychologists study, such as altruistic behaviour, group decision making or friendships.

Some of the other issues which commonly arise when social psychologists try to define and draw the boundaries around an issue are also evident when we look at aggression, as you did in Activity 1. For example, should we only look at behaviour or is the *intention* to harm a necessary part of the definition? If it is a necessary ingredient, then incidents such as those in items 3, 9 and 12 will not count as aggressive. Did you think they should be included? Does physical harm have to be actually inflicted, or just thought about (item 6), or attempted (items 5 and 8)? Does verbal aggression exist (item 10)? Is aggression defined by observers or by the people involved (item 5)? How do we describe justified acts and direct orders to aggress (items 1 and 2), acts of self-defence, and retaliation (item 11)? Can we aggress on our own (items 4 and 6)? Can only humans be aggressive (item 13)?

These are only a few of the problems encountered in defining aggression. You probably came up with others in trying to decide about the list of items in Activity 1. Social psychologists have attempted a number of different definitions. A very broad one was suggested by Buss (1961) who believed that only *behaviour* can be studied systematically and who therefore wanted to avoid any inferences about intentions and motives. He proposed that aggression is any behaviour that harms or injures another organism.

SAQ 1   (*SAQ answers are given at the end of the chapter*) Which of the behaviours listed under Activity 1 would be counted as aggressive in Buss's terms?

The list given in answer to SAQ 1 includes some items which we would not normally class as aggressive, such as items 3, 9 and 12, and it certainly seems too wide a definition. A second definition (Berkowitz, 1974), suggests that it is unrealistic and undesirable to exclude the *intention* to harm from any definition of aggression. It is the intention that is crucial, rather than the actual inflicting of harm.

SAQ 2   Which of the items in Activity 1 would count as aggressive if intention to harm is the criterion for the definition?

Whilst it seems necessary to include the intention to harm the other person for an adequate definition of aggression, it does lead to problems for some social psychologists. Intentions are not pieces of behaviour which can be openly observed and measured. Many social psychologists (like Buss) would prefer to have a definition which relies only on observable behaviour. Yet, as you have seen from Activity 1, such a definition does not express the full complexity of a phenomenon like aggression. As you have seen earlier in the book, many psychologists maintain that scientific investigations can only be based on the study of observable behaviour, others that psychological science depends on the study of meaning. This debate resounds through social psychology as well as other areas of the discipline.

For the purposes of this chapter, we will adopt a fairly broad definition of aggression, proposed by Baron (1977), which covers many of the above points and contains three key elements:

1   The aggressor must have an intention to harm the victim.

2   The victim must be another living thing.

3   The victim must be motivated to avoid such treatment.

SAQ 3   Look through the list from Activity 1 and, using a table like the one below, decide whether or not each item complies with each of the criteria in our definition. Put a tick or a cross under each criterion. Then we can categorize each item as aggressive or not depending on whether it complies with *all* of these three criteria. Consider if the definition seems reasonable to you in the light of this list of aggressive actions. What, if anything, would you add to the definition?

| Item no. | Intention to harm | Victim a living thing | Victim motivated to avoid harm |
|----------|-------------------|-----------------------|--------------------------------|
| 1        |                   |                       |                                |
| 2        |                   |                       |                                |
| 3 etc.   |                   |                       |                                |

## Summary of Section 1

- Three main issues were introduced as concerns of social psychology: the level of analysis used in explaining social phenomena; the appropriate methodology to use; and the possible ways of applying findings to the 'real world'. These will be discussed in the context of a case study of aggression.

- There are many problems in defining aggression. If only behaviour is studied, then important factors such as intentions and social norms are ignored. Instead, we have opted for a definition which includes intention to harm and the victim's motivation to avoid such harm.

# 2 | The aggressive individual

Having looked at a range of instances of aggression and considered the problems of definition, the next question to examine is what makes people perform aggressive acts. It is an appealingly simple suggestion that some people are 'born aggressors', since this places responsibility for their behaviour squarely on their biological inheritance. But is this explanation of behaviour really adequate for such a complex phenomenon? In this section we will evaluate the view that aggression can indeed be explained with little or no recourse to the social context within which it is displayed.

## 2.1  Aggressive instincts

A classic account which attributes aggression to internal instincts that drive all of us to behave aggressively was proposed by the ethologist Konrad Lorenz. Lorenz suggested a model in which aggression is derived from a self-generating instinct rather than a reaction to external events. He argued that instinctual energy builds up internally until an appropriate cue in the environment allows it to be released. If appropriate cues are not available to release the energy, then the person or animal will behave destructively, or aggressively.

As an ethologist, Lorenz (1966) closely examined animals to establish why they behave as they do, and he believed their behaviour is often best explained with reference to the operation of biological instincts. Lorenz argued that there are good biological reasons for an **aggressive instinct**, since it allows stronger and fitter animals to carve out a larger area of territory, to have access to more mates and to compete successfully for scarce resources. Lorenz suggested that the aggressive instinct, like the sexual instinct, is a source of energy which wells up over time and seeks discharge where it can. Aggression is not simply a response to threat, or pain, or attack, but is the result of accumulated energy. Unless this energy is released regularly, through such outlets as aggression or competition, Lorenz believed less and less appropriate cues would be needed to trigger an aggressive response. Observations of species such as butterfly fish supported Lorenz's view. These fish defend their territory ferociously against intruders of their own species. But when one butterfly fish has destroyed all the other butterfly fish in the aquarium, it will attack fish of other species which bear some minimal physical resemblance to their own. Deprived of its normal target for aggression, the butterfly fish directs its built-up aggressive energy elsewhere. Lorenz believed that in modern *human* society there are too few appropriate outlets for the inevitable build up of instinctual energy (such as competitive sport) and consequently there is a proliferation of aggression.

Lorenz also observed that in animal species, especially those which are equipped with lethal claws, beaks or teeth, the loser in a fight offers an **appeasement gesture** to the aggressor. This signal usually involves the loser exposing the weakest part of its body to the victor, and it has the effect of preventing further aggression. Lorenz argued that this serves to prevent wholesale slaughter during the regular hierarchy disputes and mating skirmishes. In humans, appeasement gestures are not well developed since we are not naturally well equipped for killing each other bare-handed. However, Lorenz believed that the danger of human aggression lies in our lack of appeasement gestures combined with our ability to use technology to inflict great harm.

Accounts of aggression such as Lorenz's which are based on universal instincts leave a great deal to be explained. They do not explain why some people act more aggressively than others; when someone's 'aggressive needs' will be satisfied; or how aggression might be eliminated as a way of behaving. Furthermore, extrapolations from a range of animal species to human behaviour may ignore the variety of human behaviour and the impact of the social context in determining behaviour.

## 2.2  Aggression as a drive

Lorenz's explanation of behaviour in terms of pent-up energy bears many resemblances to the hydraulic model proposed by psychodynamic theorists such as Freud. As was discussed in Chapter 4, psychodynamic theorists believe that the energy which drives human behaviour will continue to build up until it can be released in some way. The release will either be to attain the person's original goal or, where this is not possible, some form of displacement behaviour will occur; the energy will not just dissipate of its own accord. This hydraulic model was very influential in later theories of aggression, but it was difficult to test empirically as expressed in psychodynamic theory.

There have been attempts made to translate psychodynamic theory into behaviourist terms in order to subject the ideas and insights to empirical test. One example was the attempt to explain the causes of aggression made in 1939 by a team of researchers based at Yale University (Dollard et al., 1939). This influential analysis began with Freud's suggestion that the blocking of pleasure-seeking impulses of the id (either by circumstances or the operation of the super-ego) causes frustration. One of the possible responses to this frustration is aggression. By spelling out the necessary *stimuli* in the environment which cause frustration, and the aggressive *responses* to these stimuli, the Yale group worked within the behavioural tradition of studying observable behaviour. They tested their hypotheses empirically using the methods of experimental social psychology.

Dollard and his colleages used the terminology of **drives**, which refer to the internal aspects of motivation that drive behaviour. They believed that aggressive drives are in many ways like other basic drives such as hunger and thirst; just as we eat and drink to reduce our hunger and thirst, so we engage in aggressive behaviour in order to reduce our aggressive drive. However, a major difference between hunger and thirst, on the one hand, and aggression, on the other, is that hunger and thirst are governed by intrinsic physiological factors. Dollard and his colleagues believed that the aggressive drive is governed by *external* factors in the social world which block our attempts to reach a goal. They suggested that when we are working towards some goal, anything that thwarts our efforts to reach it (mostly external factors) will lead to our becoming frustrated. Frustration then arouses an aggressive drive which is only relieved by behaving in an aggressive way. This sequence is shown in Figure 14.1.

**Figure 14.1** The original frustration–aggression model
(Source: Based on Dollard *et al.* 1939)

Dollard's **frustration–aggression hypothesis** was stated boldly at the beginning of the book *Frustration and aggression*: 'This study takes as its point of departure the assumption that *aggression is always a consequence of frustration* and, contrariwise, that the existence of frustration always leads to some form of aggression.' (Dollard *et al.*, 1939, p. 1 (italics in original)).

An experiment with young children illustrates this hypothesized relationship between frustration and aggression (see Box A).

## BOX A    Frustration and aggression

Barker *et al.* (1941) frustrated young children by showing them a roomful of very attractive toys, which they were not allowed to play with. The children stood behind a screen looking at the toys, hoping to play with them, but unable to reach them. After a very long wait the children were finally allowed to play with the toys. A second group of children in this experiment were allowed to play with the toys without being frustrated first. This second group played happily with the toys, but the frustrated group, when finally given access to the toys, was extremely destructive. The children smashed the toys, throwing them against the walls and stamping on them.

On the basis of evidence from experiments such as this, and from our everyday experiences, there does seem to be the link between frustration and aggression which Dollard and his colleagues suggested. One of the important points about their hypothesis is its emphasis on the *inevitability* of the drive to aggress being triggered by frustration. This is based on the instinctual and hydraulic models which have as a central idea that the energy which drives human behaviour does not dissipate of its own accord if it cannot attain its original goal. In the context of frustration and aggression, if a person cannot aggress against the source of the frustration, he or she will not cease being angry but will **displace** the aggression onto another target. The aggressive energy aroused by frustration can only be released in some form of aggressive behaviour, although this does not always have to be overt aggression. As one of the original authors in the Yale group, Miller (1941), made clear in a refinement of the model, there may be inhibitions against behaving in an overtly aggressive way, and the energy could alternatively be released through *covert* aggression, such as aggressive fantasies. The expression of either overt or covert aggression is **cathartic**. By releasing energy the probability of further aggression is reduced until thwarting leads to further frustration (see Figure 14.1).

The frustration–aggression theory was very appealing to researchers and public alike, gaining widespread interest and acceptance. Perhaps this was due to the apparently simple way it explained the complex behaviour of aggression. Certainly it seems to accord with many everyday experiences in which aggression and hostile feelings towards others follow from being thwarted in some way.

## ACTIVITY 2

Look at some newspaper accounts of aggressive incidents and try to assess the extent to which frustration seemed to trigger the event. Is any reference made to frustration or thwarted effort? What other causes are suggested which might not be accounted for by the frustration–aggression model?

The original model put forward by Dollard and his colleagues soon began to be questioned in the light of both experimental and anecdotal evidence. As you may have found in Activity 2, there are times when aggression does not seem to have been triggered by frustration, and others where frustration does not result in any aggression. Experiments seem to suggest that aggression is most likely to be the result of frustration if a person is nearing his or her goal, expectations are high and when the frustration seems arbitrary.

A study by Harris (1974), described in Box B, demonstrates this point. This is an example of a **field study**, that is, a study which was conducted outside the psychology laboratory in the 'real world', but which employed some control of the situation. Waiting for incidents of naturally occurring frustration and aggression is time consuming and they may not be easy to observe. As a result, this study intervened to frustrate people in a natural setting in order to observe the effects on their behaviour.

This study by Harris suggests that frustration is increased when a goal is near and you are prevented from reaching it. When the interruption is unexpected, or when it seems illegitimate, the frustration is increased still further, as can be seen in an experiment by Kulick and Brown (1979) which is described in Box C.

The studies in Boxes B and C suggest that being thwarted will lead to most frustration, and hence to greater amounts of aggression, when people are near their goal, when they expect to succeed and when the blocking does not seem justified. When frustration is less, the chances of aggression resulting are much less. These findings do not contradict Dollard *et al.*'s model, but they do refine it, since they show that frustration will not *always* lead to aggression as the original hypothesis suggested.

The results of these studies may seem to be 'just common sense', and indeed many social psychological findings have this criticism levelled at them, as we

## BOX B   Aggression and nearness to a goal

Male or female confederates of the researcher pushed into queues of people in a number of different locations, such as outside cinemas, at bus stops and at supermarket check-outs. In one condition (high level of frustration), they pushed in front of the person who was second in the queue, and in the other condition (mild level of frustration), they pushed in front of the twelfth person in the queue. The first condition was expected to produce higher levels of frustration since the people who were second in line were nearer to their goal than those who were twelfth in line when they were thwarted, and this was hypothesized to have a strong effect on the level of frustration experienced. This was indeed what Harris found, as Figure 14.2 shows. The subjects' responses were recorded on a scale of 0 to 2 by observers, with 0 being no response and 1 a somewhat aggressive verbal response. (None of the subjects scored 2, for a physically aggressive response.)

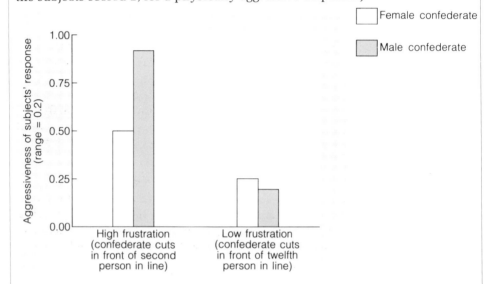

**Figure 14.2** Subjects who were close to their goal were more aggressive towards a confederate who thwarted their reaching it than subjects who were distant from their goal. (Source: Based on data from Harris, 1974)

saw in Chapter 1, Section 2. However, social psychology has the valuable role of testing out and systematizing those theories which we all hold about ourselves and other people. And whilst some studies, such as those just discussed, may confirm lay theories, others come up with counter-intuitive findings and so challenge and occasionally change 'common sense'. Some of these counter-intuitive findings will be discussed later in this chapter.

There is another challenge to the frustration–aggression hypothesis: that aggression can occur in the *absence* of frustration. Does frustration drive a bomber pilot to drop bombs on a target? Could someone who performed a copy-cat murder of a stranger based on the plot of a film plausibly claim that

---

**BOX C   Unexpected and illegitimate interruptions**

In this study, subjects were told that they could earn money by telephoning people and persuading them to make pledges of money to charity. Some of the subjects were led to expect that a high proportion of people (about two-thirds of those approached) would make pledges when asked, and others were told not to expect a very high response. The subjects then telephoned people who were in fact all confederates of the experimenter, none of whom pledged any money at all. The subjects who had high expectations exhibited more aggression than the other subjects, slamming down the phones and speaking more harshly. Some of the respondents were told to give legitimate reasons for not making pledges (such as 'I can't afford it'), whereas others gave less legitimate reasons ('charities are a waste of time and a rip-off'). Subjects who heard these less justifiable reasons also exhibited greater aggression than those who heard the legitimate reasons.

---

he or she was frustrated? Is not the definition of frustration rather stretched if we include cases where people hit out at others who have attacked them? You may like to look back at some of the newspaper reports of aggressive incidents which you found for Activity 2, and see if they seem to be the result of prior frustration. You should remember, though, that the frustration–aggression link has become firmly rooted in commonsense explanations of violence and aggression, and the reports may imply prior frustration when it either did not occur or when the cause is unknown.

It certainly seems that factors other than frustration can trigger aggression. Two main factors which we will deal with here are the *learning of aggression* and the *following of orders*. Since both of these have received tremendous coverage in their own right, and not as challenges to the frustration–aggression hypothesis, we will examine them in Section 3.

## 2.3  Limitations of individualistic analysis

Can social phenomena such as aggression be explained by looking only at individuals? In this section we have looked at two accounts of aggression using the individual level of explanation. Theories like Dollard *et al.*'s attempt to take a complex social phenomenon and explain it in terms of general psychological processes located within individuals. This move from social events to establishing the psychological processes believed to determine them is a common one in psychology. Both the instinctive and the frustration–aggression models suggest that it is something about individuals and their psychological make-up which causes aggression: an inevitable build up of energy leads to aggressive behaviour. The frustration–aggression model also looks beyond the individual, seeing the tension as being triggered by factors in the environment which thwart the individual's attempts to reach a goal. Nevertheless the explanation of aggression proposed by Dollard *et al.* lies in the individual's internally driven response to this thwarting.

Most of the frustration–aggression experiments, such as those described in Boxes A, B and C, have concerned incidents of interpersonal aggression. One person frustrates another and this then leads to an aggressive response against the frustrator. In these settings, the explanation offered by the frustration–aggression model with its individualistic emphasis may seem appropriate. But, can this model be extended to explain what is happening when a person aggresses against a member of another social group (such as an ethnic minority) simply because he or she is a member of that group rather than as a result of any personal frustration? On the face of it, the frustration–aggression model seems inadequate to explain such intergroup aggression.

Nevertheless, the second half of Dollard et al.'s (1939) monograph dealt extensively with the social implications of the frustration–aggression hypothesis, and they sought to explain a number of issues such as racial prejudice. Since then, both social psychologists (such as Berkowitz, whose work will be discussed in the next section) and political scientists have applied the theory to instances of civil turmoil, riots and revolutions.

How do frustration–aggression theorists extend their concepts to these large-scale acts of aggression? The frustration–aggression explanation of intergroup conflict is based on the notion of displacement. Dollard et al. argued that frustration is a necessary and inevitable part of living in an organized society. We have to accept certain limitations on our freedom in order to allow society to function. Social order would collapse if every individual responded with overt aggression to every frustration. For this reason, they argued that social pressures ensure that the aggression is displaced onto individuals or groups who are not part of mainstream society. These minority groups are blamed for the inevitable frustrations of everyday life and have a number of aggressive responses displaced onto them.

This account based on displacement is, however, still individually based. Despite being a group topic, it remains an essentially individual explanation. It suggests, for example, that a crowd of rioters behaves aggressively towards another group because all the rioters simultaneously experience the same level of frustration and coincidentally choose the same group on which to displace their aggression. This ignores the many factors which may be operating within the crowd; for instance, the way common goals are established and group cohesion maintained. As Turner and Giles (1981) put it, it is a bit like saying that

. . . several hundred people eating their lunch at the same time in the same cafeteria do so because, and only because, they are all hungry—an explanation which ignores such important socially determined factors as the prevailing norms about appropriate mealtimes, the time people are allowed off from work, and the availability of alternative hostelries.

(Turner and Giles, 1981, p. 45)

Turner and Giles believe that we cannot hope to explain people's social behaviour without taking into account the social context in which it naturally occurs. In social psychology recently, there has been a growing concern with studying this social context and with seeing people as members of groups, rather than as collections of individuals (Steiner, 1986). This was a strong theme of Mead's social philosophy, discussed in Chapter 2. However, it was not immediately taken up by social psychologists, perhaps because many were trained in the more individualistic discipline of psychology rather than in the more group-orientated discipline of sociology. However, Mead's belief that the group is the focal point of social psychology is now more widely held by social psychologists and the implications of this view are becoming evident in current research.

We are not in social psychology building up the behaviour of the social group in terms of the behaviour of the separate individuals composing it, rather we are starting out with a given social whole of complex group activity, into which we analyze (as elements) the behavior of each of the separate individuals composing it.

(Mead, 1934, p. 7)

In the rest of this chapter, we will be discussing social psychological explanations of aggression which place greater emphasis on the social context within which people operate, and which do not seek to explain an individual's behaviour solely in terms of internal motivational states or instinctive drives. These explanations stress the need to take into account a number of social factors which influence the emergence of aggression as a group phenomenon. Some of the explanations discussed may appear to do this more than others. It may help to think about the types of explanation available for behaviour as occupying different points along a continuum from the most individualistic to the most social. For some issues in social psychology, such as how we explain why a person is attracted to a particular other, a more individual or interpersonal explanation may be appropriate, but explanations for other issues, such as rioting, will more appropriately draw on wider group and intergroup factors. Deciding which is the appropriate type of explanation in each case is not straightforward or uncontroversial; it is a major area of debate in social psychology.

## Summary of Section 2

- Lorenz's theory of aggressive instincts suggests that an inevitable build up of energy results in aggressive behaviour which serves an evolutionary purpose for animals, in regulating fights over mates for example.

- The psychodynamic theorists propose a hydraulic model which has similarities to Lorenz's theory.

- Dollard et al. (1939) attempted to translate this model into behaviourist terms to test it experimentally. They suggested that a drive to aggress is triggered by attempts to reach a goal being thwarted, which results in frustration.

- Dollard et al.'s claims that frustration always leads to aggression and that aggression is always the result of frustration have been challenged and refined.

- The issue of the level of explanation appropriate for the study of aggression and other social phenomena is complex. A 'group' topic, such as racial prejudice, may still be explained at the individual level by the frustration–aggression model. However, the group level of explanation is generally seen as more appropriate for social psychology. A continuum between the most individual and the most social explanations was proposed.

# 3 | Individuals in context

In this section we will examine explanations for aggression which take more account of the social context in which the aggressive individual operates than the instinctual and drive theories. This is not to say that they offer entirely social explanations; they still focus on individuals, but they do place the individual into a social context. As such they can be seen as lying further along the hypothesized continuum towards social explanations than the theories discussed in Section 2.

The explanations examined here include analyses of the *cues* in the environment which trigger violence, the *imitation* of aggressive behaviour and *obeying orders* to act aggressively. Each of the studies presented comes firmly from experimental social psychology, and they provide examples of the method many social psychologists employ (the laboratory experiment), the ethical problems raised by these experiments, the type of data they generate, and the findings which emerge. Issues of methodology, data and ethics are important for social psychology generally, and we will discuss these again in more detail after considering these examples. In later sections, different methods used by social psychologists will be introduced and contrasted with such laboratory experiments.

## 3.1 Contextual cues for aggression

Berkowitz (1974) has proposed a theory which deals mainly with impulsive aggression. As he has noted, relatively few murders are the result of premeditation; most are 'spontaneous acts of passion' carried out quickly and impulsively. Aggression of this type, he argues, may be elicited by observation of aggression carried out by others or, in some cases, by the mere presence of the instruments of violence such as knives and guns.

In explaining aggression, Berkowitz, like Dollard *et al.* (1939), views frustration as an important antecedent. However, in common with others, he believes that the claims made in the original formulation were too sweeping and he has called for some modifications and qualifications to the frustration–aggression hypothesis. In his words, he is 'deviating somewhat from the letter (but not the philosophy) of the 1939 monograph' (1962, p. 49) in proposing his **aggressive cue theory**. Instead of suggesting a one-to-one relationship between frustration and aggression, he stresses the role of mediating factors within the environment. Whilst frustration still creates a state of anger or arousal, whether or not this results in aggression will depend on the existence of appropriate situational cues for aggression. Without such cues there will be no aggressive behaviour.

These **aggressive cues** can be people or objects that have acquired an **aggressive cue value** through some association with anger arousal, witnessed violence, or aggression generally. Berkowitz suggests that, once the people or objects have acquired this cue value, then their presence can elicit an aggressive response from an angered person. It follows from this that an angry person will be unlikely to behave aggressively if there are no aggressive cues in the setting at that time.

Berkowitz and his colleagues have investigated the aggressive cue value of a number of different types of stimuli. These include characteristics of people (their names or faces) and objects such as weapons. In a controversial series of experiments, Berkowitz has demonstrated a so-called **weapons effect**, by which he means that an angry person is more likely to behave aggressively towards another if he is in the presence of a weapon, and particularly if the weapon is in some way linked to the victim; see Figure 14.3. The basic experiment by Berkowitz and LePage (1967) is described in Box D overleaf.

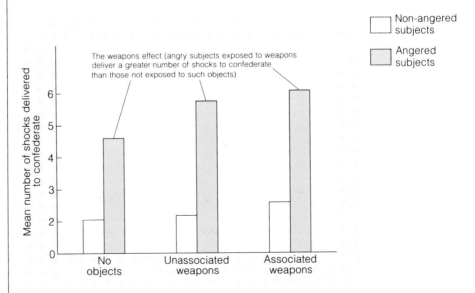

**Figure 14.3** The weapons effect. The physical presence of weapons elicited aggressive behaviour from angry subjects.
(Source: Based on data from Berkowitz and LePage, 1967)

## BOX D   Does the trigger pull the finger?

Subjects were told that they would be involved in an experiment on the effects of stress on problem solving. Each subject worked with another person who had been introduced as a subject but was in fact a confederate of the researcher. Both were asked to try to work out the solution to a problem. Stress was introduced by getting each of them to evaluate the other's solution to the problem. They had to express their evaluations by giving each other from one to ten (very mild) electric shocks.

In one condition, the confederates gave the subjects one very mild electric shock; in the second condition, the subjects were given seven mild shocks, supposedly as the confederates' evaluation of their work (but in fact randomly decided by the researcher). Whilst the subjects believed that these shocks were given to assess the effect of stress on their problem solving abilities, the experiment was really designed to see how the subjects who received seven shocks would react towards the confederate. These subjects should feel very angry towards the confederate and would therefore be more likely to aggress against him. But, according to Berkowitz's theory, they would only act aggressively if aggressive cues were present. The subjects who received only one shock should not feel angry towards the confederate because he had given them the least unpleasant feedback possible in the circumstances.

Subjects then had their turn to 'evaluate' the confederate's work. They pressed a button on a machine in front of them (the 'aggression machine') to determine the number of shocks which they wished to give the confederate. In fact no shocks were administered to the confederate as the machine was bogus. The researcher assessed the subjects' level of aggression by counting the number of shocks they believed they were administering. In one condition (the 'no weapons' condition), the subject only had the 'aggression machine' in the room with him. In another condition (the 'unassociated weapons' condition) a revolver and a shotgun were also in the room and the subject was told they were being used for another experiment later that day. In the 'associated weapons' condition, the weapons were said to belong to the conferedate who was going to use them in a study of his own later that day.

The results supported Berkowitz's theory. All the angered subjects responded more aggressively to the confederate than the non-angered subjects. Those who were angered and had been in the presence of weapons responded even more aggressively, and most aggressively of all in the 'associated weapons' condition (see Figure 14.3).

Berkowitz and LePage's results have some very far reaching implications for gun control and perhaps also the argument about arming the police force. As Berkowitz (1968) put it: 'Guns not only permit violence, they stimulate it as well. The finger pulls the trigger, but the trigger may also be pulling the finger' (p. 22). His results have stimulated much research but have also been heavily criticized (e.g. Zillman, 1978) and some researchers have not been able to replicate the effect (e.g. Buss et al., 1972). Many of the criticisms concern Berkowitz's method of studying aggression. You may yourself have wondered what this type of experiment can *really* tell us about aggression. The ethics, realism and validity of his laboratory techniques have all been called into question. However, since many of these criticisms also apply to other experimental studies which we will be discussing next, we will delay the examination of these criticisms until the end of the section where issues about all the experiments can be covered together.

Berkowitz's studies are important because they have stimulated a vast amount of research into the nature and strength of contextual cues for aggression. As we noted in our discussion of the frustration–aggression hypothesis, not *all* frustrated or angered people will behave aggressively, and Berkowitz has begun to indicate the type of factors which might determine when actual aggression is more likely to occur.

## 3.2  Social learning and imitation

Another approach to aggression suggests that, as with so much other behaviour, aggression is acquired and maintained as a result of positive reinforcement. According to **social learning theory**, aggression is a behaviour which has to be *learned* rather than being the direct result of frustration, or mediated by contextual cues. The implication is that, without learning, children would not naturally be aggressive.

It is clear in observations of children, for example, that aggression *can* become associated with positive reinforcement. The child who pushes another out of the way to reach a toy is rewarded by getting it; the winner in a playground fight is rewarded by enhanced status among the other children. This social learning approach is based on **instrumental learning**, which was discussed in detail in Chapter 6. According to instrumental conditioning theory, the probability that behaviour will be repeated on later occasions is increased as a result of positive reinforcement.

Bandura, one of the foremost proponents of social learning theory, has suggested that another process known as **modelling** is also involved in aggressive behaviour. This is the process whereby people learn new behaviour, including aggression, through observation of the actions of others (called 'models') and of the results of their actions.

## BOX E   The Bobo doll studies (Bandura *et al.*, 1963)

These studies involved aggression towards an inanimate object, a large inflatable 'Bobo doll'. Children in the experimental group watched an adult model who behaved in an aggressive way towards the doll when left in a playroom by the researcher. (Children saw the adult model through a one-way mirror.) The model performed a number of specific, novel aggressive acts towards the doll, such as striking it with a hammer, throwing it in the air, punching, kicking it and saying things like 'Pow . . . boom . . . boom'. These particular actions were used because the children would be unlikely to perform them spontaneously. Thus, if the children displayed them the researcher could be confident that they were imitating the model.

After they had seen the model, the children were left in the playroom for 10 to 20 minutes and their behaviour was observed by the researchers. A control group of children was not shown the model before being allowed to play in the playroom with the same toys as the experimental group. The experimental group's behaviour towards the doll very closely resembled that of the model, whereas the control group did not display any of these actions. These results suggested that the children who had witnessed the model's aggression had imitated the behaviour of the model.

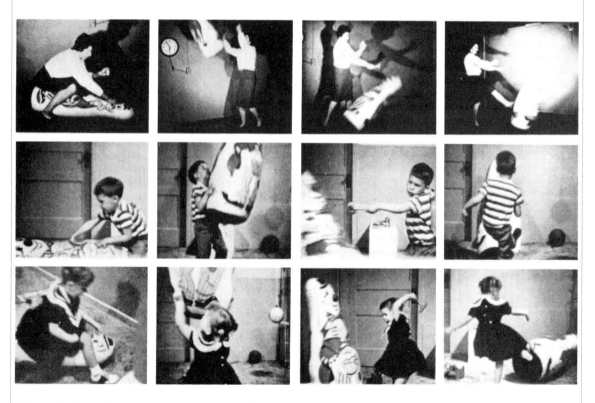

**Figure 14.4** Adult models and children attacking the Bobo doll
(Source: Bandura, 1977)

Imitation, in the minds of most people, means reponse mimicry—the exact duplication of what the model does. The term carries a very narrow connotation . . . I use the term modeling because the psychological effects of exposure to models are much broader. The more interesting effect of modeling is what I call 'abstract modeling'. From observing examples, people derive general rules and principles of behaviour which permit them to go beyond what they see and hear.

(Bandura, 1980, p. 160)

In a series of studies (see Box E), Bandura and his colleagues have shown that children display novel aggressive behaviours which they have acquired simply by observing the verbally and physically aggressive behaviour of another person (a model).

In a later experiment using the same format (Bandura, 1965), the children who saw the model acting aggressively towards the doll were divided into three groups. One went straight into the playroom. A second group saw the model being *rewarded* for the aggressive actions against the doll before going into the playroom, while a third group saw the model being *punished*. As Figure 14.5 shows, the children who saw the model being punished for aggression displayed significantly less aggressive behaviour towards the doll than those who saw the model rewarded or those who saw no consequences.

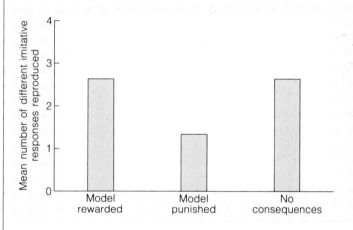

**Figure 14.5** The mean number of imitated aggressive behaviours exhibited by children after observing models being rewarded, punished or receiving no feedback for aggression. (Source: Based on Bandura, 1965)

This would seem to suggest that seeing a model punished leads to less learning of the model's behaviour. However, a further stage in the experiment yielded some interesting findings. After the children had played in the playroom with the doll, Bandura offered them all rewards to behave like the adult model had done, and asked them to return to the playroom to try to do what the model had done with the doll. The results from this part of the study are presented in Table 14.1. They show that in the first stage of the experiment the consequences for the adult had an effect on the children's behaviour. But in the second stage of the experiment the children showed that they had in fact acquired the behaviour by observing the model since they could perform it when asked, and they were given a reward for doing so.

**Table 14.1** Mean number of imitated aggressive actions by children. In the first stage, after observing models who were rewarded, punished or received no feedback for aggression. In the second stage, when the children had been asked to demonstrate the model's behaviour. (Source: Bandura, 1965)

|  | Model rewarded | Model punished | No consequences |
|---|---|---|---|
| First stage | 2.5 | 1.5 | 2.5 |
| Second stage | 3.5 | 3.6 | 3.5 |

As you can see from this second part of the experiment, the incentive offered to the children to behave like the model eradicated all the differences between them according to whether they had seen the model being rewarded or punished. It seems that those children who had seen the model being punished had still learned the behaviour, but would only behave in that way themselves if offered an incentive. Bandura suggested that a clear distinction might be made between the *acquisition* of aggressive responses and the *performance* of aggressive acts. He suggested that modelling is sufficient for aggressive behaviour to be acquired, but that reinforcement is necessary for aggressive acts to be actually performed.

Bandura suggested that there were three principal sources of aggressive models: the family, the sub-culture and the mass media. There has been considerable research interest in his idea that aggression can be acquired simply by observational learning. Of the three sources of models, the mass media and, particularly, violence on television has been most heavily investigated. If children can learn aggressive behaviour simply by seeing it enacted, then television programmes in which an aggressor is the hero could contribute to children acquiring a large repertoire of aggressive behaviours. Understandably, this issue has become a very important one for researchers since it addresses a real life problem which is important to many people, and it will be discussed further in Section 4.4.

## 3.3 Obedience to authority

We noted earlier that many acts of aggression (such as wartime aggression by soldiers and bomber pilots) do not seem to be the result of frustration but are planned and carried out as a result of other motives. These acts cannot be explained by drive or instinctual theories. We need to look at the social context, such as the hierarchy of command within the armed forces and the notion of obeying without question. These are the questions which stimulated a highly publicized research programme by Milgram (1963; 1965; 1974). Milgram made some unexpected findings about the disturbing lengths to which ordinary people would go when obeying orders (see Box F).

Milgram's results were obtained with the experimenter saying only, 'Please continue', and later, 'The experiment requires that you continue' when the subject expressed unwillingness to carry on giving the shocks. The experimenter had no real authority over the subjects to make them continue. Also, since the subjects had been paid for participating in the experiment before the session, payment did not provide an incentive to stay until the end.

## BOX F   Obedience in the laboratory

In contrast to many social psychology experiments, this research did not use university students. Men between 20 and 50 years of age were recruited as subjects for this experiment through an advert in a local paper asking for volunteers to take part in a 'scientific study of memory and learning'. Each subject was introduced to another man, ostensibly another subject, but in fact a confederate of the experimenter. The confederate had been specially trained to respond in a particular way during the experiment.

The experimenter (dressed in a white coat) told the two men that they would be assigned a role as either the teacher or learner, and the teacher would then proceed to teach the learner to remember a list of word pairs. The two men drew lots to decide who was to take each role, but in fact this was rigged so that the genuine subject always became the teacher. The subject then saw the learner being strapped into a chair and attached to electrodes (electrical connections) which linked up to a shock generator. The learner at this point mentioned that he had heart trouble but the experimenter assured him that, 'Although the shocks can be extremely painful, they cause no permanent tissue damage.' The subject was then shown into a separate room where the shock generator was placed on a table (see Figure 14.6).

The subject was told that each time the learner made a mistake in remembering the list of word pairs, he was to administer a shock by pressing one of the thirty switches on the shock generator. The first switch was labelled '15 volts—mild shock', the next '30 volts' and so on up to '450 volts—XXX', and the subject was told to start by pressing the 15 volt switch and then move one switch up the scale each time the learner made a mistake.

When all the instructions were clear, the session began. Milgram wanted to know how far up the scale of shocks the subjects would go when told to continue by the experimenter, despite hearing cries and pounding on the wall from the learner asking the subject to stop giving the shocks and, later, the learners' complete silence. The results were unexpected and dramatic; as you can see from Figure 14.7 (overleaf), 65 per cent of the men proceeded up to the 450 volt level. At the end of the session (when the subject had reached 450 volts or had refused to continue) the true purpose of the experiment was revealed and the subjects were told that no shocks had in fact been delivered to the learner.

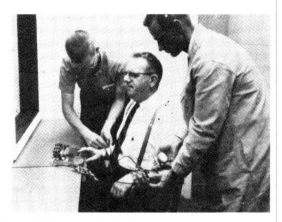

**Figure 14.6** Milgram's apparatus, and the confederate learner being attached to it
(Source: Milgram, 1963)

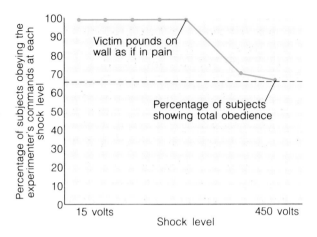

**Figure 14.7** Surprisingly, many subjects obeyed the experimenter's command that they increase the strength of electric shock to the full 450 volts
(Source: Based on data from Milgram, 1963)

SAQ 4    What factors about the experimental situation might have made the subjects feel the experimenter should be obeyed?

From Milgram's research it would seem that ordinary people are all too likely to act aggressively towards another person when following the commands of even a spurious authority figure. They do not seem to be acting from any feelings of frustration or instinct, but are responding to social pressure. Later work by Milgram emphasized the importance of such pressure. In one experiment, (Milgram, 1965), the level of obedience was reduced from 65 per cent to just 10 per cent when the subject was in the presence of two confederates of the experimenter (ostensibly other subjects) who refused to obey the commands to administer the shocks (see Figure 14.8).

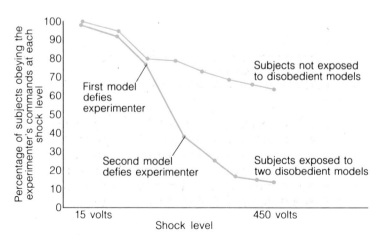

**Figure 14.8** Subjects' obedience to the experimenter's command decreased in the presence of other subjects (confederates) who disobeyed
(Source: Based on data from Milgram, 1965)

This is an effective means of counteracting the experimenter's power over the subject since he sees that disobeying the experimenter does not result in any ill-effects. The experimenter is seen to have no real power to force the subject to continue with the shocks. Also, a subject who did not wish to administer the shocks (and from the way the subjects became upset during the experiment, this would seem to be almost all of them) would have received strong social support from finding that he was not alone in these feelings. This support from his peers was powerful enough to overcome the commands of the experimenter, something most of the subjects could not do alone.

The power exerted by peers can also be seen in another variation of Milgram's basic experiment (1964). In this version, the experimenter did not require that the level of shocks should be increased after every mistake made by the learner, and was not present after the experiment got under way. Two confederates of the experimenter, posing as other subject teachers, continually urged the subject to increase the level of shock given. As can be seen in Figure 14.9 this social pressure led to an *increase* in the severity of the shocks which the subject gave the learner, as compared with other subjects who, in the absence of the experimenter and the confederates, continue to administer the lowest level of shock.

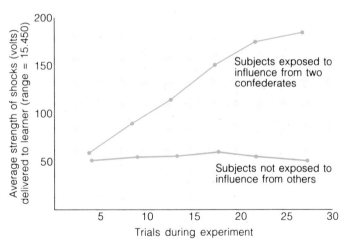

**Figure 14.9** Subjects applied stronger electric shocks when pressured to do so by other subjects (confederates)
(Source: Based on data from Milgram, 1964)

Milgram's research has pointed out some important features of the influence of social pressures of a group on a person. Someone given orders to hurt another person, either from a figure in authority or from his peers, seems to act in ways which are unexpected and disturbing. Given the support of similar other people who rebel against an unjust authority, many more people are able to resist the orders to obey. Explanations of aggression which fail to look at these powerful social forces seem unable to explain why the subjects in Milgram's research behaved as they did.

Before discussing further research on group pressures, the status of all the studies discussed in this section needs to be evaluated. The experimental research of Berkowitz, Bandura and Milgram raises questions of methodology, ethics and realism. Since such criticisms can justifiably be levelled at many social psychology experiments, we will examine some of the criticisms in more detail.

## 3.4 Experimentation in social psychology: people as subjects

Laboratory-based experimental studies have dominated social psychological research, especially in the United States, for many years. Such experimental studies are seen as having a number of advantages over other methods for studying social behaviour, notably in their ability to control factors influencing behaviour and to randomly assign individuals to different experimental conditions. As a result of this control and random allocation of subjects, many argue (e.g. Aronson *et al.*, 1985; Berkowitz, 1989) that we can learn a good deal about the causes of a particular behaviour. By altering the conditions in which groups of children watched adult models in Bandura *et al.*'s study, or the number of peers present in Milgram's experiment, for example, the experimenters can test explicit hypotheses about the causal links between factors. Correlational studies in the real world can never yield such precise information since they can only say which factors vary along with the behaviour, and not which cause it. Understanding causation, many believe, should be the principal aim of all branches of psychology. However, a number of criticisms have been levelled at this approach to studying social behaviour and many new methods have recently flourished as a reaction against such laboratory experiments. Here we will consider the major criticisms and the response to them from the proponents of the experimental approach.

A major issue with laboratory studies of phenomena such as aggression concerns their **ecological validity**. This is the extent to which we can extrapolate from the results of an experiment to real-life situations. An important factor which might limit generalization on the basis of experimental findings is the artificial nature of the laboratory. If the setting for the experiment is very contrived and artificial, then the chance of people behaving in the same way in the laboratory as they do outside can be questioned. Some psychologists would argue that to study issues such as aggression, the researcher must look for naturally occurring incidents, and that it is impossible to reproduce and study such behaviour in a psychology laboratory. As one critic of the experimental approach puts it:

Laboratory studies may tell us about certain general features of aggression, but to seek to understand a specific form of aggression such as child abuse or violence by children at school through a laboratory model would be to divest it of its specific context and meaning. Real-life acts of violence are embedded in a web of social structures, relationships, and interactions that provide them with a setting which needs to be considered in understanding their meaning.

(Archer, 1989, p. 28)

Berkowitz (1989), however, replies that it is not of prime importance for the experimental situation to mirror real life outside the laboratory. He believes that an experiment is designed in order to establish the causal link between two factors (such as the presence of weapons and the display of aggression), and that all other extraneous variables should be removed or controlled. As long as the subject sees the experiment as meaningful and gets fully involved in it, the experiment can be said to have **experimental realism**. With such realism, the subjects will be caught up in the scenario of the experiment to such an extent that they will behave realistically and provide useful data on the existence of a link between the factors. It is then the place of field studies to establish whether, in the more complex social world outside the laboratory, any link between these factors remains.

This argument does not do justice, however, to the complex social world *within* the laboratory. Silverman and Shulman (1970) suggested that doing experiments with humans is like doing chemistry with dirty test tubes. In experiments with humans, the contaminants are the needs, motives, values and expectations of the people participating in the research wherever it is conducted. The individuals participating in psychological research do not come to the laboratory like blank slates, ready to perform tasks without questioning them. They do not suspend their extensive knowledge of the real world just because they are in an experiment. They use this knowledge to make sense of the situation they are in (although by calling them 'subjects' many would argue that this 'blank slate' view is easier to maintain).

Orne (1962) has argued that people taking part in experiments act in very much the same way as anyone placed in a novel situation. People characteristically search for meaning and order in their environments. When in a new situation, they are especially likely to be looking for clues about what is going on and how they are supposed to behave. In an experiment, individuals will try to work out the hypothesis and discover what is expected of them by the researcher. To do this, they are likely to be responding to the **demand characteristics** of the experiment. These are cues unintentionally present in what the researcher says and does and in the layout of the laboratory, that suggest what the experiment is really about and how the subject is supposed to act.

---

Think about the experiments you have read about in this section, and consider what there was in the experimental setting which might have told *you* what the study was *really* about if you had been a subject.

---

In Berkowitz and LePage's study, for example, even though people are more familiar with the sight of guns in the USA than in Britain, the sight of weapons in a psychology laboratory must have set a number of the subjects wondering about why they were there and about what the guns were meant to make them do or think.

People who have taken part in social psychology experiments before are perhaps even more likely than others to look for and respond to demand characteristics, since they may well have been deceived by a previous researcher and be wary of the rationale given for the current experiment. When researchers assume that the participants in an experiment are unaware of the hypothesis and the conditions in the experiment (referred to as **naïve**

**subjects**), they should not assume that they are equally unaware of the likelihood of deception, or that they are not trying to guess the purpose of the study. This is likely to be a particular problem because many experiments use students as subjects, who participate in several studies during the year and may even learn about such studies in their courses.

SAQ 5    Who were the subjects in the Berkowitz and LePage, Bandura *et al.*, and Milgram studies?

Another factor 'contaminating' research on humans is that of **evaluation apprehension** (Rosenberg, 1969). This means that in experiments, as in the rest of our lives, we are aware of being evaluated by others. We are therefore concerned to appear in the best possible light and be judged favourably. In everyday life we are usually too busy concentrating on other things to be consciously aware of this evaluation apprehension, but there are times when we become much more aware of how we are 'performing' and how others are judging us. Job interviews, joining a new group of people and entering a psychology laboratory for an experiment are all likely to be situations of increased self-awareness.

In experiments, the individual may be anxious to perform well and so he or she will try to establish what it is the experimenter wants to happen. In searching for clues about how to behave (by using the demand characteristics in the situation), the individual will not be responding normally as the experimenter assumed. Consequently the results may not reflect how people would react if faced with such a situation in real life.

To clarify the concepts of demand characteristics and external validity further, let us now apply them to one of the studies we have discussed previously: the Berkowitz and LePage study of aggression described in Box D. The concepts are equally relevant to other social psychology laboratory studies, but it may be helpful to discuss one example in more detail.

One major criticism of the Berkowitz and LePage (1967) weapons effect study concerned the demand characteristics of the situation (Page and Scheidt, 1971). As you may yourself have felt when reading about the study, might the subjects in the study not have wondered why the guns were on the table in the laboratory and guessed their purpose? Would they have believed the researcher's explanation for the presence of the weapons? Would *you* have believed it? Page and Scheidt suggest that the subject would have inferred that the guns were meant to affect him and, casting around for the rationale, would have guessed that they were meant to make him feel aggressive. For someone anxious to perform 'properly' in the experiment, this would have been a clue about how to behave; he should be more aggressive than he really felt.

Page and Scheidt tried to replicate the weapons effect study and then conducted extensive interviews with the participants afterwards to establish the extent of their suspicions about the experiment. They found that 81 per cent of the subjects suspected that the hypothesis was concerned with revenge against the confederate, and that many of these believed that the weapons were present in order to increase their aggressive response to the confederate.

Page and Scheidt therefore concluded that the results of the Berkowitz and LePage study could be explained by the subjects co-operating with what they (correctly) perceived to be the purpose of the study.

This is not the end of the story. Berkowitz (1971) was quick to respond to Page and Scheidt's criticisms, pointing out that, in the weapons effect study, any demand characteristics and evaluation apprehension would lead to *contradictory* cues for appropriate behaviour. Demand characteristics, which Page and Scheidt claim are present in the experiment, are likely to urge the subjects to give more shocks (in the condition where the weapons were present and where the confederate had given seven shocks) than they would normally. Evaluation apprehension, on the other hand, might lead the subjects to give fewer shocks since it is not generally seen as desirable or normal to give another person electric shocks. As a result of these contradictory cues, Berkowitz claims these concepts could not account for the weapons effect. Furthermore, he suggests that, just because subjects might have guessed the hypothesis of the study, they would not necessarily be more likely to co-operate with it. Indeed they may have been motivated to behave in such a way as to disprove the hypothesis, to protest against the researcher's attempt to manipulate them. Berkowitz suggests that the view of the 'compliant subject' which LePage and Scheidt adopt is a myth. Whilst Berkowitz may be right that some subjects would try to disprove the hypothesis in order to protest at being manipulated, this is possibly only true for people who are experienced in the experimental situation, such as the many (psychology) students who often take part in experiments. The extent to which less experienced people, such as those in Milgram's study, were motivated to either prove or disprove the hypothesis is debatable.

**Ethics**

A very important consideration in examining experiments in social psychology, and particularly experiments on aggression, is ethics. There are two main issues here. The first is that of deception, where subjects are led to believe that the purpose of an experiment is other than its real purpose. The second is that people may undergo stress or loss of self-esteem as a result of taking part in the experiment.

The first problem arises because social psychology aims to study aspects of human behaviour and influences on that behaviour of which people are not always aware. If subjects were told what was being observed, they would then become aware of that behaviour and consequently change it. You can imagine that if any of the people in the experiments discussed here had been told that the investigators were studying, for example, the power of an illegitimate authority, or the effect of the presence of weapons on aggression, they would have behaved very differently in the experiment. By being alerted to these influences which normally operate below the level of awareness, they would not then be able to behave naturally.

The problem for social psychology is that attempting to study behaviour of which people may be unaware seems to necessitate some form of deception. There are two alternatives to using deception. The first is to tell subjects exactly what is being studied, and then to ask them to behave in the experiment as they would normally; that is, to **role-play** their usual behaviour. This may be a valuable strategy for some experiments, but the question remains about how the researcher can know whether this role-playing accurately represents what does happen normally. A second strategy is to observe people unobtrusively in their natural settings in a **field study**. However, even this apparently innocuous type of research has ethical problems. Should data be collected on people without their knowledge or consent? Researchers are open to the charge of invading people's privacy.

If deception is used, how can people give their informed consent to taking part in the experiment when they do not know what the experiment is really about? This raises the second main ethical issue: the possible stress or the loss of self-esteem that might be experienced by participants in the research. Where deception is used they have no reliable information about such consequences on which to base their decision about whether or not to be involved. Perhaps the most striking example of this is in Milgram's obedience studies where participants appeared very distressed during the experiment and had to face the knowledge that they had been prepared to inflict such harm on another innocent person.

Milgram responded to criticisms of his experiment in two ways. First, he explained that he did not expect the participants to go to such lengths in giving shocks to the learners. He had asked many people, including psychiatrists, what level of shocks they would expect a person to go up to in the experiment before they refused to continue. No one had expected the results which Milgram actually found, so, he argued, he had not begun the experiment with the expectation that the participants would suffer as they did.

His second response to critics (e.g. Baumrind, 1964) was to reveal the results of a follow-up study which he conducted with all the participants in his research one year later. In a survey of the participants, Milgram (1964) reported that 84 per cent of them were 'glad to have taken part in the experiment' and only 1.3 per cent were 'sorry' or 'very sorry to have taken part in the experiment'.

These responses may seem to cover the criticisms of the controversial experiment, but many social psychologists continue to question its ethics. As Kelman (1967) pointed out, many of the subjects would have experienced a loss in self-esteem from the knowledge that they were able to harm another person and were unable to resist an unjustified and inhumane authority figure. Some of these ethical problems can be alleviated by a comprehensive and carefully conducted **debriefing** after the experiment. In a debriefing session, the true purpose of the experiment is explained, any deception (such as the use of confederates and fake equipment) is revealed, and the participants are assured that their behaviour in the experiment was to be expected under those circumstances by telling them of other subjects' similar responses. The participants are also encouraged to ask questions about the study and to satisfy themselves about its purpose and what use will be made of the results.

An experiment by Ring et al. (1970), examined the value of such debriefing. They replicated Milgram's basic experiment (using female students instead of male non-students) and then one group were thanked and not debriefed.

Another group of subjects were debriefed, being told that continuing to obey the experimenter was a normal and reasonable response (as Milgram had said). The third and last group of subjects were told in the debriefing that it would have been desirable to defy the experimenter. A subsequent follow-up of these subjects found that those who had been led to think badly of their behaviour in the experiment were as upset about the experiment as those who had not been debriefed and who thought they had really hurt the learner. Despite this, only the subjects who had had no briefing actually thought the experiment was unethical or regretted being involved in it. At the follow-up stage of the study, all the subjects had the true purpose of the experiment explained to them, and they were debriefed about the reasons for it and the behaviour of other subjects in the study.

The work of Ring *et al.* does suggest that with careful and sensitive debriefing *some* of the ethical problems of experiments can be lessened. However, they studied female students, and we cannot know whether the older, non-student male population in Milgram's original study were equally reassured by this type of discussion after the experiment, despite the results of his later follow-up study. Nevertheless, the ethical guidelines for conducting social psychological studies have been considerably tightened since (and perhaps as a result of) Milgram's research. It would be almost impossible for a researcher to conduct that type of study today.

The debate will continue about the role of laboratory studies in social psychology. It is not an issue for which there is a neat solution. Some psychologists will always argue that the opportunity which a laboratory experiment provides of manipulating variables is invaluable. Others will just as strongly argue that, without the 'contamination' of human social life, the phenomenon being studied loses all real meaning.

## Summary of Section 3

- Berkowitz's aggressive cue theory suggests that frustration will result in anger, but that this will only be manifested in aggression if certain aggressive cues are present in the environment, such as weapons.

- Social learning theory suggests that all aggressive responses are learned by modelling the behaviour of other people. Seeing an aggressive model punished may inhibit the expression of aggression by a person, but will not have lessened the chance of the person having learned the behaviour.

- Milgram's study suggested that people were surprisingly obedient to a spurious authority figure who instructed them to give high voltage shocks to another person. The presence of other people in the room was shown to be crucial. If they defied the experimenter, so would the subject, but if they appeared to support the experimenter, the subject did not resist them.

- All these studies raise important ethical and methodological issues for social psychology. Laboratory experiments are seen as providing the control of variables necessary to establish causality. They are however likely to have low ecological validity, and to suffer from the effects on subjects' behaviour of evaluation apprehension and demand characteristics in the experimental setting.

- Ethical issues are difficult to resolve. In studying social phenomena, deception has become rife in social psychology, yet it means the subjects cannot give their informed consent to take part in the study and may suffer a loss of self-esteem as a result of what they find out about themselves.

- Debriefing is a way of reducing, but by no means eliminating, some of these ethical problems.

# 4 | The power of the group

In this section we will move to a rather different level of analysis. In Sections 2 and 3 we looked at an individual's aggression, caused by internal factors or the context of social behaviour. The level of explanation these theories offer is either intra-individual or, at most, inter-individual. The frustration–aggression model, for example, explains aggression as the result of external thwarting conditions arousing an internal drive to aggress. There is little reference to what actually happens in the interaction between the people involved. Milgram's research is the most 'social' perspective we have so far encountered, since this explanation of aggression lies in the relationship between the authority figure and the subject, and since the presence of other subjects had a clear impact on the level of obedience and hence of aggression.

In this section we will look at theories of aggression which use the group level of analysis. Aggression can be explained, not so much by reference to the characteristics of individuals within the group, as to the effects of the group on its members and of interactions between groups. This research suggests that there are powerful pressures to conform within a group. These pressures may result in aggression since members of a group are seen to behave in a hostile way towards non-members simply as a result of their membership of that group and the pressures within it to conform.

## 4.1 Conformity

The pressure to fit in with the expectations of a group, known as **conformity**, is a widely established finding in social psychological research. As we saw in the discussion of social comparison theory in Section 4 of Chapter 2, there are considerable rewards in being a member of a group. For example, members of a group of similar others can get the support they need for their attitudes and views of the world from finding that these views are shared by other people. If they do not share attitudes, there is considerable pressure on them either to change their attitudes to conform with the rest of the group or to leave the group. Many people fear such rejection and thus pay the cost of conformity to remain a member of the group and to receive its support.

A classic experiment in the United States by Asch (1955) influenced much of the subsequent work on groups. He clearly demonstrated the tendency of individuals to conform to the views of other members of a group (see Box G), and later work on aggression and hostility between groups has drawn on these findings a great deal.

## BOX G   Asch's study of conformity

Asch devised a novel means for studying conformity. One subject was seated in a room with six other people, ostensibly other subjects but in fact confederates of the experimenter. The experimenter told the group that the experiment was concerned with accuracy of perception and showed them two cards. On one card was a single line, and on the other were three lines (A, B and C) of different lengths. One of these lines (C) was the same length as that on the first card (see Figure 14.10).

A     B     C

**Figure 14.10** An example of the stimuli used by Asch

The experimenter told the subjects that their task was to match the single line with the line of equal length from the three-line card, and that they were to respond in turn by calling out the name of the line chosen (A, B or C). There were a number of trials with different sets of cards for each trial. For each trial, the real subject gave his response second from last in the group. Thus he heard the responses from five confederates before giving his own. In the first two trials, the confederates all gave the correct answer but, in the following 16 trials, they were only correct on four occasions. In the other trials, the confederates consistently gave the wrong response, all saying, for example, that line A (in Figure 14.10) was the same length as the single line, instead of the correct line C.

There were great individual differences in the results. About a quarter of the subjects withstood the pressure from the group of confederates and *always* gave the correct response. Others apparently denied the evidence of their own eyes and conformed to the incorrect judgement of the other members of the group in every trial, with many falling between these two extremes and conforming in only one or two trials.

A very few of the conforming subjects in Asch's experiment reported afterwards that they had actually *seen* the wrong line as correct. Others felt that the majority were probably correct (the confederates had after all established their credibility by responding correctly at the beginning of the experiment) and had consciously changed their own judgements to fit in with the majority. Still others had no doubt that their own judgements were correct, but agreed in public with the majority to avoid being the 'odd one out'. This brings us to an important distinction between *public compliance* and *private change*. Although the observed response of all these subjects was the same (i.e. of conformity to an incorrect group decision), the *meaning* of this response for each of these groups of subjects was entirely different. Some seemed to have undergone a real change of opinion and actually felt that the group decision was correct (**private change**). Others were merely complying with the group publicly, but in private their own opinion remained unchanged (**public compliance**). It might be expected that, after the experiment in the absence of the group, those who had undergone private change would continue to give the incorrect response, whereas those who had only been complying in the presence of the group would revert to their own (correct) judgement.

Asch's research appears to provide clear-cut experimental evidence for conformity to a group, but some attempts to replicate it have suggested that the picture is a little more complicated. For instance, when Milgram (1961) compared Norwegian and French students as subjects, the Norwegians conformed more than the French. Thus the finding is not universal; it does not hold for all cultures. (Incidentally, Milgram believed that the difference between the nationalities could be accounted for by the greater diversity in French lifestyles with the Norwegians being generally less tolerant of divergence.)

In 1974, Larsen replicated the Asch experiment in the United States but failed to obtain the same results as Asch had done. Larsen suggested that this was due to the changed social climate in the country over the years, with the students of the early 1970s being less conforming that those in the early 1950s. By the late 1970s, the rate of conformity amongst United States students was again similar to that of the 1950s (Larsen *et al.*, 1979), perhaps reflecting the increased concern with jobs and careers emerging at that time. Nicholson *et al.* (1985), summing up the various attempts to replicate Asch's findings on conformity, suggest that the 'Asch paradigm may provide a useful indicator of fluctuations in group cohesion over time and in changing national circumstances'.

Superficially Asch's work seems to have a lot in common with the laboratory-based studies discussed in the previous section. However, although Asch's research was conducted in restricted laboratory conditions, his focus of interest was unequivocally the group and its influence and pressure on members. As Asch put it:

We cannot do justice to events by extrapolating uncritically from man's feelings, attitudes, and behaviour when he is in a state of isolation to his behaviour when acting as a member of a group. Being a member of a group and behaving as a member of a group have psychological consequences. There are consequences even when the other members are not immediately present.

(1967, p. 9)

The studies of Berkowitz, Bandura and Milgram looked at the individual, often interacting with another individual, but not, or rarely, as a member of a group, being subjected to pressures to conform to the group's norms. In this section we will be dealing with research which builds on Asch's emphasis on the power of the group, but which examines the even stronger influences of conformity to group norms in real-life groups to which members feel a continuing loyalty.

## 4.2 Social norms, rules and roles

One of the most frequently discussed types of aggression is football hooliganism, which is portrayed in the media as senseless and unruly. The ethogenic approach to studying social behaviour, founded by the Oxford philosopher Rom Harré, (e.g. Harré, 1979), suggests that such behaviour is not unruly. Instead it is governed by many rules which are strictly conformed to by the members of a group and which can be identified through careful observation. This approach builds on and extends the work of Goffman on rule-following discussed in Chapter 2.

In the 1970s, Marsh, a colleague of Harré's, set out to investigate the extent to which football hooligans' behaviour is the result of them conforming to the rules developed and enforced by the groups of fans themselves. He conducted his research using methods such as interviews with the fans, analysis of video recordings of behaviour on the terraces, and by using the technique of **participant observation**, in which he observed the behaviour of the fans whilst attending football matches himself and travelling to matches with them. His interviews with the fans were conducted on the trains and coaches and his detailed observations were made as he shared the terraces with them. As he comments: 'Perhaps listening to what fans have to say sounds "unscientific". You can draw very few graphs in this line of work. But the story speaks for itself. It is both intelligible and meaningful to anyone prepared to give it the attention it deserves' (Marsh, 1978, p. 62).

Marsh concludes from his research that the football terraces are like mini-cultures within the main British culture. Marsh suggests that the fans' behaviour is governed by rules about how to behave in various social roles. As was stressed in Section 5 of Chapter 2, social roles exert a powerful influence on behaviour. Once a person is established in a role, it can become so much a part of his or her sense of self that efforts are made to act appropriately in that role at all costs. The person must not appear to 'lose face' since that would mean losing his or her identity within the group. In the same way as we understand the roles of parent or waiter and know the rules for how to behave at the doctor's or in a lecture, Marsh suggests that the fans know how to behave in the various situations which arise before, during and after a football match. Not only do they know how to behave 'correctly', but they also feel under great pressure to conform to these rules. Rules of this kind which are set up by a group are termed the **norms** of the group. If particular members do not conform to the group's norms, they risk being expelled from the group. This would be a major blow since, for many of the fans involved, the group is the main or the only place where they get a sense of self-worth and prestige. To keep receiving the support of the group which they need, they are therefore under great pressure to conform.

Although the behaviour on the football terraces may look like chaos, Marsh believes that there is in fact an underlying order which all the fans understand and abide by, in the same way as people generally agree to drive on the left-hand side of the road and queue for cinema tickets.

There's an organized pattern of events, I mean you know what's going to happen. Bringing a knife, I mean, probably by your own supporters sometimes it's looked down on as being a form of, you know, cowardice. There's not many people will carry knives about, there's not many who set out to harm someone. Not many people have got that killer instinct, I mean once you've sort of kicked them on to the floor and made them bleed, I mean that's it. It's left at that and they'll just say 'leave him he's had enough'.

(Fan quoted in Marsh, 1978, p 63)

Aggression seems to be part of the behaviour demanded by the group, but it is controlled, almost ritualized aggression within clear limits. Marsh argues that honour has to be satisfied, and that not backing down, 'making a stand', can be more important than actually winning a fight or causing serious injury to anyone else. This is reminiscent of Lorenz's notions of ritualized aggression and appeasement gestures described in Section 2. Lorenz observed in his studies of animal behaviour that where disputes are common, aggression is rarely allowed to proceed to the death of one of the animals. Instead, the loser will offer an appeasement gesture to the winner, who will then withdraw. Marsh's account is one of many which have documented similarly ritualized aggression in humans. Honour has to be and is seen to be satisfied, and little actual hurt inflicted. The combatants both live to battle again.

The social order which Marsh believes underlies the fans' behaviour is particularly apparent in the hierarchy of different roles which they can occupy, from the 'novices' through the 'rowdies' and the 'nutters' to the 'graduates'. For each of these roles, there are clearly prescribed rules for acceptable behaviour (acceptable, that is, as defined by the rest of the fans and not by outside groups such as the police). The 'nutters' behave outrageously, taking on a whole crowd of rivals single-handed, or going too far in beating up another fan. Marsh describes their role as almost that of court jester, providing entertainment for the other fans. Marsh claims that the very existence of the so-called 'nutters' proves that a social order exists. If random action was the norm then the 'nutters' would be indistinguishable from the rest, but they are viewed by the other fans as deviants from the social norm.

The power of rules and roles underlying much group behaviour is also well documented by Campbell in her accounts of her research on gangs of girls (1981; 1984) (see Box H). Aggression amongst girls and women is a very under-researched topic; as you may have noticed, most of the studies reported in this chapter have concerned male aggression. Perhaps the emphasis on male aggression is the result of the assumption that females are 'naturally' less

---

**BOX H    Girl delinquents**

Campbell gave questionnaires to 251 16-year-old girls from working-class areas in British cities. She also surveyed 60 girls from a Borstal. To gain more detailed information, she interviewed a sample of the girls in small group discussions. She found that every one of the girls had seen a fight, and 89 per cent of them had been in at least one fight themselves, although they did not occur very often. The girls who went around with mixed groups of boys and girls were more likely to have been involved in a fight than those who mixed only with other girls, but the fights themselves were overwhelmingly between the girls. They mainly seemed to be triggered by one girl insulting another, with a fight being seen as an inevitable response to maintain face.

---

aggressive than males. Many psychologists would, however, argue that the socialization of boys and girls is very different, with boys being rewarded for being aggressive and girls being rewarded for more passive, peaceable behaviour. Whatever the reason, a good deal of research, using a wide range of measures, suggests that males are more aggressive. Some studies suggest no difference, and only a small number find females to be more aggressive (Rohner, 1976).

Campbell (1981) sought to look at female aggression in more detail to establish how it resembled and differed from male aggression. In particular, she wanted to assess the effects on aggression of the different socialization experiences of females and males, and the rules that govern the expression of female aggression.

Campbell's research revealed rules governing female aggression similar to those found by Marsh amongst the football hooligans. Girls were expected not to take on more than one opponent at a time, not to report the fight to any authority figure, nor to use bottles or knives. Such rules defined what they thought was a 'fair fight'. The Borstal girls were less constrained by rules, apart from the proscriptions on involving the authorities, and put fewer limits on the damage which could be inflicted in a fight. They also reported having been encouraged, if not bullied, into responding aggressively by their families. It appears, then, that although we are less aware of female aggression, and it is a less well-researched area, it bears many similarities to male aggression and can equally well be analysed in terms of the rules and roles which underlie it.

## 4.3 Intergroup hostility

So far we have discussed the factors operating *within* a group which might lead to norms of aggressive behaviour being set up and adhered to. However, the football hooliganism example also pointed to another very important aspect of the group level of analysis: the relationship of one group to other groups. For the football fans, aggression was almost exclusively directed at members of other groups, usually other teams' supporters but also at times the police. Social psychologists have tried to establish whether there is something about being in a group which *inevitably* leads to feelings of hostility towards non-members, and particularly towards members of other rival groups.

An important piece of research conducted by Sherif *et al.* (1966) examined the processes of competition and co-operation which he believed underlie intergroup relations. In the naturalistic setting of boys' summer camps in the United States, the researchers (posing as camp volunteer workers) investigated the relations between groups of 11 and 12-year-old boys placed in a number of group situations; see Box I.

---

### BOX I   Competition and co-operation

The research began with a stage in which the boys engaged in sports and outdoor activities of their choice and developed normal friendships. They were then divided randomly into two groups, with friends being split up. Each group shared a dormitory, ate and played together, and spent the rest of the first week at camp engaged in a number of fun activities away from the other group, designed to stimulate a strong feeling of cohesion and co-operation within the group. By the end of the week the groups were very closely knit units and had developed norms, leadership structures and names for themselves, such as the Eagles and the Red Devils.

Following this stage of group formation, the researchers brought the two groups together. They organized a series of competitions between the groups based on a range of activities, which resulted in overt hostility between the groups. Graffiti appeared, the dorms were raided and names were shouted between the boys whenever they met. Arranging for the boys to meet in less competitive circumstances (such as watching a film or eating a meal together) did not reduce these displays of hostility.

A final stage of the study provided the warring groups with superordinate goals. To succeed in various tasks they had to co-operate rather than compete with each other (e.g. to beat a team from another camp, to rescue a truck bringing them all food). After a series of such co-operative encounters, their previous hostility to each other was supplanted by more favourable attitudes and friendly behaviour.

---

SAQ 6   What was the purpose of the first stage of the experiment?

---

Sherif *et al.*'s research was important since it showed that ordinary boys acted towards each other in very different ways depending on the social context they were in, and particularly depending on the goals they were working towards. Sherif *et al.* claimed that the results of the study showed that the boys' feelings towards each other were the *consequence* of the relationship between the two groups. Hostility and dislike resulted from the two groups being in competition, and friendship and good feeling resulted from the two groups being united in pursuing a common goal.

What does this tell us about prejudice and hostility between groups in the wider society? We would expect to find that, where groups are in real conflict, for instance in competing for scarce resources such as jobs, members of one group will feel hostile towards members of the other group. This may lead them to exaggerate the good features of their fellow members (their **in-group**) and to discriminate against the members of the other group (their **out-group**). Sherif *et al.*'s work would suggest that, to overcome this hostility, groups not only have to meet and interact with each other as equals, but have to work together to achieve a superordinate goal, and have to do this on a number of occasions because the effect is cumulative.

A number of social psychologists have suggested, however, that hostility between groups may arise even when there is no real competition between them (e.g. Billig, 1976; Tajfel *et al.*, 1971). This body of research has established the minimum conditions under which attitudes about another group are formed. **Minimal groups** are formed artificially in the laboratory from people who are not linked by any of the normal characteristics that bind people into cohesive groups. They may be allocated to groups on the basis of, for example, their eye colour, or the toss of a coin. There is no history of either competition or co-operation between the groups. As a result, the sense of social cohesion within the in-group and hostility towards the out-group ought to be low.

In Billig and Tajfel's (1973) minimal group study, once the groups were formed, members of each group were asked to make decisions about monetary rewards for unnamed members of their own group and members of the other group. Members could choose to respond by distributing rewards fairly or randomly, or to favour their own group or the other group. Most distributed the money unfairly, giving more to members of their in-group. The results suggested that simply being allocated to membership of a group is enough to lead to discrimination against an out-group, even though there were no objective reasons for this discrimination.

SAQ 7    How might demand characteristics (see Section 3.4) have affected these findings?

It appears, then, that even if people initially realize that they have become members of a group on the basis of trivial or even random criteria, the mere fact of being able to categorize themselves as members of this group is enough to set in motion a number of social processes. For example, members of a group may exaggerate the good qualities of in-group members and discriminate against out-group members who are in all respects the same type of people. This emphasis is rather different to that proposed by Sherif *et al.* who suggested that in-group identification was the consequence of *real* conflicts between groups.

Tajfel and Turner (1979) emphasize the importance of these social psychological processes in their **social identity theory**. This proposes that every group strives to maintain a positive social identity, so that its participants define themselves as members of social categories, such as women, militants or Scots. This holds true even if they do not often meet other members of that social category. What is important in establishing and preserving a particular social identity is comparison with an out-group. In order to enhance the in-group's social identity, the comparisons will tend to be made with less powerful or less prestigious out-groups. Members of the in-group seek to differentiate themselves from the out-group by any available means. Descriptions of members of out-groups emphasize their similarity to each other and their difference from members of the in-group, resulting in

**stereotyping**. When people are categorized as black, for example, stereotyping suggests that they will be seen by some whites as possessing a number of characteristics 'typical' of all black people and as being different (and usually inferior) to members of their own white in-group.

The evidence from minimal groups, when no natural groupings are involved, seems to suggest that intergroup hostility is the *inevitable* consequence of the division into in-groups and out-groups. Whilst we have seen many positive benefits of being a member of a group, such as providing support and validation for the members' beliefs, and developing friendships, the cost to be paid for this is high in terms of intergroup conflict. To overcome this hostility it is not enough for the groups to meet in co-operative activity, the division between the groups has to be broken down. This is not an easy matter. Moreover, the processes of social categorization, social identification, social comparison and social differentiation do not occur in a vacuum. Economic and cultural factors influence the categories to which we assign people and the judgements we make of them on the basis of these categories.

## Summary of Section 4

- The pressure to conform to the expectations and opinions of a group are powerful. In Asch's study, people felt pressured to say they agreed with a patently wrong decision in order to fit in with a group of strangers. A real group has much more power over its members.

- Marsh's analysis of football hooligans emphasizes the rules underlying seemingly random aggressive behaviour. The gangs strictly enforce these rules by assigning roles to the various members which determine acceptable behaviour.

- Aggression between groups was seen by Sherif *et al.* as the result of competition between them, which could be reduced by getting the groups to co-operate.

- Minimal group studies suggest that it is not competition that causes intergroup hostility, but the mere division of people into in-groups and out-groups.

- Social identity theory stresses the powerful processes involved in creating and maintaining distinctions between groups in order for each group to preserve a distinct and favourable social identity.

# 5 | Aggression in the real world

It is only in the previous section of this chapter that we have really begun to look directly at the aggression that is found 'out there' in the city streets and behind closed doors. This does not mean, however, that the findings of laboratory studies *cannot* be applied to such real-world aggression, but as we noted in Section 3.4, we have to be cautious with these findings.

Simplifying the phenomenon in order to study it in the laboratory can mean that the richness and complexity of real aggression is lost and little can be extrapolated from the findings to other situations. However, other social psychologists would argue that the laboratory experiment allows causal links to be established which can then be tested in a more complicated, natural, social context. Moreoever, many studies, such as Dollard's *et al.*'s frustration–aggression work, began with a concern about prejudice and aggressive behaviour in the real world and moved into the laboratory as the first step in attempting to explain and, ultimately, find ways of reducing such conflicts. Other methods, discussed in this last section, have attempted to look more directly at real aggression and conflict and to get out of the laboratory and use field studies. In this section we will examine different methods which have been employed to study an issue of real concern: the influence of aggressive television material on viewers.

### ACTIVITY 3

If there are children in your household, consider your views about violence on television. Write down which programmes you are happy for them to watch, and those which you would not want them to see. What do you do about the 'grey areas', such as cartoon violence or made-for-children programmes which show, for example, fantasy figures being violent? What do the children understand by the 'pretend' world of television? Do you let them watch the news on television, and if so, what is their reaction to the real violence often seen there?

The topic of violence on television and its effect on viewers' behaviour was examined in Chapter 1 as an illustration of the problems of devising and conducting systematic research in psychology. Here we will look further at some of the existing studies which examine the link (if any) between screened aggression and subsequent aggressive behaviour engaged in by the viewer.

The methods used have varied from the strictly controlled laboratory study to more naturalistic, sometimes long-term field studies of the reactions to television programmes watched at home. In all cases, however, researchers have been faced with a real methodological and ethical problem. This is, how can subjects be shown really violent material in an experiment? Ethically it is unjustifiable, especially in experiments with children and young people. However, whilst in real life many people including children are exposed to 'video nasties', the researchers have to use much less extreme images to examine the effects of screened violence on the viewer's behaviour. This may account in part for the low levels of significance and sometimes contradictory findings in some of the research.

The conclusions from these studies range from Howitt and Cumberbatch (1975), who argue that, 'The mass media do not have any significant effect on the level of violence in society' (p. vii); to Comstock and Lindsey (1975) who state that, 'the widespread belief that . . . the evidence suggests a causal link between violence viewing and aggression is correct' (p. 8). Here we will briefly examine some of these studies to give a flavour of a few of the problems involved in applying the methods of social psychology to real-world issues.

## 5.1 Experimental laboratory studies

The major studies of this type were those of Bandura described in Section 3.2, in particular those conditions where the children viewed the model acting aggressively towards the Bobo doll on a television screen rather than through a one-way mirror. Among other criticisms of these studies, the violent sequence of behaviour viewed by the participants could not be directly compared with typical television programmes and the measures of aggression used (i.e. punching and shouting at a doll) may not be considered to be representative of serious interpersonal aggression.

To answer such criticisms, Liebert and Baron (1972) conducted an experiment, using real television programmes, in which they measured children's willingness to hurt another child after viewing a programme. In a laboratory, children were shown either a track race or an aggressive programme and then allowed to either facilitate or disrupt another child's game. They could hurt the other child by pressing a button to make the handle hot which he or she was holding. The measure of helping the other child was the number of times the children pressed a button to make the other child's game easier. The aggression in this study was against a real person and not just an inanimate toy as in Bandura's studies. As predicted, the children who had seen the aggressive programme were significantly more aggressive than those who had seen the non-aggressive programme. This was particularly the case for the older children and for the boys. Moreover, when the children were later observed during a free play period, those who had viewed the aggressive programme exhibited a greater preference for playing with weapons and aggressive toys than did the children who had watched the non-aggressive programme.

Most of the experimental studies on the effects of exposure to television violence reach similar conclusions. They suggest, for example, that even young children can learn new aggressive responses from one viewing of screened aggressive behaviour, and that the more violence that is viewed, the greater is the likelihood of aggressive responses. Nevertheless, there are dangers in generalizing from such results to what happens in day-to-day viewing. In the laboratory, the experimenter ensures that the subjects' attention is focused exclusively on the screen and there are none of the typical distractions of family life to take the viewer's attention away. Neither are there any of the comments on the programme made by companion viewers which may reinterpret what is happening on the screen. Children seeing an aggressive or frightening programme may often be watching with other children or adults who will reassure them that it is 'pretend', and perhaps comment on how they would respond differently in the circumstances of the person in the programme. This type of interactional context of normal viewing is not present in the experimental setting. There is one other important difference in viewing aggressive television programmes in the laboratory. The normal restraints and sanctions against aggression are absent and it could be argued that the experimenter encourages aggression. In Liebert and Baron's study, for example, the experimenter gave the children instructions on how to both help and hurt another child and gave them the opportunity to do either without approbation. A response to such criticisms has been to conduct more naturalistic research using real programmes as they are watched in normal home settings.

## 5.2 Long-term field studies

A key feature of normal television viewing is that it occurs over long time periods. Whole series of programmes are watched and several different programmes may be seen every day over many years. Long-term field studies allow researchers to study this pattern more successfully than in one-off showings of edited programmes in the laboratory. One such study took advantage of the introduction of television into a small Canadian town to conduct a natural experiment on the level of aggression in the community before and after its arrival (Joy et al., 1977). Other researchers, such as Phillips (1986), have conducted studies which look at the effects of heavily publicized suicide and murder cases on the rates of suicide and murder in the United States. He looked at whether reports in the media were followed by rises in the suicide and murder rates, particularly in the vicinity of the original case and after heavily publicized cases. Phillips claims that from such studies there is indeed 'some evidence that mass media violence elicits serious adult aggression in the real world' (p. 208).

In other field studies, people have been exposed to controlled diets of violent or non-violent television programmes over the course of days or even weeks, and their behaviour in their natural environment has then been observed to establish whether or not the level of aggression changes as a result of their viewing. A series of such experiments by Parke et al. (1977) observed delinquent boys in the United States and Belgium (see Box J).

---

**BOX J    Naturalistic study of the effects of violence on television**

The researchers began by unobtrusively observing, for between one and three weeks, boys living in minimum security institutions behaving in their normal way. Then the boys were divided into two groups on the basis of the houses in which they lived. Over the next five evenings one group saw violent films and the other group saw non-violent films. The violent films included *Bonnie and Clyde* and *The Dirty Dozen* and the non-violent films included *Lily* and *Daddy's Fiancée*. The boys' behaviour was observed during the five days on which they saw the films, and for up to three weeks afterwards. Various different forms of interpersonal aggression were recorded, such as physical threats, verbal aggression and physical attacks, as well as aggression against objects and self-inflicted aggression. The results gave partial support for the hypothesis that viewing violent films would lead to an increase in aggressive behaviour. The boys who watched violent films did display more forms of aggressive behaviour.

---

## 5.3  Is there a link?

Results from both the laboratory experiments and the field studies seem to support the notion that viewing violent material leads to an increase in aggressive behaviour. Baron (1977) suggests three means by which this effect occurs. First, the individuals viewing violent programmes acquire new ways of being aggressive through **observational learning** (as Bandura, 1977, established). Second, the individuals may experience reductions in their restraints against aggression. They may feel that it is all right for them to be aggressive if so many others on television appear to be; this is known as the **disinhibitory effect** because it disinhibits normal constraints on aggressive behaviour. This is particularly likely where the true consequences of such behaviour are not shown. Finally, there may be a gradual **desensitization** to aggression as a result of continued exposure, such that viewers become inured to signs of pain, violence and its consequences. As a result, aggression is not treated as a significant form of behaviour and so it is not avoided.

While the evidence seems to suggest that viewing violent programmes, especially over a long period of time, will lead to increased rates of aggressive behaviour, it has also been argued that someone viewing violence on television will in fact be *less* likely to aggress as a result. In a long-term field study, Feshbach and Singer (1971) investigated the claim that watching televised violence might decrease the likelihood of the viewer behaving aggressively. Adolescent and pre-adolescent boys at a residential school were presented with a diet of either aggressive or non-aggressive television programmes over the course of six weeks. During this time, the teachers and houseparents rated the boys' daily level of aggressive behaviour. The results suggested that in some cases the boys who had seen the non-aggressive programmes behaved more aggressively than those who had seen the aggressive programmes.

The explanation for such findings is based on the notion of catharsis discussed in Section 2.2. According to the psychodynamic and frustration–aggression models, a person watching television vicariously experiences the violence by identifying with the actor on the screen and discharges any pent-up anger and aggressive feelings without actually engaging in aggressive behaviour. However, there are some problems with applying this explanation. Specifically, in the Feshbach and Singer (1971) study there were a number of methodological problems which call the results into question. The ratings of the boys' aggressive behaviour were made by untrained researchers, so we cannot know if they were consistent and accurate in their ratings. More seriously, the raters knew which condition of the study each boy was in, and this may have affected their ratings. Also, the boys in the non-aggressive programme condition were allowed to continue watching their favourite programme—*Batman*—which was considered aggressive enough to be included for viewing in the aggressive programme condition. In a later attempt to replicate the study (Wells, 1973), there was no evidence for the existence of the catharsis effect.

There are also more general problems with the catharsis notion when applied to television viewing. The concept of catharsis, as formulated by psychodynamic theorists, requires the experience of rather intense emotional involvement with the person or situation being observed, and this may not always be found in normal home television viewing where there are many distractions. Furthermore, the catharsis effect does not square with the results of correlational studies which show that more aggressive children prefer to watch, and are more likely to watch, aggressive programmes than children who behave less aggressively (Chaffee, 1972). It would seem that viewing violence on television is more likely to lead to an increase in aggressive behaviour than a decrease through the process of catharsis.

This does not mean, however, that children and adults are likely to go straight out and attack others after watching violent television programmes. The effect is likely to be much less direct than this. Viewing violent material regularly over a long period of time will tend to develop elaborate and detailed conceptions of violence; the viewers will see many examples of different kinds of violence, in many different situations. As a result, violence of one form or another may seem to be an appropriate response in a wide variety of circumstances and this will be manifested in more aggressive and violent behaviour. The influence of television violence, or indeed of a violent culture generally, upon individuals is complex and indirect. It is not only people's behaviour which may be affected, but also their attitudes, beliefs and understandings. For example, the influence seems greatest when it is in accord with other sources of information or when such other sources are absent. In this way, people with little knowledge of crime statistics who view violent programmes will tend to see the world as a more dangerous and violent place than those who know more about the statistics or who see less screened violence.

Many other factors mediate the effect of viewing violence on television. At the individual level, for example, studies by Berkowitz and Bandura (variations of those described in Sections 3.1 and 3.2) are illuminating. These studies found that people only behaved more aggressively after viewing an aggressive programme if they had been angered or frustrated first. The content of the programme itself did not have a consistent effect on all viewers.

Despite the qualifications which must be placed on the nature of the link between violent behaviour and screened violence, the research evidence does suggest that, in general, those people who watch more violent programmes will be disposed to act more aggressively in their dealings with others.

## Summary of Section 5

- In addressing the issue of whether social psychology can shed light on real-world aggression, the influence of television violence on aggression was examined.

- Findings from a range of studies raised the issues of the appropriate level of analysis and methodology for social psychology.

- The evidence suggests there is a link between screened violence and aggression. Observational learning, disinhibitory effects and desensitization all seem to play a part in making the viewer of violence behave more aggressively.

- The link between screened violence and aggression is a complex one, mediated by the mood of the viewer and the effects of the viewer's attitudes and beliefs.

# 6 | Issues revisited

This chapter has examined some key issues in social psychology using as a vehicle the case study of aggressive behaviour. The problems of studying aggression are representative of the problems social psychologists typically encounter in their studies of other phenomena, such as people's attitudes, their leadership skills and their family relationships. Perhaps the most fundamental issue which arose was that of determining the appropriate level of analysis to employ. Can aggression, which is by definition a social act, be explained by looking within the individual at instincts and drives? Is it enough, on the other hand, to look only at large-scale cultural factors which try to explain the action? On a continuum between intra-individual and intergroup levels of explanation, we saw how social psychologists typically investigate group and intergroup issues, but that they range almost across the whole continuum in the types of explanation offered. Research in social psychology often begins with a global problem, such as the cause of riots, but may then proceed to investigate narrower aspects of the problem, such as the effects of heat on aggressive feelings (in this case because many riots happen in the summer).

Another key issue, that of the appropriate methodology to employ, was discussed at length, but only a few of the many points in this complex debate could be covered. On the surface, the choice between experimental laboratory studies and naturalistic field studies seems clear-cut. If the researcher wants to make causal statements about the link between two factors then the control possible in the laboratory seems essential. However, studies of the social processes taking place in experiments show that the subjects in the laboratory react to the manipulations which the experimenter imposes and may not behave as they would do normally. The ethics of such studies were also questioned. However, this is not to suggest that there are fewer ethical problems with alternative methods such as unobtrusive observation, where invasion of privacy is difficult to avoid.

It can be argued that there are two justifications for social psychological research, despite such ethical concerns. The first is that it might bring about needed social change, and the second that it will benefit society, or science. As an example, a study conducted by Zimbardo (1975) investigated the effects on the behaviour of college students of adopting the role of prisoner or guard in a mock prison. This well-known experiment had to be discontinued before it was due to finish because the 'prisoners' had become so demoralized and depressed and the 'guards' were behaving in very authoritarian and aggressive ways. This experiment received a good deal of criticism on ethical grounds since the subjects were so obviously distressed by having taken part in it. Zimbardo replied that, although his subjects were upset, the findings could not have been established in another way, and they had a tremendously positive impact on the way prisons were organized in the United States. The prison authorities were persuaded of the impact of the institution itself since in Zimbardo's study both the prisoners and the guards were randomly chosen from people who were law-abiding and middle-class with normal personalities. Despite this, the experience of being in prison circumstances resulted in these normal people behaving in ways characteristic of the most disturbed and antisocial prisoners and guards.

The shocking results provided some of the ammunition needed to change the conditions in real prisons which led to prisoners feeling dehumanized and degraded. As Zimbardo commented:

My feeling is that if you really believe in your research and your discipline then you have to go beyond being a researcher and a theorist; you actually have to go out and bring your results to the people in question because they don't read our journals. Social change never comes merely from knowledge; it comes from the political activity that knowlege of injustice generates.

(1980, p. 210)

ACTIVITY 4

Reflect on the studies that have been presented in some detail in this chapter and consider what contribution they might have made to social change.

In recent texts on aggression (e.g. Archer and Browne, 1989; Campbell and Gibbs, 1986), the emphasis has increasingly been placed on studies of real aggression in the workplace, in schools and in the home. Hand in hand with such a move towards the study of real-world aggression, the methods adopted in such research are becoming more naturalistic. This move is characteristic of much of the work in social psychology, which is shifting towards the study of real-world social behaviour, such as naturally occurring relationships between people, their conversations and their explanations for each other's behaviour. Methods such as interviews, observations and analyses of conversations and interaction routines are found more often than laboratory studies, although some (e.g. Berkowitz, 1989) continue to insist that light can be shed on the causes of real-world aggression by laboratory experiments.

An important issue for our understanding of aggression is raised by this shift towards studying the complexity of behaviour as it occurs in the real world. This is an increasing emphasis on the different functions of aggression. In our discussion of the definition of aggression in Section 1.2, harm and the intention to harm were seen as key principles in deciding whether or not a piece of behaviour was aggressive. Since that was an introductory discussion, we did not consider the complicating issue of the very different functions aggression can serve. One broad distinction that can be made is between instrumental and expressive aggression. **Instrumental aggression** is defined as behaviour in which another person is harmed incidentally to the main goal of the aggressor. This would include fighting in self defence. In contrast, **expressive aggression** (sometimes known as angry or hostile aggression) is where the aggressive behaviour is the end in itself; the aggressor's aim is to injure the other person. However, this distinction is not as clear-cut as it first seems. In observing an aggressive act it is extremely difficult to determine which type of aggression it is. Nevertheless, viewing apparently similar aggressive actions as different on the basis of the aggressor's goals and motives allows us to move towards a richer theory of aggression. Other theorists have explored the functions of aggression further.

Tedeschi et al. (1974) suggest it is useful to view aggression as one form of coercive power. They argue that in trying to exert power over someone a person may use a number of tactics, such as threats, rewards, persuasion and physical aggression. Aggression in this analysis becomes one of a number of ways of enforcing and maintaining power, and is not so easily defined as any behaviour which causes, or has the intention to cause harm to another living being. Other functions of aggression have also been identified from studies of real-world aggression such as violence in the family. These include the functions of furthering a person's aims or self-interest, and signalling distress and hurt (Powers, 1986). The same action may well be perceived and interpreted very differently when it is serving these different functions. As a result, the focus of our research will also change depending on what functions a particular aggressive action may have within the context of the existing relationship between people or groups of people. Furthermore, wider concerns such as the distribution of power within society and the ways in which society sanctions some types of aggression must be brought into our analysis. As with many topics in social psychology, it appears that we are moving away from seeing aggression as having a single cause and towards seeing it as the complex combination of many different social processes and outcomes.

# Further reading

ARCHER, J. and BROWNE, K. (eds) (1989) *Human aggression: naturalistic approaches*, London: Routledge.

A review of naturalistic approaches to the study of aggression, which includes an interesting debate between the proponents of these approaches and Berkowitz who champions the experimental technique.

CAMPBELL, A. and GIBBS, J.J. (eds) (1986) *Violent transactions*, Oxford: Basil Blackwell.

A fairly complex, but very interesting series of papers with theoretical analysis and examples of real-world aggression.

COLMAN, A.M. (1987) *Facts, frauds and fallacies in psychology*, London: Hutchinson/Unwin Hyman.

This easy to read book has a very good chapter on Milgram's study.

NICHOLSON, J. (1984) *Men and women: how different are they?*, Oxford: Oxford University Press.

This takes up the issue of differences between male and female aggression, which has only been touched on in this chapter.

# References

ARCHER, J. (1989) 'From the laboratory to the community: studying the natural history of human aggression', in Archer and Browne (1989).

ARCHER, J. and BROWNE, K. (eds) (1989) *Human aggression: naturalistic approaches*, London: Routledge.

ARONSON, E., BREWER, M. and CARLSMITH, J.M. (1985) 'Experimentation in social psychology', in G. Lindzey and E. Aronson *Handbook of social psychology*, volume 1, Hillsdale, NJ: Lawrence Erlbaum.

ASCH, S.E. (1955) 'Opinions and social pressures', *Scientific American*, vol. 193, pp. 31–55.

ASCH, S.E. (1961) 'Issues in the study of social influences on judgement', in I.A. Berg and B.M. Bass (eds) *Conformity and deviation*, New York: Harper and Row.

BANDURA, A. (1965) 'Influence of models' reinforcement contingencies on the acquisition of imitative responses', *Journal of Personality and Social Psychology*, vol. 1, pp. 589–95.

BANDURA, A. (1977) *Social learning theory*, Englewood Cliffs, NJ: Prentice-Hall.

BANDURA, A. (1980) 'Albert Bandura', in R.I. Evans *The making of social psychology*. New York: Gardner Press.

BANDURA, A., ROSS, D. and ROSS, S.A. (1961) 'Transmission of aggression through imitation of aggressive models', *Journal of Abnormal and Social Psychology*, vol. 63, pp. 575–82.

BARKER, R., DEMBO, T. and LEWIN, K. (1941) 'Frustration and regression: an experiment with young children', *University of Iowa Studies in Child Welfare*, vol. 18, (whole no. 386).

BARON, R. (1977) *Human aggression*, New York: Plenum.

BAUMRIND, D. (1964) 'Some thought on ethics of research: after reading Milgram's "behavioural study of obedience"', *American Psychologist*, vol. 19, pp. 421–3.

BERKOWITZ, L. (1962) *Aggression: a social psychological analysis*, New York: McGraw-Hill.

BERKOWITZ, L. (1968) 'Impulse, aggression and the gun', *Psychology Today*, vol. 2, no. 4, pp. 19–22.

BERKOWITZ, L. (1971) 'The "weapons effect", demand characteristics, and the myth of the compliant subject', *Journal of Personality and Social Psychology*, vol. 20, pp. 332–8.

BERKOWITZ, L. (1974) 'Some determinants of impulsive aggression: the role of mediated associations with reinforcements for aggression', *Psychological Review*, vol. 81, pp. 165–76.

BERKOWITZ, L. (1989) 'Laboratory experiments in the study of aggression', in Archer and Browne (1989).

BERKOWITZ, L. and LePAGE, A. (1967) 'Weapons as aggression-eliciting stimuli', *Journal of Personality and Social Psychology*, vol. 7, pp. 202–7.

BILLIG, M. (1976) *Social psychology and intergroup relations*, London: Academic Press.

BILLIG, M. and TAJFEL, H. (1973) 'Social categorization and similarity in intergroup behaviour', *European Journal of Social Psychology*, vol. 3, pp. 27–52.

BUSS, A. (1961) *The psychology of aggression*, New York: Wiley.

BUSS, A., BOOKER, A. and BUSS, E. (1972) 'Firing a weapon and aggression', *Journal of Personality and Social Psychology*, vol. 22, pp. 296–302.

CAMPBELL, A. (1981) *Girl delinquents*, Oxford: Basil Blackwell.

CAMPBELL, A. (1984) *The girls in the gang*, Oxford: Basil Blackwell.

CAMPBELL, A. and GIBBS, J.J. (eds) (1986) *Violent transactions*, Oxford: Basil Blackwell.

CHAFFEE, S.H. (1972) 'Television and adolescent aggressiveness', in G. Comstock and E. Rubinstein (eds) *Television and social behaviour*, volume 3, Washington, DC: US Government Printing Office.

COMSTOCK, G. and LINDSEY, G. (1975) *Television and human behaviour: the research horizon, future and present*, Santa Monica, CA: The Rand Corporation.

DOLLARD, J., DOOB, L., MILLER, N., MOWRER, O. and SEARS, R. (1939) *Frustration and aggression*, New Haven: Yale University Press.

FESHBACH, S. and SINGER, R.D. (1971) *Television and aggression: an experimental field study*, San Francisco: Jossey-Bass.

GERBNER, G. and GROSS, L. (1976) 'Living with television: the violence profile', *Journal of Communication*, vol. 26, pp. 173–99.

HARRÉ, R. (1979) *Social being*, Oxford: Basil Blackwell.

HARRIS, M. (1974) 'Mediators between frustration and aggression in a field experiment', *Journal of Experimental Social Psychology*, vol. 10, pp. 561–71.

HOWITT, D. and CUMBERBATCH, G. (1975) *Mass media, violence and society*, London: Paul Elek.

JOY, L.A., KIMBALL, M. and ZABRACK, M.L. (1977) 'Television exposure and children's aggressive behaviour', in T.M. Williams (Chair) *The impact of television: a natural experiment involving three communities*, a symposium presented at the annual meeting of the Canadian Psychological Association, Vancouver.

KAUFMANN, H. (1970) *Aggression and altruism*, New York: Holt, Rinehart and Winston.

KELMAN, H. (1967) 'Human use of human subjects: the problem of deception in social psychological experiments', *Psychological Bulletin*, vol. 67, pp. 1–11.

KULICK, J.A. and BROWN, R. (1979) 'Frustration, attribution of blame and aggression', *Journal of Experimental Social Psychology*, vol. 15, pp. 183–94.

LARSEN, K.S. (1974) 'Conformity in the Asch experiment', *Journal of Social Psychology*, vol. 94, pp. 303–4.

LARSEN, K.S., TRIPLETT, J.S., BRANT, W.D. and LANGENBERG, D. (1979) 'Collaborator status, subject characteristics and conformity in the Asch paradigm', *Journal of Social Psychology*, vol. 108, pp. 259–63.

LIEBERT, R. and BARON, R. (1972) 'Some immediate effects of televised violence on children's behaviour', *Developmental Psychology*, vol. 6, pp. 469–75.

LORENZ, K. (1966) *On aggression*, New York: Harcourt, Brace and World, (original publication: *Des Sogenannte Böse*, Vienna, Austria: Dr G. Borothaschoeler, 1963).

MARSH, P. (1978) *The rules of disorder*, London: Routledge and Kegan Paul.

MEAD, G.H. (1934) *Mind, self and society*, Chicago: University of Chicago Press.

MILLER, N.E. (1941) 'The frustration–aggression hypothesis', *Psychological Review*, vol. 48, pp. 337–42.

MILGRAM, S. (1961) 'Nationality and conformity', *Scientific American*, vol. 205, no. 6, pp. 45–51.

MILGRAM, S. (1963) 'Behavioural study of obedience', *Journal of Abnormal and Social Psychology*, vol. 67, pp. 371–8.

MILGRAM, S. (1964) 'Issues in the study of obedience: a reply to Baumrind', *American Psychologist*, vol. 19, pp. 848–52.

MILGRAM, S. (1965) 'Some conditions of obedience and disobedience to authority', *Human Relations*, vol. 18, pp. 57–76.

MILGRAM, S. (1974) *Obedience to authority*, London: Tavistock.

NICHOLSON, N., COLE, S.G. and ROCKLIN, T. (1985) 'Conformity in the Asch situation: a comparison between contemporary British and US university students', *British Journal of Social Psychology*, vol. 24, pp. 59–63.

ORNE, M. (1962) 'On the social psychology of the psychological experiment', *American Psychologist*, vol. 17, pp. 776–83.

PAGE, M.M. and SCHEIDT, R.J. (1971) 'The elusive weapons effect', *Journal of Personality and Social Psychology*, vol. 20, pp. 304–18.

PARKE, R.D., BERKOWITZ, L., LEYENS, J.P., WEST, S. and SEBASTIAN, R. (1977) 'Some effects of violent and nonviolent movies on the behaviour of juvenile delinquents', in L. Berkowitz (ed.) *Advances in experimental social psychology*, volume 10, New York: Academic Press.

PHILLIPS, D.P. (1986) 'Natural experiments on the effects of mass media violence on fatal aggression: strengths and weaknesses of a new approach', in L. Berkowitz (ed.) *Advances in experimental social psychology* volume 19, New York: Academic Press.

POWERS, R.J. (1986) 'Aggression and violence in the family', in Campbell and Gibbs (1986).

RING, K., WALLSTON, K. and COREY, M. (1970) 'Role of debriefing as a factor affecting subjective reaction to a Milgram type obedience experiment: an ethical enquiry', *Representative Research in Social Psychology*, vol. 1, pp. 67–88.

ROHNER, R.P. (1976) 'Sex differences in aggression: phylogenetic and enculturation perspectives', *Ethos*, vol. 4, pp. 57–72.

ROSENBERG, M.J. (1969) 'The conditions and consequences of evaluation apprehension', in R. Rosenthal and R. Rosnow (eds) *Artifact in behavioural research*, New York: Academic Press.

SHERIF, M., HARVEY, O.J., WHITE, B.J., HOOD, W.R. and SHERIF, C. (1961) 'Intergroup conflict and cooperation', *The robber's cave experiment*, Norman, OK: University of Oklahoma.

SILVERMAN, I. and SHULMAN, A.D. (1970) 'A conceptual model of artifact in attitude change studies', *Sociometry*, vol. 33, pp. 97–107.

STEINER, I. (1986) 'Paradigms and groups', in L. Berkowitz (ed.) *Advances in experimental social psychology*, volume 19, New York: Academic Press.

TAJFEL, H., BILLIG, M. and BUNDY, R. (1971) 'Social categorization and intergroup behaviour', *European Journal of Social Psychology*, vol. 1, pp. 149–78.

TAJFEL, H. and TURNER, J. (1979) 'An integrative theory of intergroup conflict', in G. Austin and S. Worchel (eds) *The social psychology of intergroup relations*, Monterey, CA: Brooks/Cole.

TEDESCHI, J.T., LINDSKOLD, S. and ROSENFELD, P. (1984) *Social psychology*, St Paul, MN: West Publishing Co.

TURNER, J. and GILES, H. (1981) *Intergroup behaviour*, Oxford: Basil Blackwell.

ZILLMAN, D. (1978) *Hostility and aggression*, Hillsdale, NJ: Lawrence Erlbaum.

ZIMBARDO, P. (1975) 'Transforming experimental research into advocacy for social change', in M. Deutsch and H. Hornstein (eds) *Applying social psychology*, Hillsdale, NJ; Lawrence Erlbaum.

ZIMBARDO, P. (1980) 'Philip Zimbardo', in R. Evans, *The making of social psychology*, New York: Gardner Press.

## Answers to SAQs

### SAQ 1

Items 1, 2, 3, 5, 7, 9, 11, 12 and 13 all involve harm being inflicted.

### SAQ 2

Items 6, 8, 10 and 13 clearly involve an intention to harm another person. With other items, the picture is less clear-cut. In items 1, 2 and 11, assignment of the label 'aggressive' rather depends on a number of social and cultural norms for behaviour. We might not call these actions aggressive because they are sanctioned by society, either officially or unofficially and so the *individual's* intention is less relevant. Other problems arise with item 5, since who is to define a person's intentions—the person him or herself, or an observer? Perhaps the people were intending to tease, not harm, each other. In item 7, although the driver presumably did not intend to harm the person, he or she did intend to drink and drive which might be considered an aggressive act.

### SAQ 3

| Item no. | Intention to harm | Victim a living thing | Victim motivated to avoid harm |
|----------|-------------------|-----------------------|-------------------------------|
| 1 | √ | √ | √ |
| 2 | √ | √ | √ |
| 3 | × | √ | √ |
| 4 | √ | × | × |
| 5 | √? | √ | √? |
| 6 | √ | √ | √ |
| 7 | depends | √ | √ |
| 8 | √ | √ | √? |
| 9 | × | √ | √ |
| 10 | √ | √ | √ |
| 11 | √ | √ | √ |
| 12 | × | √ | √ |
| 13 | √ | √ | √ |

### SAQ 4

The prestige of the university where Milgram held the experiment may have influenced the men who were subjects and made them more willing to obey the experimenter. Also, on arrival at the laboratory, the white coat of the experimenter and the impressive 'scientific' looking equipment might have intimidated them into feeling that the experimenter had real power and prestige. Furthermore, the experimenter specifically took responsibility for what happened in the experiment, and this may have made the men feel they could reasonably do as he said without recrimination. They may also have believed that he would not allow real harm to come to the learner since he had assured the learner that the shocks could do no permanent damage, and since he was responsible for the learner's welfare.

## SAQ 5

Berkowitz and LePage's study used male college students; Bandura *et al.*'s study used children; and Milgram used men of between 20 and 50 years of age who were not students.

## SAQ 6

By showing in the first part of the experiment that the boys formed natural friendships amongst themselves, Sherif *et al.* could show that there was nothing to prevent the boys getting on with each other once they were split into the competing groups; there was no natural enmity there. Also, having made friends initially, it might have been expected that the boys would be unlikely to discriminate against their former friends too readily once in different groups. The fact that they did do so suggests that strong negative feelings can easily become associated with people who belong to a different group.

## SAQ 7

Demand characteristics were defined in Section 3.4 as the clues in the experimental setting or in the remarks of the experimenter which the subject could use to establish what the experimenter was investigating and how he or she wanted the subject to behave. In this experiment, demand characteristics might have led the subjects to behave unfairly towards the out-group if the procedure led them to believe the experimenter was 'expecting' unfair distribution and favouritism for the in-group. In an experiment by St Claire and Turner (cited in Turner and Giles, 1981), this possibility was examined by having some subjects observe the experiment and predict how the other subjects would distribute the money. If there were clues in the procedure then, St Claire and Turner argued, these 'observer subjects' would also pick them up and predict the unfair distribution.

However the observers did not do this; they predicted that the subjects would be fairer than they were. Furthermore, there was evidence that being fair was perceived to be the more socially desirable response, and so subjects with evaluation apprehension (see Section 3.4) would be keen to act in this desirable way and not as the subjects actually did in the study. Both these factors suggest that the subjects were not responding to demand characteristics in the experiment.

# Overview of Part VI

Now that you have read the two chapters in Part VI, we hope that you can see a common thread running through the discussion of two such apparently disparate topics, language and aggression. In both cases the major contrast is between explanations which focus on the individual level and those which stress the importance of social rules and roles in determining patterns of communicative and aggressive behaviour.

## The individual and the social dimension

The overview of Part II ended by referring to the tension between explanations at the individual level and at the social level. Theories in developmental psychology simultaneously attempt to focus on the psychological processes which characterize child development and to describe the way in which this development operates in the framework of society. The individual and the social dimensions are equally relevant in the areas of language and aggression.

In Chapter 13 the point is made that the ability to use language involves basic cognitive processes such as perception, attention and memory. Information from the environment has to be processed in order to produce appropriate linguistic responses. For instance, in Treisman's theory (Chapter 11, Section 2.3), spoken words are recognized when they trigger dictionary units, which accounts for the recognition of one's own name even in an unattended message. These dictionary units represent the meanings of words; that is, they constitute the vocabulary (the lexicon) of a language.

The description of language as a cognitive process emphasizes the individualistic aspects of knowing how to use a language. As indicated in Section 3 of Chapter 13, the implication is that each individual child has to learn how to recognize words in the lexicon and to acquire the appropriate syntactic, semantic and pragmatic rules for producing comprehensible sentences. Researchers, notably Vygotsky, have pointed out that language plays an important role in a child's intellectual and social development, supplying symbols for representing objects, events and plans.

The theories of aggression introduced at the beginning of Chapter 14 also have a distinct individualistic tinge in the sense that they focus on the underlying processes which result in individuals displaying aggressive behaviour. One such theory proposes that all animals have an internal drive which propels them to find an outlet for aggression. The frustration–aggression hypothesis (Dollard *et al.*) assumed that frustration is caused by external conditions which thwart goal-seeking behaviour. But nevertheless it is the effect on the *individual* which is important; frustration builds up within an individual whose aggressive drive then has to be released.

Even in the more socially oriented theories of aggression described in Chapter 14, Section 3, the effects of social factors are still treated at the individual level of explanation. Exposure to social cues, such as objects associated with aggression, aggressive models and instructions from persons in authority, may all predispose individuals to express their frustrations in the form of aggressive behaviour. But, once again, it is internal turmoil and conflicts which result in individual acts of aggression.

Even when full weight is given to the influence of the external social mirror in which we see ourselves and the social processes which determine our modes of action, there still seems to be a natural human tendency to think in terms of how all these social events affect 'me' as an individual. So it takes something of a leap of imagination to appreciate the message of the later sections of both chapters in Part VI. These indicate that social interactions within and between groups involve processes which 'go beyond' the intentions and actions of the individual participants. People's behaviour in groups takes on another dimension which cannot be predicted from their behaviour as individuals. As Asch and other social psychologists have emphasized, the group is greater than the sum of its individual members.

The theories introduced in Chapter 14, Section 4, concentrate on aggression as a group phenomenon. In the Sherif experiments, membership of a group led to social cohesiveness which in turn generated intense rivalry between the groups. An even 'purer' version of the effects of the group was demonstrated in Tajfel's work with minimal groups. Here the groups had no chance to get to know each other, to play or to work together. Simply to be a member of a randomly allocated group was sufficient to encourage a favourable attitude to in-group members and hostility towards the out-group.

Parallel to this in relation to language, Section 4 of Chapter 13 goes beyond the idea that people simply learn pragmatic rules in order to guide their selection of utterances. It suggests that episodes take on a 'life of their own', over and above the individual utterances of each speaker. The conversational 'dances' described by Winograd and Flores have a structure which dictates possible moves and counter-moves in a conversational episode. From Goffman's dramaturgical point of view, verbal communication is only one medium for presenting oneself in social encounters.

To sum up, it can be said that the power of the group, and expectations about norms for communication and behaviour, have an enormous, and often unacknowledged, effect on what appear to be individual acts. The extent to which people can become aware of, and possibly break out from, this social framework was touched on in the discussion of the humanistic perspective in the overview of Part IV. While it is extremely difficult to balance the influences of the individual and the social, the existence of the social dimension is an inevitable fact of human life.

### Rule-following explanations of behaviour

The other parallel between theories of language and social approaches to aggression is that both stress the importance of following rules. In the area of language, knowing how to speak a language is expressed as knowing the rules. In Chapter 13, Section 3, putting together correct combinations of words to produce grammatical and meaningful utterances is described in terms of syntactic and semantic rules. Apart from a few stereotyped phrases, which may be learned as single verbal responses, utterances will not make sense unless they respect the rules of the particular language being used. It is, of course, important to realize that these rules are automatic and not part of the consciousness of speakers, except on the rare occasions when writers are struggling with their grammar.

Syntactic and semantic rules define the knowledge each individual speaker must have in order to produce utterances that other speakers can recognize as utterances in particular languages: English, French or Turkish for instance. But equally important are the *social* rules for communication. In order to make one's intentions understood, it is necessary to master the pragmatic rules for carrying on conversations, including the selection of appropriate speech acts. In the wider sphere of social encounters, the knowledge of rules for playing a role towards others is essential for maintaining social communication.

The principle underlying this approach to social interaction is that social behaviour is governed by implicit rules. Chapter 2, Section 6, introduced the importance of social roles in the way people view themselves. Each social role we play carries with it rules with which we are expected to conform. There are rules which define the role of parent, the role of office worker, teacher, 'one of the boys', and many others. An example given in Chapter 14, Section 4.2, concerns the rules followed by football fans. Being a fan is a type of role; for each precise role, 'novice' or 'graduate', the rules of behaviour are clearly known, even if they may appear random, as in the case of so-called 'nutters'.

It is the formulation of rules as group norms that explains the powerful influence of the group in social behaviour. It may be relatively easy to change some of the rules associated with a particular role in isolation; for instance, acting as a strict or more liberal parent. But, once these rules have the support of a group to which we feel we belong, they become enshrined as norms which are hard to break without leaving the group altogether. Much of our behaviour, including the way we use language and the expression of hostility and aggression, is determined by implicit roles, rules and norms with which we identify ourselves.

# PART VII

# APPLICATIONS TO PROBLEMS

# Introduction to Part VII

Up until now, most chapters in this *Introduction to psychology* have focused on theoretical approaches to explaining and understanding human behaviour and experience. The two chapters in Part VII deal with psychologists' attempts to *apply* such approaches when dealing with psychological problems. Of course, there is no clear-cut distinction between theoretical explanation and practical application. For instance, the Freudian approach discussed in Chapter 4 offered a comprehensive explanation of human behaviour as well as a therapeutic application of this framework to helping people with psychological problems. Other theories too have practical implications. As we saw in Chapter 11, Broadbent originally developed his theory of attention to characterize the information-processing difficulties experienced by air traffic controllers. As these examples suggest, psychological principles have applications in many different fields, including clinical work, industry and education. The chapters in Part VII deal only with clinical applications.

Chapter 15 offers an introduction to the broad field of clinical psychology. The aim is to provide an account of the work clinical psychologists do. In particular, the chapter attempts to characterize the different kinds of psychological problems with which clinical psychologists have to deal. These range from conditions such as mental handicap to problems such as depression or anorexia nervosa, the causes of which may be a complex interaction of physical and social factors. The chapter describes the role of the clinical psychologist (as distinct from the psychiatrist) in assessing the nature of psychological problems, and in deciding what can be done about them. In seeking to alleviate these problems, the psychologist is shown as drawing upon different theoretical frameworks, including psychoanalysis, behaviourism, cognitive theory and humanistic psychology.

Chapter 16 presents a detailed account of one particular clinical problem: the disorder known as autism, which commences in early childhood. Autism is a syndrome in which children suffer from profound difficulties in social interaction and verbal and non-verbal communication, and have a restricted range of interests and activities. The chapter shows how psychological theories have been brought to bear in attempts to understand the causes of autism and to provide therapy and education for autistic children. It discusses the difficult process of diagnosing autism and describes also some contrasting theories about its causes and nature. Finally, the chapter deals with some of the different therapeutic approaches advocated for autistic children. It is interesting to note the extent to which these therapies are based on the different theories about autism.

chapter **15**

# CLINICAL PSYCHOLOGY

Rudi Dallos and Chris Cullen

## Contents

# 1 | Introduction: what is clinical psychology?

A useful place to start is by thinking about what clinical psychologists do. They are called upon to assist in a variety of situations when there is a **problem** that requires their specialist expertise. By 'problem' we do not mean simply that someone is seeking 'therapy' of some sort. Clinical psychologists work in a wide range of situations: with elderly people, mentally handicapped adults and children, violent offenders, seriously confused people of all ages, families, community organizations and so on.

In the great majority of cases, something will have been defined by someone as 'going wrong' in some way, and knowing what to do about it will have proved difficult. The clinical psychologist can usefully be seen as a 'consultant' who takes a 'fresh look' at the situation. This involves detailed **assessment** of the person, the attendant circumstances, and the social context within which the 'problem' is occurring. The assessment may involve the use of a variety of psychological tests. The use and interpretation of tests has traditionally been a major part of the clinical psychologist's role. Box A provides an example of the kind of work in which a clinical psychologist might be involved.

The programme described in Box A is put into practice but this is only the start of the clinical psychologist's involvement. The boy's parents are concerned by his lack of developmental progress and wish to see him

---

## BOX A    Case study

During a **case conference** (a discussion and planning meeting) at a unit for mentally handicapped children, the team—consisting of a speech therapist, a nursery nurse, a teacher, a physiotherapist and a nurse—request the assistance of a clinical psychologist. A young boy aged three and a half suffering from hemi-paresis (partial paralysis of one side of his body) is felt to be making very little progress. He can say only a few words, his mouth constantly dribbles, he has to be cleaned regularly, and he makes a mess when he is fed by dropping food from his mouth and pushing food off his plate on to the table.

The clinical psychologist starts by discussing the case with the team in order to clarify the 'problems'. This leads to the setting of some immediate goals, the first of which is to try to bring the dribbling under control and improve the boy's feeding skills. Preliminary analysis shows that the boy enjoys eating and that food can be used as a reinforcer in a training programme (see Chapter 6). An analysis of the meal-time situation reveals that the staff spoon-feed him rapidly and he loses a lot of his food. In effect, he is being rewarded for having food in his mouth rather than for swallowing. On the advice of the clinical psychologist, the team devise a simple programme:

1    The boy is required to swallow his food and keep his hands down before he is offered the next spoonful.

2    His swallowing is brought under verbal control by pairing the word 'swallow' with his swallowing of the food, and he is then required to swallow some of his saliva to gain more food.

becoming more independent, so it is proposed that he be allowed to feed himself; this would also give him something more useful to do with his hands. These features are added to the training programme, which starts to show some success, and the team decide to extend it to the boy's home. The psychologist visits the boy and his mother at home in order to assess the home situation.

As part of the assessment, the psychologist uses the **Griffiths mental development scale** to measure the progress of the boy's development. This test consists of a wide range of items which children are 'normally' expected to be able to perform at different ages. For example, a child of 21 to 24 months is expected to be able to jump off a step, know the parts of his or her body, use sentences of four words, build a tower of six or seven bricks, open a screw toy and so on. The mother's presence helps to make sure that the boy understands what is required of him for each test. Also, she is able to gain some reassurance about what he *can* do as well as seeing where his deficiencies lie, and suggestions for play and instructional activities can be developed.

The mother sees that her son is making some limited progress and agrees to continue the feeding programme at home. While visiting the home, the psychologist observes that the boy eats with his younger brother and that they compete over who is the best eater. The mother confirms that this happens frequently. Rather than trying to eliminate this, it is *utilized* and an element of competitive play is incorporated into the training programme.

Development at home is slow and steady but the mother informs the psychologist that her husband is unhappy and would like to talk about what is happening. During an interview with the whole family at home, the father complains that he sees the programme as only like 'teaching a dog some new tricks'. He thinks the *real* problems are how to control the boy, communicate with him, increase his language and play with him. The psychologist makes some suggestions about playing constructively with the boy and giving him some individual attention. The psychologist also discovers that the father feels depressed by his son's handicap and that, while both parents are weary and in need of a holiday, they feel guilty about leaving the boy with anyone else. They are reassured about this and agree to leave him at the unit regularly at weekends. This will give them a break so that they can 'recharge their batteries' and devote more attention to their son when he is at home.

The clinical psychologist continually communicates with the rest of the team. At a case conference the team agrees upon a strategy of planned respite for the family, guidance on constructive play and language training with continued use of the feeding programme.

Many other details have been omitted from this example but it illustrates how the clinical psychologist worked. One central role was to offer some clarification of the 'problems'. Using a mixture of observation, interviews with family and staff, detailed recording of behaviour and tests, new information was gained and people's perceptions of the problems changed. Obviously, in this case, the boy had a physical disability which a psychologist could not 'cure'. However, it was clear that the boy had potential abilities which needed to be explored and promoted. From an initial definition of the problem as being centred on the boy, the problem was expanded to include the parents' ability to cope with his handicap. Also it became clear that the problems at home were not the same as those at the unit.

We can now consider some of the issues raised by this case and the work of clinical psychologists in general.

## 1.1  What constitutes a 'problem'?

Defining what constitutes a 'problem' is an extremely complex matter. The best we can do here is to outline some of the key issues and briefly introduce the debates surrounding them. Throughout the chapter there are references to psychologists' attempts to help people to solve their problems. But *who* decides *what* constitutes a problem? There is no simple way of answering this question and it often generates considerable debate. In thinking about the matter the following points are relevant.

There are clearly some situations where there would be almost *universal* agreement that a person has a problem. For example, a woman who refuses to speak or to look at other people, and whose ability to look after herself is deteriorating to the state where her life is at risk, obviously has a problem. It might be more difficult, though, to agree about *why* she has that problem. Some might claim that it is directly caused by, and is one of the symptoms of, a mental illness which is *physical* in origin. Others might assert that a combination of a physical problem together with other factors (such as an unusual family background) is responsible. The view one takes can imply different approaches to treatment.

In the case described above it would be generally agreed that the woman has a problem. However, there can be disagreement about whether particular behaviour in a particular context does constitute a problem. For example, some people think that children who refuse to sit still in a classroom and who get up and wander about are 'naughty'. The solution is to get them to stay at their desks. Others, however, disapprove of this 'be still, be quiet, be docile' philosophy and argue that such children are merely expressing their natural curiosity. Their solution would involve harnessing this curiosity as part of the learning process. Again, the view taken determines the potential solution.

There can be even more dramatic cases which involve moral issues. Take the case of a man who presents himself to a clinical psychologist as a homosexual who is distressed by his attraction to other men and wants help to reorientate his sexual inclination. In the past, clinical psychologists might have accepted the case as a problem and employed a variety of 'therapies' to try to resolve it, such as presenting aversive stimuli as punishers when the man responds sexually to pictures of men, and rewards to encourage response to pictures of women.

Today it would be most unusual to find clinical psychologists who would even contemplate such a course of action. They would not see it as part of their role to act as guardians of a society's view of what constitutes 'normal' behaviour. Society's view of homosexuality is itself changing, and the clinical psychologist is now more likely to start by discussing the matter, exploring how the man sees himself and whether he is making the request voluntarily or under pressure from his family. It is more likely that the psychologist would treat the man's *distress* as the 'problem' and devise ways of helping him come to terms with his homosexual feelings. Of course, if he still wanted to change his sexual inclinations, the psychologist would help him to do so.

Not all cases with moral implications would be approached in this way. A man who shows signs of a strong sexual attraction for children *would* find himself offered therapy designed to reorientate his sexual interests. Acting upon such attractions is likely to be regarded as a dangerous 'abuse' of children by all except a tiny minority in our culture.

The work of clinical psychologists is embedded in the changing views of the society in which they work. This raises the criticism that they therefore serve as agents of control in enforcing what society deems to be 'normal' at any given time. Clinical psychologists may, of course, have personal views that conflict with society's norms, but they are subject to the codes of practice of the British Psychological Society if they are chartered psychologists, and they must operate within the guidelines of their employer, usually a Health Authority.

## 1.2  Biological and psychological causes

In many cases, the problems tackled by clinical psychologists have several causes rather than just one. They are often involved in assessing the extent to which a problem is physical rather than psychological in origin. For example, a young child may be suspected of having brain damage or an elderly person of showing early signs of Alzheimer's disease. In these cases, the psychologist works closely with medical staff to produce an overall assessment. If the causes are judged to be mainly biological in origin, the solution is likely to involve medical management, possibly using medication to control the symptoms. If the causes are seen as arising mainly from external experiences, it is more likely that the problems will be treated by psychological methods. However, as you have seen in Chapter 5, the physical and psychological are often closely interrelated. The following examples illustrate the complexity of this interrelationship.

Problems with primarily physical origins, such as many forms of mental handicap, may have attendant psychological problems. A mentally handicapped child, for example, may be socially withdrawn, hostile towards parents and care staff, show depression and so on. These behavioural problems are not a direct result of the physical causes of the mental handicap. Also, it has often been overlooked that people with mental handicaps may have the same feelings and emotional needs as other people. For example, a young woman with a mental handicap was reported by the staff to be showing 'disruptive emotional outbursts' in her residential home. A variety of treatments, such as medication, confinement and behavioural programmes were attempted without much success. Eventually a clinical psychologist who was new to the case reassessed the circumstances and discovered that the woman was being restrained from visiting her baby. A vicious circle had been set up. She was restrained from seeing her child *because* of her violent behaviour, for fear that she might damage the child. However, the distress and anger at being prevented from seeing her baby, which would have been accepted as normal in other mothers, had been overlooked in her case. When her feelings were taken into account and discussed with her, she started to behave in a less violent and angry manner. This then led to more sensitive counselling about the loss of her child.

In contrast to the above examples, problems which have a predominantly psychological basis may have serious physical consequences. For instance, depressive states following an emotional loss, such as bereavement or divorce, or the experience of constant stress and tension, can have serious physical consequences, such as cardiac and respiratory problems. Furthermore, treatment may involve the prescription of tranquillizers, and psychological and physical dependence can develop, leading to the habitual and increasing use of medication. This can result in physical damage to health, especially if the medication is misused.

## 1.3 Social contexts

It is rarely the case that behaviour can be labelled as a problem without considering the **social context** in which it occurs. A woman who talks to people who are not physically present and who reports hearing voices, might be judged to have a problem. If certain other symptoms are present, she could be described as psychotic. However, if she claims to be a medium who assists people in getting in touch with their deceased relatives, then her behaviour might be regarded as socially acceptable.

The very strong effect of context was dramatically illustrated by Rosenhan in his classic paper: 'On being sane in insane places' (1973). This is described in Box B.

Rosenhan's study suggested that the effects of such **social labelling** can be extremely powerful. Sociologists have developed similar ideas and added the concept of **secondary labelling**. This means that a person who is seen by others to act in a 'deviant' way eventually comes to accept the label, sees him or herself as 'deviant' and begins to behave in a way consistent with the label. If people are prepared to accept a professional diagnosis without demur, this raises some important ethical questions about depriving people of their freedom on the basis of such diagnoses.

Goffman (1971) points to cases of people who were initially hospitalized many years before for 'trivial' reasons, such as having an illegitimate baby. But, after having spent many years in hospital, the secondary labelling of 'insanity' resulted in people accepting that they had a clinical problem. A paradoxical situation can develop whereby some people are seen to be insane partly because they have been inmates in an institution for a long time. If they ask to leave, they may also be seen as insane because they wish to leave without the doctor having recommended it. It is important to recognize that

> ## BOX B    Rosenhan's study
>
> Eight subjects were instructed to claim that they had heard voices in order to gain admission to mental institutions. They were labelled as schizophrenics. Once in the institutions they behaved quite normally, claiming that their symptoms had gone and that now they felt fine. The other patients accepted that they were normal but most of the staff continued to believe them to be insane. They were released only when the hospitals were told about the experiment!
>
> Meanwhile some interesting incidents had occurred. One subject, who was a psychology undergraduate, kept a diary of what happened to him each day. However this writing activity was actually seen as a further symptom of his problem, as being a sign of social withdrawal, because he did not participate with the other inmates in social activities, such as card games. In desperation some experimental subjects attempted to convince the staff who they 'really' were.
>
> Again, though generally sympathetic and 'understanding', the staff continued to see these confessions as indications of further serious delusions.

the staff in the institutions are actually acting for benevolent reasons. They, too, can be caught up in confusing and contradictory organizational rules. The problem does not *inevitably* reside within a person, but is frequently a feature of a disorganized or confusing social organization.

We should also bear in mind that many people who exhibit problems can legitimately be considered to be victims of a wider social and political context, and that their problems are symptoms or side-effects of a wider problem. It may be more appropriate, and more ethical, to deal with the wider problem than the personal problem. For example, many alcoholics may be using drink as a reaction to poverty, homelessness, stress or loneliness. To attempt to control the excessive drinking without addressing these other matters would be short-sighted at best and probably doomed to failure.

SAQ 1    (*SAQ answers are given at the end of the chapter*) Consider for a moment which other kinds of social context might contribute to the development and maintenance of psychological problems.

## 1.4  Who are clinical psychologists?

Many people are confused about the difference between clinical psychology and psychiatry. The distinction is actually quite simple, although there is some overlap in roles.

**Psychiatrists** are trained initially in general medicine, which includes detailed knowledge of physical and pharmacological treatments. Like many other medical practitioners, they use the courtesy title 'doctor' even though they may have no doctoral degree. After their initial medical training they have a three-year postgraduate training in psychiatry, which includes studying some psychology, psychotherapy and various physical and pharmacological treatments.

**Clinical psychologists** must have an undergraduate degree in psychology. Postgraduate training varies, although all courses have a common core of assessment and therapy with mentally handicapped people, and with children and adults who have mental health problems. In addition, all courses provide training in specialist areas such as elderly people, general health, pain relief, psychotherapy, neuropsychology and family therapy. Clinical psychologists can only use the title 'doctor' if they have a PhD degree, which is awarded for postgraduate research.

The roles of clinical psychologists and psychiatrists overlap to some extent, as do the roles of these two professions with those of nurses, social workers and counsellors. This is because they all serve a common client or patient group, bringing to the job their own specific skills and attributes. Because people's problems cannot be conveniently split up into separate components and treated discretely, everyone needs to have interviewing skills, some form of assessment and therapy skills (although these vary between the different professional groups), and some counselling skills.

A useful definition of clinical psychology which embodies the concept of the scientist-practitioner model (which we will consider further in Section 4) is given by Kendall and Norton-Ford:

Clinical psychologists share several common attributes. They are *psychologists* because they have been trained to use the guidelines of knowledge of psychology in their professional work. They are *clinicians* because they 'attempt to understand people in their natural complexity and in their continuous adaptive transformations' . . . They are *scientists* because they utilize the scientific method to achieve objectivity and precision in their professional work. Finally, they are *professionals* because they render important human services by helping individuals, social groups and communities to solve psychological problems and improve the quality of life.

(Kendall and Norton-Ford, 1987, p. 4)

Other common confusions occur between the roles of clinical psychologists and psychoanalysts or psychotherapists. This is because some people do not realize that psychoanalysis and psychotherapy are *types of treatment* while clinical psychology is a *profession*. There are many clinical psychologists who are trained in psychoanalysis or psychotherapy just as many psychiatrists and social workers are so trained. However, not all clinical psychologists are qualified to practise psychoanalysis or psychotherapy—these approaches to treatment require further training after the basic qualification—although they will all have had some introduction to psychoanalysis and psychotherapy as part of their basic training.

# 1.5  The main areas of clinical work

The majority of cases that a clinical psychologist deals with will have been through a 'filtering process' (Goldberg and Huxley, 1980). For example, someone may feel that his or her life is becoming intolerable because of some problem such as anxiety, insomnia or an irrational fear. Frequently, other people, such as relatives or friends, will be equally, if not *more*, distressed by the problem and may have already spent considerable time trying to 'help' the person. If this 'natural therapy' has failed, then the most common next step will be for the person to approach the family doctor. Sometimes this will be done voluntarily, but often under considerable pressure from others. The doctor will conduct a preliminary assessment and then make a decision about whether to attempt to deal with the problem him or herself, for example by prescribing medication or by some form of 'brief counselling' by a counsellor serving the medical practice (if this is available). If this fails, or the problems appear too severe, the doctor may decide to refer the person on for further specialist medical examinations, or to a specialist such as a psychiatrist. Some referrals may also be made direct to a clinical psychologist. The important point is that often a variety of decisions and diagnoses have been made before the psychologist becomes involved.

Clinical services broadly fall into four areas and a clinical psychologist will usually work predominantly in one of these areas. Typically, the work is carried out in multi-disciplinary teams.

### Child psychological services

Services for children are mainly provided by Child Guidance or Child and Family Units to which children with emotional problems, such as school refusal, disruptive behaviour, phobia, bed-wetting and such like, are referred. Clinical psychologists working in these areas are involved in the initial assessment of problems, the formulation of plans for treatment, the monitoring of progress and the evaluation of change. They usually work as part of a multi-disciplinary team with child psychiatrists, health visitors and psychiatric nurses. Psychologists have come to play an increasingly important role in such teams. This has come about largely because of their training in research methods which equips them to assess problems in a systematic way and to evaluate treatments.

### Adult mental health

Until recently, most work in this area took place in large psychiatric hospitals, most of which were built on the outskirts of towns in the Victorian period. Such institutions are now being closed and, in their place, day-hospitals are being established in the centre of towns. These are smaller than the old hospitals and they provide a less anonymous and regimented environment. Working with adults, like working with children, is likely to involve a mixture of assessment, treatment and evaluation, and the work will usually be conducted in a multi-disciplinary team. Psychologists tend to work in a variety of well-established fields, such as in the neuropsychological assessment of head injuries and brain tumours, and in the treatment of psychological problems such as phobias, sexual problems and anxiety. In addition, some psychologists have become involved in the assessment and treatment of major psychiatric problems such as psychoses and depressive conditions.

In practice, the move away from large hospital-based provision to the community has not only meant care in the community but also care by the community. This means that families, and women in particular, are increasingly taking on the burden of care for mentally handicapped children, elderly relatives and the rehabilitation of children with psychological problems. Partly as a consequence of this, there is an increasing emphasis on working closely with families in order to assist the processes of rehabilitation, reduce the risk of relapse and reduce the risk of other members of the family developing problems.

### The elderly

Work with the elderly includes providing a service in public and private residential homes, as well as day centres and social support groups. Work in this area is likely to involve neuropsychological assessment to determine whether a person is showing signs of the mental illnesses that typically afflict the elderly, such as Alzheimer's disease. Recent emphasis has been on the development of techniques to maintain old people's abilities, for example, by providing opportunities for social contact to offset loneliness and the threat of depression. **Reality orientation training** consists of simple daily memory exercises about the time of day, the date, where the person is and where various places in the locality are. The elderly may be encouraged to practise their memory abilities by remembering events in their pasts (**reminiscence therapy**), such as important events and dates in their personal lives and the political events that were taking place at the time. Simple measures can also be adopted to help elderly people find their way around their homes or residential homes; for example, by providing perceptual cues, such as colour coding and clear markings on doors.

### Mental handicap

Once again, the principles of multi-disciplinary involvement and community-based provision apply. Psychologists have made a significant contribution to the treatment and management of mentally handicapped people with the application of behavioural methods. These have been especially useful for people who have very limited verbal abilities and who sometimes engage in violent and self-destructive behaviour.

Clinical psychologists are trained to be able to work in all of the areas outlined above and in other areas. However, after training, they are likely to specialize and develop further skills in working with particular client groups. Similarly, as we will discuss in the next section, they are trained to use a wide range of theoretical orientations and techniques but they are likely to develop preferred theoretical orientations, such as behaviour therapy, psychotherapy, family therapy or cognitive therapy.

# 1.6 Evaluation of services

Clinical psychologists carry out evaluation and research in all the main areas that we have just described. They may also be asked to evaluate the effectiveness of a particular type of service, for example, a system of community-based support and rehabilitation for adults recovering from various psychological problems. Box C provides an example of this type of work.

## BOX C   Case study

A clinical psychologist was asked to look at units developed for patients recovering from a variety of psychiatric problems. Many of the clients were still living at home with their families, even though some of them were middle-aged or older. The units were based upon a family home model and aimed to offer a variety of support including medical care, psychological treatment, assessment, respite for the families and rehabilitation.

The evaluation involved an attempt to clarify the perceived aims of the units and an assessment of the actual needs in the community. The psychologist interviewed staff, the adults using the units, their families and the mental health team—social workers, psychiatric nurses and doctors. He also carried out some participant observation (spending time working as part of the team) and analysis of statistics reflecting the use of the units. A simple research design was used which compared two units that differed in their location and facilities.

The evaluation revealed that the units had originally been envisaged as providing medical support, such as assessment and the administration of drugs. In practice, however, one major function of the units was found to be that they offered respite—a break from each other for both families and patients. Many of the families had problems in containing their son or daughter at home, and they tended to keep them in a 'child' role which served to retard rather than foster rehabilitation. A related problem was that misunderstandings could develop between families and staff, especially if parents felt that they were failing because their children were often less troublesome in the units than at home. It emerged that a vital function of the units should be to assist the families in enabling the patients to leave home and move towards more independent and age-appropriate accommodation in the community.

This additional feature of the units' role was incorporated, and some changes were made in the organization and training of staff. A policy of working more closely with families to assist the transition between home and alternative accommodation was established.

## Summary of Section 1

- One of the major contributions of clinical psychologists is to offer a systematic approach to the assessment of psychological problems. Following assessment they will suggest a variety of methods of treatment.

- Clinical psychologists do not focus exclusively on the biological and psychological symptoms that are presented, but attempt to treat the whole person in his or her particular social context.

- The main difference between clinical psychologists and psychiatrists is that psychiatrists have a medical training and are able to prescribe medication and other forms of medical treatment.

- Clinical psychologists spend a considerable amount of their time working in multi-disciplinary teams. Some of the boundaries between professions such as psychiatry, psychology and social work are now less rigid; knowledge and methods of enquiry are shared and the clients benefit.

- The main areas in which clinical psychologists work are child psychology, adult mental health, the elderly, mental handicap and in the evaluation of services.

# 2 | Biological and behavioural models in clinical psychology

This section shows how some of the major theoretical perspectives discussed in other chapters are put into practice. We will be mainly concerned with the implications of each approach for clinical work. We will also outline some of the developments of the theories that have occurred as a result of clinical practice and research.

It is important to remember that many of the psychological theories that you have encountered, especially psychodynamic theories, have sprung from clinical contexts. There is not space to provide details of all the treatment techniques available. Rather we will survey the way these perspectives are employed by clinical psychologists to guide their assessment and to help them formulate a plan of treatment for each case.

# 2.1 Biological perspectives

Biological perspectives and the medically-based treatments associated with them are generally regarded as the province of psychiatrists. Nevertheless, clinical psychologists usually provide assessments for psychiatrists, and psychologists need to be clear about the contribution of biological factors to a problem in order to decide how to proceed with treatment.

The assumption underlying biological perspectives (see Chapter 5 for further details) is that some psychological problems result from physical defects in the functioning of the brain and other organs. Examples of this are chromosome abnormalities, such as Down's syndrome, and accidents that result in brain damage. Some specialists extend this perspective to disorders such as schizophrenia and depression which they explain as resulting from physiological disturbances in the functioning of the brain.

In the past, the biological perspective implied that many disorders should be treated predominantly by medical methods. In psychiatry today, medical treatment is mainly by means of **psychotropic** (mood-altering) drugs. Interestingly, some of the main tranquillizing drugs were developed in order to relieve the anxieties of people waiting for major surgical operations, and were only later applied to control psychological conditions. There have been extensive debates about the value of drug-based treatments, and especially about the indiscriminate prescription of tranquillizers and antidepressant drugs. The positive aspects are that many seriously disturbed patients no longer need to be physically restrained and can live more normal lives. However, long-term use of medication can lead to addiction, damaging physical side-effects and psychological dependence. Current practice generally accepts a minimal use of medication in conjunction with attempts to replace it with psychological methods of treatment if at all possible. This is consistent with the view, also described in Chapter 5, that biological and social perspectives are complementary. For example, some people may have a biological predisposition to depression which is triggered by environmental factors such as stress.

An important part of a clinical psychologist's work involves assessing the balance of biological and psychological causes. A young child may display symptoms such as retarded speech, outbursts of temper and lack of motor co-ordination. These could be due to brain damage, to an emotionally difficult home situation or to some early traumatic experience. The clinical assessment will attempt to establish which of these explanations is most likely. It will usually involve using a variety of objective test instruments, for example measures of intellectual abilities and specific tests of memory, perceptual abilities, left–right discrimination, motor co-ordination and so on. The purpose is to determine whether further detailed medical examinations are necessary and to help identify the impairments with a view to detecting all the probable causes of a problem; see Box D overleaf.

## BOX D   Case study

Mr Wright, a man of 53, was referred to a clinical psychologist for preliminary assessment for a suspected brain tumour. He had been complaining of memory problems and disorientation, but it was not clear exactly which of his functions were being impaired nor where his suspected tumour might be located.

The psychologist conducted an assessment which is summarized diagrammatically in Figure 15.1 as a process of decision making. The first step was to clarify and discriminate between cognitive, social and emotional aspects of his impairment. Second, the question was whether the problems indicated specific deficits or a general intellectual impairment.

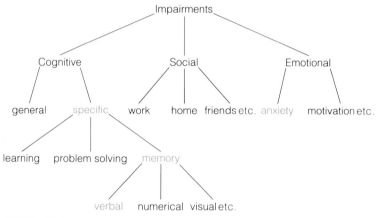

**Figure 15.1**

The psychologist constructed a profile of tests starting with the Weschler Adult Intelligence Scale (WAIS), a general intelligence test which assesses all-round performance but which also involves a set of sub-tests which can indicate specific areas of difficulty—verbal, numerical, memory, problem solving etc. (The various forms of the WAIS test were described in Chapter 7.) At the same time, indications of alternative psychological problems such as depression were explored; Mr Wright was questioned about insomnia, poor appetite, lethargy, alcoholism and so on. He was anxious but not obviously depressed, his drinking was not excessive, and there was no history of drink-related problems such as absence from work.

Mr Wright's WAIS test result indicated a specific impairment of short-term verbal memory. His long-term memory was normal, and his short-term memory for numbers, pictures and his ability to solve problems was comparatively good. The impairment revealed by the test indicated that a specific disorder such as a tumour was likely. He was referred for further neurological assessment which confirmed this picture. Subsequently, an operation was successfully carried out on a tumour in the left-hand side of his brain (in the temporal region which is associated with verbal memory abilities).

During the assessment Mr Wright appeared extremely worried about his problems and their possible implications. Time was spent during the stages of the assessment in discussing these fears and also in stressing his areas of competence as well as his deficits. This shows that, even when the main problem is entirely physical and needs surgical treatment, there are associated psychological problems which require psychological intervention.

## 2.2 Behavioural perspectives

Behavioural approaches, such as those discussed in Chapter 6, assume that some psychological problems are acquired through learning experiences, and that they are subsequently maintained by the contingencies of events in the environment. The classic example cited as evidence of this is the experiment by Watson and Raynor (1920) in which a fear (**phobia**) of white rats was created by classical conditioning in an 11-month-old boy, Albert. The boy had a pet white rat of which he was very fond. By startling Albert with a loud noise every time that he was playing with his pet, a conditioned fear response was created. Albert did not just become frightened of his pet—he would cry when he saw it; he also *generalized* this fear to other white furry objects, like a white rabbit, and even cotton wool. Once Watson and Raynor had shown that a phobia could be acquired through learning like this, they de-conditioned Albert by feeding him sweets when they showed him his pet, until he was quite happy with it again.

Behavioural treatment methods used in clinical psychology fall broadly into two classes:

1 Methods based upon classical conditioning, known as **behaviour therapy**.

2 Methods based upon operant conditioning, known as **behaviour modification**.

Both approaches are founded on the premise that treatment should concentrate on tackling the inappropriate learning that has occurred. In practice, some treatments involve considerable adaptation of and deviation from simple learning theory principles.

### Behaviour therapy

A common example of the application of *classical conditioning* is the treatment of nocturnal enuresis (bed-wetting) using the bell and pad method. The start of urination activates an alarm which wakes the child. Urination is a neutral stimulus which does not lead to waking; the ringing of the bell is the *unconditioned stimulus* which does lead to waking. Repeated pairings of the bell with urination will lead the child to wake automatically in response to sensations of discomfort in the bladder muscles and then get up to go to the toilet.

SAQ 2   Consider the process of learning in the treatment using the enuresis alarm. How do you think any *operant* conditioning might also come into play here?

Most other applications of classical behavioural approaches have attempted to *extinguish* learned responses. The process of **extinction** was described in Chapter 6, Section 2.1. One example is a technique known as **systematic desensitization** (Wolpe, 1958). This technique is typically used to assist people with phobias, such as an excessive fear of snakes or heights. It usually consists of the following stages:

1   The person suffering from the phobia is taught relaxation techniques. This enables him or her to become calm and pleasantly relaxed at will.

2   Following this, a reduced, tolerable sample of the fearful object or situation is presented so that the person remains relaxed.

3   The severity of the stimulus is gradually increased in stages. For example, at first only a vaguely snake-like object might be used; this would be followed by more realistic objects; then an actual snake would be used.

The rationale of this technique is that the person is able to employ the relaxation training in order to feel relaxed at each stage in the process. The frightening stimulus gradually becomes conditional to a relaxed state, and this replaces the association between the object and a state of fearful anxiety. In practice, considerable time might be spent on each stage until the person is ready to increase the severity of the stimulus. Using this technique the person is gradually desensitized from the original phobia.

A related but more dramatic technique is that of **flooding**. In this, the person is subjected to the feared stimulus in full rather than in gradual stages. In the example above, the person would be introduced immediately to the snake and not allowed to escape or avoid contact with it. The rationale is that this prevents avoidance behaviours from having their reinforcing effects and enables the process of extinction of the feared response to occur rapidly.

Flooding techniques are usually carried out in the real-life situation in which the problem normally occurs so that the whole range of associated stimuli can be extinguished at once. For example, a woman who is frightened of crowded places will be required to go shopping in a large supermarket or store. In severe cases, the therapist may initially accompany the patient and this provides a *model* of how to cope with the situation. The clinical psychologist will in most cases have to offer some reassurance and a rationale to persuade the person to attempt these techniques. Some argue that this reassurance and advice is as important as the technique itself.

### Behaviour modification

These treatments are directed specifically at the behaviour itself rather than at underlying causes; nor is there exploration of the patient's feelings or understandings. The focus is on changing behaviour by manipulating its consequences through *operant conditioning*. Reinforcement is chosen on the basis of detailed preliminary assessment of the person and his or her environment. In clinical work, operant procedures usually concentrate on building up desirable behaviours rather than simply eliminating undesirable behaviours (Goldiamond, 1974; Cullen *et al.*, 1981). For example, a disruptive boy's behaviour would be carefully assessed in the classroom and home situations in order to establish when he was behaving appropriately as well as disruptively. Only the appropriate behaviours would be built up using reinforcers, and the other undesirable behaviours would be gradually extinguished by making sure that they were not rewarded. Parents and teachers would manage the distribution of the rewards in order to alter the context in which the disruptive behaviour had been occurring.

Behaviour modification procedures are based on the rationale that problems, like all behaviours, are *maintained* by the situation that the person is in. In experimental work, the situation has usually been simple, consisting of buzzers, levers, and pellets of food. However the clinical situation is more complex in that it consists predominantly of *other people*: family, friends and colleagues in organizations such as schools and the workplace. The focus is on identifying the factors in a person's *present* environment which are maintaining the problematic behaviours. For example, a woman's agoraphobia (fear of open spaces) may be reinforced, perhaps indirectly, by her husband who is jealous and worried that she may start a liaison with another man when she goes out of the house. Also, the agoraphobic wife avoids some domestic duties since her husband has to do the shopping and pick the children up from school. In this way, she gains control over his behaviour. He, in turn, may gain a sense of superiority and control over his wife which reinforces his behaviour.

The application of behavioural approaches involves detailed assessment in order to identify, first, the **contingencies** maintaining the behaviour, and then potential **reinforcers** that can be used to alter behaviour. Clinical psychologists spend considerable time assessing the frequency, duration, onset and circumstances in which a behavioural problem occurs. This requires detailed record-keeping which is often carried out by the patient, prior to and during treatment. Interestingly, this self-monitoring has repeatedly been found to produce significant behavioural change in itself (Nelson, 1977). Possibly the activity of observation and recording may it disrupt the established behavioural contingencies. It may also produce some insights which help to change the behaviour.

## ACTIVITY 1

Think for a moment about one of your own phobias or the phobia of someone you know or have heard of. Write down the phobia and answer the following questions. Try to use both classical conditioning (desensitization) and operant conditioning (reinforcement contingencies) approaches.

(a) Which particular cues trigger the fear?

(b) How might the fear have been learned?

(c) In what ways might the fear be maintained, e.g. what positive consequences might it have for the person or others close to him or her?

(d) How might the person be desensitized?

If you considered your own rather than someone else's phobia in Activity 1 you may have found it hard to analyse the problem, especially the question about how the fear might be maintained. When someone suffers from a debilitating problem he or she finds it very hard to think of any positive consequences of the symptoms. But the consequences need not be external; avoidance learning suggests that avoiding the feared situation is rewarding in itself, and thereby could serve as a reinforcement to maintain a fear.

## 2.3 Cognitive–behavioural approaches

A recent significant development in clinical psychology has been the growth of cognitive approaches. Psychologists have become dissatisfied with behavioural techniques because they are protracted and not very effective for many types of problem (Rachman and Wilson, 1980). The main criticism is that many problems are not simply learned behaviours but are influenced by a person's thought processes. As discussed in Chapter 6, even within the behavioural approach there has been a split between those who accept that there is some internal mental representation and those who do not. For example, the idea of cognitive maps proposed by Tolman, is a cognitive approach to explain maze learning in animals and humans. The cognitive shift described in Chapter 6, Section 6 shows that expectation of outcome plays a significant part in learning. At a commonsense level, it is obvious that the successful treatment of humans requires their full co-operation and trust. It is necessary to understand how people see their problems, and to negotiate an agreed approach to treatment in order to avoid dissatisfaction or confusion about its aims and to prevent possible withdrawal from it before its effectiveness has been properly tested.

Aaron Beck (1987) has reviewed the cognitive approach to the treatment of depression. He suggests that depression is produced and maintained by the depressed person's characteristically gloomy and pessimistic style of thinking. These cognitions are maintained by a consistent perceptual bias towards the negative aspects of experience, and by systematic, logical errors of interpretation. A person may make excessive generalizations based upon very limited information. Also, an overly selective use of information may mean that only *negative* experiences are noted and all *positive* reactions are ignored. For instance, based upon an incident of rejection, someone may conclude that he or she is *totally* worthless and liked by *nobody*. Beck adds that **depressive thinking** is rooted in a triad of dysfunctional assumptions which lead to self-perpetuating and automatic negative cognitions:

● Negative view of self: *I am worthless.*

● Negative view of circumstances: *Everything is bleak and I cannot manage the demands that people put upon me.*

● Negative view of the future: *Things will only get worse and there is nothing I can do to change them.*

Beck proposes that these cognitions may be triggered by real-life experiences, such as loss, failure or rejection. Subsequently, though, these depressive cognitions filter and restrict a person's thinking so that he or she is virtually unable to recognize any positive experience. A similar idea was outlined in Chapter 6 in Seligman's concept of 'learned helplessness'. Seligman (1973) found that, after a period of failing to solve problems which were impossible to solve, his subjects seemed to be unable to recognize any success even when they were presented with what he regarded as clear examples of success. Instead they dismissed it as luck or because the tasks were easier.

Beck's therapy aims to teach people to modify their immediate cognitive responses to potentially upsetting situations, and then to restructure the fundamental beliefs on which their depressive responses are based. He employs extensive discussion and joint exploration of a person's beliefs using interviews and an objective test called the **Beck depression inventory** (see Box E).

---

### BOX E   Sample items from the Beck depression inventory

There are twenty-one items in the Beck depression inventory. Together they provide an overall score which is used to assess the extent of the depression. Each item is used diagnostically and explored with the patient. Three examples are given below.

(1) I do not feel sad
   I feel sad
   I am sad all the time and cannot snap out of it
   I am so sad and unhappy that I can't stand it

(2) I am not particularly discouraged about the future
   I feel discouraged about the future
   I feel I have nothing to look forward to
   I feel that the future is hopeless and that things cannot improve

(8) I don't feel I am worse than anybody else
   I am critical of myself for my weakness or my mistakes
   I blame myself all the time for my faults
   I blame myself for everything bad that happens

---

Beck regarded behaviour and cognition as reciprocally related and employed behavioural *experiments* in the form of 'homework tasks' designed to test and challenge people's negative cognitions. For example, they might be asked to confront a difficult and potentially depressing situation and keep a detailed record of what happens. An example of the type of work that might be undertaken is described in Box F overleaf.

## BOX F   Case study

Mrs Harris was severely depressed when she was referred for psychological help. She spent many hours of the day in bed and had great difficulty in doing simple tasks around the house. She was frequently tearful and reproached herself for her inadequacy as a mother, a housewife, daughter and spouse.

The first stages of therapy entailed asking her to keep a detailed record of her activities and, from this, selecting tasks that could be most easily mastered. She was seen twice a week at first and gradually, by means of structured planning and support, built up her activities. At the same time, she learned to attend to and eventually challenge her negative thinking. For instance, she frequently had the thought, 'I am hopeless; I cannot do anything right'. In therapy the accuracy of this cognition was questioned; she was asked to find and list things that she had in fact had done correctly. She learned that she could achieve many tasks provided that they were specific and small scale. When Mrs Harris questioned the value of such achievements ('Anyone can do them. They are trivial.'), therapy turned to a discussion of some of her basic assumptions and beliefs. It emerged that she had adopted a very rigid, perfectionist set of standards, which had been instilled into her from childhood.

Until her treatment Mrs Harris had not articulated these standards and she was quite surprised at how extreme and rigid they were. It became clear to her that much of her depression was directly caused by her own standards for correct behaviour. Because of their extreme nature, it was very difficult for her to succeed at anything. As therapy progressed she began to experiment with alternative ways of seeing herself and the world. Her depressed mood began to shift.

---

Other forms of cognitive treatments have developed. Meichenbaum (1977) has formulated a version of **cognitive therapy** based around self-instruction which is intended to block negative thoughts; for example . . . 'Oh it's no use, I know I won't be able to manage. I'm just in too much of a state . . . etc.' People are encouraged to develop more effective problem-solving strategies and to practise applying them. These techniques have also been extensively applied in **stress management**. People are taught to discriminate the emerging tensions in their bodies more accurately and to manage these using imagery coupled with progressive relaxation. (The technique, developed by Jacobson (1929), involves gaining a state of relaxation by progressively relaxing each part of the body, usually starting with the feet and legs and proceeding upwards.)

The emphasis in cognitive treatments is towards enabling the person to regain a sense of control over his or her life. It is recognized that some problems develop as a result of external events, such as loss and rejection, but the approach is based on the idea that people have the ability to overcome both these and *future* distressing events by developing better cognitive strategies for coping. Fennell (1983) has noted some important assumptions in this, namely that cognitive approaches provide a set of tactics for tackling problems without dealing with the person's deeper predisposition to see the world in a gloomy way, or to see more problems than other people do. In Chapter 8, you encountered the work of George Kelly who takes a broader cognitive perspective and emphasizes the need to bring about changes in a person's *core* constructs which represent their cognitions about the world.

Cognitive approaches are also used to cope with a range of anxiety-related disorders, particularly those associated with anxieties about controlling spontaneous functions. For example, in the case of sexual problems it has been suggested (Kaplan, 1974) that problems can be considered in terms of an interplay between conditioning and cognitive factors. The initial problem might develop as a result of anxiety generated by parental attitudes to sex or some initial embarrassing experience. This has been described as a **general anxiety**. This worry is likely to lead to failure in sexual relationships, such as premature ejaculation or inability to achieve orgasm. Subsequently, the person is likely to attempt to *control* him or herself to try to make the experience better, and may become extremely preoccupied with doing so. This leads to a **performance anxiety**; that is, a set of cognitions in the form of worries and insecurities about controlling the body. The overall consequence can be that the person's anxiety level is *increased* making it even more likely that he or she will not be able to achieve the desired experience.

A cognitive approach to this kind of problem would start by attempting to relieve the performance anxiety. This could be achieved by providing reassurance and offering some insights into how the performance anxiety and the general anxiety are affecting sexual behaviour. In addition, confidence is gradually built up using behavioural homework tasks to improve communication between partners and to reduce the anxiety associated with sexual intimacy.

An interesting variation of a cognitive approach is to use a **paradoxical approach** to such problems instead of a gradual, constructional one. Someone with sexual problems may be asked by the psychologist to attempt to deliberately induce the problem or to completely refrain from attempting sex for a prescribed period of time. This can provide initial relief from the performance anxiety and may even lead to the spontaneous return of enjoyable sexual activity. Subsequently, the general anxiety can be dealt with cognitively and confidence can be increased as better performance is achieved.

## Summary of Section 2

- Clinical psychologists need to be aware of biological factors and how they interact with external experiences.

- Behaviour therapy is based on classical conditioning and aims to extinguish patterns of learned behaviour. Behaviour modification, in contrast, aims to offer new patterns of rewards to establish new behaviour.

- Cognitive behaviourists take into account patients' cognitions, for example negative thoughts in explaining depressive behaviour.

# 3 | Psychotherapeutic models in clinical psychology

## 3.1 Psychodynamic approaches

The contribution of psychodynamic approaches to therapy has been very extensive and it is hard to do it justice. There is a full account of psychodynamic theory in Chapter 4. Here we will pick out a few of the most relevant points:

1  One major contribution that psychodynamic theory offers for clinical psychology is the hypothesis that clinical problems are largely rooted in negative, childhood *emotional* experiences which serve to disrupt the normal path of development throughd the psychosexual stages. Resulting problems may be manifest in childhood, adolescence or in various guises in adult life.

2  Difficulties are seen to be located in the *unconscious*. Therefore the memories of these events, including the thoughts and emotions surrounding them, are not readily accessible but need to be teased out using a variety of techniques, such as dream analysis, free association and so on. In some ways, this is the opposite of the cognitive approaches which tend to assume that cognitions are consciously available for negotiation between the psychologist and the patient.

3  Freud, and other psychodynamic theorists in differing degrees, proposed that sexuality was the cornerstone of emotional problems. The conflict between society's prohibitions regarding sexuality and a person's sexual desires is seen as resulting, for many people, in profound emotional problems which may need therapy.

4  In particular, Freud suggested that problems are related to inabilities to resolve sexual feelings within a family. The Oedipal triangle was a central concept suggesting that a young child is caught between ambivalent feelings of desire, guilt and anger as a result of his sexual feelings for his opposite-sex parent and antagonism towards the same-sex parent.

An important contribution to the practice of therapy is the emphasis on the **therapeutic relationship** and **transference**. Freud argued that his patients inevitably transferred their feelings on to him in various ways. The therapist could be seen as a punishing father about whom the patient was ambivalent; on the one hand hating and wanting to attack him and, on the other hand, harbouring unacceptable sexual feelings for him. Treatment involves the patient *working through* these feelings with the therapist and thereby becoming more aware and in control of them (strengthening the ego). Later Freudians, such as Klein and Fairbairn, emphasized that it was also inevitable that the therapist could in turn project his or her feelings onto the patient— **counter-transference**. Rather than attempting to eliminate such feelings, the dynamics of the therapeutic relationship were seen as a main point of focus.

Freud himself pioneered the technique of psychoanalysis, a one-to-one confrontation between analyst and patient, often at least once a week over many years. This is obviously a time-consuming and expensive treatment. In recent years, however, attempts have been made to apply psychodynamics using less intensive, brief psychoanalytic techniques which are more specifically focused on relieving specific problems. Many of these do not focus on sexuality and transference but take a broad range of emotional factors into account.

Group therapies are another way in which psychoanalytic therapies can be used to reach more people. These employ various techniques to bring out and work through unresolved emotional problems with other members of the group. One therapist can work with up to a dozen patients at a time, and therapeutically utilize various psychodynamic processes, such as transference, denial and projection between group members (Bion, 1961; Slavson, 1950).

A significant recent development has been family focused therapy. Here the aim is to resolve the tensions and emotions in the *whole* family as well as in the individual displaying the problems. The aim is to ensure that the family environment is subsequently more supportive and relapse is less likely to occur (Ackerman, 1966; Boszromenyi-Nagy and Sparks, 1973).

Traditionally, psychodynamic therapy has been carried out by psychoanalysts and some psychiatrists. Until recently, most clinical psychologists have had very little formal training in psychodynamic treatments, but they have absorbed many aspects of the theory, especially a recognition of the importance of the therapeutic relationship. Some behavioural therapists, such as Wolpe, criticized Freud's concepts strongly. However, when Wolpe was carrying out his technique of systematic desensitization, he recognized that the therapist–patient relationship was an important factor, especially in respect of transference and feelings of support and trust.

## 3.2 Humanistic perspectives

In Chapter 9, it was stressed that the main emphasis of humanistic psychology is on viewing people in a *holistic* way, integrating all aspects of the person—behaviour, emotions, cognitions, sensations, dreams and fantasies. There is a concern with consciousness, the awareness of self and the sense of purpose in life. People are seen as potentially integrated beings capable of acting in a self-directed and autonomous way. Humanistic therapies, such as Carl Rogers' client-centred counselling are concerned to understand how people *experience* their problems in their world. Treatment aims to provide a supportive environment in which people are able to experiment with new roles and are assisted to regain their sense of self-agency and purpose. There is an emphasis on helping people to *integrate* their feelings and their conscious awareness. This involves encouraging people to 'get in touch' with their feelings and to communicate more clearly. Rogers summarizes some of the aims of a humanistic approach as follows:

One way of assisting the individual to move towards openness to experience is through a relationship in which he is prized as a separate person, in which the experiencing going on within him is emphatically understood and valued, and in which he is given the freedom to experience his own feelings and those of others without being threatened by doing so.

(Rogers, 1967, p. 24)

There has been a massive development of group-based therapies: encounter groups (Rogers, 1970), gestalt groups (Perls, 1969) and psycho-drama groups (Moreno and Kipper, 1968), to name but a few. Most importantly, humanistic psychology has had a *political* impact on clinical psychology. Psychiatrists such as Laing (1960), Cooper (1972), Kelly (1955) and Rogers (1964) challenged the appropriateness of the medical model of psychological problems. They suggested that many problems were misrepresented as being like physical illnesses or forms of 'sickness'. Though these labels could have a temporarily benevolent effect in securing care for distressed people, in the long term they could have the unfortunate consequences of invalidating and denying the 'real' conflicts that faced such people, and their own attempts to solve these conflicts. They also vigorously criticized some aspects of the labelling process whereby people with 'problems' could become stigmatized as 'mental patients', which sometimes resulted in them being treated as inferior people (Goffman, 1961; Szasz, 1960; see also the description of the Rosenhan experiment in Section 1.3).

Most importantly for clinical psychology, the humanistic approach focused on changing the role of the therapist. It was argued that the trappings of a medical model—the image of 'men in white coats'—served to destroy people's sense of self-respect and confidence in their ability to solve their own problems. In Rogers non-directive counselling approach, the therapist attempts to avoid confusing his own needs with the client's needs by making interpretations and giving advice. All this can make the therapist feel good but may actually cause the patient to feel stupid: 'why couldn't I work that out myself?'. George Kelly also makes this point:

Some clients try to manage the interplay of roles so that they can find out what the therapist thinks, as if it would help them to get along in life without letting the therapist in on what they think. If he accepts the flattery, the therapist may waste time confiding his views to the client.

(Kelly, 1955, p. 97)

The emphasis, then, is on encouraging the patient to 'do the work' of solving his or her own problems with some assistance from a therapist in order to encourage the growth of self-confidence and respect. Some varieties of humanistic techniques go even further and dispense with the therapist role altogether. For example, in co-counselling or leaderless groups, people teach each other basic skills and then mutually assist one another in applying them to solving their own problems.

Humanistic ideas have had a considerable impact on clinical psychology and many psychologists are now involved in developing, supporting and advising various forms of self-help group in the community, such as alcoholics groups, family support groups and women's groups. Above all, there has been a recognition that prolonged forms of treatment and hospitalization can lead to states of dependence and helplessness similar to those described by Seligman in his laboratory-based studies (see Section 2.3). The clinical psychologist working in the humanistic tradition is therefore concerned, not simply to diagnose and then remove problems as effectively as possible, but to ensure that the person develops skills and confidence in managing potential future problems.

## 3.3 Family therapy

A major contribution to the understanding of clinical problems has resulted from the applications and development of Gregory Bateson's (1965) and Don Jackson's (1968) research on communication in families. Their early studies suggested that many symptoms can usefully be seen as a function of the **communication dynamics** of intimately involved people in groups such as families. Therapists repeatedly found that, following relief of people's problems in hospital, they often deteriorated on returning home. This observation led to the suggestion that a patient's symptoms could be seen as functioning to avoid, or distract attention from, other areas of conflict in the family. Jackson (1957) observed a see-saw effect whereby improvement in one person could result in deterioration in another member of the family. He went on to suggest that this represented a form of equilibrium, or resistance to change, in the family. This is known as **homeostasis**, a concept borrowed from biology where it is used to describe the regulation of physiological functions within given parameters. This offered a new way of regarding the phenomenon of resistance to change which psychodynamic and other therapists had seen as depending essentially on an individual, rather than on interpersonal interactions within the family. The argument was that to label one member of the family as 'ill' might delay or prevent change in the family as a whole. New forms of treatment developed which involved working with the family group. Box G overleaf describes an example of this type of therapy.

The *pattern* of interaction between Mark and his mother suggested a **pernicious cycle** whereby Mark's solutions to his mother's interference were to retreat into his shell, sleep a lot and cease to take care of himself. This made his mother interfere even more in his life in an angry and critical way, accusing him of being lazy and telling him to get a job. Mark would, eventually, react to this by acting in some bizarre and disturbed way which could result in another episode of hospitalization. Neither of their behaviours was seen to be consciously malicious but as forming an unfortunate and unhappy interactional sequence. This pattern had become well established over the years and was not easy to change.

Therapy involved attempts to clarify their communications and to develop their understanding of how they were both contributing to a confusing situation. As an experiment, Mark was asked to take a stand to assert his independence so that his mother could show where she would draw the line. His mother was asked to keep a detailed record of her own reactions to Mark's attempts to assert himself. Mark's feelings towards his father were also discussed, as was the extent to which his mother saw Mark as being like her

## BOX G   Case study

After moving to live nearer to his mother, Mark, a 25-year-old man, started to display disordered thinking and emotional distress, and he eventually slashed his wrists. He was admitted to a psychiatric hospital and initially prescribed medication for schizophrenic symptoms. He had a history of similar episodes which usually involved periods of stay in a psychiatric hospital.

Mark's previous treatment had focused on him as an individual. However, on this occasion, the consultant psychiatrist noted signs of conflict between Mark and his mother, and he referred them to a family therapy clinic specializing in treatment for long-term psychotic problems. The family therapy team was headed by a clinical psychologist and included a psychiatrist and two psychiatric nurses.

Assessment revealed that Mark generally felt that he was a failure, especially in comparison to his academically successful siblings; in particular, he felt that he had not come up to the high expectations of his father who had died ten years previously. Mark was well above average on intelligence tests. His mother alternated between periods of intense concern and guilt about his welfare, with periods of apparent emotional indifference and irritation at his difficult behaviour. She also tended to interfere in his life, forbidding him to maintain a relationship with a girlfriend whom she regarded as too disturbed for him. Mark, for his part, also gave mixed messages to his mother. He was vague and unable to explain what he wanted for himself and what he wanted from his mother. Instead, he occasionally stated that he resented her interference but followed this with episodes of incompetent behaviour which necessitated her assisting him.

husband and was making self-fulfilling assumptions based on this. The mother's view of Mark gradually changed and she saw him in a more positive light. In turn, Mark came to regard his mother's actions as motivated by a positive desire to help him to get back on his feet and gain adult independence. This permitted a change in their mutual roles. The mother was able to talk about her problems, especially her loneliness since her husband had died, and she admitted that Mark's problems had served to help distract her from her own distress.

Mark later discharged himself from the psychiatric hospital and gradually ceased to use medication. It is questionable whether Mark was totally 'cured' but he was able to live a more independent life. The improvements in his relationships with his mother seemed to be a vital part of this and they continued to get along more effectively.

The contrast with most of the other approaches discussed in this chapter is sharp. Freud was aware of the complexities and problems associated with family life but, surprisingly, he was strongly against the involvement of family members in therapy. He likened the involvement of relatives in the therapeutic process to an undesirable intrusion into a surgical procedure: 'Ask yourselves now how many of these operations would turn out successfully if they had to take place in the presence of all the members of the patient's family, who would stick their noses into the field of the operation and exclaim aloud at every incision' (Freud, 1963, p. 459).

The impact of a family perspective on clinical work has been far-reaching. In addition to specifically family orientated treatments, there has been a growing recognition of the need to take into account the family and social contexts of problems. This has been particularly evident in children's problems where there has been a recognition of the involvement of parents in the children's difficulties (Rutter, 1975; Haley, 1976). There has also been more recognition of the need to prepare families for the return of a member who has been in hospital, for example, in situations such as schizophrenia. Assisting families to maintain the emotional atmosphere within acceptable limits has been found to reduce the incidence of relapse and the need for rehospitalization (Brown *et al.*, 1962).

## 3.4 Common threads

There is a need to distinguish between approaches to clinical work in order to develop more effective and acceptable therapies. However, throughout this chapter, we have resisted the temptation to present clinical psychology as being divided into conflicting theoretical camps. There are sufficient common threads which it is useful to identify. The following are important features that the various approaches share.

### Empathy

Most approaches, though especially those deriving from the humanistic perspective, recognize that, irrespective of the treatment technique, successful treatment involves the need to establish a positive, trusting relationship with the patient, his or her family, and others (Yates, 1983; Rogers, 1957). If for no other reason, this is necessary in order to gain the co-operation of the patient, especially in the sometimes tedious record-keeping that is required in behavioural programmes.

### The therapeutic relationship

There is a general recognition of the need to consider the relationship between the patient and therapist. Both patient and therapist bring a history of previous experiences to the therapeutic encounter. Psychodynamic approaches particularly emphasize the issues of how transferences and counter-transferences function in therapy. The therapist has to be able to modify his or her relationship with the patient, couple or family in order to overcome their resistance to change which is a frequent feature of psychological problems.

### Communication

This may seem glaringly obvious, but it is important to stress that all forms of therapy require clear communication at different levels between the patient and the therapist. For many patients, the ability to communicate about their problems is central, and symptoms often emerge as a form of *indirect* communication, expressing what they want to say, but feel they are not allowed to say. (Slade, 1982; Owens and Ashcroft, 1982; Haley, 1976.) Perls' (1969) gestalt therapy encourages people to use an exercise that requires them to *experience* their emotions in the session. People are asked to imagine some real aspects of their lives, such as a parent sitting in an empty chair, and to express their feelings *to* the imagined person in the chair, rather than simply attempt to talk *about* their feelings and cognitions. This communicates more directly to the therapist what they are experiencing.

### Maintenance and escalation of problems

Behavioural and family therapy models share an important emphasis on analysing the factors responsible for *maintaining* problematic behaviour. It has been widely recognized in clinical psychology that it is essential to consider how and why problems are being maintained, and to discuss what *function(s)* they serve. As you will see in Section 4, this is reflected in the clinical approach of functional analysis which aims to incorporate a range of theoretical orientations in its analysis of the causes of problems.

### Pernicious cycles

Finally, a number of orientations include the idea that problems can escalate through a cycle of interaction between the behaviour and its consequences. The classic example is that of the person who starts drinking to gain some relief from worries and problems. Unfortunately, the problems become worse as a result of the alcholic's inability to deal with them effectively because of the effects of drink (Heather, 1985). This in turn can aggravate the problem. Family therapists likewise talk about 'attempted solutions' to problems, such as a father nagging a wayward adolescent child to behave more responsibly, which can further anger the child leading to more of the same behaviour.

## Summary of Section 3

- Freud's psychodynamic theory has influenced clinical psychologists' views about unconscious emotions, particularly transference and counter-transference between analyst and patient in the therapeutic situation.

- Many clinical psychologists have adapted the insights of humanistic psychologists about the need for empathy and the self-directed nature of personal growth.

- Family therapy stresses the importance of the interactions between members of a group which may result in unacknowledged resistance to change.

- Although there are different approaches to clinical work informed by different theoretical perspectives, they share many common features.

# 4 | The scientist-practitioner model of clinical psychology

Having reviewed some of the major theoretical orientations and the therapeutic approaches associated with them, we will consider how clinical psychologists make decisions about which types of treatment are most appropriate. Such decisions are not made simply on the basis of theoretical arguments. Other factors such as the length of treatment, its cost, the availability of staff trained to work with a particular method, and its estimated effectiveness have to be balanced against each other.

## 4.1 Assessment of problems and choice of models

The different psychological theories that we have outlined in the previous section imply different approaches not only to treatment but also to assessment. For example, behavioural approaches tend to focus on assessing the patterns of reinforcements that are maintaining the behaviours; cognitive approaches examine the person's patterns of thinking; a family approach focuses on the relationships within the family; and a psychodynamic approach concentrates on the patient's unconscious emotions. In other words, it is not a question of analysing a problem and then deciding on an appropriate treatment. Each theoretical approach influences the kind of analysis and its associated treatment.

So how can clinical psychologists start out from the full range of theories available and apply the appropriate type of analysis to a particular problem? What is needed, in addition to a grasp of the basic psychological theories, are some **metaperspectives**; that is, guiding frameworks which assist in carrying out a systematic assessment of the problem and the efficacy of different treatments.

A metaperspective or general framework which has gained recognition in clinical psychology as providing a model to guide the process of clinical work is known as the scientist-practitioner model. After outlining this model, we will go on to consider functional analysis, which derives from it. This offers some more specific guidelines to assist the process of clinical work. We can think of this model *not* as a theoretical approach or another form of treatment but as a **heuristic**; that is, a set of plans or strategies to assist the process of exploration and reasoning.

## 4.2 The scientist-practitioner model

In earlier chapters you have encountered the view that psychology should be a scientific discipline. There has been extensive debate regarding the applicability of a version of science drawn predominantly from the natural sciences to all types of psychological activity. For example, the psychodynamic approach embodies a variety of concepts which are difficult to assess or test in a normal scientific way (see Chapter 4). However, this does not mean that all aspects of the theory are non-scientific. The practice of good psychodynamic therapy involves the formulation of clinical hypotheses which the therapist revises as new information emerges. The theory is also potentially testable in terms of the extent to which the therapeutic interventions serve to reduce distressing symptoms.

Historically, there have been two main ways in which it has been attempted to apply science in clinical work:

1   The findings from psychological research have been applied to clinical problems. In particular, there has been an emphasis on the application of techniques that have been demonstrated in a laboratory (e.g. the use of extinction as a procedure in behaviour therapy).

2   The other approach, which we will concentrate on, conceives of clinical psychology as being guided by, and operating within, the framework of general scientific method. This involves clear descriptions of problems, the formation of alternative hypotheses guided by psychological knowledge, and the testing of the hypotheses by observation, monitoring and other forms of assessment of alternative treatments. Intuitive and qualitative observations are regarded as potential hypotheses. This is known as the **scientist-practitioner model**.

We would argue that this model has become central for clinical psychology. As you will see in Section 4.3, people who display apparently similar problems, such as a phobia, may require radically different treatments since the underlying causes and functions of the symptoms are different. Each case has unique features and treatment, and the role of the 'scientific' clinical psychologist is to select and assess hypotheses about analysis and treatment for each particular person. As Shapiro (1985) puts it: 'It seems necessary to try to make explicit the role of the scientific method in every aspect of clinical work, even in the most intimate moment-to-moment interactions with the patients. We need to develop a philosophy of scientific clinical work' (p. 2).

Shapiro goes on to give a simple example of this emphasis from his own clinical work. A woman walked in to and out of his office very slowly with apparent difficulty. However, when she had left his office, she walked down the street quickly and easily. He felt that he was being manipulated, but he then realized that his feeling was really a **hypothesis** about the reason for her behaviour. An alternative hypothesis was that the slow walking may have been caused by the 'freezing' effect of a very strong feeling, such as fear, evoked by the interview situation. Subsequently, this second hypothesis was confirmed by nurses and the occupational therapist involved with the woman who said that she typically 'froze' and withdrew into herself if anyone responded in a mildly threatening way, such as by speaking loudly.

The scientist-practitioner approach embodies the idea of **progressive hypothesizing**; that is, the formulation of one or more provisional working hypotheses based upon detailed initial observation and information gathering (see Figure 15.2). The hypotheses are expressed in a testable form in order to generate treatment interventions by the therapist. The effects of these

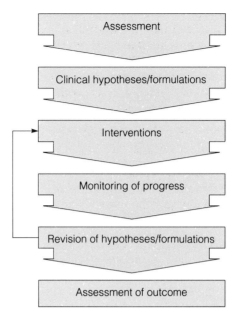

**Figure 15.2** Progressive hypothesizing

treatments are monitored using a variety of evidence, including observations of behaviour as well as subjective reports by the patient. This approach has two main advantages:

1 It helps to clarify and to maximize the accuracy of assessment since clinical psychologists have to examine their assumptions repeatedly, including their own preconceptions, needs, prejudices and moral attitudes. Likewise, the continual process of assessment reveals the effectiveness or otherwise of the treatments adopted.

2 It helps the clinician to find his way through the complexities of clinical work. A working hypothesis helps to organize and manage the proliferation of sometimes contradictory information that can otherwise become overwhelming.

Shapiro summarizes the scientific approach to clinical psychology in this way:

There is increasing concern with clinically relevant phenomena: their characterization, explanation and control, in the broad sense of that word; and scientific method appears the essential means of pursuing that concern. It produces a style which can be described in terms of five features: (1) a continuous and critical assimilation of the relevant general and critical literature; (2) a wholistic awareness of the total context of psychological, social and somatic (biological) influences upon the person's dysfunctions; (3) a critical, i.e. scientific, electicism in the selection of explanations and procedures; (4) an attention to the effects of the clinician's own emotional needs upon professional behaviour; and (5) a continuous attention to both idiographic (individual) and nomotheric (general) evaluation of both assessment and treatment procedures.

(Shapiro, 1985, p.10)

As you can see, this definition includes the important issue of **evaluation of treatments**. But it is broader and, in addition, it stresses the need for continual assessment of the psychologist's assumptions, behaviour and selection of explanatory theories. Most importantly, it focuses on the *process* of clinical work, the moment-to-moment interaction between the patient and the clinical psychologist. We can note a similarity here with psychodynamic theory's emphasis on the relationship between the patient and the clinician as a central aspect of clinical work.

## 4.3 Functional analysis

Scientists generally try to control their subject-matter by identifying and then manipulating the *causes* of what they observe. Sometimes causal relationships are relatively simple and well understood. For example, the direction of a snooker ball which is struck by the white ball with a particular force at a particular angle can be predicted with considerable accuracy. Usually, however, causal explanations are more complex. We only have to add the impact of a second or third ball, and it becomes much more difficult to predict the outcome of the impacts.

Human behaviour may sometimes be explained by relatively simple causal relationships; a woman playing a fruit machine may lead to the hypothesis that she is doing so because of the existence of powerful, expected reinforcement. Some schools of psychology would argue that this situation is rather more complex; for example, that the person is playing to punish herself.

Usually, human behaviour involves complex chains and webs of causal relationships. Why, for instance, would a woman engage in repetitive hand-washing, sometimes up to hundreds of times a day? There would appear to be no obvious reinforcement, and it adds nothing to assert that she does it because she has a compulsion. The process of identifying the causes of behaviour is called **functional analysis**. It is called *functional* analysis because the emphasis is on analysing the *functions* that the behaviour may fulfil for an individual. Is it the function of hand-washing to occupy the day, or to get rid of guilty feelings because the woman's parents thought sex was filthy? These are all preliminary hypotheses about the function of behaviour, which in turn raise issues about what environmental factors may be maintaining that behaviour. Causal questions are in effect 'why' questions; *why* is the behaviour happening?

There are of course many ways of answering 'why' questions. Let us digress briefly. An infamous American bank robber, Willie Suttom, was once asked by the prison chaplain why he robbed banks. After a few moments thought Willie replied, 'because that's where the money is'. This explanation did not help the well-meaning padre in his quest of turning Willie away from a life of crime. Nor would answers such as 'because I enjoy it', or 'because I had a deprived childhood'. We are not concerned with the correctness or otherwise of such explanations but with their *usefulness*. In a functional analysis of behaviour we are interested in identifying factors in the environment which *maintain* the behaviour. Psychologists set about doing this by *manipulating* the environment through treatments, and by *assessing* whether these bring about any change in the person's behaviour.

It is possible, of course, that there are events deep in a person's past which contribute to his or her behaviour. But this does not rule out the possibility that there are also *current* variables which are influential and accessible. Functional analysis is mainly concerned with the way that people *currently* construe past events rather than the past events themselves.

When carrying out a functional analysis, it is important to remember that behaviours which at first sight appear to be quite similar may be serving quite different functions. Likewise, behaviours which appear to be quite different may be serving similar functions. For example, a boy might whine and cry, he might hold his breath until he goes blue, cling to his mother's skirt, fall down and bang his head on the floor, throw his food and sit silently and refuse to speak. All of these appear to be different forms of behaviour. However, they could all serve the same function of attracting his mother's attention. In functional analysis they could all be treated as equivalent. Some psychologists would say that they all have the same 'meaning'. On the other hand, a scream may involve the same behaviour of opening the mouth and making a noise, but it will serve very different functions if it is a scream of terror, excitement or joy. What gives them their different meanings are their different causes and contexts.

When doing a functional analysis, it is crucial to identify the **antecedents** of the behaviour (what comes before), and the **consequences** of the behaviour (what follows). Antecedents can be thought of as the possible *causes* of behaviour. Consequences can be thought of as the results of the behaviour which are likely to be *maintaining* it. In behavioural terms, the consequences can be thought of as the *reinforcers* which maintain a particular pattern of behaviour. The three stages of investigation in functional analysis are shown in Figure 15.3.

**Figure 15.3**  The three stages of investigation in functional analysis

Let us look now at some examples of the contribution that functional analysis can make to the practice of clinical psychology. We will start by considering the case study in Box H overleaf.

It is important to recognize that functional analysis is essentially a *pragmatic* exercise, and it cannot really be carried out without trying to manipulate the consequences and antecedents. Therapy based on functional analysis has to test hypotheses systematically. Otherwise, the clinician will identify antecedents and consequences which might *not* be related to the behaviour in question. In the case study described in Box H, we used the terms 'might have included' and 'possibly included'. The only way to be sure of the analysis would be to change some of the circumstances to see what the effect would

---

**BOX H ˙ Case study**

The *behaviour*: a woman patient talked excessively, in a bizarre manner, about the pain experienced during intercourse as being like the pain of Jesus on the cross. Extensive interviews with her, observation of her behaviour and self-report measures indicated that the following analysis was possible:

Relevant *antecedents* (i.e. the causes of the bizarre talk) might have included: (a) pain during intercourse; (b) a religious background with a good deal of conflict (this was at the time Pope John forbade the use of the contraceptive pill); (c) disputes between the woman and her husband about the desirability of having a child; and (d) the presence of doctors and psychologists willing to listen.

The *consequences* of the bizarre talk possibly included: (a) getting the attention of family, friends and psychologists; (b) the avoidance of discussions about having a family; (c) removal from an environment in which difficult decisions were having to be made; and (d) the avoidance of painful intercourse.

---

be. For example, we have suggested that the woman's marital problems, involving disputes with her husband about having a child, may have been one of the antecedents (causes) of her behaviour. We could investigate this by offering marital therapy and observing whether there was a decrease in her bizarre speech if they came to some agreement about having children.

## 4.4  A case study: anorexia nervosa

We can take another example to illustrate the application of functional analysis to a problem which has previously been considered from a variety of theoretical perspectives and has generated considerable debate amongst clinicians. Anorexia nervosa is a condition consisting of an excessive and prolonged loss of appetite without any discernible physical causes (see, also, Chapter 5). It is accompanied by reduction in body weight, in some cases with a risk of death. It is a disorder predominantly found in young women. Slade (1982) identifies a number of factors which might come into play as antecedents in a functional analysis of anorexia nervosa. He arrived at these factors by studying the literature on anorexia. Although it has not always been possible to establish that each of these factors is always relevant, there is sufficient evidence for us to entertain them as likely possible causes.

**Antecedents**

1  *Low self-esteem*   This covers a number of factors of a developmental and environmental nature. Adolescent conflicts often play a role, especially when family and social difficulties are on-going. Interpersonal problems, especially with the opposite sex, are important, and the experiences of

stress and failure also contribute to the problem. These can come about because family or school have high expectations of the person, who is usually a high-achiever, and is made to feel that she must continue to strive for the top. Such expectations may be self-imposed. All these factors interact to produce what Slade calls a 'general dissatisfaction with life and the self'.

2   *Perfectionist tendencies*   This general antecedent is well established in the literature. It describes the tendency to see things in black and white terms, and anything less than perfection is considered to be failure. In the presence of this condition, Slade suggests that other key antecedents will lead to anorexia.

3   *Need for complete control*   This antecedent involves the wish for complete control and success in life or in one aspect of life. Since this goal is virtually unobtainable whenever the behaviour of other people is involved, it is transformed into control over the self. Anorexics rigidly control not only their eating, but also their sexual drive, bowel function, sleep patterns and menstruation.

4   *Specific psycho-social stimuli*   Given the other antecedents, Slade suggests that there will be specific triggers for excessive dieting. These might be: comments from peers about body shape or weight; the observation that one's friends are dieting; or the observation that slimness is valued in western society, especially for girls.

These, then, are possible antecedents for the emergence of anorexic behaviour. According to Slade, they are supported in the clinical literature, and they are widely acknowledged by clinicians. What is often overlooked or poorly researched, however, is the other component of functional analysis—the consequences. What happens to the anorexic as a result of her behaviour? Slade identifies some likely possibilities.

**Consequences**

1   *Positive reinforcement*   In the context of generally feeling a failure and having little *control* over one's environment and life, it may be powerfully reinforcing to succeed with extreme dieting and control over the bodily functions. Weight loss *in itself* is not usually a positive reinforcer, as shown by the failure of other would-be slimmers to lose weight. Weight loss in the context of seeking to gain *control* may be much more potent.

2   *Negative reinforcement*   This is reinforcement which comes about by the **avoidance** of a situation. Slade suggests that the fear of weight gain and an unacceptable body shape is avoided by anorexic behaviour. Coupled with this, the incessant preoccupation with food, weight and size allows the person to avoid some of the issues identified as antecedents. For example, the person can avoid the threat of meeting, and being possibly rejected by, members of the opposite sex at parties and other social occasions. In this way, adolescent conflicts, the worry of lacking social skills and the worry of being unattractive are avoided.

3   *Reinforcements for other family members*   The anorexic condition has a powerful controlling effect on the anorexic's social situation. Minuchin

and Baker (1976) have noted, for example, that the focus of the family members on the anorexic may function to suppress other conflicts which threaten to split the family. These divisions become submerged, but they are often revealed indirectly in disagreements between the parents about how to deal with their anorexic daughter: whether they should be tough and force her to eat, or kind and try to understand what is troubling her.

What then are the *treatment* implications of such a functional analysis? It is clear that simplistic solutions, aimed only at reversing weight loss and getting the person to eat, are unlikely to have long-term effects. They will not alter the antecedents and the consequences which are so important to the person and which play a crucial controlling role in the person's life. Efforts to persuade a girl that she does not need to pay so much attention to social fashions about slimness and that she is attractive without needing to be so slim are equally doomed to failure.

In recent years a therapeutic approach which is based on the concept of functional analysis has become influential in treating anorexia. Its originator, the American psychologist Israel Goldiamond, calls it the **constructional approach**. He defines it as 'an orientation whose solution to problems is the construction of repertoires (or their reinstatement or transfer to new situations) rather than the elimination of repertoires' (Goldiamond, 1974, p. 14). How does the approach work?

The therapist approaches the problem by asking what the client would be doing if she did not have the problem. In this way, the therapist focuses on the function of the behaviour and the construction of alternative, more desirable, repertoires of behaviour which will satisfy the client's needs. It is a contrast to more traditional clinical approaches which, as Goldiamond points out, 'focus on the alleviation or elimination of distress through a variety of means. . . . Such approaches often consider the problem in terms of pathology which, regardless of how it was established or developed or is maintained, is to be eliminated' (ibid.).

We are *not* arguing that procedures which can eliminate problems quickly and efficiently should never be used. However, in many cases, and especially in those where there are many complex factors affecting the behaviour, such as in anorexia nervosa, constructional approaches might be more effective in the long run. Slade (1982) points out several (constructional) therapeutic implications of his functional analytic approach to anorexia. He argues that a necessary precondition for therapeutic recovery is the establishment of major sources of satisfaction in a person's life: 'the anorexic needs to develop a whole new repertoire of behaviours to replace the single one of anorexic behaviour. . . . [These] include the establishment of independence from and within the family, academic and vocational training, and leisure interests, etc.' (Slade 1982, p. 178). In order to develop new repertoires, some of the important antecedents will need to be resolved. We will now consider the kinds of treatment that might be tried to achieve this.

# 4.5 Selection of treatments

One set of treatments might attempt to change the *internal* cognition of the anorexic. Kelly's repertory grid technique (see Chapter 8, Section 4.3) could be used to investigate the constructs that the anorexic uses to construe herself, her family, her friends and her life in general. We cannot assume that all people displaying anorexic symptoms see their problems in the same way. This analysis allows us to see whether the person might be able to develop her view of the world in a way which allows her to see herself as other than needing to be excessively thin. It might uncover the anxieties that the anorexic has about being in her social world as a person of normal weight, whether she is worried about sex, trying desperately to achieve academic success, or concerned about her attractiveness.

Kelly (1955) suggests that people find a massive revision of their constructs about the world extremely threatening, even when their current views and attitudes appear to be unhelpful and maintain them in a painful existence. A constructional approach might, therefore, employ a form of cognitive therapy which would not challenge an anorexic person's cognitions directly, but attempt gradually to elaborate her constructs. The approach might involve discussions with the anorexic based on her repertory grids, exploring and observing her relationship with her mother and father. The treatment might also employ psychodynamic techniques to uncover unconscious feelings about herself and her parents; for example, the origins of her perfectionist tendencies and whether these originated in the family. This might reveal issues of rivalry with other siblings for parental attention, or feelings of parental rejection which relate to unresolved Oedipal feelings. A constructional approach might deal with these by assisting the girl to resolve these feelings so that the anorexia is no longer required to serve the function of avoiding them.

Other treatments might be used to alter the *external* circumstances which may be maintaining the anorexic behaviour. These would include an analysis of the family situation, social life, school or work situation. First, at a simple level, it might be that an anorexic girl gains considerable attention from friends and family as a consequence of her condition. This may be reinforcing to some extent and also contribute to the development of a rigid and very restricted self-perception—'I am *an anorexic*'. Second, in the family and social situation, the anorexia might have more complex consequences, such as enabling others to avoid their own conflicts and family difficulties by diverting attention away from their own conflicts on to the girl. In a work situation, for instance, people will often spend a lot of time talking about and trying to help someone with a problem, but they may secretly feel relieved that they are free of such problems, feel superior in some way and submerge their interpersonal conflicts as they *unite* in discussing the person with the problem.

In the family situation, it may be possible to initiate changes to provide a more constructive environment so that the anorexic's problems are no longer needed by the family in order for the family to function. In other situations, such as work, this is harder to arrange, but the girl might find it helpful to discuss the ways in which others might feel threatened by any signs of improvement in her state and find ways of dealing with this.

The point of functional analysis is that it does not only focus on possible causal antecedents. It also provides hypotheses about the *consequences* of behaviour and so brings to light aspects of an anorexic case that might easily be missed. To the extent that the therapist can identify these, he can start to work with the patient and her family and friends to attempt to manipulate the consequences in various ways. If this leads to an improvement in behaviour, then this starts to confirm the hypothesis about the links between antecedents and consequences—a truly scientist-practitioner approach.

We can illustrate this approach further by looking at a case in which a variety of theoretical models were combined within an overall functional analysis framework to assess and treat an eating disorder. Read the initial information about the case in Box I and try to apply the framework of functional analysis to it. Try to identify some of the antecedents and consequences.

---

### BOX I    A case of bulimia nervosa

Helen was a 21-year-old student in the final year of a sociology degree. She was referred to a clinical psychologist by her GP who said that she was depressed and had become obsessed with food to such an extent that she found it impossible to work, and that she had stopped seeing most of her friends. Helen was not markedly underweight, but appeared pale and drawn. She admitted that she binged two or three times a week, eating huge quantities of food and then deliberately vomiting. At other times, she ate very little and only a selection of carefully chosen 'good' foods which she believed were not fattening.

(Adapted from Marzillier and Hall, 1987)

---

Helen's treatment fell into three parts. In the first phase, she was asked to keep a detailed record of her food consumption and to identify meals in which she felt that she was in control and those in which she felt she was not. She was advised to restrict her eating to three planned meals a day, regardless of how hungry she felt. No attempt was made at this stage to check her vomiting or modify the type of food she was eating. The therapist gave Helen as much support as possible, seeing her initially two or three times a week and providing her with corrective information about food, weight and diet. As a result, Helen gradually brought her eating more under control and the episodes of binging and vomiting were markedly reduced. Her mood lifted and she began to take up her work again.

In the second phase, Helen was seen on a weekly basis and the focus shifted to the problems and stresses that had provoked the eating disorder—the antecedents. The therapist encouraged Helen to relax her rigid restrictions and try 'banned foods' as an experiment designed to demonstrate that this would not lead to loss of control nor immediate weight gain (consequences). At this point, Helen began to talk more generally about herself and in particular about her parents. The psychologist detected that Helen had ambivalent feelings towards her family. She described her father in highly idealized terms, yet it also appeared that he was rarely at home and, when he was, he would shut himself away to work. Helen was rather contemptuous about her mother's contribution to the family ('cook and housewife'). Yet it appeared that she was emotionally quite close to her. Helen also mentioned casually, in passing, an ex-boyfriend to whom she had been very close for most of her student life. These messages alerted the therapist to the role played by disturbed relationships in Helen's problems. It was possible that some further consequences of her behaviour were in avoiding the emotional difficulties she had with these relationships. It was also possible that her problems fulfilled the function of distracting her from confronting problems within the family.

The final phase focused on the maintenance of change and preparation for possible relapse. Helen saw the therapist regularly and, as her trust in him increased, she was able to admit for the first time that she felt angry towards her parents, and her father in particular. Helen was encouraged to accept that such feelings were not abnormal and that her worth as a person was not dependent on the approval of her parents or others. Helen's self-image had been narrowly restricted to her appearance, hence her excessive concern with food and eating. The treatment allowed her to see how other aspects of herself were valuable and important.

Finally, it is important to note that the treatment Helen received proved helpful but, in general, problems of anorexia bulimia are difficult to treat. What we have tried to demonstrate is that functional analysis enabled the clinical psychologist to draw on a wide range of theoretical approaches in assessing and treating the problem, and to refine and develop the treatment as it progressed.

SAQ 3 Consider Helen's case again. Which of the other theoretical approaches described in Sections 2 and 3 could have been adopted to alter the antecedents and the consequences of Helen's symptoms?

# Summary of Section 4

- Each theoretical approach implies a particular method for assessing problems and specific treatments.

- One framework for assessing problems and selecting treatments is the scientist-practitioner model.

- The role of the 'scientific' clinical psychologist is to formulate hypotheses which can be tested by manipulating different types of treatment.

- An important method of assessment is functional analysis. This involves analysing antecedents and consequences of behaviour.

- Treatments are assessed in terms of their success in changing behaviour in relation to antecedents and consequences.

# 5 | Discussion and conclusions

## 5.1 Critical appraisals

The concept of clinical psychology as 'research' has been a theme running throughout this chapter. We have indicated that the concept of therapy as involving *progressive hypothesizing* is central to the scientist-practitioner model and specifically to the framework of functional analysis. One important implication of this view is that it helps us to abandon some of the restrictive and evaluative labels that have previously been placed on psychological problems. Functional analysis reveals that apparently similar problems can have quite different antecedents in a person's life, and that they can be maintained by quite different consequences.

A functional analysis aims to identify the relevant variables and the nature of their relationship to the problem. Research is thus directed at classes of variables defined in terms of their functional relationship, and in this sense each problem can be seen as a research process, involving the testing of hypotheses, forming models etc.

(Owens and Ashcroft, 1982, p. 184)

The approach *subsumes* a wide range of theoretical orientations. However, one criticism is that functional analysis arises from a behavioural approach to problems which stresses that, if we look closely enough, we can find factors that are responsible for the maintenance of problems. Some clinicians might not fully accept this and argue that some problems, like repetitive hand-washing or phobias, appear to have no clear antecedents or consequences that maintain the behaviour. If the antecedents or consequences are not available for change, then an eliminative, symptom-directed approach, aimed at *removing* the behaviour, might be all that can be done. This represents part of an established debate about whether some treatments merely remove the presenting symptoms without tackling the underlying causes and leave the person vulnerable to develop new symptoms—*symptom substitution*. Psychodynamic theories in particular have stressed this possibility .

We have already seen that some problems are not predominantly psychological in origin, and that a first stage in treatment is to assess the extent to which a problem has a biological basis. Nevertheless, even for such problems, there are likely to be psychological consequences which it is often necessary to deal with. An analysis which includes an assessment of potential factors that might be involved in maintaining problems *is* necessary. Functional analysis has also demonstrated its usefulness in comparison with methods aimed simply at the elimination of symptoms in a variety of problems which were hitherto regarded as extremely resistant to treatments, such as psychotic problems, anorexia and depression (Goldiamond, 1974; Slade, 1982; Owens and Ashcroft, 1982; Watzlawick, 1974).

We have also suggested that there is a need for clinical work to be somewhat *eclectic* by taking account of a wide range of theoretical frameworks to explain the causes of a problem and to guide treatment. It can be argued that an eclectic approach leads to muddled thinking and that a clinical psychologist would do better to become competent in a few techniques derived from one theory, and practise those properly. This can be countered by the argument that in applied situations more than one theoretical approach is usually required to take account of the wide range of possible factors involved. To focus narrowly on a particular theory in clinical practice might deprive a patient of other beneficial approaches. Whatever position is taken, there is general agreement that it is important that clinical psychologists attempt to discover which aspects of various techniques are effective. As we saw in Section 3.4, there are some characteristics common to a variety of theoretical perspectives.

## 5.2 A pragmatic approach

A related issue is that functional analysis is excessively *pragmatic*. In its emphasis on current factors that might be maintaining the problems, it might fail to draw out the important differences between different theoretical approaches and their implications for treatment. As a consequence, the development of psychological theories and our understanding and treatment of clinical problems may be impeded. On the other hand, some clinicians argue that we can hold one theoretical framework to explain the *causes* of a problem but utilize another to produce *change*. For example, in the case of anorexia nervosa we can explain causation in psychodynamic terms but decide that some behavioural or family/systems-based interventions are useful in producing change. Some psychologists have even gone as far as to suggest that in some circumstances we need not even concern ourselves unduly with a search for theoretical explanations of causation but operate pragmatically in terms of which factors appear to control behaviour and can be manipulated to produce change.

We have attempted throughout to show how the process of clinical work, guided by the scientist-practitioner model, involves a continual *appraisal of change* in the analysis of problems. However, the issue is more complex than this. In Section 1, we pointed out that psychologists are influenced, as are clients, by what is deemed by society to be normal at any one time. Hence, at times, they must go beyond a simple focus on the presenting problems, and consider why the person is seeking help and even whether he or she should be seeking help. The scientist-practitioner model is helpful because it stresses a need to consider an unlimited range of possible indications of change rather than being limited by a specific theoretical orientation. For example, a behaviourist might not note changes in cognitions, and a cognitive therapist changes in family structures. On the other hand, the criticisms can be made that this approach is too loose and there might be a danger of assuming too easily that change is occurring.

Most clinical psychologists evolve their own treatment styles. You will have detected this in the case studies that have been presented. This can be seen as the 'place where we start'. Based on the preliminary assessment, a psychologist is likely to veer towards a choice of treatments that he or she is familiar with. Functional analysis may be seen as an antidote to becoming complacent about the usefulness of a particular orientation in a case. If an intervention has no effect, or an effect different from the one predicted, the psychologist will be forced to revise his or her hypotheses about what is happening.

## 5.3 Clinical research

An important question related to these critical points is how does clinical psychology progress in terms of developing more effective forms of treatment?

In addition to the idea of clinical work as research, there have been developments in research designs which extend this idea to offer a more formal framework. Psychological research normally involves experiments designed in terms of comparisons between two or more *groups* of people. Usually, one group receives an experimental condition and this is compared with the performance of a control group. The statistical analysis is then based upon a comparison of the scores of the groups. This kind of design has also been employed in clinical research. One group of patients, often with a particular diagnostic category such as depression, is given some treatment, and the purpose of the experiment is to assess the effectiveness of this treatment by comparing progress with a control group which is not given the treatment.

The value and suitability of this kind of research has been questioned. Kazdin (1976) and Hersen and Barlow (1976) suggest that group comparisons tend to obscure the differences in *individual* responses to treatments. Yet for a clinician, these individual differences are of great interest. It may be that a treatment is more appropriate for people with certain psychological characteristics or backgrounds than others. Also, a clinical psychologist rarely has the time or resources to carry out such research but nevertheless wants to identify the *active ingredients* of his or her treatments—what it is that works and what does not.

## 5.4 Single-case research designs

These embody the principles of the scientist-practitioner model. The focus is on identifying the active ingredients of a treatment by carefully controlled manipulations of single cases. Systematic manipulations are made in the treatment of a single person whose psychological problems and his or her circumstances are carefully assessed:

1 *Reversal designs*   Following a recording of the incidence of the problem, (baseline), the treatment is introduced (T). Subsequently the treatment is withdrawn (B) and then introduced again (T). Consistent change at the point of introduction of the treatment suggests that it is an active producer of change.

2 *Multiple-baseline designs*   Here a number of factors such as depression score, activity level, sleep are continuously recorded. One or more treatments are systematically introduced and the recordings examined for evidence of specific predicted changes coincident with the introduction of the treatments.

Such research is more practicable and ethically defensible, since it allows the psychologist to *tune* the treatments to be more effective as they proceed. Published work in different situations with variations of a type of specific problem can be compiled to allow generalizable findings to develop. The approach has also been described as *treatment building* since it permits new ideas for treatment to evolve until they are relatively potent. This can complement group designs which can then be employed to compare treatments further.

This approach to clinical research and evaluation emphasizes that a range of criteria are involved in assessing change and clarification of these is in itself intrinsic to the process of treatment. Both *subjective* and *objective* criteria are employed. A patient may say, for example, that she feels better, can now tackle situations she could not face and finds her social contacts less stressful. Objective measures complement such subjective reports. In the case of anorexia nervosa, for instance, it is important to note whether a person gains weight, or in the case of obsessive hand-washing, whether the incidence decreases. The psychologist may attempt to observe and assess these behavioural changes directly or employ friends and family members to do so.

There is also the important question of whether there is agreement that the patient and all concerned have become more 'normal'. Often patients and their families impose excessively strict or loose criteria of acceptability, and the clinical psychologist becomes engaged in negotiating some compromise acceptable to everyone. In some cases, tests such as the Beck depression inventory may have been employed to provide an indication of how a person's initial condition compared with the social norms and how their scores changed during the course of treatment. Different criteria will apply in different cases. The treatment of each person can be regarded as a piece of clinical research.

## 5.5 Conclusions

As stated at the outset, we have attempted to give you an overview of the type of work that clinical psychologists are involved in and how this relates to the theoretical ideas discussed in the book. This account is inevitably restricted. Some areas, such as diagnosis, the use of objective assessment tests, the educational role of clinical psychologists and so on, we have only merely touched on.

Above all else, our intention has been to convey the central idea that clinical work encapsulates the contribution that psychology has made to the social sciences. Clinical psychologists have gained respect for the scientific way that they approach a variety of problems. As we have attempted to demonstrate, this involves using the scientific method as a 'working method' guiding the moment-to-moment work on a case. We have employed functional analysis as the framework for discussing this approach. Perhaps one of the most exciting aspects of this framework is that it unites clinical psychologists of various theoretical persuasions in what is considered 'good practice'.

It is important to remember, though, that functional analysis is *not* a therapeutic approach like behaviourism or psychodynamic theory. It is essentially a scientific framework for applying any or all of the psychological theories described in earlier chapters. Of the two authors of this chapter, Chris Cullen has a behavioural orientation and Rudi Dallos specializes in work with families and couples. Although we might differ with respect to some aspects of clinical work, we agree about the value of the general orientation to clinical work provided by functional analysis. This orientation may seem to be just simple 'common sense'. We hope that it does. Sometimes new ideas appear to be so simple that one wonders why they were not thought of before. But one cannot assume that everyone has always worked in this way. In fact, even for us, it is not always easy to adhere to the principles of functional analysis. It is very tempting to simply assume that one's preferred approach is the best and that it always works.

## Summary of Section 5

- Clinical psychologists are eclectic in drawing upon many different theoretical frameworks.

- Clinical research involves both traditional evaluation of treatments, using groups of patients, and the work of the scientist-practitioner in exploring antecedents and consequences to explain an individual's behaviour.

- Functional analysis is a framework which enables clinical psychologists to evaluate assessments and treatments from a variety of psychological approaches.

- A variety of criteria should be used to evaluate whether a treatment has been successful.

# Further reading

DAVIDSON, G.C. and NEALE, J.M. (1982) *Abnormal psychology: an experimental clinical approach*, New York: John Wiley.

MARZILLIER, J.S. and HALL, S. (eds) (1987) *What is clinical psychology?*, Oxford: Oxford University Press.

WATTS, A.W. (1961) *Psychotherapy East and West*, Harmondsworth: Penguin Books.

WATZLAWICK, P., WEAKLAND, J.A. and FISCH, R. (1974) *Change: principles of problem formation and problem resolution*, New York and London: Norton.

# References

ACKERMAN, N.W. (ed.) (1966) *Exploring the base for family therapy*, New York: Basic Books.

BATESON, G. (1972) *Steps to an ecology of mind*, New York: Basic Books.

BECK, A.T. (1967) *Depression: clinical, experimental and theoretical aspects*, New York: Harper and Row.

BION, W.R. (1961) *Experiences in groups*, London: Tavistock.

BOSZROMENYI-NAGY, I. and SPARKS, G. (1973) *Invisible loyalties*, New York: Harper and Row.

BROWN, G.W., MONCK, E.M., CARSTAIRS, G.M. and WING, J.K. (1962) 'The influence of family life on the course of schizophrenic illness', *British Journal of Preventative Social Medicine*, vol. 16, pp. 55–68.

COOPER, D. (1967) *Psychiatry and anti-psychiatry*, London: Paladin.

CULLEN, C. HATTERSLEY, J. and TENNANT, L. (1981) 'Establishing behaviour: the constructional approach' in Davey, G. (ed.), *Applications of conditioning theory*, London: Methuen.

EYSENCK, J. (1969) *The effects of psychological therapy*, New York: Science House Inc.

FENNEL, M.J.V. (1983), 'Cognitive therapy of depression. The mechanism of change', *Behavioural Psychotherapy*, vol. 11, no. 2, pp. 97–109.

FERRIERA, A.J. (1963), 'Family myths and homeostasis', *Archives of General Psychiatry*, vol. 9, pp. 457–63.

FREUD, S. (1917) 'Introductory lectures on psycho-analysis', in Strachey, J. (ed.) (1963) *Standard Edition*, vol. 16.

GLYNN-OWEN, R. and BARRIE-ASHCROFT, J. (1982) 'Functional analysis in applied psychology', *The British Journal of Clinical Psychology*, vol. 21, no. 3, pp. 181–91.

GOFFMAN, G. (1971) *Asylums*, Harmondsworth: Penguin Books.

GOLDIAMOND, D.I. (1974) 'Towards a constructional approach to social problems', *Behaviourism*, vol. 2, pp. 1–84.

GOLDBERG, D. and HUXLEY, P. (1980) *Mental illness and the community*, London: Tavistock.

HEATHER, N. and ROBERTSON, I. (1985) *Problem drinking: the new approach*, Harmondsworth: Pelican Books.

HALEY, J. (1976) *Problem solving therapy*, San Francisco: Jossey Bass.

HERSEN, M. and BARLOW, D.H. (1976) *Single case experimental designs: strategies for studying behavioural change*, New York: Pergamon Press.

JACOBSON, E. (1929) *Progressive relaxation*, Chicago: University of Chicago Press.

JACKSON, D.D. (1957) 'The question of family homeostasis', *Psychology; Quarterly Supplement*, vol. 31, pp. 79–90.

JACKSON, D.D. (1968) (ed.) *Therapy, communication and change*, Palo Alto, CA: Science and Behaviour Books Inc.

KAPLAN, H.A. (1974) *The new sex therapy*, New York: Brunner Mazel.

KELLY, G. (1955) *The psychology of personal constructs*, New York and London: Norton.

KENDALL, P.C. and NORTON-FORD, J.D. (1982) *Clinical psychology: scientific and professional dimensions*, New York: John Wiley.

KLEIN, L.S., DITTMAN, A.T., PARLOTT, M.B. and GILL, M.M. (1969) 'Behaviour therapy: observations and reflections', *Journal of Consulting and Clinical Psychology*, vol. 33, pp. 259–66.

KHUN, T.S. (1970) *The structure of scientific revolutions*, Chicago: University of Chicago Press.

LAING, R.D. (1960) *The divided self*, London: Tavistock.

MARZILLIER, J.S. and HALL, S. (1987) (eds) *What is clinical psychology?*, Oxford: Oxford University Press.

MEICHENBAUM, D.H. (1973) 'Cognitive factors in behaviour modifying what clients say to themselves', in Rubin, R.D., Brady, J.P. and Henderson, J.D. (eds) *Advances in behaviour therapy*, vol. 4. New York: Academic Press.

MINCHIN, S., ROSMAN, B. and BAKER, L., (1978), *Psychosomatic families: anorexia nervosa in context*, Cambridge MA: Harvard University Press.

MORENO, J.L. and KIPPER, D.A. (1968) 'Group psychodrama and community-centred counselling', in Gazda, G.M. (ed.) *Basic approaches to group psychotherapy and group counselling*, Springfield Ill: Charles and Thomas.

MORGAN, R.T.T. and YOUNG, G.C. (1975) 'Parental attitudes and the conditioning treatment of childhood enuresis', *Behaviour Research and Therapy*, vol. 13, pp. 197–9.

PERLS, F.S. (1969) *Gestalt therapy verbatim*, Moab, Utah: Real People Press.

RACHMAN, S.J. and WILSON, G.T. (1980) *The effects of psychological therapy*, Pergamon Press.

ROGERS, C. (1965) *Client centred therapy*, New York: Houghton Mifflin.

ROGERS, C. (1970) *On encounter groups*, New York: Harper and Row.

ROSENHAN, D.L. (1973) 'On being sane in insane places'. *Science*, vol. 179, pp. 250–68.

RUTTER, M. (1975) *Helping troubled children*, Harmondsworth: Penguin.

SELIGMAN, M.E.P. (1973) *Helplessness on depressions, development and death*, San Francisco: Freeman.

SILVERMAN, L.H., FRANK, S.G. and DACHINGE, P. (1974) 'A psychoanalytic reinterpretation of the effectiveness of systematic desensitization', *Journal of Abnormal Psychology*, vol. 83, pp. 313–18.

SLADE, P. (1982) 'Towards a functional analysis of anorexia nervosa and bulimia nervosa', *The British Journal of Clinical Psychology*, vol. 21, no. 3, pp. 167–81.

SLAVSON, S.R. (1950) *Analytic group psychotherapy*, New York: Columbia University Press.

SHAPIRO, M.B. (1985) 'A reassessment of clinical psychology as an applied science', *The British Journal of Clinical Psychology*, vol. 24, no. 1, pp. 1–13.

SZASZ, T. (1962) *The myth of mental illness*, London: Secker and Warberg.

WATSON, J.B. and RAYNOR, R. (1920) 'Conditioning emotional reactions', *Journal of Experimental Psychology*, vol. 3, pp. 1–14.

WOLPE, J. (1958), *Psychotherapy by reciprocal inhibition*, Stanford, CA: Stanford University Press.

YATES, A.J. (1983) 'Behaviour therapy and psychodynamic theory; basic conflict or reconciliation and integration?' *British Journal of Clinical Psychology*, vol. 22, no. 2, pp. 107–27.

## Answers to SAQs

### SAQ 1

Some obvious candidates are: the family setting, work, leisure activities and friends. At a wider level, ethnic, religious, cultural, gender and other social contexts play a part in shaping the kinds of psychological stresses and problems that people experience.

### SAQ 2

Going to the toilet is reinforced by: (a) avoiding the discomfort of a wet bed, and (b) being praised by parents. In other words, the result avoids negative reinforcement and gains positive reinforcement.

## SAQ 3

Some alternative approaches could have been attempted to deal with the consequences of Helen's behaviour. For example, a more specifically cognitive approach could have been adopted where her beliefs and attitudes about food were tackled. Alternatively, her family could have been brought into treatment in order to alter the family dynamics and thereby alter the antecedents as well as the consequences that were maintaining her behaviour.

# 16

# AUTISM

Ilona Roth

## Contents

# 1 | Introduction

Most of the chapters in this book have dealt with psychological functions and processes as they are observed in 'normal' children and adults. We have looked at the processes by which children develop the thoughts, feelings and social responses of adults, at the way in which learning takes place, at the operation of perception, memory and selective attention and at the use of language for social communication. This chapter is about **autism**, a disorder commencing in early childhood in which some, if not all, of these functions are impaired. Because of its scope and severity, autism is often described as a 'pervasive development disorder'. It affects approximately four children in 10 000 and is three times as common in boys as in girls.[1]

From an early age, children with autism develop with a marked inability to relate socially to others, as well as with deficits in language, non-verbal communication, and an inability to think or behave flexibly. Some have additional difficulties with cognitive processes such as perception and memory, and many are intellectually impaired. Most autistic children remain extremely handicapped by these difficulties as they grow older, and are unable to lead completely independent lives as adults. A small proportion manage to overcome their difficulties sufficiently to work and run their own lives, although they tend to remain socially isolated.

What is the rationale for discussing a specific and comparatively rare disorder of this kind in a general introduction to psychology? One reason is that our understanding of 'normal functioning' is enhanced by studying children in which psychological functioning is unusual or impaired. Autism is a particularly good example to use because of the distinctive combination of social and intellectual impairments with which autistic children contend. Attempts to explain this combination of impairments have shed light on the very close interaction which must exist between social and intellectual development in normal children. But above all, autism is a puzzle which has attracted the interest and imagination of psychologists from many different perspectives. In their efforts to explain what is wrong with autistic children, and to suggest ways of helping them, these psychologists have produced some very different interpretations of the 'same' problem. Autism therefore provides an excellent case study of the theoretical and ethical difficulties which arise when psychologists work with complex real-life behaviour.

## 1.1 Origins of the term 'autism'

The word 'autism' comes from the Greek word *autos* which means 'self'. Hence autism carries the connotation of being absorbed in oneself. This is the general meaning of the term in the English language. But in 1943, the

---

[1] For this reason, I have used the personal pronoun 'he', when referring to an autistic child, for ease of reading, although the points I make refer equally to female autistic children.

psychiatrist Leo Kanner adopted the term to describe a behaviour pattern he had noticed in some of his child patients. The features of the children's behaviour stressed by Kanner were their apparent isolation from the world and their withdrawal from social contact. Most of the children also had severe intellectual difficulties.

Kanner became convinced that these and other features of the children's behaviour reflected a **syndrome** (a specific disorder with a characteristic set of symptoms) to which he gave the term 'autism'. Since Kanner's pioneering work, many other psychologists and psychiatrists have also come to the conclusion that when a child displays the type of behaviour pattern described by Kanner, a specific disorder—autism—is at work. However, this view is not universally accepted, and in Section 2.2 you will find a brief account of the arguments for and against applying the term 'autistic' to a particular group of children.

Even among those who accept the use of the term, there is some disagreement about the detailed characteristics of autism, but there is agreement about the *major* characteristics. A description of the main features of autism follows.

In reading about these, it is **very important** to remember that most of the features of behaviour which are described will be shown by all children at some time or another. It is the number, severity and persistence of these features, given the age of the child, which may lead a psychologist or a psychiatrist, after careful evaluation of all the evidence, to describe a child as 'autistic.'

## 1.2 Main features of autism

Four main groups of symptoms are used in the description and diagnosis of autism. They are:

### 1 Difficulties in social interaction

Autistic children appear to lack either the skills or the motivation necessary for ordinary two-way interaction with other people. From an early age they may appear unaware of other people's feelings. For instance, they may treat parents or siblings as objects to be sat upon or used, or may appear unaware and unconcerned that other children are distressed. They may fail to seek comfort when distressed themselves, or may seek comfort in unusual ways— by repeating 'cheese, cheese, cheese' rather than by hugging a soft toy, for example. Another difficulty often observed at an early stage is the absence of a normal tendency to imitate others by waving bye-bye, smiling when smiled at and so on.

As they get older, autistic children tend not to engage in ordinary social play, preferring solitary games to co-operative ones. Not surprisingly, these children have great difficulty in making friends. Some seem to lack any interest in forming social relationships. Others may try, but fail, because they do not understand the social conventions underlying friendship. For instance, if a child insists on reading long extracts from the phone book to another child, this is likely to discourage rather than encourage friendship.

## 2  Difficulties with language and non-verbal communication

Some autistic children may not speak at all, and may display no understanding of language. Autistic children who do speak may do so in a very unusual way; for instance, in a monotonous or sing-song voice, or at a permanently high pitch. Frequently, the form or content of the speech is very unusual, restricted or stereotyped. For instance, autistic children often repeat words or phrases they have just heard, a phenomenon known as **echolalia**. Perhaps because of this, they tend to use pronouns inappropriately and to have difficulty answering questions. If asked, 'Do you want a biscuit?', a child might respond by repeating, 'Do you want a biscuit?' when what he meant was, 'Yes, I want a biscuit'. Another common problem with language is **telegraphic speech**. For example, a child who is asked where he has been might say, 'Hut stick walk', apparently meaning that he had been to the hut for a walk and found a stick on the way. Quite a number of autistic children develop fluent speech, but remain unable to initiate or sustain a conversation with other people. In normal conversation two or more people take it in turns to talk about a topic of mutual interest. Autistic children appear not to understand this turn taking. When they 'talk to' other people, these children usually conduct long monologues on one subject, and ignore attempts to break in on their flow.

**Non-verbal communication**—that is, the use of gestures, facial expressions and so on—may be equally impaired. Again, severely autistic children may make virtually no gestures and facial expressions. Autistic children who do use gestures and expressions tend to do so in an unusual way which, as with their speech, makes communication difficult. In a normal social interaction between two people, **eye contact** (one person looking the other in the eye) is used as a means of regulating the other person's behaviour. For instance, in conversation one person may look briefly at the other's eyes to indicate that he or she has finished speaking, or wishes to speak. Autistic children are more likely to look the other person fixedly in the eye or to look away while the other person is looking. This contributes to their difficulty with the kind of turn taking necessary for normal conversation.

**Pretend play** is a third area of communication difficulty. Normal children frequently adopt imaginary roles such as 'mothers and fathers' or 'Hansel and Gretel' as a way of communicating in their games. Autistic children tend to show no interest in this imaginative play, either in social or solitary games.

## 3  Restricted range of activities and interests

Some autistic children may repeat particular body movements such as flicking their wrists or banging their head over and over again, or be preoccupied with touching a particular toy. Others may insist, to an unreasonable extent, on preserving the sameness of their environment, by keeping a 'trivial' object always in the same place, for example, or always following the same route to go shopping.

As they grow older, autistic children frequently become obsessively absorbed in one particular interest, such as making arrangements of objects, or collecting facts about trains.

## 4 Onset below 36 months of age

In the three groups of symptoms just discussed, some difficulties, such as the inability to imitate or to use simple gestures, are more characteristic of very young children, under the age of about 36 months. Other difficulties, such as the inability to use speech for conversational purposes, develop as children grow older. But a diagnosis of autism is only made if some symptoms in each of the three groups have been present before the age of 36 months. Since diagnosis does not always occur as early as this, parents and family doctors may be asked retrospectively about the presence of 'odd' symptoms. As we shall see in Section 2, diagnosing a child as autistic is a complex and skilled process. However, The National Autistic Society, a body set up by parents of autistic children, has developed a schematic version of the main characteristics of autism. This has been widely circulated to health professionals and parents to increase their awareness of the characteristic behaviour of autistic children (see Figure 16.1).

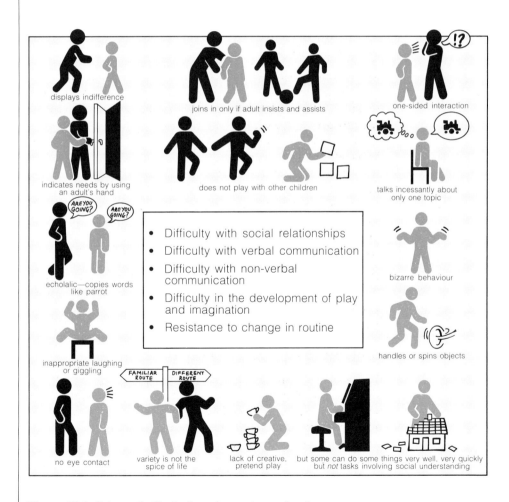

**Figure 16.1** Schematic illustration of symptoms of autism
(Source: The National Autistic Society, 1987)

# 1.3  Other deficits and skills of autistic children

The four groups of symptoms described in Section 1.2 are regarded as **criteria** of autism. That is, they *must* be present if a diagnosis of autism is to be made. However, many autistic children have additional **cognitive difficulties**, besides the language deficits included in the criteria for autism. In the **auditory modality**, some children appear unresponsive to sounds such as human voices. Yet they may be very absorbed by rhythmic sounds such as music. In the **visual modality**, some children display an inability to distinguish between stimuli such as arrows pointing upwards and downwards, and an inability to sustain attention (Hermelin and O'Connor, 1970). Cognitive difficulties are most frequent in tasks which require the capacity for abstract or symbolic thought. For instance, a child may perform well when asked to recall a list of words verbatim, but be unable to recall the meaning of a simple sentence.

Given that all autistic children have language difficulties, and some have additional cognitive difficulties, it is not surprising that the majority of autistic children perform well below average on IQ tests. But there is a wide range of ability here, and about 25 per cent of autistic children have normal and even high IQs. It is also difficult to know how far autistic children's difficulties with IQ tests are independent of, or caused by, their language difficulties. As you saw in Chapter 7, many IQ tests have verbal subtests as well as performance subtests, and all IQ tests require that the child understands the verbal instructions for completing them.

---

SAQ 1     (SAQ answers are given at the end of the chapter)

(a)  If autistic children are tested on the Wechsler Intelligence Scale for Children (WISC-R), described in Chapter 7, Section 2.1, which group of subtests would you expect them to find easier, the verbal or the performance?

(b)  Which of the following intelligence tests, described in Chapter 7, would be the 'fairest' IQ test for an autistic child with language difficulties: (i) the WISC-R; (ii) the British Ability Scales; (iii) Raven's Progressive Matrices; or (iv) the Mill Hill Vocabulary Scale?

---

So far, this discussion has drawn attention to the many deficits with which autistic children contend. But some autistic children display an outstanding skill in one particular area. For instance, children whose general level of performance on an IQ test is low, may be exceptionally good at one particular subtest such as block design, in which the child arranges painted wooden blocks to copy pre-selected designs. Many autistic children perform extremely well on tests such as the embedded figures test described in Chapter 7, Section 5.1. And a small proportion of autistic children display exceptional creative gifts. Some of these children are musically gifted, while others can perform astonishing feats of mental arithmetic. In the artistic field, a child called Stephen Wiltshire has attracted much interest with his beautiful architectural drawings (see Figure 16.2). In his original description of autism,

**Figure 16.2** A drawing by Stephen Wiltshire
(Source: Wiltshire, 1987)

Kanner referred to such special gifts as **islets of ability**, implying that other areas of the autistic child's intelligence lay submerged in a sea of communication difficulties.

## 1.4  Growing up with autism

Because of its early onset, autism is usually thought of as a condition of childhood. Many people are unclear about what happens to autistic children as they grow up, and there are several reasons for this. Psychological research has tended to focus on the skills and deficits of children. In therapeutic work the emphasis, inevitably, is on starting to help autistic children at the earliest possible age. But the main reason why relatively little is known about autistic adults is that only a few generations of autistic children have grown up since Kanner's original description. In addition, many cases of autism may have remained undiagnosed at first because it took time for Kanner's work to become widely known and accepted.

It is only in recent years that more information has emerged about autistic children as they grow up. Psychologists and psychiatrists have conducted

**follow-up studies** of particular groups of autistic children several years on. Parents have contributed much anecdotal evidence from their experiences of bringing up an autistic child.

Kanner (1971) traced the progress of all the children described in his original paper, after a gap of nearly 30 years. A small proportion of these children had made reasonably good social adjustments as adults and were leading independent lives. But Kanner was unable to trace any connection between the way children fared as adults and the way they had been treated while growing up, except that those children who had grown up in psychiatric institutions tended to remain the most affected.

Kanner speculated that the children who had fared best as adults might simply have been those least seriously affected in the first place. A review of outcome studies by Lotter (1978) tends to support this conclusion. He found evidence that the children who, from the outset, had the highest IQ scores, the most use of language, and the least severe social deficits, tended to do best in the long term.

The general picture which emerges from follow-up studies, and from parents, is that autism is a life-long condition for most children. However, the pattern of symptoms may change and become less severe as children get older. They may develop some measure of social and communicative skills and as a result become less withdrawn as adults. In Section 5 we will consider how far therapeutic work contributes to helping autistic children overcome their difficulties.

## Summary of Section 1

- Psychological studies of autism provide a good illustration of the difficulties of explaining complex real-life behaviour.

- The term 'autism' was originally introduced by the psychiatrist Kanner to describe a syndrome he observed in some of his child patients.

- Autistic children typically have difficulties in social interaction and in language and non-verbal communication, and have a restricted range of activities and interests. Symptoms in all these areas appear before 36 months of age.

- Some autistic children have additional cognitive difficulties and many are intellectually impaired.

- Some autistic children have exceptional gifts, termed islets of ability, in one particular area, such as music or art.

- In most cases autism is a life-long condition, although the pattern of difficulties may change or become less severe as children grow up.

# 2 | Diagnosing autism

The description of autism given in Section 1 is a summary of a complex range of symptoms. The detailed pattern of symptoms may vary considerably from one child to another or from one age to another within the same child. Normal children also vary in how sociable and communicative they are, and at times the behaviour of these children may appear to resemble the characteristic behaviour of autistic children. So how does a specialist decide that the behaviour of a particular child fits the description given in Section 1 sufficiently closely that it meets the criteria for **diagnosis**? In this section we will consider this process of diagnosis, but first we will examine the general assumptions underlying diagnosis of autism and other psychological problems.

## 2.1 Assumptions of the diagnostic approach

The broad assumption behind the diagnosis of a psychological problem such as autism, and others such as depressive illness and anorexia nervosa, is that these problems constitute separate disorders or syndromes. These **syndromes** are characterized by distinctive patterns of symptoms with specific causes and (in some cases) specific treatments. This assumption comes originally from general medicine. Illnesses such as measles and German measles, for example, are known to be caused by different viruses. Doctors can distinguish between the two conditions on the basis of symptoms such as where on the body a child's rash is and what it looks like. And for each of these illnesses they usually recommend a different approach to looking after the child. Measles is known to be a much more serious illness, with potential complications, while German measles in children is considered very mild.

There is, of course, an overlap of symptoms between the two illnesses such that, to the untrained observer, the two conditions may appear similar. In both cases the affected child will develop a red rash and a temperature, and will appear off-colour. The doctor, though, is usually able to distinguish between the two conditions by the precise pattern and severity of symptoms.

Many psychiatrists and psychologists believe that a broadly similar approach is applicable to some psychological problems. The rationale for this view comes from years of clinical practice and research work. This work has provided evidence that certain symptoms tend to occur regularly together, forming clusters or patterns. In some cases it has been possible to elucidate the causes underlying these patterns. As in general medicine, there is often considerable overlap between symptoms of different conditions. None the less, the overall patterns of symptoms are distinctive. To take an example, the symptom of memory loss occurs in both dementia and depression. In the first case it is associated with a progressive and irreversible process caused by degeneration of nervous tissue in the brain. In the second it is a temporary phenomenon associated with the loss of attention and concentration seen in many depressed people. It disappears when the depression lifts.

Research into the patterns of symptoms associated with different psychological problems has enabled specialists to **classify** these symptoms into diagnostic categories. Each category within such a classification is accompanied by a clear, precise description of a set of symptoms. The description of autism given in the previous section comes from a widely used classification system devised by the American Psychiatric Association and known as DSM-III-R (1987).

The importance of the classification is that it provides clear, detailed and objective descriptions of different types of psychological problem. This helps to ensure that if one group of specialists decides that a child is suffering from, say, Down's syndrome, other specialists will know exactly what the first group means by the diagnosis. This shared understanding means that any differences of opinion proceed on rational, objective lines. However, deciding on the right diagnostic category to apply to a child's symptoms is only one aspect of diagnosis. As we shall see, diagnosis also provides the basis for appropriate action on the part of the specialist. In the case of a child with Down's syndrome, this action would include treating any physical ailments, counselling the child's parents about the special problems they will face in caring for and rearing their child, and deciding on educational needs.

## 2.2  Diagnosis as labelling?

It may have occurred to you that the diagnostic approach just outlined differs in some ways from the approach to psychological problems outlined in Chapter 15. In Chapter 15 it was argued that even when two people have *identical* symptoms, the causes or antecedents of these symptoms, and therefore the most appropriate explanations and treatments for them, are likely to be different. The implication of this approach is that it is not possible to apply one diagnostic category such as autism to the pattern of symptoms displayed by different children. One child might become withdrawn because his family has behaved towards him in a rejecting manner. Another child might display the same symptoms because he has an extreme preference for solitude. The antecedents of these similar symptoms are different in each case. According to this view, diagnosing these two children as autistic merely attaches a 'label' to them. This may discourage specialists (and parents) from considering alternative explanations for the children's behaviour. It may even serve to perpetuate the symptoms because the child 'labelled' as autistic will learn that this is the type of behaviour which is expected of him. Generally, labelling will hinder the development of an appropriate strategy for the treatment, care and education of a child so 'labelled'.

This anti-labelling approach often goes hand-in-hand with the argument that diagnosis is an inappropriate application of principles drawn from general medicine to psychological problems. As we have seen, diagnosis does rest on the broad assumption that psychological problems, like medical ones, are characterized by distinctive patterns of symptoms with specific causes. And in some cases, these causes are thought to be physical, rather in the way that measles is caused by a virus. But for many psychological problems the link with medicine is no closer than that. As was mentioned in Section 2.1, clinical and research studies of patterns of symptoms have provided their own independent rationale for grouping these symptoms into different categories.

Even so, it is important to consider whether use of the label 'autism' does produce negative consequences. The first question to ask is whether it discourages specialists and parents from considering alternative explanations of why children develop autistic symptoms. In practice, the term 'autism' is used by people from a wide variety of perspectives. Some believe that biological defects lead to children developing autism. Others argue that environmental factors such as abnormalities in early social relationships between the child and his mother are the main factor. Some argue that biological and environmental factors interact. Others believe that the relative importance of biological and environmental factors varies from child to child. In short, there is no evidence that the use of the term 'autism' has produced a narrow range of assumptions about why children become autistic.

The second question to consider is whether labelling a child's behaviour as 'autistic' perpetuates a problem which would otherwise 'go away'. Given the severity of the symptoms, even at an early age, this seems very unlikely. Most specialists, as well as parents, argue quite the opposite. They argue that the decision to diagnose a child as 'autistic' frequently represents the first step towards helping the child. Many parents of autistic children experience years of perplexity and frustration because the problems of their children are not diagnosed. The diagnosis provides an explanation for their children's behaviour, helps them to understand and cope with their special and distinctive difficulties, and facilitates access to special educational and therapeutic facilities.

The need for proper diagnosis is well illustrated by the account in Extract A, given by a mother and father, of their early experiences with their child. Over quite a long period doctors came up with a series of different and conflicting 'explanations' of their child's behaviour. The diagnosis of autism was eventually made after the child's parents were referred to a specialist via The National Autistic Society.

### EXTRACT A

I felt that we weren't getting anywhere and I was very irritated to be constantly asked questions about my grandparents and breast-feeding and was my mother breast-fed, was I breast-fed, did I breast-feed Gabriel. It didn't seem to be helping Gabriel's difficulties at all and our problems with behaviour in getting him potty-trained, all these sorts of things were of concern to us and trying to help him in his development. And we felt rather guilty for raising these questions at all. And we were asked why we were worried about it. As if it were something that we ought not to be worried about and eventually I, having read some books and descriptions of autism, began to realise that maybe this was the problem with our child. Eventually I decided to come to The National Autistic Society and tell them all about my little boy and ask them if it rang bells, and I did come and see the secretary and I was saying I was very concerned with the treatment we were getting and we seemed to be going off at a tangent, and she recommended that we sought a second opinion and she gave me a list of people who might have experience in autism and we actually went privately to see one of the people on the list. It was at that stage we got referred to another child development clinic and we had a full assessment of Gabriel. This time we were allowed to be present and be there as reassurance for him and that was when the diagnosis of autism was made . . . But the fact that we got a definite diagnosis, and although we didn't like the prognosis, it did at least help us to come to terms with it. That was, I think, quite important ultimately.

To summarize, people working with autistic children, as well as many parents, argue that the advantages of treating such children as a special category outweigh the disadvantages. This does not mean that there is no debate about the use of the term 'autism'. Some of this debate concerns the possibility that there are distinct 'sub-groups' of children within the main group. In particular, attention has focused on whether children who display the social difficulties associated with autism, but have normal or high intellectual abilities, form a distinct sub-group from those who have severe intellectual impairments. It may be that the factors responsible for the development of autism differ between these two groups of children. There is also debate about the extent to which the symptoms of autism do overlap with those of other conditions. For instance, Treffert (1989) has made studies of a condition known as the 'savant syndrome'. People with this syndrome have severe intellectual handicaps coupled with spectacular 'islets of ability' such as being able to perform complex mathematical calculations or to play a piece of classical music perfectly after hearing it only once. As you will recall from Section 1.3, some autistic children have similar islets of ability, and many 'savants' display the characteristic symptoms of autism. Finally, there is debate about how widely the term 'autistic' should be applied. Some children display some but not all the symptoms of autism. Other children display the symptoms in a relatively mild form. Wing and Gould (1979) have suggested that, although approximately only four children in 10 000 conform to the full criteria, approximately fifteen to twenty in 10 000 display autistic tendencies. These points make clear that the term 'autism', like other diagnostic 'labels', does not denote a completely clear-cut category. This does not, however, render the term useless or meaningless.

To conclude Section 2, we will consider an example of the procedure used by experts to diagnose a child as autistic. It is interesting to note that, though the underlying assumptions are different, the procedure itself resembles the procedure of clinical assessment described in Chapter 15. Notice, too, that the aim of the diagnosis is not just to categorize or 'label' the child's symptoms, but to develop, in consultation with parents and health professionals, a positive strategy for helping the child and his family.

## 2.3 A procedure for diagnosis

The following account describes the diagnostic approach of the late Dr Derek Ricks (The National Autistic Society, 1985). Until recently, Dr Ricks headed a team working at a special centre for autistic children in Radlett, Hertfordshire.

The team at Radlett is multidisciplinary and includes paediatricians (doctors specializing in childhood illnesses), clinical psychologists, and social workers. The team also has access to specialists in speech and hearing difficulties, genetics, neurophysiology and biochemistry. It aims to involve parents at all stages of diagnosis, as well as consulting health professionals such as the family doctor. Diagnosis proceeds in a series of stages as follows:

*1 Initial referral*

Typically, a member of the Radlett team is called to a medical clinic by a paediatrician who is puzzled by a child's behaviour. Because autism is so rare, many doctors have never encountered a case before and have nothing with which to compare a child's behaviour. Parental pressure often plays an important part. Parents may be unhappy with assurances given by doctors that there is nothing fundamentally wrong.

*2 Preliminary assessment*

Parents are asked in detail what they feel to be the problem with their child. A member of the Radlett team explains the role of the team and offers an initial opinion based on what he or she has discovered from parents, together with an outline of how the team will proceed.

*3 Involvement of other health professionals*

The Radlett team circulates all professionals who have come into contact with the child, including family doctor, social worker and others, asking for information about any problems such as apparent hearing difficulties or odd behaviour.

*4 Observation of child at home*

Members of the team visit the child at home to make observations in the child's familiar setting, and make a video if the parents agree.

*5 Observation of child at Radlett*

Parents bring the child to the Radlett centre for observation. The child's behaviour is photographed, and a video made. The child is given tests and a detailed physical examination.

*6 Consideration of alternative diagnoses*

No two cases are identical. Some children display all the typical features of autism. Other children have these features together with other less typical features. Yet others show pronounced difficulties in some areas (such as use of language and gesture) and less pronounced difficulties in other areas. Earlier diagnoses such as 'maladjusted' or 'retarded' may have been made by other doctors. The team gives careful consideration to all the possibilities.

*7  Pooling of team opinions*

Each member of the team produces a separate report on the child, and there are group discussions. From this, a draft report is produced and discussed with parents. They are asked whether they understand and whether they agree with the findings. Following this, a final report is prepared.

*8  Consultations and negotiations about child's needs*

The team's report is presented to all other health professionals involved with the child. Advice is offered about the child's special needs in terms of care and education.

Unfortunately, this careful diagnostic procedure is not always representative of the sequence of events by which a child may come to be diagnosed. Many families have no access to specialist facilities of the kind just described. As we saw in Section 2.2, parents may spend months or years trying to establish an explanation for the odd or unusual behaviour of their child, receiving a variety of alternative 'explanations' from doctors, psychologists and social workers. In Section 5 we shall consider the question of what special provision is available for autistic children.

## Summary of Section 2

- An important assumption behind the diagnosis of psychological problems such as autism is that these problems are relatively distinct conditions, with specific causes.

- Descriptions of the symptoms of problems such as autism are organized into classifications. These provide a tool for diagnosis, treatment and research.

- Some people regard terms such as 'autism' as 'labels' which group together a diversity of problems with a diversity of antecedents. Although the boundaries of the category are not clear-cut, many people argue that the advantages of using this category outweigh the disadvantages.

- The process of diagnosing a child as autistic should include detailed observation and evaluation of the child, together with close consultation with the child's parents.

# 3 | Why do children become autistic?

Why is it that a very small proportion of children become autistic? One way that psychologists have tried to answer this question is by identifying **predisposing factors**; that is, influences which place a particular group of children at risk of developing autism. As noted in Section 2, different predisposing factors may be responsible for development of autism in different children. Or there may be an interaction between several predisposing factors for all children. In this section, we will look in turn at the main classes of predisposing factors, and at some ideas about the process by which autism develops from these influences.

## 3.1  Genetic and organic factors

One possibility is that autistic children inherit **genes** which predispose them to develop the disorder. In Chapter 5, you were introduced to the theory that there is a genetic factor in depression. The hypothesis of a genetic factor in autism follows similar lines. Chapter 7 discussed evidence for a genetic basis for IQ differences between individuals, based on correlations between identical and non-identical (i.e. fraternal) twins.

SAQ 2    From your knowledge of Chapters 5 and 7, what kinds of studies might be used to seek evidence for a genetic factor in autism?

There have been several studies of the incidence of autism in the families of autistic children, particular interest focusing upon how often it occurs in both members of identical twin pairs. These studies, using a special correlational technique, suggest that there is a higher **concordance** for identical twins than for fraternal twins. This means that the number of cases in which both members of a twin pair develop autism is greater for identical than for fraternal pairs. For instance, Folstein and Rutter (1978) studied twenty-one same-sex pairs of twins, between the age of 5 and 23, each including an autistic member. Eleven of these twin pairs were identical and ten were fraternal. Of the eleven identical twin pairs, four were concordant for autism; that is, both twins had autism. Of the ten fraternal pairs, none was concordant for autism. These findings suggest a concordance rate of 36 per cent for identical twins and 0 per cent for fraternal twins. However, in this study Folstein and Rutter made the interesting finding that almost all of the identical twins not conforming to the diagnosis of autism showed some autistic tendencies, particularly difficulties with spoken language. These findings suggest that a substantial proportion of children with autism or autistic tendencies have inherited a genetic predisposition to develop in this way. As you will recall from Chapter 7, however, there are pitfalls in the use of twin studies to draw inferences about genetic inheritance.

SAQ 3    Can you suggest an interpretation, other than the genetic one, which could be placed on the higher concordance rate found for autism in identical as opposed to fraternal twins?

In order to rule out confounding environmental factors in studies of twins, workers in this field have developed increasingly complex and sophisticated methods for collecting evidence of a genetic predisposition, but it remains a controversial area. In any case, finding a genetic factor does not on its own constitute an explanation for why autism develops. Since the reported concordance rate for fully-fledged autism in identical twins is less than 100 per cent, a genetic factor is clearly only one of many influences which might predispose a child to develop autism.

There is also the question of what type of 'defect' might be transmitted by a gene. It is often assumed that if a disorder has a genetic basis an **organic defect** will be found—a structural or functional abnormality of part of the brain, for instance. A survey by Kolvin, Ounsted and Roth (1971) reported evidence for such abnormalities in about one third of their sample of autistic children. Many of the children within this sub-group were reported to have epileptic symptoms, while others had abnormal **electro-encephalograms** or **EEGs**. An electro-encephalogram is a recording of the overall pattern of electrical activity emitted by the brain. The recording is made by attaching electrodes superficially to the scalp. Deviations from certain characteristic patterns within this activity may reflect brain malfunction.

In another study (Schain and Freedman, 1961), autistic children were found to have abnormally high blood levels of a neurotransmitter substance called serotonin (see Chapter 5, Section 2.2). **Serotonergic synapses** (synapses where serotonin is the transmitter substance) are known to occur in parts of the brain associated with arousal levels. It was therefore thought that the hyperactivity and repetitive behaviour displayed by some autistic children might be a type of over-arousal which occurs because synapses in the brains of these children contain abnormally high levels of serotonin. Treatment with a drug called fenfluramine, known to decrease levels of serotonin, has proved effective in reducing hyperactivity and repetitive behaviour in a small number of autistic children (Geller et al., 1982).

A recent study of a small group of autistic children (Courchesne et al., 1988) has reported underdevelopment of a site within part of the brain called the cerebellum. This underdevelopment appeared to be specific to autism, since it was not observed in a 'normal' control group, nor in a control group of people with other neurological disorders. The authors of the study argued that since the part of the cerebellum which displayed the abnormality is involved in a variety of cognitive and motor functions, the finding could be relevant in explaining autism.

The implications of findings suggesting organic defects are not entirely clear. In the study by Kolvin et al. (1971), only one third of the children displayed organic brain abnormalities. In the other two studies, the size of the sample was small, and it is not known whether the findings would apply to other autistic children. In all three studies there is the possibility that the abnormalities, rather than being a cause of autism, develop as a *result* of the children's autism. Krech, Rosenzweig and Bennett (1966) conducted some experiments in which young primates were deprived of the opportunity to interact with their mothers or age-mates. The absence of these normal environmental stimuli led to biochemical changes in the animals' brain cells and ultimately to a decrease in the size and number of these cells. It might be argued that the autistic child's withdrawal from normal social contacts *produces* organic changes in the same way. Even if these organic abnormalities do play a role in the development of autism, just how they give rise to autistic children's difficulties in social interaction, language and so on is unclear.

## 3.2 Emotional and environmental influences

The most immediate environment for young children is usually their family. The child's first emotional bonds are formed with members of the family, and particularly with the mother. It has been suggested that an abnormality in this early family environment may prevent a child from developing normal social bonds, and thus precipitate the development of autism.

Kanner (1943), in his original description of autism, suggested that the parents of autistic children tended to be highly intelligent, obsessive people, interested in abstractions and lacking in real human warmth. The psychoanalyst Bettelheim (1967) argued that mothers of children who develop autism lack the capacity to develop adequate emotional relationships with their children. The child of this kind of mother interprets the mother's behaviour to mean that she finds contact with him unpleasant and undesirable. The child's reaction is to withdraw from this contact, and this initiates a cycle in which the child becomes increasingly isolated from first his mother and then other members of his family.

Clancy and McBride (1969), working within the framework of family therapy (see Chapter 15, Section 3.3), made studies of fifty-three autistic children and their families. They expressed the belief that 'the mothers fall into a "type" . . . We have noted that mothers are practical, capable people, tend to be the dominant marriage partner, and carry the family through difficulties calmly and efficiently. They give great attention to detail, and become upset easily in the face of seemingly trivial incidents'.

Clancy and McBride saw this as one element in the formation of abnormal patterns of interaction between the child, his mother, and other members of his family. Another element was the early 'abnormal' behaviour of the child. Clancy and McBride conducted retrospective interviews with the mothers of the autistic children in their sample. From the mothers' accounts of how their children had behaved from birth onwards, Clancy and McBride identified a pattern of 'abnormal' behaviour, including the following features:

- Lazy sucking associated with long and tiresome feeding periods.
- Absence of the smiling response.

- Quiet, undemanding behaviour when left alone but irritation when disturbed.
- Unresponsive to human voice.

**SAQ 4**  Can you think of any difficulty that arises with the retrospective method Clancy and McBride used to identify this behaviour pattern?

Clancy and McBride argued that the behaviour identified during their interviews, in interaction with the personality characteristics of the mother, produces an 'initiating context' in which the relationship between mother and child becomes progressively more negative. For instance, when a mother tries to feed her baby, the baby's behaviour indicates indifference to the pleasures of feeding. The mother, being particularly anxious to succeed in the skill of feeding, finds her baby's behaviour upsetting. Over a short period of time, the act of feeding, instead of providing the basis for a bond, becomes aversive to both mother and baby.

It is understandable that approaches which implicate the mother (and to some extent other family members) in predisposing a child to autism, have caused profound distress to the families of autistic children. Such families have been made to feel that they are in some way to blame for their child's condition. It is therefore essential that these claims are subjected to careful scrutiny. If there is evidence to support them, then the role of parents must be acknowledged however painful this may be for them. But if the evidence is weak then there is a strong moral obligation on researchers not to exaggerate its significance.

There have been many studies of the personality characteristics of parents with autistic children. For example, McAdoo and DeMyer (1978) administered a personality test to the parents of a group of autistic children. As a control, the same test was administered to the parents of a group of children attending a child guidance clinic for problems such as behaviour disorders.

**SAQ 5**  What was the purpose of this control group?

The results of this study showed few, if any, differences between the personality characteristics of the two groups of parents. This suggests that the parents of autistic children are similar in personality to those of other children with psychological problems.

A further comparison was made between these two groups of parents (the parents of autistic children and the parents of disturbed children) and a group of people attending a psychiatric outpatients clinic. The personality scores of the two groups of parents differed significantly from those of the outpatient group, who showed evidence of psychological disturbance in their scores. Again, the implication is that the mothers of autistic children do not have exceptionally abnormal personalities.

Although some studies *have* suggested evidence of personality abnormalities among the parents of autistic children (e.g. Goldfarb, 1961), a careful review carried out by Cantwell and Baker (1984), of all studies, concluded that 'the literature does not support the hypothesis that parents of autistic children are excessively cold, introverted, undemonstrative or mentally disordered'.

Another possibility, implicit in the work of Clancy and McBride, is that there are abnormal **patterns of interaction** within the families of autistic children. That is, it is not the personality characteristics of parents which are abnormal, but the way in which all members of the family communicate with one another. Several methods have been used to gather evidence for this hypothesis, including interviews with parents and observations of families. All these methods suffer from methodological problems. Parents may knowingly or unknowingly distort their accounts of what goes on between family members. Observers of families cannot be totally objective, since they are inevitably aware that one family member has been diagnosed autistic. Cantwell and Baker (1984) have concluded that the evidence that communication problems contribute, as a predisposing factor, to the development of autism is not strong.

An important point emerges from studies of the family environment of autistic children. This environment may *well* differ from that of normal children, but as a *result* of the children's autism rather than because it is a *cause* of the problems. DeMyer (1979) has described in some detail the profound effects upon families of having an autistic child in their midst. Parents may experience disappointment and depression at the failures of their child, with consequent effects on their relationships to the child and to each other. Other children in the family may experience feelings of neglect because of the attention inevitably focused on the autistic child. It would be hardly surprising if there *were* psychological problems such as depression or difficulties in communication among the members of such families. As with the organic factors discussed in Section 3.1, care must be taken to differentiate between influences which cause a child to develop autism, and abnormalities in the child and his environment which are the effect of the child's autism.

## 3.3 Motivational conflict

The idea that autistic children lack the normal motivation to form social bonds was mentioned in the context of Clancy and McBride's work in Section 3.2. The ethologist Nikolaas Tinbergen argued that this problem is the central factor predisposing a child to autism. The **ethological approach** pioneered by Tinbergen assumes that important theoretical insights are gained by studying animals (and indeed humans) in their *natural* environment. The ethologist makes detailed observations of all the different behaviours displayed by an organism, and of the frequency with which these behaviours occur over a given period of time. The ethologist does not attempt to influence the organism's environment in any way.

SAQ 6 Does this approach differ from the studies of rat behaviour described in Chapter 6?

Ethologists use their observations to argue that organisms display instinctive patterns of behaviour which serve important motivational functions such as obtaining food, water and sexual partners. Studies of both primates and humans indicate that from birth there is a basic motivation to form social bonds with other members of the species, particularly the immediate family. Babies display behaviours such as smiles and sounds which play an important role in forming social bonds with their mothers. Older children use a wider range of behaviours to form bonds both within and beyond their families.

Tinbergen and his wife (Tinbergen and Tinbergen, 1983) made detailed studies of the behaviour of autistic children in settings such as their own home or school. They argued that, although these children possess the basic human motivation to approach other people and form social bonds, their motivation is offset by anxiety which produces an unusually powerful motivation to avoid such contact. The **motivational conflict** between these opposing forces may lead to three different kinds of outcome:

1   The 'avoidance' motivation 'wins', in which case the child behaves in ways which will protect him from contacts with others (e.g. by avoiding another person's gaze, hanging his head, looking away).

2   The 'approach' motivation wins, though only just. In this case the child will make tentative approaches to others (e.g. approaching an adult but hanging his head or standing side-on).

3   The 'approach' and 'avoidance' motivations are of exactly equal force. In this case the child is able neither to approach, nor to avoid. As a result, his behaviour may show signs of extreme frustration or anxiety. For instance, he may have a temper tantrum, bang his head or repeat the same action over and over again.

Tinbergen and Tinbergen concluded that all the behaviour patterns characteristic of autism (see Section 1) can be seen as expressions of motivational conflict, which, over the long term, inhibits the normal development of the child. Thus, the child's failure to interact socially, and to communicate with speech and gesture, occur because the child is too anxious to engage in social contact. The child's repetitive activities and restricted range of interests develop because anxiety inhibits the child from greater flexibility of behaviour.

Of course, the child's behaviour does not occur in a vacuum. Others around the child will be attempting to interact with him. In an extension of Tinbergen and Tinbergen's theory, Richer (1978) has suggested that the autistic child's anxiety-driven tendency to avoid social contact actually encourages 'approach behaviour' from adults who are unconsciously trying to overcome the avoidance. But this has exactly the opposite effect from what is intended, since it pushes the child into further avoidance behaviours. Thus, a vicious circle is established in which the more an adult tries to approach the child, the more isolated the child will become.

In support of this hypothesis, Richer cites a study in which he observed the behaviour of a group of autistic children and a group of non-autistic children, and their teachers, in a classroom. He classified the behaviours of the children into 'social approach' and 'social avoidance' and compared the amount of time each group of children spent on each type of behaviour. He also studied the amount of time the teacher spent on approach and avoidance behaviour towards each group of children. Richer found that the autistic children spent significantly less time than the non-autistic children on 'approach' behaviour such as talking and pointing. They spent significantly more time on 'avoidance' behaviour such as turning away. These results are hardly surprising. The autistic children should be, by definition, less demonstrative and talkative than the non-autistic children. The most striking feature of the results was that teachers tended to spend more time on certain 'approach' behaviours towards the autistic children, such as touching them and looking at them, than they did towards the non-autistic children. They also tended to spend less time on congratulating the autistic children. However, the teachers displayed many behaviour patterns, such as guiding a child's hand, to an equal extent with both groups of children.

In evaluating the motivational conflict theory we need to examine both methodological and theoretical aspects. The principle advantage of the ethological method is that it does not manipulate the child's behaviour or the setting in which the behaviour occurs. This makes it more likely that the behaviour observed will resemble the child's usual everyday behaviour. However, it does not necessarily mean that observations of the behaviour will be objective.

One problem is that ethologists may tend to 'observe' those behaviours that their theory predicts will occur. For instance, the motivational conflict theory implies that autistic children should engage in less eye contact than normal children, and this is what the Tinbergens and Richer have reported. But other studies (e.g. Hermelin and O'Connor, 1970) suggest that autistic children and normal children engage in the same amount of eye contact. Richer claimed to have found that 'approach behaviour' by adults accentuates the autistic child's withdrawal. But Clark and Rutter (1981) found, in contrast, that increasing the social demands made on autistic children actually increased the amount that they interacted with others.

Not only the frequency of particular behaviours, but also the interpretation placed upon them may be affected by the ethologist's theory. An ethologist may report than an autistic child is avoiding looking at other people's eyes, but this is an *interpretation* of why the child looks away when others are looking at him. Others have argued that autistic children misunderstand (rather than reject) the social function of eye contact in regulating interactions between two people. This fits with Hermelin and O'Connor's finding that the pattern (rather than the amount) of eye contact is unusual in autistic children. Similarly, Clark and Rutter found that, although they were able to encourage autistic children to interact with others, the quality of these interactions remained unusual.

An important question which the motivational conflict theory raises is *why* autistic children are motivated to avoid social bonding. Tinbergen and

Tinbergen (1983) identify a whole range of traumatic events in early childhood which, they argue, may make an autistic child abnormally anxious about the process of bonding. Their list includes an early period of hospitalization or separation from the family, or a physical problem such as loss of hearing or vision. However, this approach begs an important question. Many children experience early traumas such as a stay in hospital, separation from a parent, and even the lasting effects of losing their hearing or vision, without becoming autistic. So Tinbergen and Tinbergen's suggestions are not specific enough to explain why *some* children become autistic after such traumatic events.

To meet this criticism, Richer (1983) has argued that autistic children possess a heightened vulnerability, perhaps inherited, to such traumas. The implication is that the same type of trauma may make some children autistic, but leave others relatively unscathed. This suggestion has the merit of acknowledging the interaction of genetic and environmental factors in the onset of autism, but it is a speculative suggestion and difficult to test.

## 3.4  Conclusions

As the discussion in this section has shown, trying to explain why children become autistic is a complex and controversial problem.

One difficulty is that genetic and organic influences are often seen as interrelated while environmental influences are seen as a mutually exclusive alternative to both. In practice, there are many possible interactions between all three sets of influences. Organic problems, such as structural and functional abnormalities of the brain, are sometimes inherited. But they can also be **congenital**, which means that they can result from difficulties, such as lack of oxygen, at the time of birth. Organic problems can also arise from environmental influences, as the study by Krech *et al.* (1966) suggests. Genetic abnormalities need not manifest themselves as organic defects. As Richer has suggested, autistic children may inherit a heightened sensitivity to environmental stimuli, such as an early period of separation from parents.

Another difficulty is that there are only a few generations of diagnosed autistic children to study. Presumably there were children with the behaviour pattern now described as autistic before Kanner suggested that it was a distinct disorder, but it is not known how their behaviour was interpreted. Some of these children may have been thought to be deaf, while others would have been diagnosed as psychotic or retarded. The best way to seek evidence for predisposing factors might be a longitudinal study, in which large numbers of families are followed through the years in which they were bringing up young children. Hypotheses about predisposing factors could be confirmed or refuted by testing predictions about which families would be likely to produce autistic children. However, as Richer (1983) has pointed out, since the incidence of autism is very low in the general population, such a study would require a very large sample of children, and so would be difficult, if not impossible, to carry out.

## Summary of Section 3

- Studies of identical twins suggest that a genetic factor may play a part in predisposing some children to develop autism.

- Structural and functional brain abnormalities have been found in some autistic children.

- There is little evidence for the hypothesis that the personality characteristics of the mothers of autistic children are abnormal.

- The presence of an autistic child is likely to have a profound effect on other members of the family. Care must be taken to differentiate between influences which cause a child to develop autism, and abnormalities in the child and his environment which are the effect of the child's autism.

- Ethological studies suggest that motivational conflict between approach and avoidance behaviour inhibits autistic children from forming social bonds. Approach behaviour from adults accentuates this problem. However, this hypothesis raises both methodological and theoretical problems.

- Genetic, organic and environmental factors may interact in a complex fashion in predisposing children to develop autism.

# 4 | Deficits and skills of autistic children

The studies discussed in the last section aimed to identify the biological, environmental and emotional influences which may lead to children developing autism. As we saw in Section 1, these influences lead to profound deficits in social interaction, language and non-verbal communication, flexibility of thought and action and other cognitive skills. Many psychologists working on autism have argued that to understand the condition, one must establish whether there is one central deficit underlying all these difficulties. Until the early 1980s one popular theory, illustrated by the Tinbergens' work, was that the failure of social interaction is central: that if a child's normal motivation to interact with others is inhibited he cannot develop language, communication and other intellectual skills. At the same time, workers such as Rutter (1983) were arguing that deficits in language and other cognitive skills are central: that autistic children fail to develop these skills, and that their social and emotional withdrawal are the consequence.

The problem with both approaches is that they tend to assume a developmental sequence: either one in which social development comes before cognitive development, or one in which cognitive development comes before social development. But as Chapters 2 and 3 made clear, social and cognitive influences are closely interrelated at *all* stages of a child's development. One recent model of autism (e.g. Baron-Cohen, 1988) reflects this interplay of influences in its explanation of the social and intellectual isolation of autistic children. It sees the deficit as primarily one of **social cognition** in which the child's ability to understand the thoughts and feelings of others is impaired. As you will see, this approach draws upon the approaches to development discussed in Chapters 2 and 3. Both chapters suggested that a crucial aspect of development is the child's ability to take another person's perspective. We will look at some studies carried out to investigate whether autistic children possess this skill.

## 4.1  Taking the perspective of others

First of all, imagine a non-autistic child in the following situation. A child sits at a table on which are two small boxes, one square and one round. Two adults (Anne and Sally) are present. One adult (Anne) sits down at the table and says to the child, 'Let's hide this marble in one of the boxes'. The marble is hidden in the box of the child's choice (say, the square box) while Sally is watching. Sally then leaves the room. While Sally is out of the room, Anne says to the child, 'Let's move the marble into the round box'. The marble is moved and is concealed in the round box, after which Anne says to the child, 'When Sally comes into the room, if we ask her to look for the marble, which box will she look in?'.

SAQ 7    Which box do you think the child will indicate?

The task just described is very similar to an experiment carried out by Baron-Cohen, Leslie and Frith (1985) to test how autistic children react in this situation. This experiment is described in Box A which you should read now.

SAQ 8    Why do you think the experimenter had selected autistic children with a higher mental age than the other two groups of children?

SAQ 9    What is the purpose of (a) the Reality question, and (b) the Memory question in the experiment?

Why do most autistic children fail on the Belief question in this experiment? Clearly, it is not because they are operating at a lower intellectual level than the other two groups of children. Nor do they have difficulty in remembering where the marble was originally hidden or in understanding where it had been relocated.

## BOX A   The hidden marble experiment

At the start of the experiment, the child sits at a table on which there are two dolls (Anne and Sally) and two boxes (square and round). The experimenter names the dolls for the child, and then checks that the child has understood which is which. The scenario of hiding a marble in one of the boxes is enacted using one doll (Anne) with the other (Sally) looking on. Sally then 'leaves the room' and the marble is re-hidden in the other box. Sally then returns and the experimenter asks the child three questions:

1   'Where will Sally look for her marble?' (Belief question)

2   'Where is the marble really?' (Reality question)

3   'Where was the marble in the beginning?' (Memory question)

Three groups of children were tested (one at a time) on the task:

1   Twenty autistic children with an average age of 11 years 11 months.

2   Fourteen children with Down's syndrome with an average age of 10 years 11 months.

3   Twenty-seven normal children with an average age of 4 years 5 months.

The autistic children selected for the task had an average *mental* age (see Chapter 7, Section 1.4) of 9 years 3 months, as tested on a non-verbal intelligence test. On a verbal test their mental age was 5 years 5 months. Both these scores were higher than the mental age of the Down's and normal children. The children in all groups answered the Reality and Memory questions correctly. Eighty-five per cent of the normal children and 86 per cent of the Down's children also answered the Belief question correctly. In contrast, 80 per cent of the autistic children answered the Belief question incorrectly. That is, when asked, 'Where will Sally look for her marble?' they pointed to the marble's current location rather than to where the marble had been originally hidden before being re-hidden in Sally's absence.

Baron-Cohen *et al.* argue that the reason autistic children tend to fail on the Belief question is that they lack the capacity to imagine what beliefs another person will hold about the position of the marble. Instead of 'putting themselves in Sally's shoes', they assume that her belief about where the marble is hidden is the same as their own knowledge of where the marble really is. In another study, described in Box B overleaf, Baron-Cohen *et al.* (1986) investigated autistic children's ability to arrange sets of pictures into simple stories. As in the hidden marbles experiment, to perform correctly on certain story sequences the child had to be able to imagine what the story character was thinking.

## BOX B    Arranging pictures to tell a story

Three groups of children took part in the study: autistic children, children with Down's syndrome and normal children. As in the study described in Box A, the autistic children and Down's syndrome children were similar in average age and were considerably older than the normal children. The average mental age of the autistic children was higher than those of the other two groups. All children were tested one at a time.

A frame suitable for holding four cards in a row was placed on the table in front of the child. The first slot held a picture depicting a simple scene. Three other pictures, which together with the first could be arranged in a row to form a story, were placed in random order on the table. The child was asked to put the pictures in the frame in the correct order to form a story. After this the child was asked to tell the story he had arranged.

Each child was tested on three main conditions—Mechanical, Behavioural and Belief—each consisting of different picture sequences, defined by the type of story the pictures could be arranged to tell. These conditions are shown in Table 16.1.

**Table 16.1** Types of picture sequences in experiment by Baron-Cohen *et al.* (1986)

| Condition (type of picture sequence) | Picture 1 | Picture 2 | Picture 3 | Picture 4 |
|---|---|---|---|---|
| Mechanical | Rock on hilltop | Rock topples | Rolls down hill | Knocks tree over |
| Behavioural | Boy turns on tap | Stands under | Soaps himself | Dries himself |
| Belief | Girl puts teddy down | Turns to pick flower | Boy takes teddy | Girl sees teddy gone |

(Source: adapted from Baron-Cohen *et al.*, 1986)

In the Mechanical condition, the pictures showed a series of physical events which had to be arranged in a meaningful sequence. In the Behavioural condition, the pictures showed a series of actions which had to be arranged in a meaningful sequence. In the Belief condition, the pictures showed a series of actions which could only be arranged in a meaningful sequence if the child understood the thoughts of the story character. Figure 16.3 shows an example of each type of story sequence.

Each child's picture sequences were scored according to how closely they approximated the correct (i.e. predetermined) sequence. A completely correct sequence scored two points; a correct final card scored one point; all remaining sequences scored zero.

A summary of results is shown in Figure 16.4.

(a)

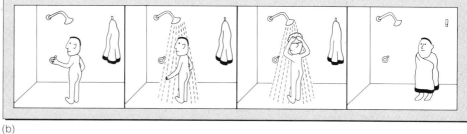

(b)

(c)

**Figure 16.3** Examples of picture sequences in the experiment by Baron-Cohen *et al.* (1986). (a) Mechanical; (b) Behavioural; (c) Belief
(Source: adapted from Baron-Cohen *et al.*, 1986)

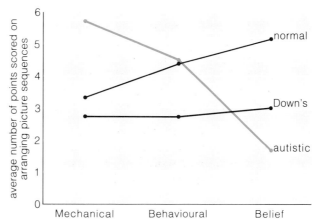

**Figure 16.4** Mean performance on picture sequencing by groups in the experiment by Baron-Cohen *et al.* (1986)
(Source: adapted from Baron-Cohen *et al.*, 1986)

SAQ 10    What does Figure 16.4 indicate about the performance of autistic children on the three main types of picture sequence?

The importance of the results of the experiment, as shown in Figure 16.4, lies in the autistic children's poor performance on the Belief story sequences, compared both with that of the other two groups and with their own performance on the Mechanical and Behavioural sequences. Baron-Cohen *et al.* argue that to place the Belief stories in a correct sequence the child needs a kind of understanding not necessary for completion of the other types of picture sequence. In the Mechanical example shown in Figure 16.3(a), the child needs to know that if a rock at the top of the hill topples, it will roll down the hill and knock down objects which are in its path. In the Behavioural example in (b), the child needs to know that when a boy stands under a tap he is likely to wash himself and then dry himself.

In the Belief example shown in (c), the child needs to understand that if a girl puts down her teddy and turns to do something else, she is likely to believe that her teddy will still be there when she turns back. She will be surprised if it is not. In this third type of sequence alone, the child needs to be able to imagine what the pictured character is thinking. Further evidence that the autistic children lack this skill of imagining or understanding another person's thoughts came from the authors' analysis of the children's narrations. The narrations of the autistic children were markedly lacking in descriptions or explanations involving the thoughts of the depicted characters.

These experiments are part of a series of studies which suggest that autistic children lack the capacity to 'put themselves in other people's shoes'. The same inability of very young normal children to take another person's perspective was first introduced in Chapter 2. Chapter 3 referred to Piaget's comparable suggestion that very young children display **egocentrism**. For instance, they may be unable to indicate how a scene such as three mountains would look when seen from another person's point of view. But autistic children perform as well as control children of the same mental age on tests of this type of **perceptual egocentrism**. Hobson (1984) conducted an experiment in which autistic children were asked to position a doll so that it could either 'see' the experimenter or 'see' themselves. He found that the autistic children were able to respond correctly in this task. Baron-Cohen (1989a) tested the ability of autistic children to identify what another person is looking at. Small toys were placed at different positions around the room. The experimenter, seated facing the child, moved his eyes under closed lids towards a toy in a particular location and then opened his eyes to look at the toy. Autistic children performed just as well as normal and Down's children controls in identifying what the experimenter was looking at. Both studies imply that autistic children, like normal children, grow out of early perceptual egocentrism. They are able to imagine themselves looking through the eyes of another person.

The normal performance of autistic children in these studies, together with their poor performance on the Baron-Cohen studies described in Boxes A and B, suggest that the egocentrism of autistic children is *conceptual* rather than perceptual. Autistic children can, literally, see the world as others see it, but they cannot apparently appreciate what others are thinking about the world. In normal children this ability to take other people's mental perspective, known as **conceptual role-taking**, begins to develop at a very early age, perhaps even as early as 2 years.

As Chapter 1 pointed out, some ability to conceptualize other people's thoughts, feelings and behaviour is essential for our interactions with them. The total absence of such 'social understanding' might be expected to have devastating consequences for the ability of any child or adult to interact appropriately with other people. At the simplest level, an autistic child may constantly misinterpret the 'meaning' of another person's smiles, waves and other gestures, and thus remain unable to respond in appropriate ways. Similarly, the child may be unable to understand what another person is feeling. We will look briefly at some studies which investigate this prediction.

## 4.2 Understanding other people's feelings

The process by which one person tries to understand what another person is thinking or feeling is a kind of **inference**. In Chapter 10, Section 4.4 you were introduced to perceptual inference as the process by which incoming cues, often in a fragmentary or incomplete form, are used by the perceptual system to form hypotheses which make sense of the real world. Similarly, since one person cannot directly observe another person's state of mind, he or she uses any available cues to form hypotheses about them. Imagine the familiar situation in which a child infers that her mother is angry with her.

SAQ 11     What kinds of cues might the child use to reach this conclusion?

Hobson (1986a) conducted some experiments designed to investigate how well autistic children can use different kinds of cues to form judgements about what another person is feeling. One of these is described in Box C overleaf.

Notice that the demands of Hobson's task, as described in Box C, are quite complex. The child has to compare several quite different kinds of information (pictures of facial expressions, videos of gestures, sound recordings and contexts) in order to identify the emotion being portrayed. There is some evidence that autistic children perform better when the task demands are simpler. For instance, in another study, Hobson (1986b) found that autistic children could match drawings depicting the gestures associated with different emotions with films of an actor making gestures to portray emotions.

Another problem with Hobson's task is that it lacks what is called **ecological validity**. That is, the task does not correspond at all closely to how people recognize and respond to emotions in everyday life. In everyday life, people use a complex interaction of dynamic cues from gestures, expression, voice and context to form inferences about how other people are feeling. These inferences provide the basis for their interactions. For instance, if a child

## BOX C   Judging emotions

Autistic children were given pictures of schematic faces which showed the facial expressions associated with different emotions such as anger, unhappiness and fear. The children were then shown videotapes of an actor portraying the same range of emotions. The children were asked to choose the appropriate face to 'go with' the emotion being portrayed at particular points in the video. The video was divided into sequences designed to present three different types of cues to the children:

| | |
|---|---|
| Gestures: | the actor appeared with a mask to obscure his face. He enacted for 10 seconds in turn bodily gestures characteristic of anger, unhappiness, happiness and fear. |
| Vocalizations: | while the screen was blank, the actor made sounds appropriate in turn to the four emotions listed above. |
| Contexts: | the actor (still masked) appeared in scenes appropriate to the above emotions—for example, for anger a jug topples over and falls on the actor; for happiness the actor is seen receiving a birthday cake. |

The autistic children performed poorly on all aspects of this task when compared with control groups suitably matched for intellectual level. Hobson suggested that this reflected the autistic children's inability to use the kind of cues normally used to make inferences about emotional states.

infers that his mother is angry, he may try to placate her, he may make himself scarce and so on. Hobson's task does not really provide a test of how autistic children behave in more realistic settings.

Even so, the inability to understand emotions and to act upon this understanding is well documented by those who come into contact with autistic children. As you will recall from Section 1, this inability to understand other people's feelings is one of the main features of autism. But autistic children also have difficulties in a number of other main areas, namely language, non-verbal communication and pretend play; focus of interests and activities; and cognitive skills. Baron-Cohen (1988) has argued that the deficits which he and others have documented experimentally, point to a common explanation for all these difficulties.

### ACTIVITY 1

Before we consider this, look back at the description of autism given in Section 1, and remind yourself of the main features.

# 4.3 What is the core problem?

As mentioned earlier, the performance of autistic children on the tasks in Sections 4.1 and 4.2 suggests a deficit in social cognition. That is, autistic children have difficulty with a type of *thinking* particularly crucial for *interacting* with other people. But Baron-Cohen (1988) has argued that this deficit in thinking might even extend to explaining why autistic children display 'odd' behaviour as individuals. He speculates that just as autistic children are unable to think about other people's thoughts, they have difficulty in reflecting on their *own* thoughts. While the first skill is necessary for complex social behaviour, the second skill is necessary for complex individual behaviour. To evaluate whether this combination of problems is a plausible explanation for the autistic child's symptoms, we will consider it in relation to each of the main groups of symptoms described in Sections 1.2 and 1.3.

Baron-Cohen's theory provides a plausible explanation for the first group of difficulties: in social interaction. Autistic children have particular difficulty in simple two-way interactions such as returning a wave or a smile, and in more complex social interactions such as making friends. As Chapter 2 showed, the ability to take the role of (think the thoughts of) another person is crucial for the success of these interactions.

The second area of difficulty is language, non-verbal communication and symbolic play. As you will recall, autistic children vary widely in their ability to use language. At one extreme there are children who grow up speaking and understanding no more than a few words. At the other extreme are children who acquire a good grasp of language. But there appears to be a common problem across all levels of ability. As the diagnostic description implied, all autistic children are deficient in their use of language for conversational and communicative purposes—what is known as **pragmatics** (see Chapter 13, Section 3.4). One example of this is the bizarre echolalia which autistic children with varying levels of linguistic ability use in response to questions. This consists of repeating the question instead of answering it. Another example is that autistic children who talk fluently, even incessantly, about topics which interest them may look blank or offer an inappropriate response when asked a simple question such as, 'Where have you been today?' The impression is often that the child is conducting a monologue rather than participating in a social dialogue.

Chapter 13, Section 4 demonstrated that for 'successful' communication between one person and another, the two people must understand not only the meaning, but the relevance of what is being said. This grasp of relevance often seems to be missing when autistic children try to communicate. For instance, a child at a special school in Nottingham asked if she could go to the toilet. Her teacher asked her to go first and ask another member of staff if she wanted a cup of coffee. The child went and issued the question, 'Do you want a cup of coffee?' but she went on her way without waiting for an answer. She had understood what she was meant to say, but not its social significance as a way of offering someone else a cup of coffee (P. Christie, 1988, personal communication).

The autistic child's lack of pragmatic and conversational skills is consistent with the core problem suggested by Baron-Cohen. As we have seen, the ability to converse and communicate is crucially dependent on one person understanding the other person's thoughts. So if a child lacks the ability to understand another person's thoughts, difficulties in using language for conversation are to be expected.

The relative absence of gestures and other non-verbal behaviour in autistic children can be explained in the same way. Even before they can speak, young children use gestures such as pointing to toys both as a way of asking for things ('Give me my lamb') and as a way of indicating them ('My lamb is over there'). Chapter 13, Section 3.4 described how 13-month-old Carlotta used pointing for both these purposes, defined as proto-imperative and proto-declarative, respectively. Careful studies of the use of gesture in autistic children have revealed a particularly interesting finding here. Autistic children much older than Carlotta appear to use and understand proto-imperative pointing, but not proto-declarative pointing. For instance, Baron-Cohen (1989a) found that if an experimenter pointed proto-imperatively to an object like a toy, autistic children could respond appropriately (e.g. by handing the toy to the experimenter). However, if he pointed proto-declaratively (e.g. to an aeroplane visible through the window), the autistic children failed to give appropriate responses (e.g. did not look in the direction of the plane).

It can be argued that proto-imperatives do not involve thinking about other people's states of mind, but merely their behaviour. Thus, by pointing to a toy which he wants to hold, a young child, or an older autistic child, treats the other person as an agent which will fetch the toy to him. In contrast, in pointing to a toy which he wants to indicate, the young child has to think about an adult's thoughts in order to influence them ('That's where it is'). So again, Baron-Cohen's theory, that autistic children lack the ability to think about other people's thoughts, fits in here.

The final feature of this second group of difficulties is the absence of pretend play. Baron-Cohen argues that this can be explained as an inability to reflect on one's own (rather than another person's) thoughts. Imagine a child playing at 'mothers and babies' with her doll. To take the role of mother and treat her doll as the baby, the child must be able to hold simultaneously in her mind two conflicting sets of beliefs. She knows that in reality she is a little girl, and her doll is a toy. At the same time she must 'think' the opposite—that she is a mother and her doll is a baby. So she must 'think about her thoughts'.

The third group of difficulties described in Section 1.2 concerns autistic children's narrow focus of activities and interests. The relevance of Baron-Cohen's theory is much less clear here. Why should the inability to think about other people's, or one's own, thoughts lead to a restricted range of interests? There is one possible answer, although it has not been directly investigated. Many of the interests of normal children and adults require some form of social communication. Many children's games require a shared understanding of, and compliance with, rules; for example, in 'snakes and ladders' players must take it in turn to move according to the number thrown on the dice. Significantly, young autistic children tend to prefer solitary activities such as jigsaws and shape sorters. Older autistic children are often obsessively interested in mechanical devices such as trains and cars, or collecting objects like stamps. Perhaps these restricted interests are the inevitable consequence of avoiding the many activities for which social understanding is necessary.

Baron-Cohen's theory has no obvious relevance to the stereotyped behaviour often seen in autistic children, such as rocking back and forth or repeatedly flipping one hand. He has speculated (Baron-Cohen, 1989b) that because autistic children find the social environment so difficult to comprehend, it is a source of great anxiety. The children use repetitive activities to impose familiarity and predictability on the environment and therefore reduce anxiety. However, this suggestion has not been tested. An alternative explanation is that autistic children find their environment monotonous and use repeated actions to enhance any stimulation which it provides.

Perhaps the biggest puzzle for Baron-Cohen's theory—and for other theories of autism—is what are broadly referred to as cognitive difficulties. You will recall that these difficulties do not form part of the *criteria* for autism. This is because there are wide variations in cognitive ability between children. In some classic experiments by Hermelin and O'Connor (1970), the children performed poorly on tests of memory and perception. Yet you may recall that the children tested in Baron-Cohen's studies (Section 4.1) performed well on memory and perception tests. In the hidden marbles study most of the autistic children had no difficulty with the Reality and Memory questions. The two types of tests may have focused on different aspects of ability, or it may be that Baron-Cohen's group of children were less severely disabled than those studied by Hermelin and O'Connor. Even so, in contemporary samples, approximately 75 per cent of autistic children have IQs below the average. At all levels of IQ, the pattern of scores across subtests tends to differ from the pattern typical of normal children. The question is whether any explanation of autism can account adequately for this complex pattern of skills and deficits.

Baron-Cohen's theory implies that all autistic children should have difficulty in one specific area of cognition—the ability to reflect on one's own thoughts. This seems most likely to affect complex skills like solving mathematical problems. But some autistic children appear to excel at mathematics, while other children have cognitive difficulties far exceeding these. This remains an area for further research.

This section has considered in some depth one theory which attempts to relate the many difficulties of autistic children to the core problem of thinking about other people's, or one's own, thoughts. As we have seen, it provides a convincing explanation for some of these difficulties but its relevance to other difficulties is more speculative. In contrast to the theories described in Section 3, it does not seek to explain *why* children become autistic in the first place, though the core problem suggested by Baron-Cohen seems more likely to have biological than environmental causes. Above all, the theory does not point to a 'cure' for autism. In the next and final section we will consider how far psychological findings such as those discussed in this chapter have contributed to the therapy and care of autistic children.

## Summary of Section 4

- Experimental studies suggest that autistic children lack the capacity to take another person's perspective, though they can literally see the world as others see it.

- Autistic children also have difficulty with tasks involving recognition of emotions.

- On the basis of such studies, Baron-Cohen has proposed that the core problem in autism is the inability to think about other people's, or one's own thoughts.

- This theory provides a plausible explanation for autistic children's difficulties in social interaction, language, non-verbal communication and pretend play.

- The relevance of the theory to autistic children's restricted range of interests and repetitive activities is less clear.

- The cognitive difficulties of autistic children present a complex pattern. The predictions of Baron-Cohen's model have not been fully tested in this area.

# 5 | Has psychology helped autistic children?

So far in this chapter, we have considered autism mainly as an intellectual puzzle. The chapter started with a description of the symptoms of autism and went on to consider the assumptions underlying the diagnosis of autism. Contrasting theories about why children develop autism were then described, followed by a look, in some depth, at one theory about what is wrong with autistic children. But has this or other psychological work had a significant beneficial effect on the lives of autistic children? Although this is a wide-ranging question which merits a chapter in its own right, it would be unacceptable to conclude without considering some of its main aspects here.

The first question which must occur to many people, and particularly to the parents of autistic children, is quite simply whether there is a 'cure' for autism. In other words, is there some therapeutic procedure which can eradicate all trace of an autistic child's difficulties? Over the years since Kanner's first description, a number of psychologists have made dramatic claims about the success of different therapeutic procedures. Indeed, Tinbergen and Tinbergen's (1983) account of their approach to autism was entitled 'Autistic' children: new hope for a cure. We will look at two therapeutic approaches which have been presented, potentially at least, as 'cures' for the condition.

# 5.1 Therapeutic 'cures' for autism?

It is not surprising that those who have made the strongest claims about therapy have mostly favoured 'environmental' and 'emotional' explanations for autism. If the cause of autism lies in the environment of the child and/or the child's emotional response to this environment, then it should be relatively easy to bring about change. Genetic and organic defects are not easy to influence. Though medical treatment has for a long time played a part in therapy for autism, it is usually thought of as a way of controlling particularly difficult symptoms rather than as a cure.

The psychoanalyst Bettelheim, whose work was mentioned in Section 3.2, was committed to the hypothesis that the mothers of autistic children have extremely abnormal personalities. In fact, he argued that these mothers entertained a 'death wish' towards their children. His therapeutic approach, described in his book *Empty fortress: infantile autism and the birth of self* (Bettelheim, 1967), involved separating children from their parents and caring for them in a special residential centre where they were exposed to an all-embracing environment of warmth and affection designed along psychoanalytical lines. His book describes the apparently dramatic improvements which occurred in the emotional adjustment, speech and behaviour of children treated in this way.

As we saw in Section 3.2, there is actually very little evidence that the parents of autistic children have abnormal personalities. They may manifest stress and other psychological problems as a *result* of the difficulties they face in bringing up an autistic child, but this is a different matter. This does not necessarily invalidate Bettelheim's therapy though. It could work for reasons other than those suggested by Bettelheim, so it merits some evaluation simply in terms of whether it succeeds.

One problem in evaluating success is whether the group of children treated by Bettelheim were really autistic at all. Most of the children described by Bettelheim had developed normally up to the age of four, after which they began to regress to earlier stages of development and withdraw from social contact. In autism, the age of onset is by definition much earlier—at under 3 years. Autistic children typically fail to pass normal development milestones, and their detachment from social interaction is present from the outset. So it may be that Bettelheim's therapy succeeded because it was used with a group of emotionally disturbed, rather than autistic, children.

Another criticism of Bettelheim's work is that he did not conduct proper 'follow-up' studies of the children who attended his centre. It is not known whether the improvements observed while the children were in his care disappeared after the children had left. As was noted in Section 1.4, there have been several long-term follow-up studies of autistic children and these provide evidence that the children who show most improvement from early symptoms of autism are those who were initially least affected. The possibility that Bettelheim achieved success simply with those children who would have improved anyway must be seriously considered.

Bettelheim's approach raises serious ethical questions since it involved separating children from their mothers on the grounds that they were to blame for their children's problems. Separation of a child from his parents can only be morally justified if there is strong evidence that the child will be harmed by their presence. In the case of autistic children, the evidence does not support the view that the parents' presence might be harmful. Under these circumstances, the total separation of the child from his parents seems therefore very likely to be harmful in itself. There is evidence that the parents rejected Bettelheim's approach, feeling unjustly victimized by the blame he attributed to them, and distressed at being separated from their children.

The second therapy to be considered here is known as **holding therapy**. Holding therapy was developed by an American psychiatrist called Martha Welch, whose work was the subject of a two-part BBC television documentary in 1988. The approach was enthusiastically advocated by the Tinbergens (1983) who saw the therapy as a logical development of their theory about what causes autism.

SAQ 12    From the discussion in Section 3.3, what did the Tinbergens see as the main factor responsible for the development of autism in children?

The Tinbergens argue that, to be successful, a therapy should 'give top priority to a restoration of the child's emotional balance'. The child's excessive anxiety is seen as inhibiting him from forming normal social bonds with his mother, and later with other people. Obviously, the mother will have developed reservations and inhibitions as a result of the behaviour of her child. So therapy must overcome both the anxiety of the child and the reservations of the mother and provide a context for bonding. Holding therapy, seen by the Tinbergens and others as the procedure for achieving this, is described in Box D.

This dramatic procedure has probably attracted more publicity than any other therapy for autism. People who have observed holding sessions, or watched them on television, usually find them upsetting because of the child's apparent distress at the procedure. Yet workers who use this technique, as well as the parents of some children interviewed about it, claim that it has produced profound changes in the children treated in this way. Most of these successes take the form of individual case histories, some of which, described by Welch and Prekop, are reported in the appendices to the Tinbergen's book. One case history describes how a 3½-year-old child progressed from being 'mute, unable to relate to people, hyperactive, developmentally retarded, bizarre looking, and obsessed with flushing toilets and aligning blocks in an exact line' (Tinbergen and Tinbergen, 1983). After 6 weeks of holding therapy, it is claimed that the child began to say words and subsequently develop language. At the age of eight, the child appeared normal, both intellectually and in his social relationships.

Unfortunately, individual case histories like the one just described are all that is available to support the claimed success of the therapy. At the time of writing, there has been no attempt to evaluate its success systematically. Yet,

## BOX D   Holding therapy

Physical contact is seen as the best way for the mother to reach through the autistic child's barrier. The role of the therapist is to help the mother to initiate this physical contact, and then to show her how to build on it. The father, or another member of the child's family, may be asked to play a supporting role, in close physical contact with the mother.

The usual position for 'holding' a young autistic child is with the child sitting on the mother's lap, facing her. The child's arms are placed around the mother. The mother holds the child's head so that she can make eye contact with the child. For an older child the mother may be asked to lie on top of the child, supporting her weight on her elbows and holding the child's head in her hands.

Initially, the child puts up powerful resistance to being held. The therapist encourages the mother to continue and to try to establish eye contact. The child may scream with rage and terror, bite, spit or strike his mother. The therapist suggests that this behaviour expresses the child's ambivalence. On the one hand he wishes to be comforted, on the other he is terrified of the comforting process.

Holding sessions are continued until, it is claimed, the child relaxes and starts to respond positively to the mother's contact. He may cling to the mother, look into her eyes, or start to speak. At this stage the therapist provides support and interpretations of what is happening in the mother's relationship with her child. The mother is encouraged to explore the conflicts which she has developed about relating to the child.

Some workers who use this technique insist that the child must be deliberately provoked first before the mother is given the opportunity to comfort him. Provocation might take the form of forcing eye contact, removing a favourite toy, or frightening the child with a loud noise.

like Bettelheim's approach, the therapy is controversial and requires the most careful scrutiny.

The criticisms which apply to Bettelheim's approach apply equally to holding therapy. The first criticism is theoretical. As we have seen in this chapter, the Tinbergen's theory, that motivational conflict is the main cause of autism, is not supported by the evidence. The evidence suggests that autistic children initially fail to *understand* what is required for social interaction, rather than emotionally withdrawing from it. If the therapy works, then it must be for reasons different from the ones suggested by the Tinbergens.

A major problem in evaluating holding therapy is that few of the children, it seems, have been through a conventional process of diagnosis. Although some of the children described displayed symptoms similar to those listed in Section 1, it is not known whether they would have met the full criteria for a diagnosis of autism. Welch (Tinbergen and Tinbergen, 1983) states explicitly that the therapy is suitable for a wide category of childhood emotional disturbances, in which autism appears to be included.

Assessment and follow-up of success is another major problem. Christie (1985) described an account of observations he made at the main British centre for holding therapy. Among his impressions he reported that 'the point at which "resolution" is reached, and the hold relaxed, was not easily discernible'. He also reported that the centre had no resources to keep systematic records on success either during or after therapy.

Given this informal, anecdotal approach to the success of the treatment, counter-claims must be given equal weight. For instance, the mother of an autistic child published an account of her failure with holding therapy, and of the harmful effects on the child:

I did holding therapy with my son for three years. In the early stages, he released a great deal of repressed anger and seemed more relaxed at the end of a session, helping us both to become in touch with our emotions. This initial 'honeymoon' period was almost inevitable, however, considering our emotional state at the time. We had all been living in a turmoil of anxious uncertainty for several years when we were offered both support and hope by the holding therapist. The relief, and the need to believe in the treatment was overwhelming. The therapist was adamant our son would recover, but during our first year of therapy, I realised he was no longer experiencing the joy of being allowed to express his natural feelings. He was being forced to become angry because somebody had *decided* he should. I began to feel my child was increasing his resistance to my approaches—the more he resisted, the more I was told to push him. This led to us becoming locked in a situation of almost unbearable tension; spontaneity disappeared from our holding sessions as I increased my efforts to do what was required. I felt a failure, which in turn made me feel I must try harder. It was a vicious circle.

We continued the therapy far beyond the point at which it ceased to help. Our therapist convinced me it would be harmful to my son if I stopped—she said he would feel I no longer cared enough to hold him. In turn, I felt she was the only person who understood my son, and believed he would get better. As far as I knew, she offered the only help available that at least attempted a cure. After I stopped the therapy, it took me a long time before I could see the whole experience in perspective and was appalled by some of the things we had done. The therapist should not have assumed responsibility for two vulnerable lives when she had neither the training nor experience to support her good intentions. Neither should she have assured us that our child would recover, with no evidence to back this up. Eventually, I realised I was trying to force my son to confront feelings with which he was not equipped to deal. Having adopted the psychologically crippling defence of autism, my son's response to our attempts to blast a way through his protective wall was to withdraw even further.

Holding therapy, I concluded, can be damaging.

(Bronwyn Hocking in *The Independent*, 3 November 1987)

To conclude, although holding therapy has given hope to some families of autistic children, its claims have never been properly evaluated. For the time being, it must be treated with caution. Like Bettelheim's approach, holding therapy raises serious ethical questions since it may inflict harm on the child and his parents. Whereas Bettelheim's approach goes to the extreme of separating the autistic child from his parents, holding therapy goes to the opposite extreme of forcing physical contact and affection upon a child who does not understand, and may be frightened by this behaviour. As we saw, there is anecdotal evidence that this produces deterioration in the condition of some children.

By contrast, some psychologists who favour environmental explanations of autism have developed therapeutic procedures which seem unlikely to harm either the autistic child or his parents, and may well produce benefits. Even if these psychologists are incorrect about the *causes* of autism, their procedures have an important practical contribution to make in helping autistic children and their families.

## 5.2 Therapeutic procedures for helping autistic children

One therapeutic approach mentioned briefly in Section 3 was family therapy. Clancy and McBride (1969) argued that autism arises from an early abnormal pattern of interaction between a mother and her child. The personality traits of the mother in interaction with the 'strong contentment of the child in the absence of human contact' were seen as producing an initiating context for the child's autistic behaviour towards all members of his family. The procedure which Clancy and McBride designed to reverse this trend treats the family as the 'unit of therapy'. Some aspects of this therapy are described in Box E.

### BOX E   A family therapy

The objective is to encourage first the development of bonds between the child and his family, and then the acquisition of behaviour such as language. The therapy takes place in stages. At each stage the therapist initiates the process and then hands over to the appropriate member of the family.

At the first stage the child and his mother are admitted to hospital to maximize the opportunities for guidance by the therapist. The therapist may start by tackling practical problems such as feeding fads, in which the child refuses to eat anything but the most restricted range of foods. The therapist deals with this by introducing a series of new foods, initially camouflaged by the food the child prefers, at each mealtime. To start with, the child usually ceases eating altogether. When he becomes very hungry, he begins to accept the new foods, first with, and then without, the camouflage of the preferred food. Once the child is eating normally (claimed to be within a week), the mother is given responsibility for continuing under the therapist's guidance.

The therapist encourages the mother to treat feeding as a playtime, so that it becomes pleasurable rather than aversive for the child.

In parallel, the mother is encouraged to involve the child in interacting with her via his favourite games (typically rough and tumble, water play etc.). Increasingly strong demands are placed on the child, starting with eye contact, then sounds, then words to achieve what the child wants. The mother is encouraged to cuddle and comfort the child. Once basic bonds are established (claimed to be within one week), the mother and child return home although they remain in regular contact with the therapist.

At this stage the therapist attempts to involve other members of the family in specific activities such as feeding and playing, using the procedures just described in order to encourage the child to interact. Some of this work is carried out at a special day centre where the child is also encouraged to develop more complex skills, particularly language.

Clancy and McBride (1969) reported that in a small group of children treated using this method, feeding difficulties were overcome and a normal diet established. A bond was established between mother and child. This carried over to other members of the family, although not much beyond. Children developed some use of language, although the progress in this area was limited. There were some setbacks in all these developments when the child returned home, and Clancy and McBride stressed the need for both family and therapist to keep up pressure on the child.

Like Bettelheim and the Tinbergens, Clancy and McBride's account of follow-up is sketchy and does not distinguish between spontaneous improvements and those due to the treatment. It is not clear how they decided that bonding had occurred between the child and his family, and they acknowledged problems with the therapy once the child returned home. Above all, Clancy and McBride appear to have had little success in tackling problems of language, communication and so on at a fundamental level. However, the child's behaviour appears to become less difficult and more sociable. The mother and other family members are given an active role in helping the child and are made to feel less inadequate and isolated as a result.

Over the last 20 years, many psychologists have realized the practical potential of family therapy, and have used it as a framework to help families of autistic children. Not only the behaviour of the child, but also the problems of the parents may be ameliorated using this approach.

You probably noticed that the techniques used by Clancy and McBride to encourage social responses from the children rested loosely upon **behaviour modification** (see Chapter 15, Section 2.2). Mothers were shown how to make situations, which had initially been aversive for the child, positively reinforcing. Feeding was made pleasurable by treating it as a play session. Responses such as smiles or words were accompanied by positive reinforcement in the form of the child's favourite play activities.

Other psychologists working with autistic children have made the behavioural approach central to their work. Initially, this perspective, like family therapy, was linked to a specific theory about the cause of autism. Thus, Ferster (1961) argued that autism resulted from the failure of social stimuli to acquire reinforcing properties for the child. For normal children, for instance, events such as physical contact with another person, a parent's smile or verbal approval come to be reinforcing (see Chapter 6, Section 4). Ferster suggested that this does not happen for the autistic child. This theory no longer has a major impact as an explanation of why children become autistic, but it has generated an influential model of how the difficulties of autistic children should be tackled. The views of one of its best known proponents, Lovaas, are summarized in Box F.

In the 1960s and 1970s, behavioural techniques were widely used to tackle difficult behaviour in autistic children. There have been positive developments of this approach but also a recognition of its drawbacks.

One development was that therapists succeeded in expanding the range of behaviours tackled using the behavioural method. They also recognized that food was not the most suitable way of rewarding autistic children. They found

## BOX F   A behavioural model of therapy

Lovaas (1979) argues that *most* approaches to autism, whether theoretical or therapeutic, assume that there is a specific illness or disease underlying autism, and that if the illness can be cured, the behaviour will be changed. Lovaas argues that this assumption is not *useful* in treating autistic children. Regardless of cause, therapy should concentrate on breaking down the behavioural difficulties of autism into 'manageable' components, and tackling these using principles based on learning theory.

Lovaas cites evidence that a number of different behaviours can be tackled using behaviour modification. In particular, therapists have succeeded in eliminating autistic children's repetitive behaviours, which are often self-destructive; they have taught autistic children to imitate gestures

such as waving and smiling; they have established elementary language responses (such as single words) in previously mute children. Lovaas also claims considerable success in establishing complex language behaviour, including the use of grammar and semantics. In early applications of these treatments, food was used to reward children for desired behaviours. Withdrawal of attention or physical punishment were used in order to extinguish undesired behaviours.

Lovaas' approach conforms to the 'scientist-practitioner model' (see Chapter 15, Section 4) in that he stresses the need to evaluate each therapeutic procedure in terms of its successful use with a particular child, and to modify the procedure in the light of this evaluation.

that it was possible to employ more natural *social* rewards such as praise, attention and giving the child the opportunity to engage in a favourite activity. In addition, the harmful consequences of physical punishment, as a means of extinguishing undesired behaviours, were recognized and alternative techniques substituted.

The most important development was a shift from hospital-based or clinic-based treatments, in which the therapist took a central role, to home-based treatments in which parents were given major responsibility for the therapy. Once parents were trained to use operant conditioning procedures with their autistic children, it was found that the home provided the best setting for therapy. Therapy at home could focus on the child's natural everyday behaviour, rather than on how he performed in the clinic. Also, as in Clancy and McBride's approach, the use of parents as 'behavioural therapists' encourages parents to feel involved and responsible, rather than helpless and alienated. There is, in practice, considerable overlap between this approach and family therapy.

One disadvantage of the behavioural approach is that it demands a tremendous commitment of time and energy on the part of the child's therapist and his parents. As you saw in Chapter 6, reinforcement contingencies must be applied consistently or the organism will not learn the required response. Parents do not necessarily find this easy. A second problem is that although behaviour modification may be successful in eliminating difficult behaviours such as temper tantrums and repetitive actions, it has had, despite Lovaas' claim, limited success in tackling the autistic child's central difficulties in social interaction, language and other forms of communication.

Careful studies (e.g. Churchill, 1978) have shown that while autistic children can be behaviourally trained to make appropriate verbal responses such as 'Can I have a biscuit?', this behaviour does not generalize into a command of grammar, syntax and, above all, pragmatics. This is hardly surprising since, as Chapter 13 demonstrated, the behaviourist model of how children acquire language completely fails to explain the development of complex language behaviour. Similarly, autistic children can be trained to make social responses such as waving and smiling but this does not necessarily mean that they have grasped an understanding of how to use these gestures appropriately in complex social interactions.

To summarize, behavioural treatment, like family therapy, provides a useful tool for therapists working with, and parents living with, an autistic child. But these procedures do not address themselves directly to what many contemporary workers see as the central problems for autistic children. As a final conclusion to this chapter, we will look at how current attempts to help autistic children overcome their difficulties are guided by theoretical insights like those discussed in Section 4, as well as by the practical tools discussed in this section. It is important to realize that therapy, in contemporary terms, is not a 'treatment' which is 'applied to' autistic children at particular times. It is more accurately a general framework of principles which are brought to bear in the education and everyday care of autistic children. This shift in therapeutic emphasis has occurred as a result of theoretical developments in the field of autism and changes in public attitudes, which have brought about a change in the special provision made for autistic children. We will briefly consider these changes as background to current trends.

## 5.3 From theoretical shifts to current trends

This chapter has documented some of the theoretical shifts which have occurred since Kanner first described autism in 1943. Although his original description of the symptoms of the condition remains largely intact, views about the causes and essential nature of autism have changed.

At first, many psychologists and pyschiatrists were influenced by Kanner's suggestion (which he later abandoned) that children became autistic in response to abnormal parenting. Therapies based on this assumption, such as Bettelheim's psychoanalytical therapy mentioned in Section 5.1, were common in the 1950s and 1960s, particularly in the United States. The most prevalent alternative at that time was probably medical treatment using drugs. As mentioned in Section 3.1, some specialists did believe that fundamental organic defects could be alleviated using drugs such as fenfluramine. But in most cases drugs were used because they provided the only way of controlling the more difficult behaviours of autistic children. It should be remembered that at this time knowledge of autism was relatively limited and there was little or no special provision for autistic children. Children with more extreme symptoms were often admitted to psychiatric hospitals. Others were cared for at home by parents, sometimes with the stigma of blame, and often with no back-up from specialists familiar with the condition. Educationally, the best that parents could hope for was a place for their children at schools for mentally retarded children.

One landmark in the change of professional and public attitudes was the publication in 1964 of a book written by the psychiatrist Rimland, himself the father of an autistic child. In this book, Rimland presented balanced and convincing arguments against the hypothesis of 'parental pathology' and, as we saw in Section 3.2, research evidence has continued to refute the hypothesis.

Specialists working on autism began to entertain a much wider range of hypotheses about causes, central deficits and therapies. Although purely environmental hypotheses about causes were still favoured by some, there was a growing emphasis on the contribution of genetic and organic predisposing factors like those discussed in Section 3.1. Interest focused increasingly on approaches like Baron-Cohen's (Section 4.3) which see social cognition as the central component in the autistic child's deficits.

On the therapeutic side, psychologists were exploring the potential of many different procedures. As described in Section 5.2, family therapy and behaviour modification were initially used by psychologists theoretically committed to these approaches. Other treatments were developed by psychologists with theoretical interests in communication and language deficits. But quite often these psychologists incorporated elements of family therapy and behaviour modification as practical tools within their overall procedure.

This opening up of professional attitudes and approaches to autism coincided with a growing concern, on the part of parents, that parents themselves should do something to improve the image of autism and the provision for their children. In 1962, a group of these parents formed The National Society for Autistic Children (now known as The National Autistic Society). This society, and regional societies which have grown from it, have done a great deal to change public attitudes towards autism, and to press for the special facilities which autistic children need. Such facilities include access to proper diagnosis, special schools, and provision for the children when they grow up. The first special school for autistic children—the Sybil Elgar School in Ealing—was set up by The National Autistic Society in 1969. Other schools linked to the society have followed. The fees of children attending these schools are paid for by local authorities.

As a result of these changes over the last three decades, there has been a marked improvement in the diagnostic, educational and therapeutic facilities provided for autistic children. Unfortunately though, many autistic children still do not have access to these facilities. The needs of individual children differ too. For the majority of autistic children, education in a special school is most appropriate. A minority may manage in a normal school provided extra help and support is given. At home, some families may be able to take a major role in therapy, while others need intensive support from specialists.

Therefore, in trying to describe contemporary trends in caring for autistic children, one cannot generalize about the facilities that are available or appropriate for every child. We will consider the approach of one special school for autistic children—the Sutherland House School in Nottingham.

The fact that we are considering the work of a school, rather than a hospital, clinic or individual therapist, gives some indication of how attitudes towards caring for autistic children have changed. Education and therapy are seen as integral elements within the overall aim of helping autistic children overcome their difficulties. As the head of the school has commented:

The particular pattern of impairments present in autistic children is so fundamentally disabling to their development as people, who have relationships with others, that what they need to learn and experience in an educational setting is wider than that for any other group of children. In most school settings the teacher/child relationship is seen as the vehicle for the child's learning. With autistic children the establishment, maintenance and development of that relationship becomes an aim in itself.

(Christie, 1985)

The school's assumptions about the nature of autism are similar to those outlined in Section 4. Autistic children are thought to suffer from a fundamental deficit in social cognition which impairs their ability to interact socially, to develop language and other communicative skills, and which disposes them to repetitive actions and restricted interests. The aim of therapy and education within the school is to help children overcome this deficit, initially through the acquisition of simple pre-verbal skills (pointing, eye contact etc.) on which language and other intellectual abilities and interests can then be built.

An important feature of the school is a very low staff to child ratio (approximately one member of staff to every two children). Autistic children find it very difficult to learn in a group setting, and forming a close relationship with one member of staff is an essential part of overcoming their difficulties. Another special feature is a highly structured and organized environment. This is necessary so that the child is exposed to a limited amount of information at any one time, and is aware of what is expected of him. In this way the child can be helped to progress towards a series of carefully defined goals.

A mixture of procedures is used to achieve these goals. There is a great emphasis on involving the family in the process of education and therapy. For instance, parents are encouraged to attend special workshops to help them acquire teaching and therapeutic skills similar to those used at the school, to use with their children at home. The influence of behavioural methods is seen in the use of rewards when a child performs an appropriate response. However, changing a child's behaviour is not seen as an end in itself, rather as one step towards making social interactions with other people. The ultimate aim of the process is that the child will gain reward from understanding the world from another person's point of view (see Section 4.1).

Some of these principles are illustrated by the procedure used at the school to teach pre-verbal autistic children the skill of taking turns. As Section 4

## BOX G   Using music to teach turn taking (from Christie and Wimpory, 1986)

The aim of the therapy is to provide the autistic child with experience of taking turns in an interaction with another person. This turn taking is seen as an essential requirement for communication, whether non-verbal or verbal. Music is used to provide a context of repeated and exaggerated experiences of turn taking.

Three people are present at the session: a musician (pianist or guitarist), a teacher, and a child. The teacher plays physical rough and tumble games with the child, such as lifting him or swinging him in the air, chasing him and so on (many autistic children enjoy rough and tumble games). As she does so, the teacher improvises to or with the child action songs which describe their activity. For instance, if she is chasing the child, she might sing, 'I'm going to get you'. To begin with, the teacher initiates most of the activity, but she looks for opportunities for the child to initiate an activity. Any spontaneous activity on the part of the child, such as touching a ball, is interpreted by the teacher as if it were intentionally communicative. For instance, if the child touches a ball, the teacher might sing, 'Bounce, bounce, bounce the ball' and then stop doing so until the child touches the ball again. The musician plays music in such a way as to reinforce this turn taking. For instance, if the child initiates an activity such as jumping, the musician commences a new sequence of music to accompany the jumping, and stops when the child stops.

Observations of these sessions suggest that children begin to initiate activities and to join in with activities initiated by the teacher. In other words, they begin to develop a capacity to take turns with another person in a shared activity. Some autistic children develop specifically social responses, such as making eye contact with their teacher, or imitating sounds and words.

---

demonstrated, this skill is essential for social interaction and conversational use of language. The procedure is described in Box G.

This is just one of the techniques used within the school to 'take autistic children through' the early stages in developing social responses. The idea is that if the child acquires a grasp of the basic elements required for an interaction with another person, this will develop into a more sophisticated grasp, and ultimately into an understanding of the other person's point of view.

Does this approach achieve any more than the various approaches to therapy described earlier? Certainly teachers using this method do not make dramatic claims for it. They see it as just part of a wide-ranging programme of educational and therapeutic procedures used with autistic children who attend the school. Evaluation is possible because the progress of each child attending the school is carefully monitored over the lengthy period (several years) for which a child attends the school. Some children can be monitored beyond this point, because they go on to attend an affiliated adult centre for people with autism.

As a tentative conclusion, the majority of children benefit considerably from the approach to education and therapy offered by schools like this one. Above all, the school's approach is guided by understanding rather than misunderstanding of the nature of autism. In the long run, this must offer the best prospect for helping autistic children. But, as this chapter has shown, many aspects of autism remain a puzzle. As long as the puzzle remains, so too will the problem.

## Summary of Section 5

- Therapies suggested by Bettelheim and by the Tinbergens have been claimed to 'cure' autism. However, these claims have not been properly evaluated and both procedures raise ethical problems.

- Family therapy and behaviour modification both offer practical procedures which can be used in helping autistic children and their families.

- The shift of theories about autism, and the change in public attitudes, have helped to improve special provision for the diagnosis, education and treatment of autistic children.

- Contemporary therapy is often carried out as an integral part of an autistic child's education in a special school, though parents are also encouraged to take responsibility for therapy.

- A typical therapy in a special school aims to tackle the autistic child's deficits in social understanding. First steps involve helping the child to develop early precursors of communication such as gestures and turn taking. Behavioural procedures may be used to achieve this goal.

### Personal acknowledgements

I would like to thank Simon Baron-Cohen for his invaluable comments and advice during the preparation of this chapter, and Scilla Read for her most helpful suggestions for Section 2.

## Further reading

RUTTER, M. and SCHOPLER, E. (eds) (1978) *Autism: a reappraisal of concepts and treatment*, New York: Plenum Press.
This is an important reference work and includes chapters by leading workers on all aspects of autism.

SCHOPLER, E. and MESIBOV, G.B. (eds) (1984) *The effects of autism on the family*, New York: Plenum Press.
This work forms part of a series of very informative books, edited by E. Schopler and G.B. Mesibov, on different aspects of autism.

T<small>INBERGEN</small>, N. and T<small>INBERGEN</small>, E. (1983) *'Autistic' children: new hope for a cure*, London: Allen and Unwin.
The Tinbergens' account of autism is an intriguing, if idiosyncratic, one, presenting the authors' arguments in favour of the motivational conflict hypothesis.

F<small>RITH</small>, U. (1989) *Autism: Explaining the enigma*, Basil Blackwell.
*Autism: Explaining the enigma* is an up-to-date account of theory and research on autism, including a discussion of the social cognition approach (described in Section 4 of this chapter).

P<small>ARK</small>, C.C. (1978) *The siege*, Hutchinson.
This book is now out of print but may be available through libraries. I list it here because, if you are able to get hold of a copy, it will give you a *parent's* account of life with an autistic child.

W<small>ILTSHIRE</small>, S. (1987) *Drawings*, and W<small>ILTSHIRE</small>, S. (1989) *Cities*, London and Melbourne: J.M. Dent and Sons.
These two books contain the marvellous architectural drawings of the autistic boy Stephen Wiltshire.

# References

B<small>ARON</small>-C<small>OHEN</small>, S. (1988) 'Social and pragmatic deficits in autism: cognitive or affective?', *Journal of Autism and Developmental Disorders*, vol. 18, pp. 379–402.

B<small>ARON</small>-C<small>OHEN</small>, S. (1989a) 'Perceptual role-taking and protodeclarative pointing in autism', *British Journal of Developmental Psychology*, vol. 7, pp. 113–27.

B<small>ARON</small>-C<small>OHEN</small>, S. (1989b) 'Do autistic children have obsessions and compulsions?', *British Journal of Clinical Psychology*, vol. 28, pp. 193–200.

B<small>ARON</small>-C<small>OHEN</small>, S., L<small>ESLIE</small>, A.M. and F<small>RITH</small>, U. (1985) 'Does the autistic child have a "theory of mind"?', *Cognition*, vol. 21, pp. 37–46.

B<small>ARON</small>-C<small>OHEN</small>, S., L<small>ESLIE</small>, A.M. and F<small>RITH</small>, U. (1986) 'Mechanical, behavioural and intentional understanding of picture stories in autistic children', *British Journal of Developmental Psychology*, vol. 4, pp. 113–25.

B<small>ETTELHEIM</small>, B. (1967) *Empty fortress: infantile autism and the birth of self*, New York: Free Press.

C<small>ANTWELL</small>, D.P. and B<small>AKER</small>, L. (1984) 'Research concerning families of children with autism', in Schopler, E. and Mesibov, G.B. (eds) *The effects of autism on the family*, New York: Plenum Press.

C<small>HRISTIE</small>, P. (1985) 'Education in school for autistic children "What's so special about autism?"', paper presented at a day conference at Nottingham University, 27 April 1985.

C<small>HRISTIE</small>, P. and W<small>IMPORY</small>, D. (1986) 'Recent research into the development of communicative competence and its implications for the teaching of autistic children', *Communication*, vol. 20, no. 1.

C<small>HURCHILL</small>, D.W. (1978) 'Language: the problem beyond conditioning', in Rutter, M. and Schopler, E. (eds) *Autism: a reappraisal of concepts and treatment*, New York: Plenum Press.

CLANCY, H. and McBRIDE, G.M. (1969) 'The autistic process and its treatment', *Journal of Child Psychology and Psychiatry*, vol. 10, pp. 233–44.

CLARK, P. and RUTTER, M. (1981) 'Autistic children's responses to structure and to interpersonal demands', *Journal of Autism and Developmental Disorders*, vol. 11, pp. 201–17.

COURCHESNE, E., YEUNG-COURCHESNE, R., PRESS, G.A., HESSELINK, J.R. and JERNIGAN, T.L. (1988) 'Hypoplasia of cerebellar vermal lobules VI and VII in autism', *New England Journal of Medicine*, vol. 318, pp. 1349–54.

DeMYER, M.K. (1979) *Parents and children in autism*, New York: Wiley.

DSM-III-R (1987) 'Diagnostic and statistical manual of mental disorders', revised 3rd edn, Washington, DC: American Psychiatric Association.

FERSTER, C.B. (1961) 'Positive reinforcement and behavioural deficits of autistic children', *Child Development*, vol. 32, pp. 437–56.

FOLSTEIN, S. and RUTTER, M. (1978) 'Infantile autism: a genetic study of 21 twin pairs', in Rutter, M. and Schopler, E. (eds) *Autism: a reappraisal of concepts and treatment*, New York: Plenum Press.

GELLER, E., RITVO, E.R., FREEMAN, S.J. and YUWILER, A. (1982) 'Preliminary observations on the effect of fenfluramine on blood serotonin and symptoms in three autistic boys', *New England Journal of Medicine*, vol. 307, pp. 165–9.

GOLDFARB, W. (1961) *Childhood schizophrenia*, Cambridge, MA: Harvard University Press.

HERMELIN, B. and O'CONNOR, N. (1970) *Psychological experiments with autistic children*, Pergamon Press.

HOBSON, R.P. (1984) 'Early childhood autism and the question of egocentrism', *Journal of Autism and Developmental Disorders*, vol. 14, no. 1, pp. 85–104.

HOBSON, R.P. (1986a) 'The autistic child's appraisal of expressions of emotion', *Journal of Child Psychology and Psychiatry*, vol. 27, pp. 321–42.

HOBSON, R.P. (1986b) 'The autistic child's appraisal of expressions of emotion: a further study', *Journal of Child Psychology and Psychiatry*, vol. 27, pp. 671–80.

KANNER, L. (1943) 'Autistic disturbances of affective contact', *Nervous Child*, vol. 2, pp. 217–50.

KANNER, L. (1971) 'Follow up study of 11 autistic children originally reported in 1943', *Journal of Autism and Childhood Schizophrenia*, vol. 1, pp. 119–45.

KOLVIN, I., OUNSTED, C. and ROTH, M. (1971) 'Six studies in the childhood psychoses. V. Cerebral dysfunction and childhood psychoses', *British Journal of Psychiatry*, vol. 118, pp. 407–14.

KRECH, D., ROSENZWEIG, M.R. and BENNETT, E.L. (1966) 'Environmental impoverishment, social isolation and changes in brain chemistry and anatomy', *Physiology and Behaviour*, vol. 1, pp. 99–104.

LOTTER, V. (1978) 'Follow up studies', in Rutter, M. and Schopler, E. (eds) *Autism: a reappraisal of concepts and treatment*, New York: Plenum Press.

LOVAAS, O.I. (1979) 'Contrasting illness and behavioural models for the treatment of autistic children: a historical perspective', *Journal of Autism and Developmental Disorders*, vol. 9, pp. 316–22.

McAdoo, W.G. and DeMyer, M.K. (1978) 'Personality characteristics of parents', in Rutter, M. and Schopler, E. (eds) *Autism: a reappraisal of concepts and treatment*, New York: Plenum Press.

Richer, J. (1978) 'The partial non communication of culture to autistic children—an application of human ethology', in Rutter, M. and Schopler, E. (eds) *Autism: a reappraisal of concepts and treatment*, New York: Plenum Press.

Richer, J. (1983) 'Development of social avoidance in autistic children', in Oliverio, A. and Zappella, M. (eds) *The behaviour of human infants*, New York: Plenum Press.

Rimland, B. (1964) *Infantile autism*, New York: Appleton-Century-Crofts.

Rutter, M. (1983) 'Cognitive deficits in the pathogenesis of autism', *Journal of Child Psychology and Psychiatry*, vol. 24, pp. 513–31.

Schain, R.J. and Freedman, D.X. (1961) 'Studies of 5-hydroxyindole metabolism in autistic and other mentally retarded children', *Journal of Pediatrics*, vol. 58, pp. 315–20.

The National Autistic Society (1985) *What can the matter be? Report on parents' pursuit of a diagnosis for their autistic child*, London: The National Autistic Society.

The National Autistic Society (1987) *Review 1986–87 'Building a better future for autistic people'*, London: The National Autistic Society.

Tinbergen, N. and Tinbergen, E. (1983) *'Autistic' children: new hope for a cure*, London: Allen and Unwin.

Treffert, D. (1989) *Extraordinary people*, Bantam Books.

Wiltshire, S. (1987) *Drawings*, selected and with an introduction by Sir Hugh Casson, London and Melbourne: J.M. Dent and Sons.

Wing, L. and Gould, J. (1979) 'Severe impairments of social interaction and associated abnormalities in children: epidemiology and classification', *Journal of Autism and Development Disorders*, vol. 9, pp. 11–29.

## Answers to SAQs

### SAQ 1

(a)  Autistic children find the performance subtests of the WISC-R easier than the verbal subtests.

(b)  Raven's Progressive Matrices test is probably the best test for obtaining a true measure of an autistic child's IQ. As you will recall, the items test skills such as choosing the correct pattern to complete a series of patterns. These require perceptual and logical abilities. Verbal abilities are not tested. However, some understanding of language is required for the child to carry out the instructions for completing the tests.

## SAQ 2

Evidence of a genetic factor can be obtained from studies of how often autism affects other members of the families of autistic children. Studies which compare the frequency of autism in identical twins compared with fraternal twins are particularly important because identical twins, unlike fraternal twins, have identical genes. Environmental factors are assumed not to differ between these two types of twins in such studies.

## SAQ 3

Some people argue that not only genetic inheritance, but also the environmental context are much more similar for identical twins than for fraternal twins. For instance, the families of identical twins will tend to treat both twins identically, while the families of fraternal twins will treat each child differently. To overcome this problem, psychologists have studied the similarity in, for example, behaviour and intelligence between twins who have been separated. Because autism is a rare condition, this has been difficult to do in this case.

## SAQ 4

The problem with Clancy and McBride's method is that they did not *observe* the behaviour pattern of lazy sucking etc. They obtained the information from retrospective interviews with the mothers. The mothers' memories of how their babies behaved soon after birth may well have been distorted or inaccurate, particularly since they had subsequently experienced the stress of coping with an autistic child. Even so, many mothers of autistic children do report having had the feeling that 'something was wrong' from a very early age.

## SAQ 5

The purpose of the control group was to provide a group of parents who would be directly comparable with the autistic children's parents in terms of factors such as anxiety and stress. Any 'abnormalities' due to these difficulties should be at a similar level for both groups. Any additional abnormalities observed in the autistic children's parents could then be interpreted as indicating something intrinsic to their personalities.

## SAQ 6

Most of the studies of rat behaviour described in Chapter 6 were experimental. The rats were studied in the unnatural environment of the laboratory, and the rats' behaviour was carefully manipulated by the experimenter to observe what effect particular stimuli would have on the rats' responses. However, as Chapter 6, Sections 6 and 7 illustrated, modern studies of learning rely increasingly on naturalistic methods like those of the ethologists.

## SAQ 7

Normal children over the age of four invariably indicate, correctly, that Sally will look in the square box, in which she watched the marble being hidden. Very young children sometimes point to the round box.

## SAQ 8

The reason the experimenter selected autistic children with a higher mental age was to rule out the possibility that autistic children would perform less well on the tests simply because they were less intelligent. By taking this precaution, the experimenter can be sure that poorer performance on the part of the autistic children is due to a specific difficulty in handling this task.

## SAQ 9

(a) The purpose of the Reality question is to ensure that all children tested in the experiment understand the events which have taken place. A child who does not understand where the marble has been re-hidden cannot be tested on the Belief question. He might give either a correct or an incorrect response simply because he does not understand where the marble really is.

(b) Similarly, the purpose of the Memory question is to ensure that all children remember where the marble was initially located. A child who has forgotten this may not have followed the 'deception' of relocating the marble in Sally's absence. So again, this child could not be meaningfully tested on the Belief question.

## SAQ 10

The autistic children perform better (score more points) than either the normal children or the Down's children on the Mechanical picture sequences (this difference was statistically significant). They perform as well as the normal children and (significantly) better than the Down's children on the Behavioural sequences. In contrast, on the Belief sequences the autistic children perform less well than the other two groups. Again, this difference was significant.

## SAQ 11

The child might infer that her mother is angry from her facial expression (e.g. frowning or scowling), from her gestures (e.g. wagging her finger), from her voice (e.g. shouting or speaking very quietly and deliberately), or from something which has happened (e.g. the child has poured paint all over the floor).

## SAQ 12

The Tinbergens see as the main factor a conflict between the basic human motivation to form social bonds and anxiety, which produces an unusually powerful motivation to avoid human contact.

# Overview of Part VII

The common theme running through Chapters 15 and 16 is that of psychological principles being put to use. You may have noticed that this application of psychology to real-world problems can operate in a number of different ways. In Chapter 15 the focus is on clinical psychologists carrying out therapeutic work with people on a day-to-day basis. For these psychologists the primary role of psychological methods and theories is to guide their choice of therapeutic strategies for working with individuals. Research is seen as an integral part of the clinical process of evaluating the efficacy of these therapeutic strategies.

In Chapter 16 much of the discussion concerns psychological research designed to test theories about the causes and nature of autism. A number of the studies described used the experimental method and involved comparing the performance of groups of autistic children with that of control groups. It might perhaps seem ethically questionable to use autistic children as 'guinea pigs' for such studies. But therapy stands a greater chance of success if it is informed by clear theoretical insights based on careful research.

### The nature of psychological problems

Both chapters confront the question of how to define a 'psychological problem'. It may seem obvious that an adult's extreme fear of open spaces, or a child's social withdrawal and inability to use language, constitute problems. In both these examples the person's behaviour appears to depart from what is considered 'normal'. But, as both chapters indicate, the difference between normal and abnormal is by no means clear cut. Chapter 15 points out, for example, that homosexuality might be seen as normal or abnormal, as a problem requiring treatment, by some people but not by others. And Chapter 16 makes it clear that the characteristic symptoms of autism occur to some degree, or at some times, in all children.

The two chapters adopt somewhat different solutions to this difficulty. In Chapter 15, the definition of 'psychological problem' is intentionally left somewhat loose, so that the clinical psychologist is left free to judge each individual case afresh. The point is made that two people may display very similar symptoms, but for entirely different reasons. The implication is that one cannot assume that the underlying 'problem' is the same in each case. In contrast, Chapter 16 assumes that, when different children have the same symptoms of extreme social withdrawal and of language and communication deficits, these reflect the common underlying problem of autism. The implication here is that, although each child's symptoms have some unique features, the overall pattern of symptoms falls into a recognizable category, making it possible to apply a diagnosis of autism.

Chapter 16 sets out the advantages and disadvantages of grouping symptoms into categories such as autism for purposes of diagnosis and treatment. The main disadvantage, to which Chapter 15 refers, is the danger that a diagnostic category, such as autism, may serve as a 'label' which constrains the process of understanding and treating the problem. It is interesting to compare the case study of a child with hemiparesis, cited in Chapter 15, Section 1, with the account given by parents of an autistic child in Chapter 16, Section 2.2. The first example emphasizes the parents' rather negative feelings about their son's condition: it seemed that the label of hemiparesis had discouraged the parents from considering the positive potential their son might have. It was the skilled intervention of the clinical psychologist which helped the parents to overcome their negative feelings. In contrast, the parents of the autistic child described the moment when their child was finally diagnosed as autistic as a positive step for them. Careful and sensitive diagnosis can thus play an important role in helping parents come to terms with a child's problem, providing it is combined with suitable therapeutic support. And, as Chapter 16 points out, clinicians and researchers must remain open to the possible variety of factors causing a problem, even if they agree about the diagnostic features.

This debate about 'diagnostic labelling' echoes a theoretical tension which has cropped up in earlier chapters. Essentially, the debate is about whether psychologists should treat individual cases (in this case individual people's problems) as unique, or whether they should draw out the shared, common features of different cases. It is worth remembering that the difference between the two approaches is always one of degree rather than of kind. The clinical psychologists whose work is described in Chapter 15 inevitably draw some general conclusions from a comparison of individual cases. And, of course, at times they make use of 'labels', such as depression or anorexia nervosa, as a concise description of commonly occurring patterns of symptoms. Psychologists need to make use of general categories if they are to simplify and make sense of their extremely complex subject matter. On the other hand, psychologists (clinical and others), who work with autistic children, do not treat each child's problems as identical. It is recognized that there are individual variations in the pattern and severity of symptoms, as well as in external factors such as how the child's family reacts to the problem.

## General principles of therapy

The emphasis in Chapter 15, on assessing the profile of factors involved in each individual case, affects not only the psychologist's initial conception of people's problems, but also the approach to therapy. As each case is seen as different, clinical psychologists are often eclectic and pragmatic in their therapeutic choices. This might give the impression that clinical psychology operates in an *ad hoc* fashion, lacking a general framework to guide its decision process. But the scientist-practitioner model is seen as providing such a framework. The idea is that clinical psychologists should follow the general principles of scientific method. They should give clear descriptions of a person's problems and formulate alternative hypotheses about how to proceed. These hypotheses should be 'tested' by observing and monitoring the outcome of any therapy offered to the person. If one approach fails, the psychologist should be prepared to try out and evaluate alternative approaches.

Chapter 16, with its assumption that autism is a syndrome with the same symptoms, and perhaps the same causes, in different children, stresses that therapy should be informed by theoretical insights into the nature of autism, based on research. All of the therapeutic approaches discussed in Chapter 16 draw on specific theories about autism. However, as Section 5.1 indicates, certain therapies, based too rigidly on particular theoretical assumptions, have raised ethical problems in their handling of autistic children and their families. It is interesting to note that, while contemporary approaches to therapy are informed by recent research on social understanding, they are also characterized by an eclectic use of therapeutic procedures. For instance, both family therapy and behaviour modification are described as having a useful role to play in therapy. Even though it is not thought that autism is caused by 'faulty mothering' or by a failure of conditioning, these therapies can be used to tackle the many and varied difficulties which arise at home and at school. This eclectic use of therapeutic procedures is in keeping with the scientific-practitioner model which can be seen as a general description of good clinical practice.

A second general principle for clinical practice, described in Chapter 15, is that of functional analysis. This assumes that, when a person has symptoms such as depression or anxiety, these may produce consequences which serve the function of maintaining the symptoms. For instance, by displaying the kind of helplessness associated with depression, a person may achieve the consequence of avoiding responsibilities which he or she finds threatening. Accordingly, the psychologist should identify those functions that a person's symptoms are performing, and design therapy so as to break up the functional cycle.

It is important to consider just what is implied by this approach. Many people might find unacceptable the suggestion that an unpleasant symptom, such as helplessness or involuntary starvation, serves a function for the person who experiences it, even if, as Chapter 15 implies, the person is unaware of the symptom's maintaining function. Similarly, it seems strange to suggest that autistic symptoms, such as social and language difficulties, produce consequences for the child which serve to maintain the child's autism. The implication seems to be that autism is 'avoidable', whereas the evidence described in Chapter 16 suggests that it is a profound and lifelong disorder in which genetic and organic factors play a part. There is, however, an important principle embodied in functional analysis. This is that all psychological problems, however 'fixed' they may be, have *features* which are changeable. Psychologists should focus on identifying these features in order to bring about change. In this way the need for theoretical insights into the causes of psychological problems can be balanced against a therapeutic emphasis on those aspects of problems for which therapy will have the greatest effect.

# PART VIII
## REVIEW

chapter **17**

# UNDERSTANDING PSYCHOLOGY

Judith Greene and Kerry Thomas

## Contents

# 1 | So what is psychology?

The introductory chapter in Volume 1 raised some questions about the subject-matter of psychology and the methods commonly used by psychologists in their attempts to understand people and what makes them tick. One of the problems that was discussed was whether it is appropriate to think of psychology as essentially the same as the scientific study of any other domain of the physical world. Or do people's minds and their behaviour have properties that set them apart from atoms, crystals, wave motion, electromagnetism or anything else that science has set out to explain? When it comes to explaining and understanding people, is there an essential difference between human beings and objects?

## 1.1  Setting the scene

Imagine you are glued to watching snooker on television. Even if you have only a hazy idea of the rules of the game, it is easy to find the spectacle hypnotic. The presentation of snooker on television is certainly theatrical. There is the spotlight on the table, the darkness almost hiding the audience, and the contrast between the two competitors, one playing and the other watching and reflecting. There is the tense drama of the longer breaks when each successive move is executed with a staggering degree of technical precision, until a tiny miscalculation, or a lapse of attention, leads to a mistake and the termination of the break. It is as though a snooker match, particularly when viewed from the vantage point of well-placed television cameras, demonstrates, in a microcosm, two systems which guide and constrain human experience and behaviour. On the television screen it is possible to see both the physical world in motion and people in action.

Because the players are so skilled, once they apply some initial energy to the cue ball through impact with the cue, what follows looks like a series of predictable movements played through to a pre-ordained goal. The movement of the snooker balls is a clear, and reassuring, demonstration of the physical laws of motion. We know that, if a snooker player applies a particular amount of force at a specified angle to the cue ball, this will cause it to move at a certain velocity toward, say, the red ball in its path. We know that the cue ball will hit the red ball and cause it to roll toward the pocket and drop in. All of this can be described in terms of physical concepts, such as the standard mass of snooker balls, the standard friction of snooker table baize, force, temperature, perhaps humidity, and so on. Furthermore, by studying many instances of the same forces and movements, expressed as mathematical equations, it is possible to construct a series of general statements which allow us to describe and predict the movements of other snooker balls on other tables in other championships.

But what about the actual players? Without their actions nothing would have happened. And this is where we get to the point of the story, the conjunction of the two domains, people and things. There is the potentially controllable and predictable physical world of the laws of motion; and there is the essentially private world of the players, their different strategies, their reactions to each other's tactics, their intense concentration on playing the game, their emotions and their personalities. A player's behaviour, too, can be described in terms of a series of physical movements which can be analysed objectively. But this does not tell us what the player *thinks* he is doing. Much of the pleasure of watching a championship player comes from trying to understand the man himself: 'Why is he making that shot?', 'Why did he make that mistake?', 'Why is he off form today?' or, on a slightly different tack, 'Why did he become a snooker player in the first place?'. Psychologists (like the rest of us) have to make inferences about thoughts, feelings and motivations which go beyond observed behaviour.

Another problem with explaining people's intentions and actions is that each individual person reacts in a subtly different manner. One only has to watch famous snooker players paired against each other in championship matches to note the extraordinary differences in the way they behave, either rushing at shots or deliberating endlessly, sitting down calmly between breaks or nervously sipping a drink. Viewers are left in no doubt about the personalities of the players, those that they find attractive or dislike. So how far is it possible to construct general laws which will permit us to predict exactly what *all* snooker players will do? There are, after all, many things which are common to all snooker players. They have to be able to perceive the colour of the balls and to concentrate on applying the cue to the white ball and not to any other ball. They have to be familiar with the rules of snooker. Players of championship standard will have played many thousands of games in order to learn the tricks of the trade. They also need to have the motivation and determination to succeed, the ability to play their best even in the presence of millions of viewers. So, despite all their personality quirks, there is an overriding similarity between the co-ordinated actions of top snooker players.

Some of the chapters in these two volumes have been mainly concerned with processes which are common to all humans, indeed to all animals. Others have attempted to explore each individual's abilities and experience. However, if you think back over what you have read, you should realize that this is not always an easy distinction to make. Freud, for instance, thought of himself as proposing general laws about the development of personality, yet psychoanalysts aim to bring to light the defence mechanisms adopted by individual patients. Individual differences in IQ scores, or personality disorders like depression and autism, may be partly explained by general biological and environmental factors. A person's potential for self-reflection and personal growth may be undermined by the universal tendency to adhere to social norms and expectations. A challenge for psychology is how to reconcile similarities between people with the essence of each person's distinctive experience; to provide explanations which capture both the general principles that govern behaviour and individual variations.

# 1.2 Models and paradigms

Throughout this final chapter there are two threads to follow. The first concerns psychologists' basic assumptions about **models of the person** which encapsulate a view about what people are like. Are people automatons at the mercy of every circumstance, or are they self-determining agents, or are they primarily social beings? These are the kinds of assumptions that underpin (often implicitly) psychological theories. Second, there are arguments about which are the best psychological methods for trying to understand and explain people and their behaviour. These two threads must be followed in parallel because it is impossible to separate ideas about the fundamental nature of what is being studied from the kinds of methods used to gain knowledge.

Issues concerning the nature of what is being studied, which methods to use, what sort of evidence to look for, and what sorts of criteria to apply to explanations, are issues in epistemology. **Epistemology** is a philosophical term for knowledge and how it is acquired. Questions about whether more knowledge is gained by using experimental methods to study humans and other animals, or by using psychometric methods for testing people, or by using observational methods to categorize behaviour, or by asking people to reveal their feelings—all these are epistemological issues.

The combination of a theoretical model with a particular method for acquiring knowledge is known as a paradigm. A **paradigm** is a framework of interlocking assumptions about the proper aims and methods for investigating and gaining knowledge about those aspects of behaviour the researcher is interested in. As in other fields of study, the paradigms that have been applied to psychology have varied with the period and culture in which the quest for psychological knowledge is embedded. The earliest attempts in Wundt's and other early laboratories to systematize psychological phenomena treated introspection as a paradigm for studying conscious awareness of perceptions and events. But, with the demonstration in physical science of the power of theories and hypotheses tested by experimentation, there was a move to treat psychology in the same way. This was part of a general espousal of **positivism**, a school of thought which believes that the aims and methods of natural science should be applied to all realms of knowledge, including the study of people. Initially, this approach was mainly evident in the work of the behaviourists, but it became the dominant paradigm for studying universal psychological processes, such as memory, perception, attention and learning.

The application of the natural science paradigm to studying mind and behaviour reflects the underlying assumption that people are creatures whose behaviour is determined by biological and behavioural factors. This implies that the factors which affect behaviour are potentially open to description and amenable to the formulation of general laws. According to this view, a person's behaviour is capable of complete explanation and prediction in just the same way as the movements of a snooker ball.

But there are other diametrically opposed views about what it means to understand human beings. The example which is most different from the natural science paradigm is that of humanistic psychology. Here the underlying model of the person is of an essentially autonomous creature.

Humanistic psychologists are concerned with understanding conscious experience, personal meaning and the experience of what it is to be human, rather than explaining behaviour through general laws. The humanistic movement in psychology is a reaction against the constraints of the experimental method, and the assumptions of natural science, in the face of the individuality, awareness, agency and self-determination of people.

However, there are many intermediate positions between the determinism of scientific psychology and the humanistic view of personal autonomy. For instance, there are models of the person which assume that people are essentially social beings, constrained by social norms and the conventions of society. Other models reflect the cognitive shift by emphasizing the ability of people to form mental representations of their environment which guide their behaviour. These intermediate models have implications for how we believe a child learns to think and to become a social being. In general, they represent a stance which is not wholly deterministic and yet allows for the biological and environmental constraints which influence the way we develop as people, with distinct personalities and typical modes of interacting with the world around us. In the remaining sections of this chapter we will attempt to spell out some models of the person which underlie the various approaches to psychology discussed in this book.

## Summary of Section 1

- People's behaviour can be analysed both as externally observable actions and in terms of inner intentions.

- It is a challenge for psychology to reconcile the general biological and social constraints which determine behaviour with the human capacity for individual experience and choice.

- Different approaches to psychology are based on different models of the person which have led psychologists to adopt different paradigms for studying people's behaviour and experience.

# 2 | Psychology and science

Many psychologists favour treating the study of people and their psychological processes as a science like any other. Jeffrey Gray, a physiological psychologist, has said that the difference between one science and another 'turns on the nature of the observations that are made. Chemists make observations on molecules, physicists on atoms and psychologists make observations principally on behaviour' (Open University, 1981). The basic assumption is that the behaviour of animals can be manipulated and predicted in the same way as physical objects. This does not necessarily imply that animals, including humans, are simple systems. Think of all the complex mathematical equations required to predict the stresses and strains involved in building a bridge. However, the natural science paradigm does make two claims: that behaviour is determined, and that, given enough resources, it is possible to discover all the causes of that behaviour. Thoughts and emotions may be very difficult to predict because they are 'internal' and have many causes but, according to the natural science paradigm, they are in principle predictable.

Scientific laws have to be formulated in such a way that the scientific community can agree exactly which phenomena they refer to, which events they predict and the nature of the evidence upon which they are based. When carrying out experiments, psychologists have to agree about what they are doing when they manipulate an independent variable, and predict the effect on a dependent variable. They have to agree about terms, definitions and measurements. Objectivity can be defined as this consensus between researchers about the measurement of variables.

## 2.1 Biology and psychology

Looking back over the two volumes, it may strike you that one area which is 'naturally' scientific is the biological approach described in Chapter 5. Surely, biological descriptions are rooted in natural science since they imply that all behaviour can be explained in terms of heredity and physiological functions. **Biological models** of the person appear to carry the strong implication that behaviour is completely determined by our genes and by the way our bodies function, as described in Box A overleaf.

How far should we take biological explanations? Are there limits to how far we can go in reducing the explanation of the person to the neural nuts and bolts of the nervous system? For some psychologists, biology provides most, if not all, of the answers to the fundamental questions of behaviour. For others, the biological level of explanation is inevitably fraught with misconceptions and dangers; people are not like rats, or are they? Arguably, biological factors are essential in trying to explain something like depression or aggression. Genes, neurons and hormones doubtless play a vital part in any convincing account of human behaviour. Biology has a role in determining behaviour but, reciprocally, the environment in part determines our biology as well. For

## BOX A    Biological models of the person

The person as a biological system consists largely of cells; for example, neurons and the junctions between them, known as synapses. The brain and spinal cord are made up of many millions of such neurons (Chapter 5). Information about events in the outside world is carried towards the central nervous system by neurons, as demonstrated in the account of the visual system in Chapter 10. Information is carried from the central nervous system towards the muscles by other neurons. Chemical transmitters, such as serotonin and noradrenaline, convey information from one neuron to another across synapses.

Biological explanations also make an appearance in Chapter 8 in the context of Eysenck's personality theory; differences between extraversion and introversion were explained in terms of different activity levels in the brain's ascending reticular activating system, and the dimension of neuroticism versus stability was associated with differences in the lability of the autonomic nervous system. The kind of nervous system that each person has is determined by genes. Genes were discussed in the context of a genetic bias towards disorders such as depression and autism (Chapters 5 and 16) and the possibility that a genetic factor determines differences in intelligence (Chapter 7). Another aspect of biology, the intrinsic build-up of energy and drive, was mentioned in the discussion of Freud in Chapter 4 and reappeared as a biological instinct of aggression in Chapter 14. All these approaches are based on the paradigm that psychological processes can be explained in terms of biological functions and processes.

instance, depression is not merely the expression of deviant neurotransmitters which run their inevitable course in a vacuum. Depression is part of a broader matrix of social relationships that are, in part, determined by, but may also *determine*, underlying biological events. Genes do not determine behaviour in any simple one-to-one way. Rather, from the time of conception, the developing cell is surrounded by an environment. The environment of the womb is influenced by the biological state of the mother. The infant is surrounded by stimuli that impinge upon neurons and so can change its biological state.

These examples demonstrate the full complexity of the interaction between biology and the environment. Nevertheless, biologically-based models do fall within the scientific paradigm. However complex biological systems are, there is still an assumption that it is possible to discover general laws which specify the precise relationships between external events and their biological consequences. While biological explanations at present fall far short of accounting for, say, the content of our conscious experiences, physiological psychologists have investigated physiological indicators associated with states of sleep, dreaming and awareness. The drive for biological knowledge is fuelled by the belief that general causal laws will emerge eventually which will explain the factors which determine most, if not all, aspects of human behaviour and experience.

## 2.2 Explaining observable events

Biological models can be thought of as theories about internal physiological events, albeit in reaction to external events. Another equally influential version of the scientific deterministic model takes almost the opposite tack, regarding external events as being responsible for all learned behaviour. Events in the environment—that is, observable inputs (stimuli) and observable outputs (responses)—are the only admissible scientific data. The assumption is that the behaviour of animals can be predicted solely in terms of observable events, as in other sciences. For instance, in chemistry the amounts of substances which are to be combined in an experiment can be objectively and precisely measured, as can the substances which are the outcome of the experiment. It is these kinds of assumptions which underlie the psychological school of behaviourism.

Classic behaviourism can be thought of as an input/output model because of its reliance on observable external events. Note, too, that a version of the input/output approach was also apparent in the earliest information processing models developed in the 1950s with their notion of information flowing from a stimulus input through to the production of a final response output. This is shown in its simplest form in Figure 11.1 in Chapter 11 (reproduced here as Figure 17.1), which demonstrates the similarity between behaviouristic and information processing models. Both behaviourism and information processing models are described as **input/output models** in Box B.

---

### BOX B   Input/output models of the person

In the earliest classic formulations of behaviourism, the person can be thought of as an empty 'black box', the outputs of which are determined by inputs. All learning can be explained in terms of relationships between inputs, ouputs and their consequences, as explained in Chapter 6. Manipulation of events by the experimenter will lead to predicted outcomes. The information processing framework, which underlies much of the research described in Chapters 10, 11 and 12, also concentrates on relationships between inputs from the environment and eventual outputs. Although there are several internal 'black boxes' in an information processing model between stimulus and response (representing selective filters, short-term and long-term memory) information processing progresses in an orderly direction from input to output; Figure 17.1.

Of course, behaviourism does not really imply that our heads are empty boxes. Watson assumed that connections between neurons were being made in the brain and Broadbent and others viewed the brain as an information processor. The crucial point is that all conclusions about internal events are based on observable events which can be objectively measured; for example, the way a rat turns in a maze.

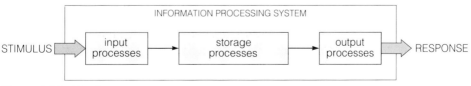

**Figure 17.1**   The input/output model

How do these models fit in with the scientific approach to psychology? As we have seen, scientific explanations are in terms of general laws, which would explain behaviour in terms of **cause and effect**. According to the behaviourist paradigm, a rat's behaviour can be caused by the pairing of a response and a reinforcement in an instrumental contingency. Information processing models are used to predict attentional behaviour in accordance with general laws about the operation of a selective filter. The implication is that, irrespective of the complexity of the biology of the brain and of psychological processes, given enough time, effort and skill, it is possible to explain all behaviour by general laws. A deterministic model of this kind implies that it is possible in principle to predict in advance what people will do in certain well-defined circumstances.

But what happens if people are conscious of what they are doing? Watson enunciated most clearly the claim that, although thinking, feelings and other mental events obviously exist, they are completely irrelevant to predicting behaviour. Even supporters of the cognitive shift assume that a rat's cognitions can be studied and manipulated in order to produce *predicted* results; for example, whether a rat will react to a tone based on its previous expectations. But suppose people's conscious awareness of their own cognitions allows them to reinterpret what is happening to them. Perhaps this is a crucial difference between rats and humans. Because of their ability to use language to reflect on their own thoughts and to discuss things with their fellow humans, it may be possible for people to reinterpret the events which appear to constrain their behaviour. In the next section we will consider this possibility that the peculiarly rich mental life of human beings crucially affects all aspects of behaviour.

## Summary of Section 2

●  The natural science paradigm is based on the assumption that the behaviour of animals is ultimately determined and predictable.

●  Experiments carried out to discover the causes of behaviour have to specify objective measurements of observable events.

●  Biological models of the person are concerned with identifying the genetic and physiological determinants of behaviour, intelligence and personality.

●  Input/output models of the person predict testable relationships between inputs from the environment and response outputs in order to discover general laws of cause and effect.

# 3 | Psychology: the science of mental life

The title of this section indicates that we are still working within a scientific framework but that the focus has shifted towards putting the 'mental' back into psychological theories. The aim is to allow for the influence of mental processes on people's behaviour and experience. However, this does not mean that we have left behind the experimental paradigm. Under the influence of positivism, the early behaviourists and psychologists who developed information processing models supported experimentation, almost as a matter of principle, to demonstrate that the causes of human behaviour can be investigated in exactly the same way as the behaviour of atoms or gases. The modern use of experiments shares the same objective of ensuring that psychological theories are tested against observations to rule out other possible explanations for their findings. The problem, however, is how to devise experiments that will reveal people's thoughts, self-concepts and feelings.

In these two volumes there are many ingenious research studies of this kind. Experiments have shown that children's ability to take another's point of view depends on what sense they can make of a situation; for example, the 'hiding from policemen' study reported in Chapter 3, Section 5. Other experiments have demonstrated the importance of memory representations of knowledge, for instance, the work of Collins and Quillian on the way memory is organized as a hierarchy of concepts (Chapter 12, Section 5.2). In Chapter 14, Section 3.4, there is an extended discussion about the advantages and disadvantages of using experiments to study people as subjects. Often it is more appropriate to use observational methods or to gather self-ratings and verbal reports from people about their personality traits or attitudes. But researchers still need to specify the aims of their studies and to indicate clearly what kinds of evidence would support their theory.

## 3.1 Mental representations: the cognitive shift

The concept of mental representations is ubiquitous in psychology. It is generally accepted that people cannot function intelligently without a mental life in the form of cognitions representing the physical and social world. Without an internalized model of the world stored in memory, we would not be able to benefit from past experience or formulate expectations about what is likely to happen next. We would not be able to recognize objects or remember anything that has happened to us. Intelligent behaviour arises from interactions with the environment which enable us to develop new skills. For instance, it is only from constant practice at the snooker table that novice snooker players acquire expert knowledge of the game, developing mental representations which enable a player to select the easiest, and at the same time the most valuable, shot to attempt.

Because of the close relationship between mental representations of knowledge and the development of intelligence, it can be argued that cognitions are responsible for everything which people are capable of learning, thinking about and acting upon. Theories which attempt to explain human behaviour in terms of mental representations are based on underlying **cognitive models** of people functioning as intelligent systems, as described in Box C.

---

### BOX C    Cognitive models of the intelligent person

Piaget describes the growth of intelligence as an unfolding process of developing more sophisticated mental representations (Chapter 3). He sees the stages of cognitive development as universal, although the full emergence of the final stage of formal operations, the ability to think logically and hypothetically, may depend on being exposed to certain kinds of intellectual opportunities. As described in Chapter 7, many IQ tests rely on formal logical skills which may account for individual differences in IQ scores found in later life. Whatever the reason for these differences, cognitive strategies for dealing with problems are clearly important.

Intelligence can be thought of as consisting of a constellation of abilities, including basic cognitive processes, such as perceiving, attending and remembering (Chapters 10, 11 and 12). Without such basic cognitive processes, people cannot function as intelligent human beings. When cognitions 'go wrong' they can lead to malfunctioning of various kinds, as is demonstrated by the failure of autistic children to develop normal modes of thinking (see Chapter 16).

---

## 3.2  Social rules and social roles

So far we have highlighted the intellectual aspects of cognition. But much of what we think of as mental life is concerned, not just with the privacy of our own personal thoughts, but with representations of other people and ourselves in relation to other people. A great deal of our thinking time is taken up with considering the impressions we make, whether people like us, and whether they live up to our social expectations. In fact, it is easy to get completely obsessed with thoughts of this kind. But are we really free to think whatever we like about ourselves in comparison with other people? Do we choose whom to be friendly with and how to act so as to meet the expectations of other people? An important trend in social psychology is to emphasize that most of what we think of as social behaviour has its roots in the earliest interactions with carers in infancy. Socialization into gender roles, for instance, is largely at the dictate of society, mediated through the actions of parents and teachers. According to this view, most of our social actions are automatic, as if we are following a well-trodden set of social rules.

In general, rules can be thought of as mental representations like any others, which incorporate the knowledge required to act appropriately. However, the particular flavour of rules is that they are so embedded in our experience that our actions as a mother, worker or sports enthusiast seem to be part of our very nature. When we first learn the rules of a game, this may seem to be a conscious and laborious task. But, once learned, playing the game becomes as automatic as driving a car or typing, leaving us spare capacity to attend to the finer points and our own individual strategies. Similarly, children begin to learn from their earliest years the rules of the social game. **Rule-following models**, which incorporate these aspects of social life, are discussed in Box D.

## BOX D  Rule-following models of the person

The idea of rules is used so commonly in everyday life that it is tempting to think of a rule-following person as someone who passively conforms to a set of prescriptions. But the concept of rule following is complicated and used differently by different theorists. An important distinction is between rules as a set of relatively specific directions (as in a recipe) and rules which can allow many varieties of behaviour within the constraints of the rules (as in a game). In this sense, rule following is like the rules of tennis which constrain the kinds of shots that are permitted but do not specify what the precise sequence of shots in a rally will be, nor a tennis player's personal style for executing a backhand. The ability to speak a language has been defined as the implicit knowledge of rules for generating grammatical, meaningful and appropriate utterances, but the content will vary according to the needs of the conversational episode (Chapter 13). The notion that social behaviour is governed by rules associated with particular roles was introduced in Chapter 2 and further discussed in Chapter 14, with special reference to the rules imposed by groups and the need to adhere to group norms in order to achieve acceptance as a group member.

You may wonder where following rules comes in the self-determination continuum. If rule following is automatic, what freedom do we have to vary our behaviour? Rules as specific directions lead to predictable behaviour. Rules in the flexible sense of a general game plan are considerably less predictive; they allow room for individual variation and interpretation. This implies that individuals can, to some extent, select their own roles and impose their personal style on their social behaviour. For example, the rules of greeting and initial social interactions between strangers can be followed like a script for a play. One important aspect of Goffman's dramaturgical theory is the idea that in social situations people present themselves as different 'personae' to perform a variety of roles. Of course, all this assumes that everyone is equally skilful at adapting him or herself to the requirements of communicative and social rules. However, in Chapter 16, it was argued that autistic children are deficient in just these respects, failing to develop the understanding of other people's states of mind which is essential for all kinds of social interaction.

Another constraint on the development of personal rules and roles is that they are largely determined by the accepted conventions of a particular culture and society. People are mostly quite unaware of the way they conform to implicit rules about how to behave, at least until someone breaks a rule by behaving oddly. Occasionally, it may seem that roles are potentially open to change. If there is a general shift in views about the position of women at work, for example, some of the rules and norms for someone playing the role of a working woman may gradually change. However, other aspects of a woman's role may seem cast in stone. So, is it possible for individuals to change their roles or to decide to violate a particular rule? To do so requires that rules are brought into consciousness where they can be thought about and decision-making can take place. While rules remain unconscious and automatic it is difficult, if not impossible, to break out from society's mould. This is what is meant by the term 'consciousness raising' as applied to women's groups and other disadvantaged groups. By discussing things at a conscious level, it becomes possible to think the previously unthinkable and to consider how to change the rules.

Contemplating the possibility of personal choice and change challenges the implication that humans are wholly determined by their immediate physical and social environment. If people can make individual choices, then it can be argued that human behaviour becomes essentially *unpredictable*, the antithesis of the experimental paradigm. One implication of this is that, rather than using the scientific paradigm in an attempt to explain the causes of human behaviour, psychologists should be content with describing and understanding the accounts people give of their own experiences and their reasons for acting as they do. This particular approach to psychology, which is still the subject of much debate, will be discussed in the next section.

## Summary of Section 3

- Psychological theories about mental representations are tested by research studies which provide evidence of internal models of the environment.

- Mental representations of the environment and the consquences of one's actions are necessary to function as an intelligent person.

- Especially important are mental representations of appropriate social behaviour and the probable reactions of other people.

- These are often formulated as rules for communicating with other people and performing social roles. Within the general framework of these rules and social norms some personal variation is possible.

# 4 | The role of understanding in psychology

From this point in the chapter, the word 'understanding' is used in a rather specific way. It is used to describe studying people in terms of their own perceptions and their own intentions, motivations and actions. In contrast to the natural science approach to people, with its search for general laws, models of understanding accept that everything that we experience has a unique meaning for each of us. This meaning is essentially personal, although it may have been communicated to us by other people and have emerged from our social context.

Those psychologists who want to move away from the natural science paradigm place more emphasis on subjective experience and people's verbal accounts of their experience. In other words, they treat people's **accounts** of their actions, thoughts and feelings as legitimate data, rather than only relying on observable events. But, nevertheless, such psychologists still attempt to reach a consensus about what events and actions mean to the people concerned. Agreement is arrived at by trying to see the world through the eyes of subjects themselves. In practice, this may be achieved by long periods of observation of the subjects, usually in their own social contexts rather than in psychological laboratories. Or it may be the result of participant observation, perhaps even living and interacting with the subjects of the research for fairly long periods, as Marsh did with the football fans (Chapter 14). According to this approach, objectivity and understanding are based on negotiated accounts. If you stop to think about it, this is really very close to how we use the word 'understanding' in everyday language.

The basic assumption is that humans are capable of using language to communicate accounts of themselves, and that such accounts are relevant to any explanation of their behaviour. You have encountered many examples in previous chapters where people are 'interrogated': for example, some of Piaget's early work involved asking small children questions such as, 'What makes the clouds move?'; researchers studying friendship asked children of different ages about what they expect of their friends; analysts and other therapists use language to explore the motivations and feelings of their patients; and theories of personality are based on people's accounts of their probable behaviour in specified situations, like socializing at a party.

## 4.1  The quality of human experience

Chapter 9 presented the humanistic psychologist's case for studying mental life in its own right. The emphasis is on people as unique individuals, each of whom experiences life, social context and 'self' through an extremely complex 'stream of consciousness'. A humanistic psychologist tries to tap this essentially 'inner' source of data in order to understand what it means to be a person, exploiting to the full the fine detail of perceptions, feelings and memories of past events. **Humanistic models** of psychological understanding are based on a set of assumptions about the nature of people that is very different from the more deterministic models we have already seen; see Box E.

---

**BOX E    Humanistic models of the person as a conscious agent**

In these models people are seen as essentially human; that is, as something more than the most highly developed member of the animal kingdom. The characteristics of such humanity are: first, a conscious awareness of existence; second, a capacity to reflect on conscious experience; and third, an ability to use this awareness to make sense of the world, to direct personal action and to achieve personal growth. For instance, Kelly's personal construct theory (Chapter 8) is concerned with how an individual construes his or her world. This theory has been used in therapy to bring about self-change and growth. Maslow and Rogers (Chapter 9) have developed motivational theories concerned with self-actualization. Both theorists suggest that, given the right preconditions (for Maslow, satisfaction of more basic needs and for Rogers, unconditional regard), people will naturally choose growth-enhancing alternatives.

---

One problem with viewing people as conscious and purposeful agents, as self-directed rather than determined, is that so much behaviour is constrained by human physiology and biology. Even more crucially, each person's uniqueness is limited by social encounters. Many psychologists would argue that people can only choose to become what they value, and that their values are determined by the society in which they live. Someone who is living in a community which is very short of food is obviously going to be more concerned with Maslow's basic needs than with the higher levels of self-actualization. A patient who is suffering from a psychotic or neurotic syndrome, or who is locked into a mutually destructive pattern of family life, will have less opportunity for personal growth. One of the aims of therapy is to release psychological inhibitions to allow for the possibility of change, although, as you will remember from Chapter 15, concepts of mental health and mental illness are often themselves determined by society's needs.

In view of all these influences and pressures, what room is there left for personal agency and choice? To what extent can people think of themselves as being able to choose actions in a rational way, independent of other people and social context? The model of people as conscious, purposeful agents assumes that all humans have the ability to become aware of their own experience and to conceptualize a range of alternative goals and paths to goals. So, even within a particular biological and social framework, each person should be able to fulfil his or her own potential.

## 4.2 But are these the real reasons for action?

This model of people as conscious agents assumes that we are all fully aware of the reasons for our past, present and future intentions and actions. But think about some important commitment you have made to another person in your life, perhaps getting married, or deciding to have a child. Are you aware of the real reasons for such decisions? Or think about how you voted in the last election. Why did you vote as you did? Questions like these should illustrate some of the problems associated with accepting people's reasons as explanations. Often there are several reasons, and some or perhaps all of them might be the 'real' reasons. There is no doubt that our reasons are often very complex and sometimes they are not available or are only partly available to our consciousness. We might repress our reasons because they are unacceptable either to ourselves or to the person who is asking the question. And, of course, someone who is asked to give reasons for an action might lie. Ultimately, all a researcher can do is establish as good a relationship as possible with subjects, listen carefully and attempt to draw out as complete an account as possible, giving weight to all the reasons a person might articulate. Other evidence is often brought to bear in an attempt to reconcile different accounts, self-explanations and other people's views.

Although many psychologists are optimistic about reaching agreement with their subjects about the real reasons for their actions, those in the psychodynamic tradition, in particular, work with a set of assumptions about people which suggests that much of behaviour is *not* under the control of conscious rationality. **Psychodynamic models** present a view of human nature as determined by unconscious forces. Freud stressed the importance of innate instincts and the unconscious influences of early conflicts. Yet, at the same time, in the psychoanalytic situation, people can be helped to some degree to become open to conscious consideration and rational change (see Box F).

In the light of Freudian explanations for even the slightest slip of the tongue, is it reasonable to place total reliance on what people say and accept their conscious reasons for behaviour which may be caused by unacknowledged early conflicts? Do people's expressed attitudes always match their actual behaviour? Quite apart from the effects of unconscious emotional conflicts, a great deal of our behaviour consists of actions that are carried out automatically. Chapter 11 drew particular attention to over-learned behaviours, like driving and typing, which are carried out unconsciously and so allow us to direct conscious attention to other aspects of our environment. Similarly, rules for communication and social interactions are so ingrained in us that we often appear to run through some conversational and social encounters on automatic pilot. How can we give an insightful account of behaviour we are not even aware of?

It is for these reasons that psychologists *observe* people's actual behaviour as well as explore their feelings. Therapists of all kinds, from Freud to Rogers, took care to observe the behaviour of patients in the therapeutic situation. Piaget developed the observation of children's abilities to a fine art, which in turn led to various manipulations to tease out the crucial conditions for intellectual and social development. Marsh's study of football fans was based

## BOX F   Freud's psychodynamic model of the person

Like many psychologists, Freud used a mechanical image to describe the distribution of psychic energy (libido): a hydraulic model in which the psychic energy of the id builds up, is pushed down by repression and seeks to find other outlets. Ideas of determinism and a search for causes occur throughout Freud's work. The energy-providing motivations of the id are biologically determined; the super-ego is determined by the influence of society and culture, acting largely through the child's parents during socialization; and experiences in childhood are seen as the causes of certain personality types. So how can self-direction be possible in a model which sees all behaviour as determined? Even slips and mistakes are not accidental but the result of unconscious motivations.

In therapy, unconscious feelings and motivations need to be brought into consciousness and worked through before restructuring of cognitions and behaviour can begin. The whole idea of psychoanalysis seems to be built on a contradiction: that it is possible to bring into conciousness mental representations and emotions which are essentially *unconscious* determinants stemming from past experiences. With the help of an analyst, these insights enable patients to attempt to change themselves. As in most forms of psychotherapy, it seems that we cannot easily stand outside our personal experience without help from other people.

on observation of their behaviour at matches which helped to illuminate the self-reports of individual fans. As we shall see in the next section, such a combination of observations and individual accounts allows the possibility of discovering general explanations of the processes underlying the variety of human behaviour.

Thus far we have mainly considered understanding people as individuals, in terms of their own idiosyncratic meaning systems. When a person gives a reason for an act it is an explanation of a kind, a self-explanation. But notice that this sort of explanation does not in itself rest on any general law. Understanding individuals in this way, often in great depth, can be very satisfying to the researcher. Psychologists who wish to include subjective experience as legitimate data are often content to achieve 'understanding alone'. They believe that, provided the method of negotiating accounts is done carefully and systematically, and no 'theories' are forced on to the verbal accounts, meanings will emerge which guarantee genuine understanding of people's experiences. Other psychologists (probably the majority) believe that, while enquiries of this kind can be systematic, they are of limited value, other than as the starting point for research designed to produce generalizations about behaviour.

# 4.3 The search for generalizations

How can psychologists make use of the understanding they gain of individuals in the search for more general explanations which will generate solutions to real-life problems? How can they, for instance, test whether the introduction of a new method of teaching reading, or a different method for treating depression or autism, will have a measurable and general effect on people's behaviour and experience in the predicted direction?

The problem is that people are unique and see the world differently. Even when researchers agree on the accounts of their subjects, the details of these will be different from one subject to another. The next step is for researchers to agree on categories which *classify* types of accounts and observations of behaviour. For instance, in order to test a general theory about the influence of the media on violent behaviour, researchers have to agree about what constitutes a violent television programme or aggressive behaviour. To build theories it is necessary to generalize about similarities and differences between categories of behaviour and groups of people.

The tension between respecting each individual's personal experience and, at the same time, building and testing general theories is a particular problem for psychologists, because their subject-matter is other people. Freud, for example, spent a substantial part of his working life listening to individual patients' verbal reports of their dreams, their streams of consciousness and their feelings. No doubt his understanding of each patient was deep and unique; so too was the detail of his therapeutic intepretations. But psychodynamic theory was developed by *abstracting* patterns of behaviour that were common to several patients, and recurrent themes of experience over a patient's lifetime. Freud's psychodynamic therapy depended on strong general principles which relate personality development and everyday behaviour to determinants in people's past experiences. But the willingness to understand people as individuals and help them to overcome the influence of past events by actively restructuring their views of the world still remains part of a more humanistic 'meaning and agency' approach.

Studying people's own reasons for their actions enables social psychologists to explore systematically the relations between what people do in the social world and the influence of social contexts mediated through their own internal models of what the world is like. Even in experiments, people bring many different interpretations to the way in which they construe the situation, with the result that the researcher-imposed definition of the problem may be irrelevant to the real reasons for the way subjects behave. Generalizations about people's actions provide the data for developing explanatory theories, but these explanations will only be as good as the psychologist's understanding of how people experience the world.

## Summary of Section 4

- In order to understand people's motivations and reasons, it is necessary to listen to their own accounts of experiences and reasons for actions. This method relies on negotiation between the researcher and the people whose experience is being studied.

- Humanistic psychology stresses the capacity of humans to act as autonomous conscious agents capable of making choices and giving reasons for their actions.

- Psychodynamic models of the person lay equal stress on the unconscious influences of past experiences and the possibility of acquiring conscious understanding of one's actions through psychoanalysis and other forms of therapy.

- Understanding individual experience is important in its own right but consensus about categories of experience and behaviour can lead to generalizations based on observations of common patterns of human action.

# 5 | Psychological understanding

This chapter has pursued several themes in parallel. We have considered a series of questions about how to approach the understanding of people and their psychological processes. In doing this we have had to draw on the history of psychology, the development of ideas about what psychology is or should be, and in particular its status as a science. Since people are the major subject-matter of psychology, another thread has been the way that models of the person have developed hand in hand with changing conceptions of psychological paradigms, each representing a different approach to developing theories and appropriate methodologies.

As you will have appreciated from reading through the earlier chapters, psychologists draw on many different levels of explanation even when tackling the same topic. For instance, the approaches to explaining aggression range from biological instincts to explanations in terms of inter-group hostility. These theoretical approaches bring with them their own typical methods, experiments, observations and personal accounts. The point about the six models of the person introduced in Sections 2, 3 and 4 of this chapter is that each represents a general paradigm for understanding psychology.

## 5.1 Six models of the person

1   The biological model was described as being closest to the traditional natural science paradigm. The person as a biological system is characterized in terms of internal physiological structures interacting with the environment.

2   Input/output models conceptualize the brains of animals, inluding humans, as systems for processing information. The relationships between inputs and outputs may be exceedingly complex but the aim is to describe the underlying causes of observed behaviour. These models assume that behaviour is determined in the sense that it is ultimately predictable.

3   The cognitive model of intelligence implies that the behaviour of animals is mediated by the cognitions they use to represent the environment. In humans in particular, the availability of language opens up seemingly unlimited mental representations for all kinds of cognitions which may influence behaviour.

4   Social models, which incorporate mental representations of other people and one's own roles in life, help to explain the far from straightforward relationships between what happens and a person's mode of response. The rules imposed by a society define the limits within which role behaviour can develop.

5   The humanistic-inspired model of people as conscious agents gives full reign to individual experience and the attempt to understand personal reasons. The aim is to explore possibilities for action and the potential for change and personal growth.

6   The Freudian psychodynamic model is characterized by an interesting dilemma. Behaviour and personality are considered to be influenced by unconscious emotions and habitual automatic reactions of all kinds. Yet psychoanalysis is founded on the proposition that unconscious motivations can be brought into consciousness, thus releasing a potential for changing cognitions and behaviour.

## 5.2 Internal and external perspectives

Another way of viewing the six models is from an inside or outside perspective. There is an important distinction between models which assume that people's behaviours are determined solely by aspects of the context *external* to them and those which admit that *internal* mental representations influence our understanding of the situation we are in. George Kelly in particular emphasizes the importance of internal constructions of the world, seeing people as forming expectancies and hypotheses about the outside world which guide their choices of action.

This external/internal dichotomy also guides the methods favoured by different schools within psychology. One approach is to study people from the outside, making predictions about their behaviour. This approach highlights the distinction between the psychologist as researcher and the subjects he or she is studying. The other research mode is to try to enter into the thoughts, feelings and reasons of other people. This approach highlights the similarities between the researcher and the people who are contributing to the research. It is because psychologists are human beings themselves that they are able to negotiate shared meanings and experiences.

Underlying these approaches are different criteria for what constitutes an explanation in psychology, the discovery of general laws based on external observations versus the search for people's internalized explanations. Put like this, it may sound as if there are irreconcilable conflicts between the two major paradigms. However, many, perhaps most, of the approaches discussed in this book represent 'in-between' positions. For instance, general theoretical predictions about hostile feelings are tested using observational as well as experimental methods. A good example is the Sherif and Sherif study in which in-group cohesiveness and inter-group hostility was manipulated in the naturalist setting of a boys' summer camp (Chapter 14). Humanistic theories derive generalizations from subjective experience, for instance, Maslow's hierarchy of needs, which he presents as explaining the general principles which underlie personal choice.

The opposing paradigms are really more like frames of mind. The amount of weight to be given to the 'scientific' investigation of causes by manipulating predicted outcomes, as opposed to exploring individuals' accounts, will vary from approach to approach, from psychologist to psychologist. The mix will also depend on the stage of research and also its purpose. Whether the aim is to add to 'pure' psychological knowledge, or to help people to deal with psychological problems, different emphases will be more or less congenial to a particular researcher.

## 5.3 Research stages: how far should psychologists go?

So how do psychologists go about studying their subject-matter? Despite all the arguments about the worth of different paradigms, the procedures used have more in common than you might sometimes think. Look at the research stages shown in Figure 17.2, which depicts what can be thought of as a working description of psychological research. First comes an exploratory stage in which understanding the problem in terms of human understanding and experience should be paramount. The next step is to draw out some generalizations which are not too abstract, so as not to lose the richness of the original human experience. From this, the psychologist might go on to develop a full-scale theory which attempts to explain many different aspects of behaviour as being the result of one or more underlying principles. In order to test the theory, the researcher may come up with some hypotheses predicting what should occur. Finally, some sort of research study would be carried out in as naturalistic a setting as possible, but at the same time controlling for irrelevant variables. This should make it possible to draw conclusions as to whether the data obtained from subjects were due to the predicted cause rather than to any other alternative explanations.

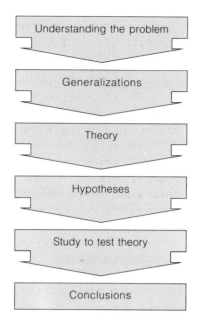

**Figure 17.2**  The stages of research

If you look right back to Chapter 1, Sections 3 and 4, you will see that Figure 17.2 encapsulates the various stages outlined there for investigating the influence of television violence on children's behaviour. Having become interested in the problem, the researcher came up with some generalizations, based on observed experiences and existing work, formulated a theory, designed a controlled study to test the theory, and drew appropriate conclusions.

The stages set out in Figure 17.2 do not represent a blueprint for all research. In the first place, not all research follows this exact sequence of stages. A psychologist might, for instance, be studying one aspect of memory and suddenly notice that subjects are behaving in an odd way and follow that up instead. An experimental researcher might start with a theory based on an earlier research paradigm, rather than beginning with an exploration of human experience. The aim would be to test whether a theory about the cause of a process needs to be modified. In another case, conclusions from a study may lead to a complete reformulation of the original problem. The stages set out in Figure 17.2 should perhaps be thought of more as a *spiral*, with feedback occurring between the different stages as research progresses.

Even more importantly, various researchers will consider that some of the stages are much more important than others, and indeed that some stages are unnecessary, or even detrimental to studying human beings. A psychologist within the humanistic paradigm might want to step off right at the beginning, feeling that understanding a problem in terms of people's own experiences and meanings is sufficient. Other psychologists interested in development, personality and therapy might want to go no further than to draw out significant generalizations about common patterns of behaviour. Trying out a range of treatments may help clinical psychologists to refine their functional analysis of the antecedents and consequences of maladaptive behaviour. The aim of this kind of research is less to make predictions or to test out theories than to understand a patient's response, perhaps through following up a single case study.

Similarly, psychologists applying the psychometric paradigm, may discover correlations between measures of personality and intelligence which indicate the existence of underlying dimensions that account for differences in the way people react to their environment. Other psychologists, working within a more conventional scientific experimental paradigm, may believe that theories about the causes of biological, cognitive and social processes can only be investigated by controlled experiments.

## 5.4 Understanding minds; understanding people

One impression that we hope you will have gained from this *Introduction to psychology* is that there is no single right and proper way to conduct psychological enquiries. In the current state of psychological knowledge, all the paradigms contribute at some level of analysis towards understanding how the mind works and what makes people tick. But what are the implications for a general psychological model of the person? Let us call this final speculative model 'the understanding person'. This term has been purposely chosen to reflect both what a fully understanding person might be like *and* how psychologists attempt to understand what it means to be an understanding person. This point is expanded in Box G.

Humans have the capacity to be aware of their own awareness and their capacity for speech and other forms of symbolic representation. These two capacities are the essential prerequisites which enable people to make plans, to provide themselves with commentaries on what they are doing and to justify their actions after the event. The understanding person can be thought of as an agent, a watcher, a commentator, a critic and a planner.

Perhaps the understanding person possesses a view of the world which, although heavily influenced by social and physical context, is not a simple one-to-one replica of everything which has been experienced. Is there a unique creation resulting from the interaction of genes, external social environment and internal representations which provides the person with a sense of individual identity—a self? Given a particular environment, a particular genetic endowment and a particular problem to solve, is it inevitable that the understanding person will act in a predictable way? Suppose that psychologists reached the point at which they claimed they could predict what everyone would do, and suppose that an 'understanding' person gets to know about this claim. What would that person do? Something different perhaps?

## BOX G   The understanding person

An understanding person is like a scientist, who goes out and searches actively for explanations, trying to make sense of phenomena out of curiosity but primarily for survival. Like the psychologist attempting to understand people, the understanding person generalizes, looks for cause-and-effect relationships and tries to empathize with other people's experiences. Such a person tries to discover regularities in the world, in the form of rules, both to make the world predictable and to simplify the business of living. The understanding person tries to come to terms as much as possible with unconscious motivations, developing flexible strategies for modifying behaviour patterns to take account of new circumstances.

This may indeed be considered an 'ideal' concept of what people are like. It also represents an ideal conception of the psychologist's role in understanding people. Cognitive, social, psychodynamic and humanistic psychologists are all concerned with understanding people. In humanistic psychology, it is the phenomenological experiences of private events, however they are represented internally, that is the main concern. Cognitive psychology focuses on the nature of internal representations and the organization and processing of information from the environment. In social psychology, and much of psychodynamic theory, the symbolic content of people's models of the world is all important. The understanding person is more than just intelligent, by virtue of the feeling, emotive side of human nature, the complexity of personal meaning systems, and the capacity for self-direction.

# Summary of Section 5

- Six models of the person have been described in this chapter: biological and input/output models; cognitive models of the intelligent person and social models of the rule-following person; the person as conscious agent and Freud's psychodynamic model.

- These models vary in their view of the extent to which people are determined by biological and external social factors or are capable of making choices based on internalized models of experience.

- The understanding person represents an ideal, both of a person who acts with full understanding, and of psychologists' attempts to understand and explain people's behaviour and experience.

# Reference

OPEN UNIVERSITY (1981) 'Four psychologists on psychology', DS262 *Introduction to psychology*, Audio-cassette 1, Milton Keynes: The Open University.

# Acknowledgements for Volume 2

Grateful acknowledgement is made to the following sources for permission to reproduce material in these chapters:

**Text**

B. Hocking in *The Independent*, 3 November 1987.

**Figures**

*Figure 10.1*: P. H. Lindsay and D. A. Norman (1972) *Human Information Processing: An Introduction to Psychology*, Academic Press, Inc., ©R. C. James (photographer, whom we were unable to contact); *Figures 10.3, 10.24 and 10.25*: J. G. Beaumont (1988) *Understanding Neuropsychology*, Basil Blackwell Ltd; *Figure 10.9*: C. G. Gross *et al.* (1972) 'Visual properties of neurons in inferotemporal cortex of the macaque', *Journal of Neurophysiology*, vol. 35, pp. 96–111, The American Physiological Society; *Figure 10.12*: J. Pomerantz (1981) 'Perceptual organization in information processing', in M. Kubovy and J. Pomerantz (eds) *Perceptual Organization*, Lawrence Erlbaum Associates, Inc. Copyright 1981 by The American Psychological Association. Reprinted by permission; *Figure 10.17*: R. L. Gregory and E. H. Gombrich (eds) (1973) *Illusion in Nature and Art*, Duckworth & Co. Ltd; *Figure 10.18*: Courtesy of Eastern Counties Newspapers Limited; *Figure 10.26*: J. J. Gibson (1986) *The Ecological Approach to Visual Perception*, Lawrence Erlbaum Associates, Inc. Copyright 1979, 1986 by The American Psychological Association. Reprinted by permission; *Figure 10.27*: E. J. Gibson and R. D. Walk (1960) 'The visual cliff', *Scientific American*, April 1960, reproduced by permission of Scientific American and William Vandivert (photographer); *Figure 10.28*: R. L. Gregory (1972) *Eye and Brain*, George Weidenfeld & Nicolson Ltd; *Figure 11.6*: D. Kahneman *Attention and Effort*, ©1973, reprinted and adapted by permission of Prentice Hall, Inc., Englewood Cliffs, New Jersey; *Figure 12.3*: F. C. Bartlett (1932) *Remembering*, Cambridge University Press; *Figure 12.6*: L. R. Peterson and M. J. Peterson (1959) 'Short-term retention of individual items', *Journal of Experimental Psychology*, vol. 58, copyright 1959 by the American Psychological Association. Adapted by permission; *Figure 12.11*: G. Cohen *et al.* (1986) *Memory: A Cognitive Approach*, Open University Press; *Figure 12.14*: G. H. Bower *et al.* (1969) 'Hierarchical retrieval schemes in recall of categorized word lists', *Journal of Verbal Learning and Verbal Behaviour* (now called *Journal of Memory and Language*), vol. 8, Academic Press, Inc., *Figures 12.15 and 12.16*: A. M. Collins and M. R. Quillian (1969) 'Retrieval time from semantic memory', *Journal of Verbal Learning and Verbal Behaviour*, vol. 8, Academic Press, Inc.; *Figure 12.17*: A. M. Collins and E. F. Loftus (1975) 'A spreading activation theory of semantic processing', *Psychological Review*, vol. 82, copyright 1975 by the American Psychological Association. Adapted by permission; *Figure 13.2*: T. Winograd and F. Flores (1986) *Understanding Computers and Cognition*, Ablex Publishing Corporation; *Figures 14.2, 14.3, 14.7, 14.8 and 14.9*: R. A. Baron (1977) *Human Aggression*, Plenum Publishing Corporation; *Figure 14.4*: Courtesy of Dr Albert Bandura; *Figure 14.6*: Courtesy of Mrs Alexandra Milgram; *Figure 16.1*: Graphics by kind permission of The National Autistic Society, based on illustrations used by Prof. J. Rendle-Short, Australia and National Society for Autistic Children, USA; *Figure 16.2*: S. Wiltshire (1987) 'The Circus, Bath', *Drawings*, J. M. Dent Ltd, copyright Stephen Wiltshire; *Figures 16.3 and 16.4*: S. Baron-Cohen *et al.* (1986) 'Mechanical, behavioural and intentional understanding of picture stories in autistic children', *British Journal of Developmental Psychology*, vol. 4, pp. 113–25, figure 2, The British Psychological Society.

# Name index for Volumes 1 and 2

(NOTE: Page references 1–472 refer to Volume 1; page references 473 and above refer to Volume 2.)

# Concept index for Volumes 1 and 2

Page numbers in bold indicate where a concept is defined.
(NOTE: Page references 1–472 refer to Volume 1: page references 473 and above refer to Volume 2.)